THE

CREATOR

IN THE

COURTROOM
"SCOPES II"

THE
CREATOR
IN THE
COURTROOM
"SCOPES II"
The 1981 Arkansas Creation-Evolution Trial

Dr. Norman L. Geisler

in collaboration with

A. F. Brooke II

and

Mark J. Keough

**MOTT
MEDIA**

THE CREATOR IN THE COURTROOM: SCOPES II

Leonard George Goss, Editor
Cover photo: Harold M. Lambert Studios, Inc.
Cover design/illustration: Joe Ragont
Typesetting: G. A. Bradley
Printing: BookCrafters

Manufactured in the United States of America

ISBN 0-88062-020-X

Table of Contents

Foreword

No one is better prepared than Dr. Norman Geisler to write an account of the Arkansas creation/evolution trial. Professor Geisler was not only present during the trial, but he was the lead witness for the creationist side and one of its most brilliant witnesses. His testimony, in my view (I was present during the entire trial) effectively demolished the most important thrust of the case by the ACLU. Unfortunately, in my opinion, no testimony, no trial effort, no matter how brilliant, could have won the case for the creationist side. Judge Overton accepts the ACLU mind-set that anything that hints of God, even scientific evidence for creation, must be barred from public schools. Secular humanism will now be our official state-sanctioned religion, if Judge Overton's decision is allowed to stand.

Professor Geisler's account is carefully and thoroughly documented. His description of the actual course of the trial is interesting and his critique of Judge Overton's official decision is incisive, thorough, and accurate. Professor Geisler's account of the trial is in refreshing contrast to the usual (not always) distorted and biased accounts which appeared in the mass media and a relief from the sophistry that appeared in so many scientific journals. No eyewitness account can be accurate in all details, but I can certainly recommend this book as a fair and thorough account of the famous 1981 Arkansas creation/evolution trial.

—Duane T. Gish, Ph.D.
Associate Director
Institute for Creation Research
May 24, 1982

Preface

The creation-evolution controversy is one of the most significant and far-reaching controversies of our day. In 1925 a Tennessee judge declared the teaching of evolution illegal. By 1982 an Arkansas judge declared an Act for teaching creation (alongside of evolution) unconstitutional. This is one more court decision in a long line of precedent-setting court decisions that will have far reaching effects on the continued secularization of our society.

Some of the most significant decisions in this trend include:

1961 *(Torcaso vs. Watkins)* - Secular humanism recognized as a religion protected by the First Amendment.

1962 *(Engel vs. Vitale)* - State-required devotional prayers banned from public schools.

1963 *(Abington vs. Schempp)* - State-required devotional Bible reading forbidden in schools.

1968 *(Epperson vs. Arkansas)* - Laws against teaching evolution are unconstitutional.

1980 *(Stone vs. Graham)* - Posting Ten Commandments in classroom is unconstitutional.

1982 *(McLean vs. Arkansas)* - Law mandating the teaching of creation (with evolution) banned in Arkansas.

The Arkansas trial was appropriately billed by many as "Scopes II." Media attended from all over the world. Since a secular outlook dominates the media,* their reports were understandably slanted. An even greater disappointment was the strange and conspicuous absence of the Christian media, for not a single reporter from any Christian magazine or paper was assigned to attend the trial. Consequently, even their stories were largely based on the slanted and distorted reports in the secular press.

Since the collaborators of this book were eyewitnesses to the entire trial, and since we had direct access to all the trial documents, witnesses, and attorneys, we feel an obligation to share the truth of what happened. With the exception of chapter two, this book is almost entirely documentary. The first chapter is a brief chronology of events while the third chapter gives a summary of the legal arguments for and against the Act. What transpired at the trial is found in chapters four through seven. This is an eyewitness account derived from the three author's notes, plus those of a newspaper reporter (Cal Beisner). The final (eighth) chapter is the written decision of Judge William Overton.

We hope that this book will help overcome both widespread factual distortion of the trial and misunderstanding of the issues. What happened in Arkansas should arouse all freedom-loving people. It should also serve as a powerful reminder that the survival of a free nation demands not only a free press but a *fair* press. One final lesson that should be learned from Arkansas is that the judgment of one man can have absolutely devastating consequences for the pursuit of truth in the public schools, as well as the freedom of teachers to express the truth. *For on January 5, 1982, a federal judge in essence ruled for the first time in American history that it is unconstitutional to even imply the existence of a Creator in a public school science class or to teach any scientific theory that is not purely naturalistic.* This is a long way from the "unalienable rights of the Creator" envisioned by our founding fathers. Indeed, what we saw discussed in Arkansas was not merely creationism in the classroom: We saw the Creator go to court and "lose"!

_____

*   See Chapter Two.

*We hold these truths to be self-evident,
that all men are created equal,
that they are endowed by their Creator
with certain unalienable rights . . . .*

—The Declaration of Independence

Chapter One

Introduction: History of Act 590

A Brief Summary of the History of Act 590

The history of the Arkansas creation-evolution Act 590 is as follows:

1. In 1977 Paul Ellwanger, a Roman Catholic layman from South Carolina, formed "Citizens for Fairness in Education" group which introduced creation-evolution bills in numerous state legislatures.

2. Using a model bill prepared by Wendell Bird, staff Attorney for the Institute for Creation Research, Paul Ellwanger drafted Act 590.

3. On February 24, 1981, Senator Holsted introduced it as Senate Bill 482 where it was read for the first and second time.

4. On March 3, 1981, the Senate judiciary committee recommended that Bill 482 receive a "do pass."

5. On March 12, 1981, the Bill was read for the third and final time and passed by a vote of 22 to 2.

6. On March 12 the Bill was read for the first time.

7. On March 13 the Bill was read for the second time.

8. On March 13 the House Education Committee held a brief hearing on the Bill.

9. On March 17 the Bill was read for a third and final time in the House of Representatives. It passed by a vote of 69 to 18.

10. On March 19, 1981, Governor Frank White signed the Bill into law.

11. On May 27, 1981, the American Civil Liberties Union filed suit challenging the constitutionality of Act 590.

12. On December 7-17, 1981, the trial was held in Federal Judge William Overton's court, Little Rock, Arkansas.

13. On January 5, 1982, Judge Overton ruled the Bill was an unconstitutional violation of the First Amendment.

14. On February 4, 1982, one day before the deadline for appeal to the 8th Circuit Court of Appeals (St. Louis), the Attorney General, Steve Clark, announced that the state would not appeal the ruling.*

The Complete Contents of "Act 590 of 1981"

"AN ACT TO REQUIRE BALANCED TREATMENT OF CREATION-SCIENCE AND EVOLUTION IN PUBLIC SCHOOLS; TO PROTECT ACADEMIC FREEDOM BY PROVIDING STUDENT CHOICE; TO ENSURE FREEDOM OF RELIGIOUS EXERCISE; TO GUARANTEE FREEDOM OF BELIEF AND SPEECH; TO PREVENT ESTABLISH-MENT OF RELIGION; TO PROHIBIT RELIGIOUS IN-STRUCTION CONCERNING ORIGINS; TO BAR DISCRIMI-NATION ON THE BASIS OF CREATIONIST OR EVOLU-TIONIST BELIEF; TO PROVIDE DEFINITIONS AND CLARIFICATIONS; TO DECLARE THE LEGISLATIVE PURPOSE AND LEGISLATIVE FINDINGS OF FACT; TO PROVIDE FOR SEVERABILITY OF PROVISIONS; TO PROVIDE FOR REPEAL OF CONTRARY LAWS; AND TO SET FORTH AN EFFECTIVE DATE."

BE IT ENACTED BY THE GENERAL ASSEMBLY OF THE STATE OF ARKANSAS:

SECTION 1. Requirement for Balanced Treatment. Public schools within this State shall give balanced treatment to creation-science and to evolution-science. Balanced treatment to these two models shall be given in classroom lectures taken

---

*   For the defense attorneys' rationale for not appealing see Appendix One.

as a whole for each course, in textbook materials taken as a whole for each course, in library materials taken as a whole for the sciences and taken as a whole for the humanities, and in other educational programs in public schools, to the extent that such lectures, textbooks, library materials, or educational programs deal in any way with the subject of the origin of man, life, the earth, or the universe.

SECTION 2. Prohibition against Religious Instruction. Treatment of either evolution-science or creation-science shall be limited to scientific evidences for each model and inferences from those scientific evidences, and must not include any religious instruction or references to religious writings.

SECTION 3. Requirement for Nondiscrimination. Public schools within this State, or their personnel, shall not discriminate, by reducing a grade of a student or by singling out and making public criticism, against any student who demonstrates a satisfactory understanding of both evolution-science and creation-science and who accepts or rejects either model in whole or part.

SECTION 4. Definitions. As used in this Act:

(a) "Creation-science" means the scientific evidences for creation and inferences from those scientific evidences. Creation-science includes the scientific evidences and related inferences that indicate: (1) Sudden creation of the universe, energy, and life from nothing; (2) The insufficiency of mutation and natural selection in bringing about development of all living kinds from a single organism; (3) Changes only within fixed limits of originally created kinds of plants and animals; (4) Separate ancestry for man and apes; (5) Explanation of the earth's geology by catastrophism, including the occurrence of a worldwide flood; and (6) A relatively recent inception of the earth and living kinds.

(b) "Evolution-science" means the scientific evidences for evolution and inferences from those scientific evidence. Evolution-science includes the scientific evidences and related inferences that indicate: (1) Emergence by naturalistic processes of the universe from disordered matter and emergence of life from nonlife; (2) The sufficiency of mutation and natural selection in bringing about the development of present living kinds from simple earlier kinds; (3) Emergence by mutation and natural selection of present living kinds from simple earlier kinds; (4) Emergence of man from a common ancestor with apes; (5) Explanation of the earth's geology and the evolutionary sequence by uniformitarianism; and (6) An inception several billion years ago of the earth and somewhat later of life.

(c) "Public schools" mean public secondary and elementary schools.

SECTION 5. Clarifications. This Act does not require or permit instruction in any religious doctrine or materials. This Act does not require any instruction in the subject of origins, but simply requires instruction in both scientific models (of evolution-science and creation-science) if public schools choose to teach either. This Act does not require each individual textbook or library book to give balanced treatment to the models of evolution-science and creation-science; it does not require any school books to be discarded. This Act does not require each individual classroom lecture in a course to give such balanced treatment, but simply requires the lectures as a whole to give balanced treatment; it permits some lectures to present evolution-science and other lectures to present creation-science.

SECTION 6. Legislative Declaration of Purpose. This Legislature enacts this Act for public schools with the purpose of protecting academic freedom for students' differing values and beliefs; ensuring neutrality toward students' diverse religious convictions; ensuring freedom of religious exercise for students and their parents; guaranteeing freedom of belief and speech for students; preventing establishment of Theologically Liberal, Humanist, Nontheist, or Atheist religions; preventing discrimination against students on the basis of their personal beliefs concerning creation and evolution; and assisting students in their search for truth. This Legislature does not have the purpose of causing instruction in religious concepts or making an establishment of religion.

SECTION 7. Legislative Findings of Fact. This Legislature

finds that:

(a) The subject of the origin of the universe, earth, life, and man is treated within many public school courses, such as biology, life science, anthropology, sociology, and often also in physics, chemistry, world history, philosophy, and social studies.

(b) Only evolution-science is presented to students in virtually all of those courses that discuss the subject of origins. Public schools generally censor creation-science and evidence contrary to evolution.

(c) Evolution-science is not an unquestionable fact of science, because evolution cannot be experimentally observed, fully verified, or logically falsified, and because evolution-science is not accepted by some scientists.

(d) Evolution-science is contrary to the religious convictions or moral values or philosophical beliefs of many students and parents, including individuals of many different religious faiths and with diverse moral values and philosophical beliefs.

(e) Public school presentation of only evolution-science without any alternative model of origins abridges the United States Constitution's protections of freedom of religious exercise and of freedom of belief and speech for students and parents, because it undermines their religious convictions and moral or philosophical values, compels their unconscionable professions of belief, and hinders religious training and moral training by parents.

(f) Public school presentation of only evolution-science furthermore abridges the Constitution's prohibition against establishment or religion, because it produces hostility toward many Theistic religions and brings preference to Theological Liberalism, Humanism, Nontheistic religions, and Atheism, in that these religious faiths generally include a religious belief in evolution.

(g) Public school instruction in only evolution-science also violates the principle of academic freedom, because it denies students a choice between scientific models and instead indoctrinates them in evolution-science alone.

(h) Presentation of only one model rather than alternative scientific models of origins is not required by any compelling

interest of the State, and exemption of such students from a
course or class presenting only evolution-science does not provide an adequate remedy because of teacher influence and student pressure to remain in that course or class.

(i) Attendance of those students who are at public schools is
compelled by law, and school taxes from their parents and
other citizens are mandated by law.

(j) Creation-science is an alternative scientific model of
origins and can be presented from a strictly scientific stand-
point without any religious doctrine just as evolution-science
can, because there are scientists who conclude that scientific
data best support creation-science and because scientific
evidences and inferences have been presented for creation-
science.

(k) Public school presentation of both evolution-science
and creation-science would not violate the Constitution's prohibition against establishment of religion, because it would involve presentation of the scientific evidences and related inferences for each model rather than any religious instruction.

(l) Most citizens, whatever their religious beliefs about
origins, favor balanced treatment in public schools of alternative scientific models of origins for better guiding students
in their search for knowledge, and they favor a neutral approach toward subjects affecting the religious and moral and
philosophical convictions of students.

SECTION 8. Short Title. This Act shall be known as the
"Balanced Treatment for Creation-Science and Evolution-
Science Act."

SECTION 9. Severability of Provisions. If any provision of
this Act is held invalid, that invalidity shall not affect other
provisions that can be applied in the absence of the invalidated
provisions, and the provisions of this Act are declared to be
severable.

SECTION 10.   Repeal of Contrary Laws. All State laws or
parts of State laws in conflict with this Act are hereby repealed.

SECTION 11. Effective Date. The requirements of the Act
shall be met by and may be met before the beginning of the
next school year if that is more than six months from the date

of enactment, or otherwise one year after the beginning of the next school year, and in all subsequent school years.

Approved,

Frank White
(Governor)
3 - 19 - 81

[It] is bigotry for public schools to teach only one theory of origins.

**—ACLU Attorney, Clarence Darrow
Scopes Trial, 1925**

Chapter Two

Observations and Implications of The Arkansas Case

Several aspects of the trial require comment. We shall limit our observations only to those aspects which in view of potential historic significance and public reaction seem most worthy of inclusion. These will include the media, the bill, the trial attorneys, the judge, and the ruling.

The Media Coverage

Reporters swarmed into the court from all over the world. Excitement was high, especially for the first few days. This enthusiasm often faded as the long, highly technical, testimony continued. By the last few days of the trial there were plenty of empty seats in the courtroom.

Since we have no access to records of TV and radio coverage, and since these did not vary significantly from the printed media, we will base our comments largely on the printed record. In a single word, the media reporting was largely *slanted*. It was pitched to the "religion vs. science" theme even before the trial began.

No sooner had the bill been signed into law (March 19, 1981) than the *Arkansas Gazette* headlined a story (March 22, 1981): " 'Creation-science' Bill Prompted By Religious Beliefs, Sponsor Says." The sponsor, Senator Holsted, is quoted in bold print under his picture as saying, "I can't separate the bill from that belief in a Creator." He is further cited as saying, "the bill probably does favor the viewpoint of religious fundamentalists." The article then narrates Holsted's "born again" conversion and his agreement with the Moral Majority, even though he is not a member.

Even when the article later grudgingly admits that Holsted affirmed the bill was against establishing religion, the Gazette quickly adds: "But he could not explain why the bill does not state that the intent also is to prevent the establishment of conservative or fundamentalist religions."

Similar slanted reporting persisted during and after the trial, despite the Associated Press' reporting an NBC poll (November 18, 1981) a month before the trial showing that "three of four Americans say they believe that both the scientific theory of evolution and the Biblical theory of creation should be taught in public schools."*

As the trial began, the same "religion vs. science" motif continued. Scientific evidence for creation was usually indicated in quotes. For example, the Dallas Times Herald (December 9, 1981) headline read "Scientists Ridicule 'Evidence' of Creationists." The Arkansas Gazette (December 11, 1981) headed its articles "Creationism is Bound to Religion, Educators Say in 4th Day of Trial" and "Creationism Can't Be Divorced From Religion, Educators Say in Act 590 Trial."

When the Defense witnesses took the stand the press invariably sensationalized the irrelevant. The judge correctly noted in his ruling that "the court would never discredit any person's testimony based on his or her religious beliefs." Unfortunately, however, the mostly undiscerning public does not always grant this same courtesy, and the press knows it. In effect, they count on it. Typical of the reporting was The Milwaukee Journal (December 12, 1981) headline: "Trial zeros

---

*   But even here the poll used the slanted words "biblical" versus "scientific" to describe the views.

in on fundamentalist Christian beiefs." *The Arkansas Democrat* gave front page headlines to the first creation scientists entitled "Clark to call 7 avowed Bible believers." This despite the fact that no witness so described himself. Nonetheless, the witnesses were asked irrelevant questions (over the objections of defense attorneys*) about their religious beliefs. The papers almost unanimously described these witnesses by perjorative terms such as "biblical literalist."

Despite days of scientific testimony of creation scientists, the *Arkansas Democrat* (December 15, 1981) described it in headlines as "Salvationist view of human origins." *Time* magazine headed their article "Darwin vs. the Bible" and put creation science in quotes, suggesting that it is merely an *alleged* science. When zoologist Dr. Harold Coffin gave abundant scientific evidence for the creationists' view, the *Dallas Times Herald* (December 16, 1981) reported: "Zoologist bases belief of origins on Bible." The *Arkansas Gazette* (December 16, 1981) headed their article on the scientific testimony: "Religious Dimensions of 'Creation Science'." Other papers were more subtle in their bias. The *Tampa Tribune-Times* (December 13, 1981) entitled their report "Creative Testimony at Creationism Trial," suggesting the possibility that it was clever but not necessarily correct. *The Wall Street Journal* article (December 28, 1981) claimed creation science was not really a science. When we responded in a letter to the editor (January 14, 1982) with evidence to the contrary (Appendix Three), they headed the section with an indirect retort: "World's Beginning Stirs No End of Creative Theorizing." This again alerts the reader to beware of ingenious opinions.

One of the most scientific and factual testimonies for creationism was that of Dr. Donald Chittick. Despite his unwillingness to assent to the contents of a Bible Science Association news letter written by someone else, the *Arkansas Democrat* (December 16, 1981), in the lead paragraph about

---

*   See Appendix Two.

him, read: "But one witness confirmed he was a member of the
Bible Science Association, which was putting 'Christ and the
Bible and the power of the Holy Spirit back into science as one
of the most powerful methods of witnessing in the church today'." This was a flagrant case of guilt by association.

By far the worst example of sensational reporting was the
world-wide headline that Dr. Norman Geisler had testified
about UFO's as the work of Satan. Headlines read "Theologian
Contends UFO's Work of Satan" (Arkansas Gazette, December
12, 1981), and "Witness in creation trial links UFO's to Satan"
(Los Angeles Herald Examiner, December 12, 1981). Perhaps
the most exaggerated and embellished report of all was the
Washington Post (December 13, 1981), where the headline
read: "Creationist Tells of Belief in UFO's, Satan, Occult." The
article begins "The defense of the Arkansas creation law
opened today with a spectacular courtroom fireworks
display . . . . "*

The truth of the matter is: (1) Dr. Geisler had not even mentioned UFO's in his testimony; (2) the ACLU lawyer brought up
UFO's in the cross-examination attempt to discredit Geisler's
testimony; (3) the total testimony took about two hours and
the mention of UFO's (by the ACLU lawyer) only a few seconds!
Despite this the science magazine Discover spent half of its article on Geisler's testimony relating this incident. This promp-

---

* This exaggeration and literary embellishment led someone half way
around the world to write the Post saying: "Dear Sir: The main daily
newspaper in this part of the world, 'The West Australian,' based at the
city of Perth, included a report on December 15 by your reporter Mr.
Philip J. Hilts on the court case in Arkansas concerning the teaching of
creation science in pubic schools. A copy of the report, which is enclosed,
attributes to the opening creationist witness 'a spectacular courtroom
fireworks display . . . . ' Most of the report reads fairly objectively, but
one looks in vain for the alleged 'spectacular courtroom fireworks
display.' Was it perhaps in the fancy of Mr. Hilts? It seems so. Evidently,
he is personally opposed to creation-science. While he is quite free to
hold that view, why does he use his supposedly-factual report to discredit
the opening witness? . . . Yours sincerely, ... "

ted the following letter to *Discover:*

> Dear Editor:
> Your article on the Arkansas Creation-Evolution trial gave me new insights into how evolution has maintained itself in the absence of substantial evidence for over a century . . . . When you emphasize the irrelevant, omit the essential, and forbid the opposing view a hearing, it is easy for a theory to long outlive its evidence. Myths die hard. [See Appendix Four for the complete letter.]

In several other ways the media* generally and effectively distorted the issue: (1) The media failed to stress the highly respectable scientific credentials of the defense science witnesses. Both the court and the ACLU recognized them all as "experts." (2) It neglected to report the anti-creation stand of the ACLU witnesses. Many were active in organizations geared to fight creationism. (3) The media usually failed to report that many evolution witnesses admitted that scientific evidence for creationism *should* be taught in the schools. (4) The media omitted the beliefs of the evolutionists; most were either liberal, agnostic, atheistic, or Marxist.

The reason for the media bias was stated well by Professors Robert Lichter and Stanley Rothman in the *Washington Post* in an article on "The Media Elite." Their surveys revealed:

> A predominant characteristic of the media elite is its secular outlook. Exactly 50 percent eschew any religious affiliation. Another 14 percent are Jewish, and almost one in four (23 percent) was raised in a Jewish household. Only one in five identifies himself as Protestant, and one in eight as Catholic. Very few are regular churchgoers. Only 8 percent go to church or synagogue weekly, and 86 percent seldom or never attend religious services.
> Ideologically, a majority of leading journalists describe

---

* The reports in the Christian media were largely based on the secular media, since no reporters from the major evangelical magazines and papers were assigned to attend the trial (see Appendix Eleven).

themselves as liberals. Fifty-four percent place themselves to the left of center, compared to only 19 percent who choose the right side of the spectrum.

Chemistry and Engineering News (Jan. 18, 1982) so distorted the testimony of an agnostic evolutionist who testified for the Arkansas creation-evolution act that he wrote this in a letter to the editor *(Chemistry and Engineering News,* March 29, 1982):

> Sir:
>
> Rudy M. Baum in his article on "Science confronts creationist assault" (C&EN, Jan. 18, page 12) characterizes my testimony in the Arkansas trial as consisting "of self-serving diatribes." He needs to consult his dictionary. What I spoke in defense of was "openness of inquiry" and "fair-play for minority opinion in regard to controversial issues." Considering that I am agnostic and an evolutionist—both included in my testimony but neglected by the media generally—the "self-serving" factor is obscure at best.
>
> Apparently any spoken response in open court above that of a Caspar Milquetoast qualifies as a diatribe, unless, of course, one represents the camp of entrenched opinion. As a "news analyst" Baum qualifies for the "Paul Goebbels" award, which is granted only to those showing expertise in (1) belittlement, (2) innuendo, (3) prejudice, and (4) reporting out of context . . . .
>
>   W. Scot Morrow
>   Associate Professor of Chemistry
>   Wofford College, Spartanburg, S.C.

We believe that the unquestionably slanted, biased, and even incorrect media coverage before, during, and after the trial has given the American public a distorted picture of what actually occurred at this historic event. We hope this book will help correct this situation. The following discussion will help put matters in better perspective.

The Bill

Our positive comments on the Act were summed up in an article for *Christianity Today* (See Appendix Five), which we will now summarize here. First, we commented on some misconceptions about the Act and then gave a rationale for supporting it.

Misconceptions About Act 590

1. It mandates teaching the biblical account of creation (it actually forbids that).

2. It is opposed to teaching evolution (it actually mandates teaching evolution alongside of creation).

3. It refers to God or religious concepts (there is no reference to God and it forbids teaching religion).

4. It forces teachers who are opposed to creation to teach it anyway (actually, the teacher doesn't have to teach anything about origins and/or they can have someone else teach the lectures they do not want to teach).

5. It is a "Fundamentalist" Act. (Actually, the "Fundamentalists" of the 1920's were categorically opposed to teaching evolution and for teaching only the Genesis account of creation. This Act is contrary to both of these stands of the 1920's "Fundamentalists.")

Rationale for Supporting the Act

First, we argued along with Clarence Darrow (ACLU lawyer for the Scopes trial, 1925) that it "is bigotry for public schools to teach only one theory of origins." And if it was bigotry when the creationists were trying to keep the evolutionists out, it is still bigotry when evolutionism attempts to exclude creationism.

Second, we insisted that in the interest of openness to the scientific endeavor the "loyal opposition" should be permitted their "day in court." In fact, many court decisions would have been premature (and even wrong) had they not waited to hear both sides of the issue.

Teaching scientific creation is no more or less teaching religion than is teaching evolution from a scientific perspective. Both are consistent with certain religious worldviews, but neither is the essence of religion. Either could be used to imply certain religious conclusions, but neither should be excluded simply because it has been so used (or misused).

Fourth, scientific progress depends on allowing the presentation of alternative theories. Copernicus' view that the earth revolves around the sun was once a minority view. So was Einstein's theory of relativity; yet without this theory much of modern physics would not have been possible.

In short, the Act was clear (even the judge agreed), fair (in that it permitted both sides to be taught), and not unconstitutional on its face.

Some Difficulties with the Wording of the Act

Even though creationism is science and not religion, it seems to us that Act 590 could have avoided any *appearance* of being religious if it had done the following: First, instead of speaking of "creation out of nothing" it could have used the words "the sudden appearance of the universe" or of life. Second, it could have avoided similarity with Genesis 1 by the word "kinds" of life for a less objectionable and more scientific term such as "forms" or "types." ("Species" could not be used since creationists do not believe in the fixity of the taxonomical category of species.)

Third, the inclusion of points 5 and 6 (catastrophism and young earth) is an unnecessary red flag for those opposed to the Act. As many creation scientists have observed, a "long time" is not really helpful to the evolutionist view, but it does not hurt the creationist's view. Dropping colored paper from an airplane at 10,000 feet is less likely to spell your name on your roof than dropping it from 5,000 (where it has less time to fall). Regardless of how much time is allowed, however, intelligent intervention into these randomly moving elements is needed in order to direct them and "inform" them exactly what they are to spell.

In view of the actual irrelevance of long time periods to the basic arguments for creation, it is ill-advised to wave unnecessary red flags in front of the evolutionists. Why provide them with one more excuse to proclaim the creationists' view religious (since many believe only the Bible teaches a young earth)? After all if creationism is taught, then the scientific evidence for a young earth will have an opportunity for presentation even if it is not spelled out in detail.

Fourth, the Arkansas Act unnecessarily gives the *impression* that one must choose between one of two complete "packaged" positions, each containing six points. Technically the Act does not say this. It simply contrasts six major areas of disagreement to which either an "evolution" or "creation" interpretive model may be applied. It thus leaves the door open for one to choose some explanations from one side and some from the other. However, the way the two views are separated does make it possible that some may read the Act as detailing two mutually exclusive packages where one must choose all of one or all of the other.

Fifth, the Act could have been improved by *mentioning* theistic religions among those it opposes being established. Without this it leaves itself open to the charge that it may favor theistic religions despite the fact that it explicitly states its opposition to establishing *any* religion.

Although Act 590 could have been improved, it was a good Act and in our opinion was not unconstitutional.

The Trial Attorneys

Attorneys for the Defense

The press gave much attention to the charges by certain groups that the Attorney General, Steve Clark, and his staff (Attorneys David Williams, Rick Campbell, and Callis Childs, and Assistants Tim Humphries, Cindy English, and W. W. "Dub" Elrod) did not do a good job of defending the law. This conclusion is based on several allegations made by attorney Wendell R. Bird. The allegations of poor defense centered mainly around the following situations reported by the media (see Appendix Six). It was alleged: (1) that Clark had refused expert legal help from the attorneys Wendell Bird and John Whitehead; (2) that Clark's defense was not adquately prepared; (3) that Clark was not dedicated to defending the law, having allegedly sold out to the ACLU as evidenced by a gift of $25 to the ACLU a few weeks before the trial.

As far as we can tell, none of these allegations is true. Before we can draw implications, let us discern the facts of the matter. (1) First, the Attorney General Steve Clark did not turn down all legal help from ICR. What he turned down was the attorney's request to be the "counsels of record," which means official trial attorneys.* (2) Second, Steve Clark neither attended the ACLU function nor gave them $25. What he did was give two free lunches for the purposes of a raffle. (3) The main attorneys for the defense (and the ones who signed the Defense brief) were Dave Williams and Rick Campbell, both of whom are evangelical Christians.

It is our impression, based on first-hand observations of the entire trial and direct communication with the attorneys before, during, and after the trial that (1) they executed their duties well. This was the unanimously expressed opinion of all the defense witnesses at the trial, including Duane Gish. (2) The Attorney General was penetrating in his cross-examining of those ACLU witnesses he handled. (3) There was no question in our minds about the dedication of the defense attorneys, though they were far outnumbered by the ACLU.

The ACLU Attorneys

The lead attorney for the ACLU was Robert M. Cearley, Jr. (of Cearley, Gitchel, Mitchell, and Bryant, P.A., Little Rock, Arkansas). Immediately following the trial, twelve ACLU attorneys posed for the *Arkansas Democrat* (December 18, 1981). The Plaintiff's Brief lists the following (nine) names: Robert Cearley, Philip Kaplan (of Kaplan, Brewer, and Bilheimer, P.A., Little Rock), Bruce Ennis, Jr. and Jack Novick (of ACLU Foundation, N.Y.), and Peggy L. Kerr, Gary E. Crawford, and Mark E. Herlichy (listed as "of counsel"). In addition, acknowledgment is given to two legal students (of

---

*   See Appendix Seven for a statement of the Creation Science Legal Defense Fund (Wendell Bird, Legal Counsel) on the alleged mishandling of the case by the State's Attorney.

Fordham University School of Law), Kathryn Keneally and Kathryn S. Reimann. The media reported that there were a total of seventeen, and one source as many as twenty-two, ACLU lawyers and assistants who worked on the case. Compared with four defense attorneys and their three legal assistants, the ACLU outnumbered the State by about three to one.

Furthermore, it appears obvious that with this larger staff, the attorneys of the ACLU had a definite legal advantage. And judging from the volumes of books and exhibits presented at the trial, it was clear that the ACLU legal staff had done their homework.

Another interesting feature of the ACLU attorneys was obvious theatrical abilility. They understood playing to the press (by bringing up irrelevant but sensational matters, like UFO's), and appealing to the Court (by milking the religious background and associations of those in favor of the creation-evolution act). Probably most observers (whatever side they were on) would agree that the ACLU simply presented a more persuasive case than the Attorney General. In order to do this, however, the ACLU attorneys had to twist, distort, and even misrepresent some things. For example, they carefully concealed the unfalsifiable nature of the general theory of evolution; they hid the scientific nature of creation.* They also successfully painted supporters of creationism as Protestant "Fundamentalists," though many were agnostics, Buddhists, Roman Catholics, evangelical protestants, and others.

In some cases, the ACLU flatly misrepresented the facts. For example, they represented one witness as teaching a "science" class at Dallas Seminary, despite his clear disavowal of this in his deposition where he said "This is a theology course." And by presenting the class in *religious* anthropology as though it were *scientific* anthropology, the ACLU could make his five religious views about origins look like it contradicted the posi-

---

*   See Appendix Ten.

tion of Act 590 which lists two *scientific* positions on each point of origins (see Plaintiff's Brief): The full text reads like this:

Q. "And all of the references there in this anthropology course are to the Bible in that section?"

A. "That's correct."

Q. "And there are no—in that section there are no scientific statements whatsoever?"

A. "That's correct. This is a theology course."

There is no question that the ACLU lawyers were well trained at this kind of twisting and distorting of the facts, a talent the defense did not exercise. In short, they continued the "religion vs. science" scenario the media had already presented, and the judge bought it.

The Judge

Some have implied that the judge accepted the ACLU "story" because he was part of their plot. This seems clearly false. Although the judge was one of over 250 new judges installed by President Carter, and had little experience in First Amendment matters (his legal practice had been largely devoted to insurance claims), he gave no evidence of being against creationists. But whereas the judge was not bigoted against creationists, he was in our opinion overtly biased against creationism. We offer the following evidence for this conclusion:

1. The judge was a theologically liberal Methodist who did not believe in creationism as defined by Act 590.

2. The judge is the son of an evolutionary biology teacher who attended every session of the trial.

3. The judge's theologically liberal Methodist Bishop was the first witness against teaching creationism.

Some felt that this above fact alone should have disqualified the judge. One citizen wrote to the *Arkansas Democrat* (December 15, 1981) saying:

> Dear Editor:
>   In the creation science trial, there is a question of neutrality on the part of Judge Overton. When the

Methodist Bishop of Arkansas testified for the ACLU, how could the judge not be influenced? After all, he is a Methodist and surely must respect the head Methodist of the state. You can be well assured that if the judge were a "Fundamentalist Christian" the ACLU would cry and scream "partiality."

4. The judge manifested bias against creationism by several outbursts of personal opinion during the trial. Once, the judge chided a high school science teacher. The record reads as follows:

"Witness [Townley]: Why narrow your possibilities to only one when—

The Court [the judge]: Well, because it's not Sunday School. You're trying to teach about science." (From the Court Record.*)

5. The judge denied a motion by the defense which would have eliminated irrelevant religious opinions being included in the record (and thus reported by the press).**

6. Before the trial the judge said he would rule from the bench (as though his mind was made up), but later reversed course when he was criticized by witnesses and citizens as being biased.

7. Despite nearly a week of testimony from numerous Ph.D.s in science (some of whom were evolutionists) insisting that creationism is as scientific as evolution and is not based on the Bible, the judge still referred to scientific creationism as "the biblical view of creation." His basic mind-set had never been changed: evolution is to be learned in the public school, and creation is what you learn in Sunday School!

8. The judge's decision reveals an absolutistic naturalistic bias, as will be clearly seen in the following discussion on the ruling.

---

*   See Chapter Four for another example.

** See Appendix Two.

The Ruling

It was the almost unanimous opinion of those present on both sides after the trial that the judge would render a negative ruling. No one was greatly surprised then, on January 5, 1982, when Judge Overton predictably struck down the law and ruled it an unconstitutional violation of the First Amendment. We will divide our comments on this ruling (see Chapter Eight) into several sections: factual, logical, legal, and religious.

The Factual Errors

There are a number of factual errors in the ruling worthy of note. First, the judge is clearly wrong in saying the term "scientific creationism" did not gain currency around 1965 after the publication of *The Genesis Flood* but, instead, around 1974 following the publication of Morris' *Scientific Creationism*.

Second, the judge is again wrong in asserting that Paul Ellwanger was "motivated by . . . [the] desire to see the Biblical version of creation taught in the public schools." He desired a *scientific* version taught in public schools.

Third, the judge is mistaken in believing that creation and flood stories are unique to Genesis. They are found in many ancient cultures, including Babylonian, Sumerian, and others.

Fourth, the creationists' concept of a "recent earth" is not based on the genealogy of the Old Testament, but on their scientific arguments for a young earth.

Fifth, it is not true that no witness gave evidence of refusal to publish creationists' articles. Robert Gentry gave ample evidence of this in his testimony.

Sixth, the judge wrongly affirms that Mr. Ellwanger believes "both evolution and creation are religion." Ellwanger believes both are scientific views.

Seventh, the ruling incorrectly affirms that the improbability argument is used by creationists to support "a worldwide flood . . . and a young earth." It was used only to show the need for positing a designer of life.

Eighth, the judge misrepresented one witness' testimony about Fundamentalists' beliefs in "Five Fundamentals." In fact, he testified that there were two overlapping sets of five which made six "Fundamentals."*

Ninth, he incorrectly asserts that the scientific community does not consider the origin of life as part of the overall theory of evolution. Spontaneous generation of life is often discussed by evolutionists as an explanation of how life began in the primeval "soup."

Tenth, the judge falsely asserts that a defense witness testified that there were more than two basic scientific positions on origins. What he affirmed was that there were only two *scientific* views on the various points of origin (either life and life forms began by chance or by a creator). What he said was there are many *religious* ways to conceive of this "creator."

These are only some of the more obvious mistakes. The ruling as a whole badly distorts many statements crucial to the case. Close examination would indicate that the ruling is based on the pre-trial mind-set of the judge, since he sometimes cites the witnesses ideas from their pre-trial deposition rather than from the more clearly thought out statements they later gave in court testimony. In fact the judge's opinion seems to be based largely on the ACLU Brief.

---

* The judge wrongly asserted (in footnote 4 of his ruling) that: "Dr. Geisler testified to the widely held view that there are five beliefs characteristic of all Fundamentalist movements, in addition, of course, to the inerrancy of Scripture: (1) belief in the virgin birth of Christ, (2) belief in the deity of Christ, (3) belief in the substitutional atonement of Christ, (4) belief in the second coming of Christ, and (5) belief in the physical resurrection of all departed souls."

What Geisler had said in the Deposition testimony was: "And those essential doctrines were: (1) the virgin birth of Christ, that Jesus was virgin born; (2) the deity of Christ, that Jesus was God; (3) the atonement of Christ, that Christ died on the cross for the sins of the world; (4) the bodily resurrection, that Jesus bodily rose from the grave; (5) and the inspiration of the Bible, that the Bible is the word of God. (6) Now, some added a 6th one, but these were the five fundamentals. The 6th one that they added is that Jesus is going to return to this earth someday, the Second Coming of Christ."

The judge made two mistakes. He confused the bodily resurrection of Christ with the bodily resurrection of all believers. And he didn't add correctly, since the "five" he noted plus the inspiration of scripture equals six fundamentals, as the witness said.

The Logical Fallacies

The ruling is a field day for fallacy hunters. First of all, the heart of the legal opinion is the *genetic fallacy*. For it argues that since the *source* of creationism is a religious book (Genesis) then creationism must be religious. But as had been pointed out in testimony from both sides (Dr. Ruse for evolution and others for creation), the *source* of a scientific theory has nothing to do with its *status* as science. No one ever rejected the Kekulé model of the benzene molecule or Tesla's alternating current motor because they came from visions, or Socrates' view because it came from a prophetess!

The *source* of a scientific idea is quite irrelevant; it is its *justifiability* that counts. If one is to throw away a science because its inspiration comes from the Judeo-Christian Bible, then much of early modern science should be discarded since Bacon, Kelvin, Newton, and others admitted their source was the biblical view of creation. This is a widely held understanding even by non-creationists, from Alfred N. Whitehead to Ian Barbour. Furthermore, if a science is ruled illegal because its source is the Bible, then much of near eastern archaeology should be likewise prohibited because the source and inspiration for much of it came from the Bible. But despite the fact that this was all carefully pointed out to the judge in precise testimony, he still ruled that the Bill was religion because its *source* is Genesis.

Second, the fallacy of *misimplication* is evident. The judge stated and implied that many would draw religious implications from teaching creation. But the same also applies to evolution. For if creationism should be rejected because it is consistent with the beliefs of "Fundamentalists" (though it was never one of the stated "Fundamentals"), then evolution should also be rejected because it is one of the stated beliefs of Religious Humanists (indeed, it is one of their fundamental beliefs). Furthermore, many scientists have elevated evolution itself into a "god" or the equivalent. In later life, for example, Darwin referred to "my deity Natural Selection" as replacing the function of the Deity in creating the species. Ernest Haeckel deified the process of evolution, as did Herbert

Spencer. Julian Huxley refers to his religion as the "religion of evolutionary humanism." Now, so far as we know, there are no informed creationists who have ever made creationism into a god or religion (though it is a part of the religious beliefs of many). In view of this, one could argue that the danger of the theory of evolution becoming a religion is more likely than that of creation. At any rate, if creation (which is a belief in a religious system) is thereby religious, then so is evolution.

Third, one notices the fallacy of *emphasizing the accidental.* The classic example of this logic is the man who became intoxicated whether he drank wine and water, whiskey and water, or gin and water. He reasoned that the element of water, since it was common to all three, was the cause of his intoxication. So he gave up water! Now the judge has said in essence that since all Fundamentalists have creationism as part of their religious belief then it must be the *essence* of their religious belief. This does not logically follow. For what is only accidental to a system (even if it is always present) is not necessarily the essence of that system. And creationism has never been declared the essence of any Fundamentalist religion. In fact, not all Fundamentalists believe in creationism as defined in Act 590. Most historians acknowledge that one of the characteristics of much of modern Fundamentalism is the belief in dispensationalism. The most widespread version of this was largely influenced by the Scofield Bible. Yet this reference Bible accepts the Gap Theory, that there may be long geological ages in the alleged "gap" between the first two verses of Genesis which is in conflict with points 5 and 6 in the definition of creationism. Furthermore, some of the earliest Fundamentalists who wrote in the famous book called *The Fundamentalists* (1910 - 15) (such as James Orr, B. B. Warfield, and G. F. Wright) were willing to accept modified evolutionary positions. So if creationism (as defined in Act 590) is not even universal among Fundamentalists—to say nothing of *essential* to it—then the judge erred in rejecting creationism on the grounds it was essentially religious.

Fourth, the judge's ruling commits the fallacy of *overlooking the essential.* The essence of religion is worship or *commitment* to an Ultimate (whether God, a person, or an idea). Religion is not simply acknowledging that there is a First cause to the universe. This is no more a religious act than recognizing that some person would make a good spouse makes one married. It takes *commitment* to make religion (or marriage). If approaching an object in a purely scientific way represents religion, then the study of Christ from the evidence of history is automatically teaching "religion." The judge has failed to account for one of the most fundamental distinctions of the court in this matter: the teaching *of* religion is wrong in public school, but not the teaching *about* religion. In like manner, the teaching *about* an object of religion (the Creator) is not the essence of religion. Rather, it is presenting some alleged teachings *of* the Creator. In short, belief *that* God exists cannot be thought to be religious (Aristotle believed that God exists but did not worship Him). It is belief *in* God (trust, commitment) that is religious.

Fifth, since the judge failed to make the above essential distinction, a *reductio ad absurdum* follows. The absurd consequence of his position that a creator cannot be implied as an explanation of the origin of life is that even Darwin's *Origin of Species* cannot be taught in public schools, since the last lines of that book refer to the creator of the first form (or forms) of life.

Sixth, the fallacy of *equivocation* is committed on the word "science."* On the "strict" definition, science is something observable, repeatable, and falsifiable. On this view neither the general theory of evolution nor creation are any sort of science. So the judge apparently applied a "broad" definition to evolution (which calls for a model which can make certain testable predictions). However, on this definition, creation is just as much a science as is evolution. At any rate, an equivocation occurs with the word "evolution," since on the broad definition of evolution as a *fact* or happening, evolution is not falsifiable. Only on the narrow definition of evolution as

---

*   See Appendix Ten for documentation and elaboration of this point.

a *means* can evolution be falsified. But Act 590 deals with evolution in the broad sense, and in this sense it is no more falsifiable in the strict rendering than is creationism.

Seventh, there are also cases of *special pleading*. Suppose we accept the widely held belief reflected by the judge that creation *ex nihilo* (out of nothing) is unique to certain Judeo-Christian views. Even so, it is special pleading to make this "an inherently religious concept" any more than making creation *ex deo* (out of God), as in pantheistic systems, or creation *ex hulas* (out of preexisting stuff), as in dualistic systems, inherently religious concepts. Why single out only one of the three basic views of origin—the one represented by "creation-science" in the Act—and make it alone "inherently religious"? Is this not a clear bias against one view of origins?

Eighth, Judge Overton violates the *law of excluded middle*, which demands that there can be only two views when one is the logical opposite of the other. Both witnesses and defense attorneys insisted that on any given point of origin the beginning was either (a) caused by natural forces or (b) caused by some supernatural force. Despite this logically obvious disjunction, Overton insisted that there could be more than two theories about origins. The judge ignored the obvious fact that things either began by chance or else by design—a fact that even evolutionists acknowledge (see Appendix Eight).

Ninth, there are *non sequiturs* (does not follow logically) in the ruling. For example, the judge insists that Section 4 is wrong because "evolution does not presuppose the absence of a creator or God . . . . " By this Judge Overton apparently means that Act 590 wrongly assumes that evolution implies atheism. This of course is not true, since theistic evolution is a logical possibility. What Section 4 implies is that there is *no direct involvement* of any supreme being in the origin of the various forms of life. It does *not* imply that there is no God at all nor that one could not be indirectly involved.

Tenth, there is *petitio principii* (begging the question). The judge defines any discussion of a Creator as an "inescapably religious discussion." He then easily concludes such a discussion is unconstitutional. He says the same of "creation out of nothing." But once these concepts are pre-judged to be religious and this conclusion is then used as the basis for determining whether they are a religious violation of the First Amendment, the judge has used his conclusion as his premise. This is the logical fallacy of begging the question.

The Legal Implications

There are serious legal questions raised by the judge's ruling. The debate turns on two different interpretations of what the First Amendment means. One view is that it entails a wall of separation between Church and State. This view is clearly reflected in Judge Overton's ruling, as is evidenced by his closing quotation about "good fences make good neighbors," his ruling out any supernaturalistic interpretation of scientific data, and his conclusion that any reference to or implication of a "creation" is automatically religious.

The other interpretation is that the First Amendment intends to build no "wall of separation" between Church and State but was designed to guarantee "religious neutrality" on the part of the State toward religion by opposing the "establishment" of any religion over others. This view is reflected in the articles by Wendell Bird and John Whitehead (who will together defend the upcoming Louisiana creation-evolution case).* The essence of their argument is that the First Amendment is not for completely *separating* church and state, but is against *establishing* or favoring any one religion above others by the aid of the state. The First Amendment reads: *"Congress shall make no law respecting an establishment of religion, or prohibiting the free exercise thereof."* And in the

---

*   Wendell R. Bird, "Freedom of Religion and Science Instruction in Public Schools," 87 *Yale Law Journal* 515-570 (Jan. 1978).

Wendell R. Bird, "Freedom from Establishment and Unneutrality in Public School Instruction and Religious School Regulation," 1979 *Harvard Journal of Law & Public Policy* (June 1979).

John W. Whitehead, *The Separation Illusion.* Milford, Michigan: Mott Media, Inc., Publishers, 1982.

famous Everson case (1947), Supreme Court Justice Black stated that this means "neither a state nor the Federal Government can set up a church." And neither can it "pass laws which aid one religion . . . or prefer one religion over another."

Now if the First Amendment is really an anti-*establishment* clause, as it says, and not a complete separation clause, as it does not say, then the basis for the judge's ruling is wrong. One thing seems certain, if the Constitution meant to separate God and government, then the Declaration of Independence is unconstitutional! For it speaks of the "unalienable rights of the Creator." And since pronouncing the Declaration of Independence unconstitutional is absurd on its face, we are left with the only reasonable conclusion that the Constitution does not separate God from government or public governmental schools.

But let us suppose for the sake of argument that the First Amendment be understood as a separation clause (and not an anti-establishment clause). Even on this interpretation Judge Overton's decision is contrary to the First Amendment, since it allows *only* a naturalistic evolutionary view to be taught, which view favors the beliefs of religious humanists. In fact the judge's decision not only *favors* the religion of Humanism, but it *exclusively* favors it. For the ruling allows *only* non-theistic evolutionistic and naturalistic views to be taught, which accords precisely with the views of religious humanists. In brief, if one takes an "anti-establishment" interpretation of the First Amendment, then the Arkansas creation-evolution act is constitutional, for it does not establish any *one* view or religion over another. In fact, it mandates teaching *both* views. On the other hand, if one takes a "wall of separation" view (as Overton apparently does), then his ruling is a violation of the First Amendment, since it not only allows but favors non-theistic religions over theistic ones. In either case, the ruling seems to violate the Constitution, not uphold it.

Judge Overton rejected this anti-establishment interpretation saying that "The argument has no legal merit." He perjoratively referred to Bird's scholarly article in the *Yale Law Review* as "a student note." It is difficult for non-lawyers to enter this battle on the meaning of the Constitution. It seems to us that much of the current legal "reading" of the Constitution is contrary to the general interpretative practice of humankind. Certainly experience shows that the vast majority of people expect readers to understand by their words what they meant by them, not what the reader would like them to mean. Now from what we can discern from the statements of the framers of the Constitution, and its understood meaning by contemporaries and immediate successors, the anti-establishment interpretation of the First Amendment seems to be the correct one. If this is so, Judge Overton's decision is based on a misinterpretation of the Constitution.

For those who defend the interpretation of the First Amendment more in terms of *what it means to us today* rather than what the framers meant by it, we ask the following question: Do these interpreters want *their* words to be interpreted by succeeding generations *according to what they meant by them* or according to what the readers decide they *mean to them*? If they expect us to accept *their* meaning (and not read *ours* into it), then should they not give the original framers of the First Amendment the same courtesy? On the other hand, if they insist that others can take their words to mean something other than what they meant by them, then why can't we (or others later) take their words to mean that the Constitution should be interpreted in the way we want and not in the way they meant? Despite the fact they intend to give their interpretation of the Constitution, why can't we say their words are really to be understood in the other way, since that is what they mean *to us*? Such, it seems to us, is the dilemma of this mistaken interpretation of the First Amendment.

Surely Judge Overton does not desire his ruling to be (mis)interpreted in a way he did not mean. If so, then should he not have ruled the other way? For his ruling was based on an interpretation which reads his own meaning *into* the Constitutional framer's words, rather than reading their clear meaning out of their words. Surely the good judge believes in the Golden Rule, which being translated into this situation means: "Give the same meaning to other's words as they gave them, just as you would have others do the same for your words."

The Religious Implications

Judge Overton ruled that Act 590 would establish the religion of "Fundamentalism" in public schools and was thereby unconstitutional. But it seems to us that in ruling the way he did the judge has in effect established the religion of "Secular Humanism" in the public schools. Judge Overton accomplished the opposite of what he thought he was doing. For in trying to avoid giving what he called "Fundamentalist" beliefs *one* voice (among two voices), he gave "Humanists" the *only* voice.

Two Overlooked Factors

There are two significant factors to keep in mind which Judge Overton apparently overlooked. First, in a balanced treatment *two*-model approach (such as Act 590 provided), there is no way one can reasonably argue that only *one* view is being favored. The Act mandates teaching *both* views (if either is taught). So if Overton's reasoning is right, then the Act is also unconstitutional because it mandates teaching evolution (which is consistent with a humanistic religious system). But the judge clearly acknowledged (via the Epperson case, 1968) that teaching evolution is not teaching religion. If the Act *equally* mandates teaching both (if either), then it is unreasonable to reject the Act because it allegedly favors one of two equally mandated views.

Second, there is no way the Act could establish one view over another since it doesn't mandate teaching either. It is only an *"if, then"* law. It says *if* one view is taught—and it need not be—then the opposing view must also be taught. Now we fail to see how a law mandating the teaching of nothing could be *establishing* anything.

Of course, it is argued that with such an Act many teachers would opt not to teach either view and would thereby rob the student of a valid educational experience. But the possibility of missing "a valid educational experience" is neither unconstitutional nor uncommon (there is simply far too much knowledge to teach everything).

The Establishment of a Humanistic Religion

Granting as we do the good intentions of Judge Overton, his decision has *in effect* done exactly the opposite of what he desired. The judge wished to uphold the First Amendment by avoiding the "establishment" of religion in Arkansas public schools. This is a noble task for which he was trained and took the oath of office. Unfortunately, the judge has accomplished the reverse of his stated desires. For by trying to avoid favoring the religion of "Fundamentalism" he has in effect "established" the religion of "Humanism."

Let us outline the reasoning for this conclusion:

1. Humanism has been defined as a religion by the U.S. Supreme Court.
2. Non-theism, evolution, naturalism, and relativism are the central beliefs of religious Humanists.
3. Overton's decision in effect exclusively favors the teaching of the above beliefs.
4. But whatever in effect favors central beliefs of one religion over another is a violation of the First Amendment.
5. Therefore, Overton's decision in effect is a violation of the First Amendment.

Now let us examine each of these premises.

Humanism is a Religion

Humanism is a religion by its own acclaim and by legal recognition. This is evidenced by the following facts: (1) The *Humanist Manifesto I* (1933) declares: "to establish such a religion [of Humanism] is a major necessity of the present." The words "religion" or "religious" occur some 29 times in the six-page Manifesto. (2) The *Humanist Manifesto II* (1973) continues to expound the belief that Humanism is a religion, using the words religion (or religious) some nineteen times. It proclaims that "Faith, commensurate with advancing knowledge, is also necessary." (3) An influential journal is dedicated to these beliefs. It is called the *Religious Humanist*. (4) Many proponents of this religion have written books and articles describing their humanistic beliefs as a *religion*. Julian Huxley called his beliefs, "the religion of evolutionary humanism." *(The Humanist,* Jan.-Feb., 1962.) Michael Kolenda's book on humanistic religion is entitled *Religion Without God* (1976).

Not only do humanists recognize humanism as a religion (or as religious), but the Supreme Court has also recognized by name Secular Humanism as a religion. The process of this recognition came about gradually when many agnostics and atheists claimed First Amendment protection for their beliefs against discrimination in jobs or in the military. The Supreme Court ruled (in the *Everson* case, 1947) that "neither a State nor the Federal Government can constitutionally force a person to profess a belief or disbelief in any religion. Neither can [it] constitutionally pass laws or impose requirements which aid all religions as against non-believers." Also, the court ruled *(Torcaso* case, 1960) that those who do not believe in God can still have a conscientious objector status on *religious* grounds (i.e., First Amendment). The record of the Torcaso case specifies some non-theistic religions, saying, "Among religions in this country which do not teach what would generally be considered a belief in the existence of God are Buddhism, Taoism, Ethical Culture, *Secular Humanism,* and others" (emphasis added).

So not only do humanists claim there is such a religion as Secular Humanism, but the Supreme Court has officially noted this religion by name.

Non-theism, Evolutionism, and Naturalism

There are four central beliefs of religious Humanism: (1) Non-theism, (2) Evolution, (3) Naturalism, and (4) Relativism (of human values). These beliefs are confessed in *Manifestos I and II* and throughout the writings of most humanists.

Manifesto I begins, "We therefore affirm the following:

First: Religious humanists regard the universe as self-existing and not created [non-theism].

Second: Humanism believes that man is a part of nature [naturalism] and that he has emerged as the result of a continuous process [evolution]".

It thirdly denies any supernatural explanations in points 3, 4, 5, 6, and 11. *Humanist Manifesto II* (1973) reaffirms these same three beliefs (see "Preface" and "Religion," sections one and two).

The "Secular Humanist Declaration" (1981)* again reaffirms these exact beliefs in points 4, 6, 8, and 9. Under the last point they say, "There may be some significant differences among scientists concerning the mechanics of evolution; yet the evolution of the species is supported so strongly by the weight of evidence that it is difficult to reject it." They conclude saying, "Secular humanism places trust in human intelligence rather than in divine guidance." Again secular humanism acknowledges no need for God, a naturalistic explanation for everything, and a belief in evolution. So far as we can determine, all secular humanists hold these three essential beliefs which form the core of the religion of humanism. Indeed, if one appealed to God, the supernatural and/or creation, he would by definition be excluded as a secular humanist; he would in fact be some kind of theist.

In addition to these three beliefs—non-theism, evolution, and naturalism—secular humanism believes in the relativity of human values. In *Manifesto I* (point 5) it reads: "Humanism asserts that the nature of the universe depicted by modern science makes unacceptable any supernatural or cosmic guarantee of human values." If this is so then *Manifesto II* correctly notes, "Ethics is *autonomous* and *situational,* needing no theological or ideological sanction" (point 3). In short, if God is not needed for the origin of life, then godliness is likewise not needed as the basis for living life. Each man must decide his own values. Thus, the first three central beliefs of secular humanism imply the fourth. And these four are core beliefs of the religion of secular humanism.

Overton's Ruling Favors Religious Humanist's Beliefs

Of the four central premises of secular humanism, Judge

---

*   See the humanist magazine, *Free Inquiry* (Winter 1980-81).

Overton directly ruled that three of them (while implying the fourth) are the *only* ones that can be taught in Arkansas science classes. For he ruled that teaching any non-naturalistic or non-evolutionary theory would be unconstitutional. He ruled that even the implication of a "creator" or supernatural cause is a violation of the First Amendment. In the judge's own words, scientific creationism "is not science because it depends upon supernatural intervention which is not guided by natural law." It cannot be science, the judge added, because "it is not explanatory by reference to natural law . . . . " In fact, the judge pontificated, "there is *no* scientific explanation for these limits [of created kinds of animals] which is guided by natural law and the limitations, whatever they are, *cannot* be explained by natural law" (emphasis added). And as for the creationist contention for separate origins for ape and human, the judge ruled this "explains *nothing* and refers to *no* scientific fact or theory" (emphasis added). In addition, the judge said "the concepts and wording convey an *inescapable* religiosity" (emphasis added). Indeed, he called the scientific claim for "creation of the world" the ultimate religious statement because "God is the only actor." And "concepts concerning . . . a supreme being of some sort are manifestly religious" (see Chapter Eight, *passim*).

Favoring One Religion Violates the First Amendment

The First Amendment of the United States Constitution says nothing about the *separation* of Church and State. It does, however, forbid the "establishment" of a religion by the State. It reads: "Congress shall make no law respecting an establishment of religion, or prohibiting the free exercise thereof; . . . . " In the famous Everson case (1947), Supreme Court Judge Black stated that this means "Neither a state nor the Federal Government can set up a church." And neither can it "pass laws which aid one religion . . . or prefer one religion over another." Thus any judicial decision which so aids one religion over another is a clear violation of the First Amendment.

Some may not consider Humanism a religion. But even here

the Supreme Court has ruled (Abington School case, 1963) that "the State may not establish a 'religion of Secularism' in the sense of affirmatively opposing or showing hostility to religion" and thereby "preferring those who believe in no religion over those who do believe." Further, in the Reed case (1965), a district court similarly ruled that for government "to espouse a particular philosophy of secularism, or secularism in general" may be a violation of the First Amendment.

The Inescapable Conclusion

On January 5, 1982, Federal Court Judge William Overton in effect established Secular Humanism as a religion in the Arkansas public schools. For he ruled that only humanist beliefs. including non-theism, evolution, and naturalism, can be taught in public school science classes. These beliefs not only favor humanism, but are central beliefs of the religion of Secular Humanism. Perhaps the judge did not *intend* to do this, but this is none the less the *effect* of his decision. History will record that in Judge Overton's federal court (December 7-17, 1981) the Creator went to his court—and "lost"! The irony of history was that this very court which dishonorably dismissed God began each day by the U.S. Marshal saying (praying?), " . . . God save the United States and this honorable court." Amen!

A pluralistic, open democratic society allows all points of view to be heard.

—Secular Humanist Declaration (1981)

Chapter Three

The Legal Briefs For and Against the Creation-Evolution Act

Part I
The Plaintiff's Brief Against the Creation-Evolution Act

PRELIMINARY STATEMENT*

Twelve clergymen have joined with religious and educational organizations, teachers, parents and a state legislator in this constitutional challenge to Act 590. Plaintiffs believe that the mandate of Act 590 that "creation-science" be given "balanced treatment" with evolution in Arkansas public schools establishes religion in violation of the First Amendment to the Constitution of the United States. Moreover, it establishes a *particular* set of religious beliefs that is inconsistent with the religious views of many of the plaintiffs.

---

*   This section is taken verbatim from the pretrial legal brief of the ACLU.

Although "creation-science" is religion rather than science, Plaintiffs do not seek to "censor" it or any other view. *Cf.* Defendants' Preliminary Outline at 4, 7. Rather, out of respect for science and out of reverence for religion, they seek to maintain the separation of church and state the First Amendment to the Constitution of the United States commands: let religion be taught from our hearths and our pulpits; let science be taught in our public schools.

"Creation-science" embodies the belief of religious Fundamentalists that, in a relatively recent six-day week, God created the world as we now know it, save for the havoc later wreaked by a worldwide flood survived only by Noah and his companions in the Ark. *See* Genesis 1:1-31; 2:7; 5; 6:13; 8:19; 10; 11 . . . .

Fundamentalists believe that evolution is not only wrong but "evil;" even those people who (like many of the plaintiffs) believe both in evolution and in the Bible, holding that evolution was God's way of bringing today's world into being, are accused by Creationists of theological error. *See, e.g.,* H. Morris, *Scientific Creationism* 16 (Creation-Life Publishers, 1974) (public school edition); App. 2. *See also* H. Morris and M. Clark, *The Bible Has The Answer* 80, 90 (Creation-Life Publishers, 1976); App. 3. By cloaking their essentially religious beliefs with "an accumulation of asserted inconsistencies or insufficiencies in the evolutionary model" (Morrow Dep. at 104; App. 4), Creationists have come up with a doctrine to combat the "evils" of evolution in the public school classroom.

Mandatory inclusion of "creation-science" in the public school curriculum therefore poses a choice, which plaintiffs believe to be a false choice, between good and evil, science and religion and, ultimately, between science and God. Such a divisive doctrine—damaging to science, to education in general and to religion—has no place in our public schools.

STATEMENT OF ISSUES

Issue No. 1: Does "creation-science" constitute a religious belief, notwithstanding its claims that (a) it is an "alternative scientific model" to evolution and that (b) it has legitimate educational value?

Issue No. 2: Does Act 590 reflect a religious legislative purpose?

Issue No. 3: Does Act 590 advance a particular religious belief?

Issue No. 4: Does Act 590 entangle the government with religion?

Issue No. 5: Does Act 590 abridge the academic freedom of teachers and students in Arkansas public schools?

Issue No. 6: Is Act 590 unconstitutionally vague?

SUMMARY OF PROOF

Plaintiffs' proof falls into three closely related segments, which for the sake of convenience can be referred to as the "religion," the "science" and the "education" cases.

(1) Summary of the "Religion" Case

The "religion" proof will show a legislative history of Act 590 evincing a religious purpose. Act 590 is a legislative adoption of portions of the Biblical Book of Genesis, as literally interpreted by Fundamentalists who have a history of religious belief in the factual inerrancy of the Bible and of an equally religious opposition to modern science, particularly evolution.

Proponents of Act 590 claim that, regardless of its religious roots, "creation-science" is legitimate science which, if limited to "scientific evidences," can be taught in the public schools without contravention of the Establishment Clause. The concept of a "Creator" or "supernatural Creator" which inheres in "*creation*-science" (emphasis added), however, does not differ from the concept of "God." See H. Morris, *Scientific Creationism, supra,* at 17; App. 2 ("The creation model . . . supposes that the universe was simply called into existence by the omnipotence, in accord with the omniscience, of the Creator. Not only the matter and energy of the cosmos, but also the laws controlling their behavior, were specially created *ex nihilo,* or perhaps better, *ex Deo.*"; D. Gish, *Evolution: The Fossils Say No!* 1 (Creation-Life Publishers, 1978) (public school edition); App. 5 ("The creation model . . . postulates that all basic animal and plant types (the created kinds) were brought into existence by acts of a supernatural Creator using special processes which are not operative today.").

Act 590, moreover, has hallmarks of Fundamentalist missionary zeal, seeking to find a ground or language common to Fundamentalists and non-Fundamentalists alike that they can use to defend their religious position and to win adherents to their religious views. This is a technique known as "apologetics," a respected form of religious argumentation, except when the audience is a captive one consisting of public school children.

(2) Summary of the "Science" Case

The use of scientific techniques and terminology does not make "creation-science" science. Plaintiffs' expert science witnesses—with the concurrence of many of the defendants' witnesses—will testify that science is rooted in natural laws, not in supernatural persons, events or processes. A system of belief that has as its center the interruption, suspension or nonexistence of natural laws and, in lieu thereof, the intervention of a supernatural and omnipotent Creator (God) is not science. Even if some of its minor premises look, smell, taste, feel and sound scientific, its major premise—God—is not subject to testing or to disproof and, accordingly, is not scientific. Such a system of belief, not being science, is religion instead. "Creation-science" is precisely such a system.

(3) Summary of the "Education" Case

The secular educational value of "creation-science," if taught as science, is nil. Without God, "creation-science" is a motley assortment of facts and assertions, bound to puzzle and confuse. With God, "creation-science" is religious, forbidden by our Constitution to be taught in public schools. This educational dilemma cannot be avoided by judicious redaction of the existing "creation-science" materials or the authorship of new ones. See Defendants' Preliminary Outline at 6. Even the smallest child is likely to recognize God in the concept of a Creator.

Part II
The Defense Case for the Creation-Evolution Act

I. Act 590 Does Not Establish Religion*

1. The establishment clause of the First Amendment prohibits State legislative action which: (1) does not reflect a secular purpose, (2) advances or inhibits any religion and (3) fosters an excessive government entanglement with religion. *Tilton v. Richardson*, 403 U.S. 672, 678 (1971). Act 590 does not violate the establishment clause under this three-pronged test.

2. Act 590 has a valid secular purpose in that it does not "hinder the quest for knowledge, restrict the freedom to learn, or restrain the freedom to teach." *Epperson v. Arkansas*, 393 U.S. 97 (1968). The Act attempts to give students a broad overview of the subject of origins.

3. The purpose of Act 590 is to ensure a neutral presentation of two scientific models of origins. It does not attempt, as did the statute in *Epperson, supra,* "to blot out a particular theory because of its supposed conflict with the biblical account." 393 U.S. at 97 (1968). On the contrary, its purpose is to assure that if either model of origins is discussed in the public school classroom, the alternative model will also be taught.

4. Creation-science as defined in Act 590 is to be taught as a science—it leaves absolutely no room for religious indoctrination and, in fact, specifically prohibits it. *See* Section 2 of Act 590 of 1981.

5. Creation-science is at least as non-religious as evolution-science. The words "creation" and "creator" are not *inherently* religious. References to "God" in the pledge to the United States flag or to "In God is our trust" in the National Anthem in

---

* This section is taken verbatim from Defense Attorney's pretrial document, "Conclusion of Law."

public school class rooms has been held not to violate the establishment clause. *Engel v. Vitale,* 370 U.S. 421, 435 (1962); *Aronow v. United States,* 432 F.2d 242, 243 (9th Cir. 1970). The religious heritage of the United States has been recognized by the United States Supreme Court. *Engel v. Vitale,* 370 U.S. 421 (1962); *Zorach v. Clauson,* 343 U.S. 306 (1952); *Holy Trinity Church v. United States,* 143 US. 457 (1892); *Bogen v. Doty,* 456 F.Supp. 983 (D. Minn. 1978) aff'd 598 F.2d 1110 (8th Cir. 1979). "Many of our legal, 'political, and personal values derive historically from religious teachings. Government must inevitably take cognizance of the existence of religion and, indeed, under certain circumstances the First Amendment may require it to do so." *Abington School Dist. v. Schempp,* 374 U.S. 203, 306 (1963) (Goldberg J. Concurring); *see also, McGowan v. Maryland,* 366 U.S. 420, 421 (1961) where the Court said:

> The establishment clause does not bar federal or state legislation of conduct whose reason or effect merely happens to coincide or harmonize with the tenets of some or all religions. In many instances, the Congress or State Legislatures conclude that the general welfare of society, wholly apart from any religious considerations, demands such regulation. Thus, for temporal purposes murder is illegal. And the fact that this agrees with the dictates of Judeo-Christian religions while it may disagree with others does not invalidate the regulation.

See also *Davis v. Beason,* 133 U.S. 333, (1890); *Reynolds v. U.S.,* 98 U.S. 145, (1878); *Maluak v. Yogi,* 44, F. Supp. 1284, 1317 (D.N.J. 1977) aff'd 592 f.2d 197 (3rd Cir. 1979).

6. It is uniformly conceded that the State has a legitimate right to prescribe the curriculum for schools. *See Epperson v. Arkansas* 393 U.S. at 107; at 115-116 (Stewart, concurring); *Meyer v. Nebraska,* 262 U.S. 390 (1923), *Epperson v. Arkansas,* 242 Ark. 922, 416, S.W.2d 322 (1967), rev'd on other grounds, 393 U.S. 97 (1968). Further the State of Arkansas' authority over its schools is clearly recognized in Arkansas law. Ark. Const., Art. 14, §1 grants to the State the plenary authority over education and states:

> Intelligence and virtue being the safeguards of liberty and

bulwark of a free and good government, the state shall ever maintain a general, suitable, and efficient system of free schools whereby all persons in the state between the ages of 6 and 21 years may receive gratuitous instruction.

7. It is a well-established known principle of statutory construction that courts will refuse to consider testimony by members of a legislative body to prove legislative intent. *E.g., United States v. Emmons,* 410 U.S. 396, 93 S.Ct. 1007, 35 L.Ed.2d 379 (1973), *United States v. United Mine Workers of America,* 330 U.S. 258, 67 S.Ct. 667, 91 L.Ed. 884 (1947); *City of New York v. Ruckelhaus,* 358 F.Supp. 669 (D. D.C. 1973); *Sutherland, Statutory Construction,* §48.16 (4th Ed. 1973). A corrollary principle also uniformly rejects any reference to the motive of a member of a legislature in enacting a law, except as these motives are expressed in the statute itself. *Galvan v. Press,* 347 U.S. 522, 74 S.Ct. 737, 98 L.Ed. 911 (1954); *Algoma Plywood and Veneer Co. v. Wisconsin Employment Relations Board,* 336 U.S. 301, 69 S.Ct. 584, 93 L.Ed. 918 (1949). The Supreme Court in *Epperson v. Arkansas* specifically acknowledged that a court cannot inquire into the legislature's motives behind a law's enactment:

> It is not for the court to invalidate a statute because of the court's belief that the "motives" behind its passage were improper; it is simply too difficult to determine what those motives were.

Epperson v. Arkansas, 393 U.S. 97, 113, 89 S.Ct. 266, 21 L.Ed. 228 (1968); *see, e.g., United States v. O'Brien,* 391 U.S. 367, 382-383, 20 L.Ed.2D 672, 683, 684, 88 S.Ct. 1673 (1968). *See Karen B. v. Treen, Vol. 653* F.2d *P. 897,* No. 80-4003 (5th Cir. Aug. 5, 1981). In *Karen B.,* the Court struck down a Louisiana statute allowing daily prayer in schools. In striking the statute, the Court noted that the personal testimony of the individual proponents of a bill, given in court after the enactment of the statute, is far less persuasive than the intent embodied in the statute, since the personal testimony "reflects only the partial perspective of those legislators and not the collective intention of the entire body." Similarly, in the instant case, the intent of any one legislator is not probative of what the intent of the entire Arkansas Legislature was in passing Act 590.

8. A state legislature may require diversity in presentation of theories of origin wherever the subject of origins is to be presented. [Cf. Daniel v. Waters, 515 F.2d 485 (6th Cir. 1975).] This is exactly what Act 590 is designed to do and it accomplishes its result without the inclusion of any religious writings or teachings.

9. The establishment clause does "not call for a total separation of church and state," and the requirement, "far from being in fact a 'wall' is a blurred, indistinct, and variable barrier . . . . " Lemon v. Kurtzman, 403, U.S. 602, 614 (1971). The establishment clause is not, as plaintiffs suggest, a complete wall of separation between church and state.

10. The mere fact that the scientific evidence for creation-science may coincide with the tenets or beliefs of some religions clearly does not result in the establishment of those religions. See Harris v. McRae, 448 U.S. 297, 100 S.Ct. 2671, 2689, 65 L.Ed.2d 784 (1980). In Harris, the Supreme Court summarily rejected the argument that limiting medicaid funds for abortion violated the establishment clause because such a requirement incorporated into the law of the doctrines of the Roman Catholic Church. The Court reasoned that:

> Although neither a State nor a Federal Government can constitutionally "pass laws which aid one religion, aid all religions, or prefer one religion over another," Everson v. Board of Education, 330 U.S. 1, 15, it does not follow that a statute violates the establishment clause because it "happens to coincide or harmonize with the tenets of some or all religions." McGowan v. Maryland, 366, U.S. 420, 442.

448 U.S. at 319.

II. Act 590 Does Not Unconstitutionally Abridge Academic Freedom Rights

1. Academic freedom is not a constitutionally protected right which limits state action, but is rather an interest which may be weighed against state education interests. Pickering v. Board of Education, 391 U.S. 563, 568 (1972). Furthermore,

the commentators are in general agreement that the cases create no fundamental right of academic freedom. S. Goldstein, *The Asserted Constitutional Right of Public School Teachers to Determine What They Teach,* 124 Pa.L.Rev. 1293, 1298 (1976).

2. The state has an "undoubted right" to establish the curriculum of its schools. *Epperson v. Arkansas,* 393, U.S. 97, 107 (1968), *West Virginia State Board of Education v. Barnette,* 319 U.S. 624, 631, (1943), *Meyer v. Nebraska,* 262 U.S. 390, 402 (1923). All subjects can't be taught; it is therefore within the power of the state to choose which subjects will be included in the curriculum and which will be left to other sources. *Mercer v. Michigan State Board of Education,* 379 F.Supp. 580, 586, (N.D. Mich. 1974) aff'd mem. 419 U.S. 1081 (1975).

3. The state has a legitimate interest in establishing a curriculum that reflects the value systems and educational emphasis which are the collective will of those whose children are being educated and who are paying the costs. *Cary v. Board of Education,* 598 F.2d. 535, 543 (10th Cir. 1979). *See also Mercer v. Michigan State Board of Education,* 379 F.Supp. 580 (E.D. Mich. 1974) aff'd mem., 419 U.S. 1081 (1975); *Griggs v. Cook,* 272 F.Supp. 163, (N.D. Ga. 1967); *Ahern v. Board of Education,* 456 F.2d 399 (8th Cir. 1972).

4. Courts do not and cannot intervene in the resolution of conficts which arise in the daily operation of school systems and which do not directly and sharply implicate basic constitutional values. *Epperson v. Arkansas,* 393 U.S. 97, 104 (1968). The inclusion of objective, scientific study in the curriculum is a valid exercise of the state's power to determine the curriculum of its schools which does not implicate constitutional values.

5. Teachers have no constitutional right to override political decision-makers as to the proper content of courses taught. *Cary v. Board of Education,* 598 F.2d. 535, 544 (10th Cir. 1979); *Palmer v. Board of Education,* 603 F.2d. 1271, 1274 (7th Cir. 1979); *Adams v. Campbell County School District,* 511 F.2d 1242, 1247 (10th Cir. 1975); *Clark v. Holmes,* 474 F.2d. 928, 931 (7th Cir. 1972).

6. Academic freedom embraces the interests of both

students and teachers to inquire, to study, and to evaluate, to gain new maturity and understanding. *Sweezy v. New Hampshire,* 354 U.S. 234, 249 (1957).

7.   Public schools should provide students with a variety of concepts rather than limiting students to the ideas of only those in authority. *Keyishian v. Board of Regents,* 385 U.S. 589, 605 (1967). Students may not be confined to the expression of only those sentiments that are officially approved. *Tinker v. Des Moines School District,* 393 U.S. 503, 511 (1969). Students should be trained through wide exposure to that robust exchange of ideas which discovers truth out of a multitude of tongues rather than any kind of authoritative selection. *Keyishian v. Board of Regents,* 385, U.S. 589, 603 (1967). Without Act 590, Arkansas' Public School System would present only one view of origin—evolution. The actions of local school boards, school officials, and groups such as the Arkansas Education Association and the Classroom Teachers Association which seek to prohibit the teaching of scientific evidences which support creation-science violate the academic freedom interests of students and teachers to learn useful knowledge. Act 590 is an attempt by the State to enhance academic freedom.

8.   While the State cannot adopt a course of instruction which would aid or oppose any religion, it is free to adopt programs and practices for use in the public schools which insure religious neutrality. *Yoder v. Wisconsin,* 406 U.S. 205, 234-35n.22 (1972); *Abington School District v. Schempp,* 374 U.S. 203, 295 (Brennen J., concurring) (1963); *Chess v. Widmar,* 635 F.2d 1310, 1317 (8th Cir. 1980).

III. Act 590 Is Not Unconstitutionally Vague

1.   Act 590 sets forth with specificity a definition of creation-science. Section 4(a) of Act 590 defines creation-science to mean:

> The scientific evidences for creation and inferences from those scientific evidences. Creation-science includes the scientific evidences and related inferences that indicate:
> (1) Sudden creation of the universe, energy, and life from

nothing; (2) The insufficiency of mutation and natural selection in bringing about development of all living kinds from a single organism; (3) Changes only within fixed limits of originally created kinds of plants and animals; (4) Separate ancestry for man and apes; (5) Explanation of the earth's geology by catastrophism, including the occurrence of a worldwide flood; and (6) A relatively recent inception of the earth and living kinds.

Sections 2 and 5 of the Act specifically limit treatment of both evolution-science and creation-science to the scientific evidences for each model and explicitly prohibit the use of any religious instruction or references to religious writings.

2. Act 590 provides no penalties or sanctions for failure to give "balanced treatment" to the two models of origins. There can be no adverse affect on a teacher's "liberty and property interests" when there are no sanctions to impose.

3. The standard for vagueness is whether the statute is set out in terms that the ordinary person exercising ordinary common sense can sufficiently understand and comply with the statute. *E.g., United States Civil Service Commission v. National Association of Lettercarriers,* 413 U.S. 548 (1973)' *Broadrick v. Oklahoma,* 413 U.S. 601 (1973). Act 590 will be implemented by professionals (teachers) capable of assimilating difficult material and then explaining it to students in a simplified form. Professional educators will have no difficulty in giving "balanced treatment" within the meaning of Act 590. It will allow teachers to use their training and professional judgment to formulate their own treatment of both creation-science and evolution-science without chaining them to rigid standards or guidelines with which they might not feel comfortable.

4. The term "balanced treatment" is enlarged upon in Section 1 of Act 590, which states:

> Public schools within this state shall give balanced treatment to creation-science and to evolution-science. Balanced treatment to these two models shall be given in classroom lectures taken as a whole for each course, and textbook materials taken as a whole for each course, and library materials taken as a whole for the sciences and taken as a whole for the humanities, and in other educational programs in public schools, to the extent that such

lectures, textbooks, library materials or educational programs deal in any way with the subject of the origin of
man, life, the earth, or the universe.

Section 5 of Act 590 clarifies what is meant by "balanced
treatment":

> This act does not require or permit instruction in any
> religious doctrine or materials. This act does not require
> any instruction in the subject of origins, but simply re-
> quires instruction in both scientific models (of evolution-
> science and creation-science) if public schools choose to
> teach either. This act does not require each individual
> textbook or library book to give balanced treatment to
> the models of evolution-science and creation-science; it
> does not require any school books to be discarded. This
> act does not require each individual classroom lecture in a
> course to give such balanced treatment, but simply re-
> quires the lectures as a whole to give balanced treatment;
> it permits some lectures to present evolution-science and
> other lectures to present creation-science.

Act 590 leaves it to the professional judgment, training, and
discretion of the teacher in the classroom on how the treatment of both evolution-science and creation-science should be
balanced.

5. It is entirely speculative to argue that Act 590 is unconstitutionally vague inasmuch as it is not yet in effect. Constitutional questions do not arise merely because they are
raised and a decision is sought. *McElroy v. U.S.* 361 U.S. 281
(1960). Legislation, when interpreted by the courts, carries
with it a heavy presumption of constitutionality. *U.S. v. Raines,*
362 U.S. 17 (1960). *Annistan Manufacturing Company v. Davis,*
301 U.S. 337 (1937). In *Mercer v. Michigan State Board of
Education,* 379 F.Supp. 580 (E.D. Mich. 1974) a statute involving family planning classes was challenged because it might
have caused teachers to refrain from constitutionally protected speech. The Court found that the plaintiff's contention
that the statute was vague could not be reached. The parties
were attempting to obtain an abstract adjudication of the facial
invalidity of the statute prior to the occurrence of any concrete
problems. Challenges addressed to the alleged unconstitu-

tionality in the application of a statute must be supported by facts "cold and hard as concrete instead of hypothetical." 379 F.Supp. at 587. *Accord, Maryland Casualty Company v. Pac. Coal and Oil Company,* 312 U.S. 270 (1941); *Electric Bond and Share Company v. Securities and Exchange Commission,* 303 U.S. 419 (1938).

6. "Allegations of a subjective 'chill' are not an adequate substitute for a claim of specific present objective harm or a threat of specific future harm . . . ." *Laird v. Tatum,* 498 U.S. 1, 13, 14 (1972). Such generality of objection is really an attack upon the political expediency of "the act challenged . . . not the presentation of legal issues. It is beyond the competence of the courts to render such a decision." *Texas v. Interstate Commerce Commission,* 258 U.S. 158, 162 (1922).

*If you limit a teacher
to only one side of anything,
the whole country will eventually have
only one thought, be one individual.*

**—John Scopes of the
1925 Scopes Trial**

Chapter Four

Record of Plaintiffs' Religion and Philosophy Testimony

Summary of Plaintiffs' Testimony
Monday, 7 December 1981
Plaintiffs' Witnesses Hicks, Vawter, Marsden, Nelkin, Gilkey

The trial opened at 9:30 a.m. in the crowded fourth floor courtroom of the Little Rock Federal Building with the words of the U.S. Marshall: " . . . God save the United States and this honorable court." Lawyers for both the plaintiffs and the defense presented opening arguments summarizing their briefs, then the first witness for the plaintiffs was called.

Bishop Kenneth Hicks

Bishop Kenneth Hicks, of the Arkansas conferences of the United Methodist Church, was the first witness to take the stand. Hicks, himself one of the plaintiffs, testified that the Act was clearly a "transgression of the First Amendment." Hicks outlined three specific objections he had to the Act. First, he said, he objected to the bill's definition of creation-science, as it limited scientific inquiry to the six areas specified in the bill and reflected a literalistic interpretation of the Genesis account in the Bible. His second objection was to that part of the Act which stated as part of its purpose "preventing establishment of Theologically Liberal, Humanist, Nontheist, or Atheist religions." (Section 6) Hicks claimed that such language, with its "undefined labels," contains an element of alarm and imposes constraints on these views. Hicks also objected that the Act was a mixture of philosophical and theological beliefs designed to limit scientific inquiry.

Bishop Hicks concluded by saying "The Bible is important to my life. I hold very dearly and intently to the opening words of Genesis: 'In the beginning God created . . . . ' To go beyond that, and to try to circumscribe the way in which he did it, belittles both God and the theological process."

On cross examination, Hicks admitted that the Act specifically prohibited religious instruction in defense of creation-science (Section 2: "must not include any religious instruction or references to religious writings.") Hicks also admitted that any "limits" to free inquiry were based on his assumption that the definitions of creation-science and evolution-science were meant to be comprehensive. Hicks agreed that his perception of "creation" was necessarily religious because of his training, and that he would have difficulty considering "creation" in a scientific sense.

Father Francis Bruce Vawter

The second ACLU witness was Father Francis Bruce Vawter, a Roman Catholic priest and professor of theology at DePaul University, Chicago. He testified to the religious nature of the Act. He characterized the book of Genesis as an explanation of religious convictions concerning human origins and the origin of the world. He argued that as there were no witnesses to creation, Genesis should not be taken as a factual account (which could only be derived from a direct witness). Vawter contrasted the Biblical literalists' view (which would take the account at face value), with the historical-critical view (which accorded more closely to his own approach). Vawter testified that Act 590 was consistent with a literalistic interpretation of Genesis.

"This Act," he said, "in its description of what it calls creation-science, has as its unmentioned reference book the first eleven chapters of Genesis." He gave several specific references. Vawter pointed out that the term "kinds" in the Act (Sections 4(a)(3) and 4(b)(3)) had as its source the King James translation of the Bible. Vawter also noted that "catastrophism" and a "world-wide flood" (Section 4(a)(5)) must refer to the Noahic deluge recorded in Genesis, though he later admitted that this was also paralleled by a similar Babylonian myth. Vawter concluded, "I do not know of any other creation story (except in Genesis) that embodies those parts."

On cross examination Vawter was pressed on this point, and he admitted that many points of creation-science could not be found in Genesis according to his view of the book. Specifically, he agreed that Genesis neither affirmed nor denied the "insufficiency of evolutionary mechanisms." (Section 4(a)(2)) Similarly, he said that "changes only within fixed limits" (Section 4(a)(3)) are not required by the Genesis account, nor must separate ancestry for man and apes (Section 4(a)(4)) be understood from the text. Vawter testified that the only evidence for "catastrophism" (Section 4(a)(5)) to be found in the Genesis account was the occurrence of the Noahic flood, and that even the "sudden creation of the universe" (Section 4(a)(1)) was not required by the Biblical account of origins.

Vawter agreed that he was not a competent judge of the scientific evidence, and that he had always studied "creation" in a religious context. Vawter said that the idea of evolution was not at all inconsistent with Genesis, and that he saw no conflict between the concepts of creation and evolution.

On redirect examination, Vawter re-emphasized some points in his original testimony, and restated his conclusion that the source of Act 590's description of creation-science was the book of Genesis.

Dr. George Marsden

The third witness called by the plaintiffs was Dr. George

Marsden, professor of History at Calvin College, an evangelical Christian college in Grand Rapids, Michigan. Marsden's area of testimony concerned Fundamentalism. Marsden typified Fundamentalists as "militantly anti-modernist" and chiefly concerned with "spreading the faith." He testified that while anti-Darwinism was not as important a facet of Fundamentalist belief as usually thought, Darwinism was (especially in the South) a symbol of secularism. The Fundamentalists of the 1920's held to a model of origins based on the Bible and had a "dualistic outlook" in viewing creation and evolution. Marsden said the creation-science movement is "strikingly similar" to the Fundamentalist movement in its approach to origins. He based this view on several observations. Creation scientists, he said, hold a literalistic view of Genesis, oppose all forms of evolution (including theistic evolution) and use the Bible as the primary source for their beliefs. Marsden quoted from Henry Morris' *The Troubled Waters of Evolution* and Duane Gish's *Evolution: The Fossils Say No!* in order to show the religious intent and source of creationists' beliefs.

At this point Defense attorney David L. Williams objected on the grounds of relevance, saying, "Merely because someone calls it creation-science somewhere out in the world doesn't mean it complies with Act 590." The plaintiffs argued that Marsden's testimony was relevant to their contention that all creationist literature advanced religious goals. Overton overruled the objection, saying, "If the people who are writing about creation-science are borrowing their ideas from religious movements I would think that is relevant. These writers can't wear two hats; they can't call it religion for one purpose and science for another."

Marsden continued, concluding that Act 590 represented a Fundamentalist view of origins. Before cross-examining Marsden, defense attorney David Williams pointed out that the books Marsden had quoted from were printed in two editions, one intended for public school use and one (containing an explanatory notice inside the front cover) intended for Christian schools.

On cross-examination, Marsden admitted that Act 590 was not exclusively a product of Fundamentalism. In particular, he noted that many Fundamentalists believe that the creation happened in six literal twenty-four-hour days—a view not found in the Act. Additionally, while Fundamentalists typically oppose evolution, Marsden agreed that Act 590 does not, and that not all Fundamentalists would be able to accept the Act. Marsden conceded that he was not a scientist, and since his training was religious, he could not distinguish between "religious" and "scientific" creationism. Marsden concluded by agreeing that it was typical to talk of Fundamentalists as champions of scientific inquiry.

Ms. Dorothy Nelkin

The next witness was Ms. Dorothy Nelkin, a professor of Sociology at Cornell University. The substance of her testimony concerned the relationship of Act 590 to the creation-science movement. She testified that Fundamentalists were opposed to evolution, and that they make use of science to "legitimatize" their religious beliefs. She claimed that the aim of creation-science was to convince others of their beliefs, and that they "believe it's necessary to give their ideas a sense of scientific credibility." Nelkin stated that creationists only give negative evidence against evolution, rather than evidence for creation. She noted that many of the creationists' books came in public school and Christian school editions.

On cross-examination Ms. Nelkin agreed that speculation or intuition could legitimately lead to a scientific theory that could then be tested. She said that evolution was not based on any a priori assumptions. She admitted that Julian Huxley had formed a naturalistic religion based on evolution, but said that in so doing he abused evolution.

Nelkin testified that while the scientific community is theoretically a meritocracy, historically it has not been neutral, and in fact scientific opinion has been influenced by society.

Nelkin confessed that she had entered her study of the creation-science movement with the presupposition that creation-science was not truly scientific. She also agreed that as she was not a scientist, she was not competent to judge the validity of the scientific evidence for creationism.

Defense attorney Williams asked Nelkin whether theories of origins were testable. She agreed that such theories were not *directly* testable by observation. When asked whether evolutionary theory presupposed the non-existence of a creator, she said "No" (thus contradicting her deposition; she explained this inconsistency by saying "I was confused.").

When asked whether creation-science should be taught in schools to the extent that there was scientific evidence, she called the question a "contradiction in terms" (though she had answered the same question in her deposition "Of course."). Nelkin was asked whether a religion could be based on science, and answered in the negative, though she later admitted that this, too, was inconsistent with her deposition. Finally, she said "People can take science and use it any way they choose."

The last questions directed at Nelkin concerned the availability of textbooks presenting the balanced view advocated by Act 590. Nelkin agreed that textbook publishers would probably produce such texts, if the law were upheld. "Sure, there's money in it," she said.

Dr. Langdon Gilkey

The final witness to take the stand Monday was Dr. Langdon Gilkey, professor of theology at the University of Chicago School of Divinity. Gilkey's testimony concerned the definition of "religion" and the relationship of religious and scientific knowledge. Gilkey defined religion as having three essential parts. He said (1) a religion involves a view of ultimate reality: it deals with the basic problem of human existence and provides an answer to the problem through myths, stories, truths, and teachings, (2) a religion is a way of life finding its source in the ultimate reality, and (3) a religion involves a community structure expressed for example in worship. He stated that in Western religions "God" is the source of ultimate reality. Gilkey said that all that is religious is related to God, and that all that is related to God is religious. Gilkey claimed that creation "ex nihilo" (from nothing) was the most religious of all statements since God was the only actor. He added "A creator is certainly a God if he brings the universe into existence from nothing." He said that since creation necessitates a Creator, Act 590 "is unquestionably a statement of religion." He said, though, that a creative force is not necessarily religious, though a creative being must be.

Gilkey testified that the attempt to distinguish the "Creator" from a God to be worshipped was similar to the Marcionite and Gnostic heresies which plagued the Church in the first century, and which led in part to the adoption of the Apostles' Creed as a statement of orthodox faith.

Gilkey's testimony next turned to the relationship of religious and scientific models. He characterized Act 590 as a religious model of origins rather than a scientific model, and gave several differences between the two. Gilkey said that religious and scientific models differed in the experiences and facts appealed to and in the types of questions asked. Scientific models, he said, deal with facts that are observable, repeatable, and objective. A religious model, though, refers to the facts "as a whole," to "inner facts," and to facts which are not objective. Science asks what? and how? questions, said Gilkey, but religion asks why? He said that science appeals to a sense of coherence and elegance which is confirmed by the scientific community, but that religious authority resides in "revelation" and the "interpreters of revelation."

Gilkey claimed that scientific laws are universal and necessary, and that no non-naturalistic process may be appealed to within the bounds of science. He said that religious theories use symbolic, not objective, language, and concern personal causes and intentions.

Gilkey's testimony then moved to the area of apologetics. He testified that creation-science was in fact apologetics, not science, that it was an effort to "spread the faith." Continued Gilkey, "There's nothing wrong with apologetics, I've written some, the only problem is when one has two hats on and hides one." Gilkey claimed that Act 590 represented a "dualistic" approach to origins because it assumed that there were only two views on origins and that these were mutually exclusive. He challenged this assumption, saying that there were other views (e.g., theistic evolution) and that some people believed in God and evolution.

On cross-examination by Defense counsel Rick Campbell, Gilkey was asked to comment on primary and secondary causality in scientific and religious knowledge. (In philosophical language the primary, or *ultimate* cause of an event is distinguished from the secondary or *direct* cause of an event.) Gilkey said that while not all questions of ultimate origins are religious, for scientists to talk about primary causality is for them to stray afield. Gilkey agreed that the Bible does not refer to primary and secondary causality, but said that these might be inferred from the text.

Gilkey stated that the Bible was the guide in his own life and in his understanding of the world. He said that it influences the fields of philosophy and science as well as his own views. Gilkey said that scientists were not the only ones to define science, and that for example historians have reminded scientists of cultural influences on science.

Campbell then asked Gilkey whether a scientist should be permitted to talk in a classroom about creation-science if he felt that there was evidence. Gilkey modified the response that he gave in his deposition ("Of course, of course"), saying that this would be appropriate only if the teacher could argue that creation-science was a theory (since according to Gilkey, science resides in theories, not in facts). He said that while a professional should be able to decide, the ultimate authority would reside with the biological community. Gilkey added that he was against *requiring* that creation-science be taught, not against teaching it.

Gilkey conceded that apologetics was not always religious, that there were atheist apologists giving a defense for atheism. He cited Bertrand Russell as an example.

Campbell asked Gilkey where the "why?" questions were in Act 590. Gilkey said that there were none, that there were no questions at all, only answers. Campbell asked whether science could answer "why?" questions. Gilkey said that science could not deal with questions of ultimate origins, and conceded that if evolution were to do this it would not be science, but theology.

Gilkey agreed that there are religions which hold evolution as part of their creed, such as the religious beliefs espoused by

Spencer and Huxley. When asked whether evolution was "atheistic," Gilkey replied that science does not talk about God. When asked whether this exclusion of God from science was a presupposition, he said that properly speaking there were two types of presuppositions. In the first category were "characteristic presuppositions" of Western culture or of the scientific community, such as the reality of the material world. In the second category were "canons," or "rules of the road," which might be based on presuppositions, but were not themselves presuppositions in the same sense. The principle of falsification, for instance, is a canon, as is the exclusion of God.

Gilkey, when asked, admitted that creative leaps of imagination were part of the history of science, though those who took such leaps were not part of the scientific mainstream. He said that, for example, Copernicus, in making his break with established thought, was not entirely within the mainstream of science.

On redirect examination, Gilkey said that a secular statement was not necessarily atheistic. He also repeated his opinion that science cannot appeal to a supernatural cause.

Tuesday, 8 December 1981
Plaintiffs' Witnesses Ruse, Ayala, Holstead, Dalrymple

The court reconvened at 9:00, and the judge revealed his ruling on a Defense motion seeking "an order in limine excluding all evidence addressing either the validity or invalidity of evolution-science and/or creation-science as a 'scientific theory' on the ground that such evidence is irrelevant to the determination of the constitutionality of Act 590 on its face." Overton denied the motion. Defense attorneys then requested that Ms. Nelkin's deposition be received into the record as evidence. The deposition was accepted, and the first witness of the day took the stand.

Dr. Michael Ruse

Dr. Michael Ruse, professor of Philosophy at the University

of Guelph, in Ontario, Canada, testified concerning the nature of science, particularly biology. Ruse defined science as consisting of four essentials. First, science must explain events by means of natural law, or "unguided natural regularities." Also, science must be "explanatory," "testable," and "tentative." Ruse said "explanatory" means that science must predict and confirm events, so that science is self-generating, it is constantly moving into new areas. To say that science must be "testable," or "falsifiable," means there must be at least potential for evidence against a scientific belief. As an example, Ruse cited the theory of evolution. Evolution is thought to be unidirectional, that is evolution is thought to continually lead to more and more complex forms of life. If scientists were to find evidence that evolution sometimes proceeded in the direction of less complexity, this aspect of the theory would be falsified. The fourth essential of science is that it be "tentative." This means that a scientist must always be willing to modify his understanding of the data. Ruse said that a scientist's work should be objective, without personal bias, public, repeatable, and honest.

Ruse said that the way in which contradictory evidence is dealt with depends both on the nature of the evidence and the theory attacked by the evidence. Unless the evidence were to be quite strong, it could not overturn a well-supported theory.

Ruse said that "observability" is not an essential in science, although creation-science literature often listed it as such. He said that sometimes direct empirical evidence simply is not necessary.

Ruse, who wrote *Darwinism Defended*, an examination of the attack of the creationists on evolution, testified that evolution is not under attack by credible scientists. He claimed that there is a double use of the word "evolution," to indicate either the "happening" of evolution or the "mechanism" of evolution. He said that usually the "theory" of evolution is used as a synonym for "mechanism" of evolution, while the "fact" of evolution refers to the "happening" of evolution. Ruse said that, other than creation-scientists, no scientists challenge the happening of evolution, though of course evolutionists do disagree about how it happened.

Ruse testified that Act 590 is a statement of scientific creationism, and is "very closely" related to the creationist literature, "so closely, I'd say they were identical." The Act, he said, has a dual model approach to the question of origins, contains the six points usually covered in books on scientific creationism, and used the term "evolution-science." (Section 4(b)(1), etc.). He said that the wording of the bill implies the existence of a creator in the word "creation." (Section 4(a)(1)) Ruse said that the word "kinds" used in the Act (Sections 4(a)(3), 4(a)(3)) is not a scientific word, that it is not a taxonomic category, but rather is derived from the book of Genesis. He criticized the Act's description of evolution-science as inadequate, saying that it implies that all six points are to be taken as a package deal, though not all evolutionists would agree with the definition.

Ruse said that evolution doesn't say anything pro or con about the existence of God, nor does it inquire into the origin of life. Ruse gave as an example of evolution the change in predominant coloration of the population of certain species of moth in industrial England. He said that creationists respond to such examples, "We admit the evolution the evolutionists have found—that's just not enough." When asked whether creationists explain why evolutionary change should be limited, Ruse said, "Not really, no." He said the assertion was "an ad hoc device that creation scientists have had to think up to get away from some of the things evolutionists have come up with."

Ruse further objected to the points under the definition of creation-science that dealt with the flood (Section 4(a)(5)) and with a young earth (Section 4(a)(6)) as not really important to the question of origins. He also objected to the contrast between "catastrophism" (Section 4(a)(5)) and "uniformitarianism." (Section 4(a)(5)) He said that the Act polarizes the two views, and implies that disproof of evolution is equivalent to proof of creation.

Ruse said that "creation-science is not science, it's religion," and that it "invokes miracles." He added, "Nobody's saying religion is false, they are saying it's not science." He said that creation-science does not rely on "natural law" and is not "ex-

planatory." He said that there is too much dependence in creation science on "ad hoc explanations," and that though it has
explanations, they are not "scientific explanations." He added
that "something that can explain everything is no explanation
at all." Ruse said creation-science also fails to be "testable"
and "tentative," and that it employs an improper
methodology.

Ruse said that creationists often quote evolutionists out of
context, that they imply that there is disagreement about
whether evolution happened, not just how it happened. He
referred to this practice as "dishonest" and "sleazy."

On cross examination, Dr. Ruse admitted that he had no
training in biology, nor had he done any significant independent study.

He agreed that many scientists believe that life was
generated from non-life. He said that the ultimate origin of the
universe might be an area for scientific concern and that the
"Big Bang" model certainly is within the realm of science.
Ruse said that the theory of evolution does not extend to the
source of life, that it takes life as a given. He added, however,
that the origin of life is also a matter for scientific inquiry.

Defense attorney Williams asked how a theory of origins
might be tested, since there were no direct observations. Ruse
said that such a theory might be tested by observation in an
analogous situation, by controlled experimentation in the
laboratory, or by computer modeling. He added that this would
not make the work unscientific. He agreed with Williams that
these methods would be dependent on the conditions assumed
to be on the earth at the time of the origin of life, though these
conditions could not be known with certainty.

Ruse admitted that at least one philosopher of science, Karl
R. Popper, considers both evolution and creation to be equally
unscientific, because of the impossibility of falsifying either.

Williams asked Ruse to distinguish between a "fact" and a
"theory." A "model" could be thought of as an "explanation,"
and would be "narrower" than a "theory."

Williams asked Ruse further about the example of evolution
he had given in his direct testimony. Ruse agreed that,
although it is often cited as an example of observed evolution,

no new species were formed. He said that there were two forms of moth both before and after.

Williams pressed Ruse on the question of the "polarization" of the two models, asking whether it was true that either there *was* a creator or there was *no* creator. Ruse avoided the question, but then admitted that if two models *were* mutually exclusive, then evidence against one would be evidence for the other.

Ruse agreed that the books produced by the Institute for Creation Research would not be permitted under the Act because of the religious content. When asked about his personal teaching method in the classroom, Ruse said that he did give a "balanced treatment," but that this does not mean that he teaches all theories ever held. Ruse said that teaching evidences for creation-science would be meaningless "unless you are talking about a theory."

Ruse characterized himself as "somewhere between a Deist and an Agnostic." He agreed with Williams that religious people can be competent scientists. He said that while creation from nothing is not consistent with his belief, evolution is inconsistent with the beliefs of some students.

Williams asked whether some scientists believe that the theory of evolution is not falsifiable. Ruse said that most believe that it is falsifiable, though some, including Karl Popper (whom he called an "old man"), do not.

The plaintiffs objected to the relevance of this line of questioning as evolution was not on trial. The judge overruled the objection after a short recess.

Ruse was asked to define "teleology." He said it was an attempt at understanding in terms of purpose rather than causes. He agreed that teleology could be either theological or non-theological.

Ruse said that there are no authorities in the area of philosophy of science. He agreed that "What is science?" was a question for philosophers of science, and that there is no agreement on its answer.

Ruse said he objected to Act 590 because it was a foot in the door of science classrooms for religion, that it was "the thin edge of a very large wedge" of an attempt to teach religion as science. He said that he was against Biblical literalism, and was concerned for what might happen if the law were to stand. He further said that he was "shocked" that a creationism display had recently been put up in the British Museum.

Ruse said that it is possible for scientists to become emotionally attached to their theories, both individually and as groups. He said his purpose at the trial was to "fight a battle" against creationism.

Ruse agreed that ideas from outside science could be sources of scientific theories, and said that to other scientists it is more important that the theories fit the data than what the source was. He gave as an example the work of Dr. Stephen Jay Gould, a Marxist paleontologist. He said that though Gould "pushes" Marxism the source of his science isn't important. Ruse said that he did not accept Gould's theory personally, but that is because of lack of evidence, not because of the theory's source. He said that Darwin had developed his theory of evolution because of his personal religious Deism.

On redirect examination, Ruse repeated his assertion that data without a theory are not science. He said that it is not possible to separate evidence from a theory. He said once again that evolution is science.

On recross examination, Williams asked, "Is evolution a fact?" Ruse replied in the affirmative. Williams asked, "How then is it tentative?"

The plaintiffs' testimony turned from philosophy and religion to the scientific and educational portion of their case.

The plaintiffs' religious and philosophical testimony was reported in the following manner.

Sample Media Coverage*

Chicago Tribune, Tuesday—December 8, 1981:

Creationism Trial Arguments Begin
Little Rock (AP)—An Arkansas law that requires schools to give equal weight to so-called "creation-science" if they

---

*   The samples from the media articles are usually the lead paragraph(s).

teach evolution is a clear and dangerous violation of the
1st Amendment, an attorney told a judge Monday.

But the state defended the law, saying it "broadens"
teaching of the origin of human life.

The Boston Globe, Tuesday—December 8, 1981:

Evolution Trial Launched

By Bill Simmons
Associated Press

LITTLE ROCK, Ark.—A federal judge yesterday began
hearing a suit against an Arkansas law requiring public
schools that teach evolution to give equal time to creationism, the theory that the universe was created suddenly
from nothing.

In opening arguments, lawyers for the American Civil
Liberties Union (ACLU), which brought the suit, called the
law a "dangerous violation" of the Constitution. But the
state maintained that it would broaden the knowledge of
school children and did not require the teaching of
religion.

Dallas Times-Herald, Tuesday—December 8, 1981:

Creationism Trial Opens in Arkansas

By JERE LONGMAN
Staff Writer

LITTLE ROCK—The American Civil Liberties Union,
which made its reputation a half a century ago by
recruiting substitute biology teacher John Scopes and
defense attorney Clarence Darrow to challenge Tennessee's ban on teaching evolution, returned to court
Monday to test the constitutionality of Arkansas' creation-
science law.

The non-jury trial before U.S. District Judge William R.
Overton is being called another "monkey trial" and
"Scopes Two." It has attracted national media attention
like the 1925 Scopes trial and has the same far-reaching
implications, yet in many ways it is hardly similar.

St. Louis Post-Dispatch, Tuesday—December 8, 1981:

Creation Law Goes On Trial

LITTLE ROCK, Ark (AP)—The book of Genesis is the
"reference book" for an Arkansas law requiring public
schools to balance the teaching of evolution by teaching
the creationist theory of the origin of the universe,

religious experts have testified.

The constitutionality of the law went on trial Monday in federal court. The American Civil Liberties Union, which has filed suit to overturn the law, says it is a dangerous violation of First Amendment guarantee of the separation of church and state.

The state insists that the creationist theory is scientific, not religious. The theory says the universe began suddenly from nothing, and that men and apes have a separate ancestry.

The New York Times, Tuesday—December 8, 1981:

Arkansas Creation Law From Bible, Judge Told

LITTLE ROCK, Ark., Dec. 6 (UPI)—A Methodist bishop and a Roman Catholic priest testified today that Arkansas's new creation-science law was obviously taken directly from the Book of Genesis.

"This act in it's description of what it calls creation-science has as its unmentioned reference book the first 11 chapters of Genesis," said the Rev. Bruce Vawter, a priest and chairman of the Department of Religious Studies at DePaul University in Chicago.

New York Daily News, Tuesday—December 8, 1981:

"Creation" Law Under Attack in Ark. Court

Little Rock, Ark. (AP)—Lawyers for the American Civil Liberties Union yesterday called an Arkansas law requiring public schools that teach evolution to give equal time to creationism—the theory that the universe was created suddenly from nothing—a "dangerous violation" of the United States Constitution.

But the state maintained that the law would broaden the knowledge of schoolchildren and did not require the teaching of religion . . . .

Opening witnesses for the ACLU said the law reflects a literal interpretation of the biblical book of Genesis and is not rooted in science.

Chicago Sun-Times, Tuesday—December 8, 1981:

"Creation" Law Called Obviously a Danger

LITTLE ROCK, Ark. (UPI)—Witnesses at the opening of the trial of a suit against Arkansas' new creation-science law testified Monday that the law obviously is based on the

Bible's book of Genesis and is a "dangerous" threat to the First Amendment.

The Detroit News, Tuesday—December 8, 1981:

Creation Texts, Bible Allowed in Trial
By George Bullard
News Staff Writer

LITTLE ROCK, Ark.—Creation science can't wear "two hats"—be religion for one purpose and science for another—a federal judge said.

The judge, William Overton, made the comment on the opening day of a trial over an Arkansas law that permits teaching about creation in public schools.

The comment came in an Overton ruling favoring the American Civil Liberties Union (ACLU), which is challenging a new Arkansas law giving equal public school time to evolution and to beliefs that a divine creator made the world.

Arkansas Gazette, Little Rock, Tuesday—December 8, 1981:

Religious in Nature, Theologian Testifies
God is "Agent" Under Theory, He Contends
By George Wells
Gazette Staff

Act 590 of 1981 is "unquestionably a statement of religion," a noted theologian testified Monday during the opening day of a trial testing the constitutionality of the law, which requires public schools that teach evolution to give balanced treatment to creation-science.

Dr. Langdon B. Gilkey, professor of theology at the Chicago University Divinity School and author of a book on creation called *Maker of Heaven and Earth,* also testified that "in creation, God is the only actor—the only agent is the divine."

Washington Post, Tuesday—December 8, 1981:

Battle Joined In Arkansas Creation Trial
By Philip J. Hilts
Washington Post Staffwriter

LITTLE ROCK, Dec. 7—The Arkansas attorney general said in court today that he will prove evolution, a guiding principle of modern biology, is not science.

With that opening shot, the Arkansas creation trial leaped past the famous Scopes trial of 1925 and others

since then that have evaded the direct battle between creation and evolution.

Los Angeles Times, Tuesday—December 8, 1981:

Arkansas Trial Seeks to Resolve School Issue
Is "Creation-Science" Old-Time Religion?
By RONE TEMPEST, Times Staff Writer

LITTLE ROCK, Ark.—It began with the traditional in-
vocation from the U.S. Marshal: "May God bless the
United States and this honorable court."*

But the celebrated "creationism" trial, which opened in
federal court here Monday, quickly evolved into another
species—a constitutional test of whether "creation
science" is nothing more than that old-time religion.

Arkansas Gazette, Little Rock, Tuesday—December 8, 1981:

Attempts Thwarted To Limit Testimony

Deputy Attorney General David L. Williams tried unsuc-
cessfully throughout the first day of the creationism trial
to have testimony limited or excluded as irrelevant.
Federal Judge William R. Overton indicated that he would
let all the evidence in and then decide what weight to give
it.

The trial began Monday on a lawsuit contending that
Act 590 of 1981, which requires public schools teaching
evolution to give balanced treatment to creation-science,
is an unconstitutional violation of the principle of church
and state.

At one point Williams argued that a witness was using
materials that clearly could not be used in classrooms
under the law because they were religious in nature.

The Christian Science Monitor, Tuesday—December 8, 1981:

"Monkey Trial" in Reverse Opens in Arkansas Court
Little Rock, Ark.

An Arkansas version of the famous "Scopes Monkey
Trial" opened Monday as the American Civil Liberties

---

*   The exact wording of the Marshal's statement was " . . . God save the
     United States and this honorable court."

Union attacked the constitutionality of a 1981 state law that forces schools to teach the view that man and the universe were created by a supernatural event all at once about 6,000 years ago.

Chicago Tribune, Wednesday—December 9, 1981:

Science Issue Relevant: Judge

By Lee Strobel
Legal Affairs Editor
Chicago Tribune Press Service

LITTLE ROCK, Ark—A federal judge Tuesday refused to block testimony about whether creationism is scientific theory, as an updated version of the "Scopes Monkey Trial" went into its second day.

The court is hearing a challenge to an Arkansas law that says the creationism concept must be given equal time with evolution in public schools.

U.S. District Judge William Overton rejected a motion by Arkansas Atty. Gen. Steve Clark, who argued that the issue isn't whether creation and evolution theories are scientific, but whether the law is constitutional.

The New York Times, Wednesday—December 9, 1981:

Professor Contends That Creationism Is No Science

By REGINALD STUART
Special to *The New York Times*

LITTLE ROCK, Ark., Dec. 8—The creation theory of the origins of the universe fails to meet accepted standards for consideration as a science, opponents of a new Arkansas law contended today in Federal court. The law requires public schools to teach creation science as well as evolution.

The opponents are seeking to have the law ruled unconstitutional on the ground that it violates the First Amendment requirement of separation of church and state and the equal protection clause in the 14th Amendment. They include educators and practitioners of Protestant, Roman Catholic, and Jewish faiths.

Today's testimony by Michael E. Ruse, a doctor of history of philosophy science at the University of Guelph, in Ontario, Canada, was the first to question the state's acceptance of creationism as a science . . . .

The 41-year-old professor testified that creation science was a religion rather than science, saying that it was based on the belief that a supernatural power created the earth and all living things.

The New York Times, Thursday—December 10, 1981:

Mood of Trial on Creationism
Is Different from Scopes Case

By REGINALD STUART
Special to *The New York Times*

LITTLE ROCK, Ark., Dec. 9—The trial in Federal court here of a challenge to the Arkansas creation science law may have been billed as a repeat of Tennessee's famous Scopes trial of 1925, but there are distinctive differences, not the least of which is the way the trial here is being conducted . . . . "

Sparring Has Been Minimal

The mood in the large courtroom of Federal District Judge William R. Overton is tranquil. Sparring between lawyers representing opponents of the law and its defenders has been minimal.

*One of the objectives of universal
free education is to develop in children
the intellectual capacities required
for the effective exercise of the rights
and duties of citizenship. Experience
demonstrates that this is best
accomplished in an atmosphere
of free inquiry and discussion.*

—ACLU Academic Freedom Committee
December 3, 1976

*We are committed to an open and
democratic society. We must extend
participatory democracy in its true sense
to the economy, the school [and]
the family . . . .*

—Humanist Manifesto II

Chapter Five

Record of Plaintiffs' Science and Education Testimony

Summary of Plaintiffs' Testimony

Tuesday, in the early afternoon, the thrust of the plaintiffs' testimony turned to the scientific case against creationism. The first scientist was called to the stand.

Dr. Francisco J. Ayala

The first science witness called by the ACLU was Dr. Francisco J. Ayala, professor of Genetics at the University of California at Davis. He testified concerning the scientific validity of creation-science.

Dr. Ayala testified that creation-science, as expressed in the Act was not science, because it was neither naturalistic nor was it falsifiable. He gave as an example the creationists' assertions that there are limits to evolutionary change. Creation-scientists make use of the term "kind," said Ayala, to delineate the limits of change, but this word is "religious," not scientific.

Ayala then explained the significance of the phrase "natural selection," the idea that, because of the harshness of nature, animals with physical and genetic weaknesses will die younger and have fewer offspring. This, according to evolutionists, would have the effect of encouraging useful genetic change. Ayala said that creationists do not dispute the action of natural selection, but do give limits to the amount of change it may generate. Ayala said, however, that there was nothing self-limiting about natural processes. Ayala's testimony became increasingly technical as he spoke of the role of genetics in evolutionary science. He explained several ideas concerning the mechanisms of evolution and said that the Act's definition of evolution-science was inadequate. He said that evolutionary theory does not include the concept of life from non-life, but that it presupposes the existence of life. Ayala said that evolutionists do not accept "the sufficiency of mutation and natural selection," (Section 4(a)(2)) but recognize the existence of other mechanisms, such as recombination, genetic drift, and the founder effect. Ayala then discussed the importance of mutation in evolution. He said that while most mutations are harmful to the organism, many are beneficial, and the harmful ones are almost immediately eliminated by natural selection. He said that although creation scientists often assert that mutations must present immediately beneficial results in order to be successful, in so doing they ignore the fact that latent genetic traits can be retained, and become useful later.

Ayala said that "the emergence of life from nonlife," (Section 4(b)(1))is not actually part of evolutionary theory. He said that the theory of evolution deals only with existing processes such as mutation.

He also objected to the Act's contention that there were only two models of origins. He said that one can never claim that there are only two models. Instead, he said that the creation-science model is not a scientific model at all, and that there are several evolutionary models.

He spoke of the scientific validity of evolution, and explained some of the evidences for evolution. He said that the similarities between human and animal proteins implied evolution. At one point, he handed Judge Overton a chart showing these similarities. Ayala said, "It's simpler than it looks." Replied Overton, "I sure hope so."

Ayala contended that it was not necessary to observe evolution directly and said that it is not possible to observe macroevolution. He noted, however, that "speciation," the splitting of one species into two, has been observed in the laboratory. Ayala said that evolution does not presuppose the nonexistence of a creator, but that "a creator, a God can create the world any way he chooses." He said that God might "establish the laws by which the world evolves. God may have created the mountains. He may have created the processes by which the mountains are formed. Science is neutral." Ayala said that a creator would be a personal God by necessity.

During cross-examination by Defense attorney David Williams, Ayala agreed that he had been president of the Society for the Study of Evolution, and had formed an educational committee, with the purpose of countering movements which were opposed to the teaching of evolution. He admitted that the creation-science movement was one of these movements. He also admitted that he had been instrumental in the attempts of two other organizations, the National Academy of Science and the Committee of Correspondence, to limit anti-evolution movements.

Williams asked Ayala whether it was true that there either was or was not a Creator. Said Ayala, "The law of contradiction still holds."

Ayala said that "testability," not "observability," was a necessity for a scientific model, and said that some of the most interesting aspects of science were not observable. He called science "a creation of the mind," and said models could be used to make predictions, which could then be tested. He agreed that conclusions based on such a technique would be inferences.

When asked to define the term "religion," Ayala, who holds the equivalent of a doctorate in theology, quoted from the writings of theologian Paul Tillich. Ayala said that religion was a concern for the ultimate reality, which would require religious convictions, but not belief in a creator. He agreed that humanism could be a religion. He said that evolution might cause some students to reject their religious beliefs.

Ayala said that he believed that life arose from non-life

through naturalistic processes. He said that this was a testable theory, and that it should be taught in the public schools. He agreed that to the extent that there were scientific evidences for creationism, they should be taught in the classroom. Ayala said that while academic freedom is "a right and a privilege," a teacher need not agree with an idea in order to teach it.

Senator Jim Holsted

The next witness for the ACLU was Senator Jim Holsted, an Arkansas state senator, and sponsor of the bill which became Act 590. Holsted testified concerning the source of the bill and his own motivations in introducing it.

Holsted testified that he received the bill from a business associate, Carl Hunt, and later learned that the bill had been drafted by Paul Ellwanger. (Ellwanger formed the South Carolina-based creationism organization, Citizens for Fairness in Education.)

He testified that the bill was passed in the Senate without being referred to a committee, and said that the bill received "fifteen to thirty" minutes of discussion on the Senate floor. Holsted said that no one spoke against the bill. In the House, the bill was sent to the Education Committee, where it received a short hearing before being returned to the floor.

Holsted testified that his motivation in introducing the bill partly involved his personal religious convictions. Of the bill, he said, "Certainly, it would have to be compatible with something I believed in. I'm not going to stand before the Senate and introduce something I don't believe in."

He admitted that the bill was strongly supported by religious fundamentalists, and agreed that the Act favored Biblical literalists. Holsted admitted that the term "creation" presupposes a creator, but said that the Act did not violate the First Amendment, because "it doesn't mention any particular god."

The cross-examination of Holsted was very brief. Holsted agreed that because of the nature of the Arkansas legislature, which meets for only 60 days every two years, it is not unusual for a bill to be passed with little or no debate.

Dr. G. Brent Dalrymple

The next witness to be called, late Tuesday afternoon, was Dr. G. Brent Dalrymple, a geochronology expert and geologist with the U.S. Geological Survey. His testimony concerned the age of the earth and the relevance of geochronology to creation-science as expressed in Act 590.

Dalrymple testified that, though creationists usually claimed an age for the earth of about 10,000 years, there was no evidence that the earth was young, but rather that the evidence indicated that the earth was about 4.5 billion years old. Dalrymple indicated that on this point, at least, creation-science could be falsified, and that indeed it had been falsified. Dalrymple said that theories which have been shown false should be discarded, and said that the theory of a young earth was "in the same category as the flat earth hypothesis and the hypothesis that the sun goes around the earth; all are absurd hypotheses."

Dalrymple explained that in order to date the age of the earth, scientists must rely on measuring the action of some process which is constant over time. He discredited several arguments made by creationists, saying that they were based on processes which are not constant. He gave as examples the measurement of the earth's cooling, the small amount of dust on the moon and the supposed decay of the earth's magnetic field, each of which, according to creationists, point toward a young earth.

Dalrymple said that more widely accepted values for the age of the earth were based on a technique known as radiometric dating. This technique relies on the decay rates of certain radioactive elements, which, he said, are known to be constant to within a few percent. He said that one creation-scientist, Harold Slusher, of the Institute for Creation Research, had argued that the decay rate of iron-57 was not constant. Said Dalrymple, "The problem with this is that iron-57 is not radioactive."

The court adjourned at the end of Dalrymple's direct testimony.

Wednesday, 9 December 1981
Plaintiffs' Witnesses Dalrymple, Morowitz, Gould, Glasgow

The third day of the trial opened with the cross-examination of Dr. Dalrymple by Defense attorney David Williams. Williams questioned Dalrymple about the validity of radiometric dating. Dalrymple testified that "as far as we know," the radioactive decay rate of an element is constant, but in response to a question by Williams, said that it didn't make any difference whether the decay rate was constant before the formation of the solar system, about 4.5 billion years ago.

Dalrymple said that all methods for calculating the age of the earth rely on the constancy of radioactive decay rates, and said that "in a certain sense," this was an assumption of the methods.

He said that for the rate of decay to change, there would need to be a change in the physical laws of the universe. He testified that the rate of decay is found to be constant in the laboratory, and from theoretical considerations. He also said that radioactive testing gives consistent results.

Williams asked where in the Act Dalrymple found a figure for the age of the earth of 10,000 years. Dalrymple replied that this was not a part of the Act itself, but was a common figure given by creationists. Williams then asked whether Dalrymple would consider "several hundred million years" to be recent. Dalrymple agreed that on a geological time scale this would be recent.

Judge Overton interrupted at this point to ask Williams just how the state intended the phrase "relatively recent" to be taken. Williams said that the state was not tied to any particular figure. Overton disagreed with Williams' opinion that the question would not be raised in the biology classroom. "I'm puzzled as to what the teacher is supposed to say," said Overton.

When questioning of Dalrymple resumed, he was asked about the use of radiometric dating in conjunction with fossils. He agreed that this method was the best way of dating fossils found in a particular geological formation, and agreed that much of the case for evolution relied on this method. He agreed that because of its importance in this area, evidence about the accuracy of radiometric dating should be studied.

Williams then asked Dalrymple whether he knew of any reputable scientist who had called into question the validity of radiometric dating. Dalrymple said, "No," but when pressed, he admitted that one who *had* done so was Dr. Robert Gentry of Oak Ridge National Laboratories. Dalrymple said that, according to Dr. Paul Daymon, professor of Geosciences at the University of Arizona, if Gentry's conclusions were correct, they would cast doubt on all of geochronology.

Dalrymple said that Gentry had made a proposal for the falsification of his theory, but that it was not clear whether it was valid. Dalrymple said that Gentry had claimed that if a "hand-sized piece of granite" could be synthesized, then he would consider his theory falisified. Dalrymple said that this was a difficult technical problem, but that he did not see its relevance to Gentry's claims. He admitted that Gentry was a competent scientist.

In response to a question from Williams, Dalrymple said that he was a member of the American Geophysical Union, and admitted that he had drafted an anti-creation proposal for that organization. He said that an abbreviated resolution had been adopted by the A.G.U. on 6 December 1981, the day before the trial had begun.

Dalrymple said that he had read "about two dozen" books and pamphlets by the creationists, and that "every piece of creationist literature I have looked into so far has had very, very serious flaws—and I think I have looked at a representational sample." He admitted however, that while he was aware of Gentry's work, he had not made an attempt to examine it more closely before the trial. Dalrymple said that Gentry had raised "a tiny mystery," for which "I suspect we will eventually find an explanation."

Williams asked Dalrymple whether he believed in God. Dalrymple said the question was "highly personal," but said that he was "half way between an agnostic and an atheist," though he had "reached no final conclusions." He said that there was no evidence for God's existence, but that a religious person could be a competent scientist.

On redirect examination, Dalrymple was asked further about the recently adopted A.G.U. resolution and read the resolution into the record. Dalrymple agreed that Gentry's theory depends on supernatural causes and that his proposed test for falsification was "meaningless."

Judge Overton interrupted to ask for an explanation of Gentry's theory. Dalrymple explained at some length the content of Gentry's research and the conclusions which Gentry had suggested.

On recross examination, the subject of Gentry's work again arose, and Dalrymple said that the source of a theory might be important in assessing the validity of that theory.

Dr. Harold Morowitz*

After the conclusion of the cross-examination of Dalrymple on Wednesday morning, the plaintiffs called Dr. Harold Morowitz, professor of biophysics and molecular chemistry at Yale University. Morowitz testified that because "sudden creation assumes supernatural causes" it is "outside the realm of science."

Morowitz complained that the "two model" approach to origins outlined in Act 590 implied that under that law, only those two strictly defined models could be taught, and no others. This, he said, would be limiting on science teachers who might want to take positions not quite identical to either of the two models.

Morowitz said most creationists argue that the complexity of living things indicates that they could not have occurred by chance. Creationists, he said, "move from complexity to improbability," and added, "but the fact of the matter is that we do not know the ways in which life came about," and said

---

*   From this point on the account follows that of the *Times* (Cal Beisner) of Pea Ridge, Arkansas (Dec. 30, 1981), except supplements noted by brackets.

science could one day learn of completely mechanistic processes by which complex living organisms first came into existence.

He said creationists also rely on arguments based on the second law of thermodynamics. This law, he said, states that natural processes in closed systems tend toward maximum randomness, a breakdown in complexity. However, he said, creationists ignored the fact that the earth is not a closed system, but receives energy from the sun, making it an open system in which temporary, local processes can occur in a direction opposite that described by the second law—that because of the energy the earth receives from the sun, growth in complexity and therefore the naturalistic origin of life are possible.

"Evolution," he said, "rather than being contrary to the laws of thermodynamics, is an unfolding of the laws of thermodynamics." He said while science could know that the ordering effect of the flow of energy through the system had caused the origin of life, it was not clear how this happened.

Under cross-examination, Morowitz testified that he had calculated the chance combination of elements to form life at about one to $10^{1,000,000,000}$, the number one followed by one billion zeroes. He said, however, that those odds could not be applied to the surface of the earth, since the earth is not a closed system and therefore not directly subject to the second law of thermodynamics.

Asked if anyone had yet created life by the flow of energy through various mixtures of elements, Morowitz said that in the thousands of experiments done, no one had yet succeeded in creating life.

Asked how he would define the scientific community, Morowitz said it consists of those who make their livings within the field of science. He said science was a "social activity," and that essentially science was, in the words of defense attorney David Williams, "what is accepted in the scientific community."

Dr. Stephen Jay Gould

The plaintiffs then called Stephen Jay Gould, professor of

geology at Harvard University, and a proponent of a view called "punctuated equilibria," which holds that evolution took place through fairly sudden, rapid changes in life forms, which is the reason that the fossil record contains so few plausible examples of transitions from one form of life to another.

Gould said that creation science tries to explain the geological record, which he said shows the age of the earth in billions of years, on the basis of a single major catastrophe, a worldwide flood. Such a view, he said, is not "scientific, because it calls on a creator to suspend the laws of nature." [He said that the Act creates an artificial dualism when it refers to uniformitarianism and catastrophism. (Sections 4(b)(5) and 4(a)(5)) Modern geology, he said, accepts both uniformitarian and catastrophic occurrences as responsible for the geological record. He said that there were two meanings for the word uniformitarianism: (1) the constancy of natural law, or (2) the constancy of the rate of sedimentation. Modern geology accepts only the first.]

Gould said that on the basis of a flood model of geology, one would conclude that all forms of life were alive simultaneously, at least before the flood. However, he said, the fossil record preserved in the strata of sedimentary rocks in the earth shows that the animals were not mixed together, but are "rather well ordered in a sequence of strata, from the old to the new," and this, he said, showed the flood theory to be wrong. [Gould said that creation scientists account for the sequence of fossils by so-called "sorting mechanisms," but that these mechanisms are not consistant with the observed fossil record.]

Asked if, relative to paleontology (the study of fossils), creation science were "scientific," Gould answered, "Certainly not, because it calls upon the intervention of a creator . . . . " The fossil record, he said, shows gaps between various types of life, but while creation science calls on a creator to explain the gaps, and therefore is not scientific, evolution can explain the gaps as resulting from the rapid, short-term changes that occurred from time to time along the branches of the evolutionary tree, and from the incompleteness of the fossil record.

Gould said that creationists misrepresent his view of "punctuated equilibria," claiming that he says entire evolutionary sequences can be produced in single steps. This, he said, is not what his theory says, but rather that minor changes occur suddenly. The traditional view of evolution, he said, could be compared with rolling a ball up an inclined plane—the fossil record for such a view should appear fairly smooth. His view, however, would be comparable to bouncing a ball up a set of stairs—because he postulated sudden changes, the fossil record should reflect gaps from one step in evolution to another. [Gould referred to the fossil record as "woefully incomplete." He illustrated the fossil record as an old book in which there were few pages remaining, on which there were few lines remaining, in which there were few words remaining, of which only a few letters remained. He said that, because of the difficulty of fossilization, the "resolution" of the fossil record was probably not sufficient to show speciation—which would occur quite rapidly according to Gould. Gould then gave some examples of the transitional forms which do occur in the fossil record. Two examples mentioned were *Archaeopteryx*, a bird-like creature with some reptilian characteristics, (thought to be a transitional form between reptiles and birds) and "Lucy" (a fossil hominid classified as *Australopithicus afarensis*), apparently a human ancestor, thought to be about 3.5 million years old. He gave other examples of hominid transitional forms, such as *Homo habilus* and *Homo erectus].*

Asked if evolutionary theory presupposed the absence of a creator, Gould replied, "No, evolutionary theory functions either with or without a creator, so long as the creator works by natural laws."

Under cross examination, Gould said science was not his only motive for opposing creation science, but that another was his political liberalism. [Gould is an outspoken Marxist.] Asked if the term "creator" were inherently religious, Gould said, "not inherently." He said it had some "metaphorical senses in the vernacular," and was used that way by Darwin and Einstein. He also said that while the "best judgment of the scientific community" was that "life arose naturally," that was "subject to question and being proved wrong, just like anything else in science." [When questioned by Williams, Gould agreed that logically there were only two alternatives—either there was a creator, or there was not.]

Dr. Dennis R. Glasgow

The plaintiffs then called Dr. Dennis R. Glasgow, supervisor of science education in the Little Rock schools, who coordinates curriculum development for science courses in those schools.

Glasgow testified that creation science has never been treated in the science curriculum for the Little Rock schools, while evolution is treated under 18 concepts. He said all science courses, from kindergarten through twelfth grade, would be affected by Act 590, and that no materials of scientific merit are available to balance the two views in the state's public schools. "There aren't any materials available at all that I know of," Glasgow said.

He said the principle of evolution is reinforced by analogy at all levels of nature, and that therefore that principle provides a unifying theme of whole books in the science courses. This, he said, would require massive restructuring of the science education curriculum in his schools, and he didn't know how that could be done since he was unaware of any legitimately scientific materials on creation science.

Asked if he understood the term "balanced treatment" as used in the act, he said he didn't know what it meant, but that he had made an operational definition in his own mind which was that it required "equal emphasis or equal legitimacy" to be given to each view. For this reason, he said, teachers could not give their professional viewpoints on the models, because that would be unequal emphasis and would imply unequal legitimacy.

Glasgow testified that one sample curriculum for teaching two models, prepared by Dr. Richard Bliss of the Institute for Creation Research, would not be usable under Act 590 because it made value judgments and implied that there were only two views, while in fact there are many. The defense objected, saying that this was irrelevant, since no one had required Bliss's curriculum to be used in the Arkansas schools.

Asked how he would implement Act 590 as a curriculum developer, Glasgow said, "I don't think I *can* implement the provisions of Act 590 to provide balanced treatment," and added that creation science could not be taught without religion and that none of the materials about it he had seen were acceptable to him.

He also said teaching two views without allowing teachers to give their professional opinions would "damage the security of students" and "lower the student's opinion of the teacher," and would lead the students to be skeptical of information in class on other issues because they would think that at least some was untrustworthy, since one of these views had to be wrong, and therefore others might be untrustworthy as well.

He said there was no educational purpose in teaching creation science in accord with Act 590 and that such teaching would be "damaging as far as education is concerned." He also said it would hinder the hiring of good teachers in Arkansas, because they would not want to teach where they were required to present something unscientific.

Under cross examination Glasgow said a study of the effects of presenting two models by Bliss indicated students increased in cognitive development and critical ability when both models were presented. He acknowledged that the law would not necessarily require "equal time" to be given to the two views, and that nothing in the law specifically said teachers could not make a professional judgment to their students as to the validity of either theory. He said students should be free to question various ideas, but that they had not yet developed the capability to judge between views well before they were old enough to leave the public school systems.

He also said that his belief that it would be impossible for teachers and administrators to devise a curriculum for balanced treatment presupposed his belief that creation science is not science but religion. He also said one reason he objected to Act 590 was that he was offended that the legislature might restrict his discretion as a curriculum advisor.

Thursday, 10 December 1981

Ronald W. Coward

Thursday morning, the plaintiffs called Ronald W. Coward, a teacher of biology and psychology, from the Pulaski County School District. Coward said what determines what he teaches as science is his own ability to "decide what is good science and what is not," and that he must consider the interests of his student. Creation science, he said, is something he does not consider to be "real science."

Coward said that in reviewing for the Pulaski County School Board a creation science textbook called *Biology: A Search for Order in Complexity*, he was "surprised" at the religious references the book contained, and did not consider it scientific. He said the book attributed certain phenomena in the natural world to an intelligent creator/designer, and that therefore it was not scientific.

[Attorney General Steve] Clark objected to consideration of the text because it had not been shown that that book would be used by Arkansas schools.

Coward said he considered it impossible to implement Act 590 because scientific materials were not available to teach creation science. He said he would have to tell his students that there simply is no scientific data for creation science, and since he would not be able to teach creation science, then he would not be able to teach evolution science either, since the two would have to be balanced if either were taught.

Coward said there would be a "tremendous time-frame problem" because "evolution is interwoven virtually through every page of the textbooks," and that the textbooks depend on evolution as "the glue that holds it all together."

He said Act 590 would require some changes in how psychology is taught, too, because some experiments in psychology to learn about human behavior presuppose an evolutionary relationship between humans and various other animals. This, he said, would require balance by a creationist view, but if creationism were true, he said, then there would be "no interrelationships" between man and other animals, and therefore such psychological studies would be "irrelevant to us."

He said trying to balance creationism with evolutionism would hurt his teaching because if he "tried to be impartial, as I believe 590 would require, then students would see that and my credibility would be destroyed." He said that if he resorted to teaching neither evolution or creation, that would hurt teaching, too, since evolution is the "key to science and biology," and without an understanding of evolution his students "would be unprepared for college." His inability to balance the teaching of the two, however, would force him to stop teaching evolution, he said.

Under cross examination, Coward said he had made no independent effort to find other materials presenting creation science, and had not tried to obtain and read the writings of any of the defense witnesses since the publication of their names. He also said he never inquired into the validity of scientific concepts in the textbooks currently used in science courses in the state's public schools. He acknowledged, in response to a question by Clark, that it might not be beyond the ability of students to examine and evaluate arguments on evolution and creation, if scientific arguments for creationism could be found.

He also said that academic freedom would be overstepped by any teacher who tried to teach creation science because that would be contrary to professional ethics, since creation science is not scientific but is religious doctrine.

He said academic freedom for students meant their right to pursue available information in a field, but that his responsibility as a teacher was to sort out and select what information was legitimate for the students to examine. Clark asked him if his sorting limited the students' academic freedom, and he said it did, though he also said that the right of academic freedom for students was an "absolute" right.

Although Coward said he thought "balance" in Act 590 would require equal time to be given to the two views, he said that one could teach two ideas, both soundly, without giving them equal time.

Bill C. Wood

The plaintiffs then called Bill Wood, a science teacher in the Pulaski County Special School District, who testified that he had been a member of a committee in that school district to review creationist literature. He said the committee had concluded that there was no science to creation science, and that the materials they reviewed had no science in them.

Wood said he believed "balanced treatment" would require that the two views be given "equal dignity, equal treatment, equal time, and equal basis for inclusion into the body of scientific knowledge," and complete objectivity. He said he did "not like [scientific creation] because I don't think it's science, I think it's religion." He said the reason he thought it was religious was that its ideas came from the book of Genesis in the Bible.

He said he believed the results for his students of a two-model approach would be injurious to their ability to see broad pictures in science.

On cross examination, assistant Attorney General Callis Childs asked Wood to read a portion of material prepared for balanced treatment in the Pulaski school district which questioned the relationship of man to *Ramapithecus* and *Australopithecus,* alleged ancestors to man. Childs asked him if that were "evidence implying separation of man and other primates" in ancestry, and Wood said it was.

Ed Bullington

The plaintiffs next called Ed Bullington, a teacher of American history, sociology, government, and other social science courses in Pulaski County. Bullington testified that Act 590 would affect the way he would have to deal with the origin and development of human society in his courses, and that because he is not competent to deal with scientific issues, he would not be competent to present a balance of evolution science and creation science in those courses.

He said that in some of his courses he already deals with religion sociologically, and that that is not against the First Amendment, but that if he were to advance a particular religious point of view, that would be unconstitutional, and said Act 590 would do that.

Bullington also testified that if Act 590 were upheld, students would "monitor" teachers to see if their presentation were "balanced," and some "could become vigilantes," leading to complaints against teachers which would affect the renewal or non-renewal of their contracts.

Marianne Wilson

The next witness called by the plaintiffs was Marianne Wilson, science coordinator for the Pulaski County Special School District, who testified that she had been involved in an attempt to develop a "two-model" curriculum but that those attempts were futile because the committee charged with the task could find no scientific evidence for creationism.

She explained she had first heard of creation science when, in Dec., 1980, Larry Fisher, a science teacher in her school district, showed her a resolution he wanted to present to the Pulaski County School Board. The resolution called for balanced presentation of creation science and evolution. The school board passed the resolution and then asked her to form a committee to implement it. That, she said, was the first time she actually read the resolution. She said it "reminded me of Genesis," causing her to "raise my eyebrows."

She said the committee reported to the board that they did not think it possible to design a balanced curriculum because creationism wasn't scientific. The board, she said, essentially told them that it hadn't asked their opinion, it had just given them a job to do and the committee should get to it.

She asked Fisher for materials, and he gave her a number of creationist writings, which the committee reviewed. She then contacted experts in the fields of biology, geology, paleontology, and other science fields, for help in "finding legitimate sources," made a general outline for the curriculum using Act 590, and tried to build a positive case for creationism, as opposed merely to a negative case against evolutionism.

When asked if she had ever found documentation from the scientific community for so much as one single point of the creationist arguments, she said she had found none. Still, she said, she had devised the curriculum unit because her school board had ordered her to do so, but said it was "by no means" in teachable form. She also said the curriculum did not "support creationism scientifically."

When asked whether she had tried to make use of the two-model approach designed by Bliss, she said she had not because it referred to a creator, so she "threw it in the trash."

Under cross examination by Clark, Wilson said she did not believe the state has a right, through legislation, to prescribe curriculum for its schools. She also said that a belief in a recent origin of man and the earth need not be religious. She acknowledged that although four texts now used in the public schools in her county mention creation science, she had not contacted the publishers of those texts to see if they could provide further information on it.

Clark asked her if she were familiar with work done by Robert Gentry on polonium haloes in granites, and she said she had seen something about it, but had thrown it out. He asked her if she had thrown it out because she couldn't understand it, and she said, "No." He then read from her pre-trial deposition a statement in which she said she had thrown it out because she couldn't understand it. She replied that that was only one of the reasons, that other science teachers she had talked with also knew nothing about it, and that if science teachers had a hard time understanding it, it would be unreasonable to expect students to deal with it.

Dr. William V. Mayer

Dr. William V. Mayer, professor of biology at the University of Colorado and director of the Biological Sciences Curriculum Study, Boulder, Colo. was called late Thursday as the plaintiffs' last witness.

Mayer said since the inception of the BSCS in 1960, he was sure that their decision to make more open reference to evolution in the textbooks they produced would "wave a red flag before certain fundamentalists" and lead to conflict. However, they had decided that evolution was so central to understand all of science that for the sake of quality textbooks in the sciences they would have to discuss it in more depth than had been the case before 1960.

He said evolution is the only thing that ties biology all together, and added that students can't understand one organism if that organism is not related to other organisms, because comparison is necessary for understanding.

Asked by ACLU attorney Robert Cearley whether biology could be presented without evolution, Mayer replied, "not with any cohesiveness." He said that evolution does not properly include the actual study of the origin of life, but that normally that was touched upon in teaching biology, and the various ideas presented on that included chemical speculations, pan spermia (the idea that the universe if filled with the "seeds" of life), spontaneous generation (the idea that life came about suddenly by random chance combination of elements), and the "steady state" theory, which says that life and the universe have always existed.

These views, he said, all have in common the fact that they are based on evidences and observations, that they speak of entirely naturalistic mechanisms and that there is no appeal to a creator. The court recessed at this point in Mayer's direct testimony.

Friday, 11 December 1981

When the court reconvened, Dr. Mayer continued his direct testimony. Mayer said creationism is sometimes mentioned in textbooks on biology, not as science, but rather as a religious way of explaining life. He added that all biology texts teach evolution.

He objected to the term "evolution science" in Act 590 on the basis that it implied that there was such a thing as a science which was non-evolutionary, which he said is not true. He also said the act's description of evolution was not accurate, but that its description of creation science was precisely what he has found in some 27 years of reading creationist literature. He said dividing views on origins into just two basic positions, was an "artificial dichotomy" which forced students to decide between evolution and belief in God, while in fact many evolutionists also believe in God.

Mayer said the effect on students of teaching creationism would be confusion and division in the classes, causing more problems than it would solve by mixing theology and science in a way that "damages both and is helpful to neither." In addition, he said, it would "throw an unnecessary roadblock in front of students by asking them to understand science and also to adjudicate between science and religion. He said it offered them too many alternatives, including choices between believing in a worldwide flood and not believing in it; believing that mutation is sufficient for evolutionary changes, and not believing it; and other such dichotomies.

When asked if it were "proper" to "let students decide" on controversial scientific issues such as this, Mayer said that these were not the only two alternatives in understanding origins, and that one teacher and his students in a class would not be capable of treating the issue in an intelligent way and coming to "a proper conclusion" in fifty minutes of class time. He added that teaching the two views would not foster the growth of cognitive abilities.

Mayer said the difference "between science and creation science" is that between two different epistemological systems, two different ways of approaching knowledge. He compared it with the differences between the ways of stating truth used by a poet and a historian. It would be illegitimate, he said, for one to say the other's way of saying things was wrong and his own right, because they are two different ways of looking at the world.

He said the source of creation science was a belief in supernatural, divine "revelation," and this was reflected in creationist literature, which often referred to the Bible as the Word of God. He said religion is the "unifying theme" in creationist writings, not science. He quoted numerous references to religious beliefs in creationist literature.

He said the effect of such references in the literature would be to "imprint the students with the idea of a creator," and confuse them by making them think there are two alternatives which are not really alternatives at all, because one is science and the other is religion.

When asked if he thought it were impossible to teach creationism without religion, he said, "Yes, that's what's in the literature and demanded by [creation science]." He said BSCS had considered and rejected the idea of including creation science in its texts for that reason.

He referred to *Biology: A Search for Order in Complexity*, a major creationist textbook, and said it differed from other biology textbooks in that it had no "unifying principle," and it "attempted to prevent students from seeing relationships" among animals, and that it was religious. He said he knew of no similar biology textbooks.

Asked if evolution favored any religious position, Mayer replied that it did not because it was non-theistic, not a-theistic. In other words, evolution doesn't address the question of the existence of a god or creator, while creation depends on the existence of a creator.

Mayer also testified that the idea of "balance" as talked of in Act 590 was "vague," and so publishers of textbooks would not know whether they were fulfilling Act 590 or not. Furthermore, he said, even if they wanted to balance the two, they would violate the act if they put creation science in because the act prohibits teaching religion, and creation science is inherently religious. He estimated that the cost of preparing balanced textbooks and curriculum for the state's public schools, even if it could be done, which he denied, would probably be about $1.6 million.

Mayer said it would also be unwise to teach scientific evidences against evolution and for creationism as isolated elements without reference to a religious belief because that would "pit a few minute, isolated data against a huge, complex, well-ordered scientific view of evolutionary theory."

Mayer testified that Act 590 would come into play not only in biology, but also in geology, sociology, psychology, history, and even literature, most of them fields in which the teachers, because not competent in science, would be unable to deal with the scientific issues and so couldn't provide for balance.

When asked what "balanced treatment" might mean, Mayer said he had "no idea," but added, "This is not an act for balance, but for imbalance. It would make creationism the single most pervasive idea running through all of the state's education system."

Under cross examination by Clark, Mayer said he could not say that any of the present creationist literature would be used in implementing Act 590. He acknowledged that because science is in a sense the "state of the art" in each of its fields, it is subject to change daily.

When Clark asked whether the traditional concept of "scope and sequence" in curriculum development included the idea of balancing various issues in the curriculum, Mayer said it didn't but rather included the principle of selection among various ideas that could be treated.

Clark referred to Mayer's earlier statement that he could find no reputable science text which dealt with creationism in any way other than as an idea held in history or as religion, and then called his attention to *The World of Biology*, a commonly-used biology text by Davis and Solomon, and directed Mayer to read a portion of page 415, which listed six of the arguments creationists use. Clark then asked Mayer which of those he would understand as religious instead of scientific arguments, and Mayer named none of them. Clark then asked which were historical references instead of scientific arguments, and again Mayer acknowledged that none of them were historical. He agreed with Clark that none of the arguments was presented in that textbook as any more historical or religious than a book which would present arguments for evolution.

When asked if the evolution of life from non-life lent itself to statistical analysis, Mayer said that it did not. He also told Clark he believed science could not legitimately deal with the supernatural. He said though he believed life on earth had a beginning, he did not know how it began, and that no one had yet synthesized life in a laboratory.

Clark, referring to Mayer's pre-trial deposition, asked if Mayer had said it "may well be that creationism is correct about origins," and Mayer said he had said that, but that he added that "even if it were correct, it's not scientific."

Clark then asked Mayer if he believed students had a right to examine controversies, to see several sides to controversial issues, and to take positions on controversial issues without fear of discrimination from their teachers, and Mayer answered all three questions, "Yes."

With the conclusion of Clark's cross examination of Mayer, the plaintiffs rested their case, and it came time for the defense to call its first witness.

The plaintiffs scientific and educational testimony was reported in the following manner.

Sample Media Coverage

The Washington Post, Wednesday—December 9, 1981:

ACLU Opens Attack on "Creation-Science"
By Philip J. Hilts
Washington Post Staff Writer

LITTLE ROCK, Ark., Dec. 8—One witness characterized the methods of so-called "creation-scientists" as "sleazy" and another said he knew of no creation-scientist who had ever submitted a paper to a scientific journal for publication, as the plaintiffs in the Arkansas creation trial got its [sic] argument under way here.

The plaintiffs, represented by the American Civil Liberties Union, are seeking to show that what is called "creation-science" in no science at all, but merely religious apologetics for the word-for-word literal reading of the Bible.

Arkansas Gazette, Wednesday—December 9, 1981:

Creationism Premises False, Twist Science, Trial on Act 590 Told
2nd Try Fails To Get Limit On Testimony
By GEORGE WELLS
Gazette Staff

Creation-science is not science, its main premises are false, and its writers frequently twist the work of accepted scientists to meet preconceived notions, a series of witnesses said Tuesday in federal court.

Two scientists and a science historian testified as expert witnesses for the plaintiffs in the second day of a trial challenging the constitutionality of Act 590 of 1981, which requires state schools that teach evolution to give balanced treatment to creation-science.

State Senator James L. Holsted of North Little Rock, who sponsored the bill that became Act 590, also testified that he got "a model" law from creationists and sponsored it in the Senate partly because of his deep religious convictions. He testified that he believes in a literal interpretation of the Bible.

Saint Louis Post-Dispatch, Wednesday—December 9, 1981:

"Creation-Science" Law Assailed

LITTLE ROCK, Ark. (UPI)—Requiring teachers to teach "creation-science" along with evolution would be "dreadfully wrong," a geneticist testified Tuesday as scientists continue to criticize the Arkansas creation-science law word by word.

Creation science "is not science," said Francisco Ayala, a genetics professor at the University of California at Davis, and no evidence exists to back up the theory as explained in the Arkansas statute.

The Atlanta Journal, Wednesday—December 9, 1981:

Experts Say Creation Science Law in Arkansas Unsupported by Facts

United Press International

LITTLE ROCK, Ark.—Scientists dissecting Arkansas' creation-science law word-by-word testified that no evidence exists to back up the theory as explained in the statute or as presented in the literature.

Requiring teachers to give balanced treatment to creation-science would be "dreadfully wrong" because creation-science "is not science," said Francisco Ayala, a genetics professor at the University of California at Davis.

Jacksonville Journal, (Jacksonville, Florida), Wednesday—December 9, 1981:

Creation-science is "absurd," geologist tells Arkansas court

LITTLE ROCK, Ark. (AP)—The creation-science which Arkansas law says should be taught alongside evolution in its public schools is as absurd as the theory that the Earth is flat, according to a geologist.

G. Brent Dalrymple of the U.S. Geological Survey was one of four witnesses called yesterday by American Civil Liberties Union lawyers as they attacked the state law as an unconstitutional establishment of religion.

Dallas Times Herald, Wednesday—December 9, 1981:

Scientists Ridicule "Evidence" of Creationists
United Press International

LITTLE ROCK, Ark.—Scientists testifying against Arkansas' creation-science law Tuesday said evidence intended to back up the concept is based on outdated or discredited research, errors, and misleading statements.

The creation-scientists' claim that the Earth is no more than 20,000 years old, for example, ranks with the "flat Earth hypothesis and the hypothesis that the sun goes around the Earth," said Brent Dalrymple of the U.S. Geological Survey

The Boston Globe, Thursday—December 10, 1981:

Creationists Misapply Theory, Court Told
By Bill Simmons
Associated Press

LITTLE ROCK—Creationists consistently misstate and misapply a fundamental law of physics to support their contention that evolution cannot be true, a biophysicist said yesterday.

Harold Morowitz of Yale University testified during the third day of trial of an American Civil Liberties Union Lawsuit attacking an Arkansas law that says creationism and evolution must be given balanced treatment in public schools.

The Detroit News, Thursday—December 10, 1981:

3.5-million-year-old "Witness" Takes Stand
By George Bullard
News Staff Writer

LITTLE ROCK, Ark—A prehistoric ape-woman and a feathered bird-reptile are transitional life forms that boost the theory of evolution

That was the testimony yesterday by a nationally known scientist, Stephen Jay Gould, a witness in the federal trial over teaching creationism in Arkansas public schools.

The Atlanta Journal, Thursday—December 10, 1981:

Educators Say "Creation-Science" is Wrong, Impossible to Teach
United Press International

LITTLE ROCK, Ark.—"Creation-Science" would be impossible to teach in schools because it is not supported by scientific evidence and is based on fallacies like the biblical flood, witnesses testified in Arkansas' version of the Scopes "monkey trial" . . . .

Harvard paleontologist Stephen Jay Gould said the scientific community does not accept creation-science and that it is filled with fallacies, such as the worldwide flood.

Jacksonville Journal, Thursday—December 10, 1981:

Creationism Bad for Classes, Official Says

LITTLE ROCK, Ark. (AP)—Enforcement of Arkansas' creation statute would turn classrooms into circuses, with students trying to catch teachers disobeying it, says a school official who opposed the law.

"If you implement the law, students would have ample opportunity to catch the teacher doing wrong," Dennis Glasgow, science director for Little Rock schools, testified yesterday in the federal court trial of a lawsuit challenging the statute's constitutionality.

Arkansas Gazette, Thursday—December 10, 1981:

No Way to Explain Creationism
Without Creator, Judge Told
Scientists Hit Contentions of Creationists

By George Wells
Gazette Staff

"How are you going to explain to students a sudden creation without a creator, a divine creator?" federal Judge William R. Overton asked Dennis Glasgow, the Little Rock School District science supervisor, Wednesday. "Do you have a way?"

Glasgow responded that he did not.

Judge Overton asked the question near the end of testimony in the third day of the trial challenging the constitutionality of Act 590 of 1981, which requires Arkansas public schools teaching evolution to give balanced treatment to creation-science.

Dallas Times Herald, Thursday—December 10, 1981:

School Official Cites Conflict in Teaching
Creation-Science Under New Arkansas Law

United Press International
LITTLE ROCK, Ark.—Teachers could not possibly tell

their students about creation-science under Arkansas' new law without discussing religion, the science supervisor for Little Rock schools testified Wednesday.

Testifying in Arkansas' version of the Scopes "monkey trial," Dennis Glasgow said: "The first time I came across any of these ideas was in my Sunday School class."

Arkansas Gazette, Friday—December 11, 1981:

Creationism Is Bound To Religion, Educators Say in 4th Day of Trial

By GEORGE WELLS
Gazette Staff

Three teachers and a science co-ordinator in the Pulaski County School District testified Thursday in federal court that they believed creation-science could not be divorced from religion and that biology couldn't be taught properly without references to evolution.

The four were witnesses during the fourth day of the trial in which Act 590 of 1981, the state creation-science law, is being challenged as unconstitutional.

Dallas Times Herald, Friday—December 11, 1981:

Creation-Science Curriculum Not Based on Science, Arkansas Witness Claims

Washington Post Wire

LITTLE ROCK, Ark.— The chief of science curriculum for the largest school district in Arkansas said in court Thursday that she was forced to write a so-called "creation-science" curriculum for her district that had no scientific foundation and contained religious material.

In the last day of testimony for the plaintiffs in the Arkansas creation trial, Marianne Wilson, science coordinator for the 31,000 student Pulaski County School District, said she found it impossible to write a creation-science curriculum backed by evidence and without religious references.

The Detroit News, Friday—December 11, 1981:

Teachers Reject Creationism

By George Bullard
News Staff Writer

LITTLE ROCK, Ark.—Teaching creationism in Arkansas public schools means the state's students will get cheated out of a valid science education.

That was the indication yesterday from high school science teachers testifying in a federal court case over an Arkansas law requiring "balanced treatment" between evolution and creationism in public schools

The teachers contended that creationism is not science. Given that, they could not teach it and therefore could provide "balanced treatment" only by not teaching evolution, they said.

Dallas Morning News, Friday, December 11, 1981:

Creationism Law Criticized
Arkansas Statute Would Cheat Pupils, Teacher Testifies

Associated Press

LITTLE ROCK, Ark.—The State of Arkansas' creation science law would deprive students of "the cornerstone of biology" and send them to college unprepared, a high school teacher testified Thursday.

Ron Coward, a biology and psychology teacher in Jacksonville, Ark., was called to testify by the American Civil Liberties Union, which wants a federal judge to overturn a law requiring balanced treatment of creation science and evolution in schools.

Jacksonville Journal, Friday—December 11, 1981:

"Evolution" Key Word, Textbook Official Says

LITTLE ROCK, Ark. (AP)—Creationists began lobbying for their point of view to be taught in public schools after a leading biology textbook organization decided to use the word "evolution" in its books, the group's director testified in federal court.

The word is "a red flag to fundamentalists," William V. Mayer testified yesterday in the trial of an Arkansas law that requires balanced treatment of creationist thought and evolution if the latter is taught in schools. Mayer is the director of the Biological Science Curriculum Study in Boulder, Colo.

Newsweek, December 21, 1981:

Creation Goes to Court

Perhaps Charles Darwin was wrong. The more things evolve, the more they seem to remain the same. Fifty-six years after the famous Scopes trial, ten lawyers stood in an

Arkansas courtroom last week debating once again the competing—and occasionally complementary—truths of science and religion. Instead of a traditional assault on Darwin's ideas, the case displayed a new mutant of the attack on evolution. At issue was the constitutionality of an Arkansas law which requires that whenever evolution is taught, teachers must give equal time to "creation science," a set of theories that look a great deal like the Biblical account of Creation dressed in a lab coat. Supporters of the law, mainly fundamentalist Christians, say they are merely seeking a fair hearing in the secular schools. Opponents argue that the law is not only poor science, but bad law, in that it violates the First Amendment ban against the official establishment of religion.

Time, December 21, 1981:

Darwin vs. the Bible
"Creation Science" Goes on Trial in Arkansas

All 70 seats reserved for the press were full, and so were the 175 places for spectators. A lonely demonstrator wandered in and out of the courthouse in a monkey suit. But U.S. Marshal Charles Gray was not impressed by the hubbub. "When this is all over," he reflected, "it won't have changed anyone's mind." Gray surely has it right. The federal trial that began last week in Little Rock, Ark., will lead to a legal ruling on whether "creation science" (secular evidence for, among other things, the supernatural origin of the universe) may be required in public schools where the theory of evolution is taught. But after all the lawyers and experts have finished, after the press has gone, the old Bible Belt battle between Darwin and the Good Book will go right on.

The lessons of history are clear:
wherever one religion or ideology
is established and given a dominant
position in the state,
minority opinions are in jeopardy.

—Secular Humanist Declaration (1981)

Chapter Six

Record of Defense's Religion, Philosophy, and Education Testimonies

Summary of Defense Testimony
Friday, 11 December 1981
Defense Witness Geisler

Dr. Norman L. Geisler

Dr. Norman L. Geisler, professor of theology and philosophy at Dallas Theological Seminary was the first witness called by the defense [to testify] about the philosophical presuppositions of science and religion and their interface with each other. He said he had done his doctoral dissertation on this interface, and in so doing had studied a great deal of the history of science and had found much of modern science to be built on Christian understandings of the principles of the universe as established by a creator.

Geisler said one of the key issues in the trial and in understanding Act 590 was one's definition of religion. He said contrary to much popular belief, the main common denominator in religious belief is the idea of "transcending" oneself, making ultimate commitments of oneself to some object of ultimate concern. [Referring to the definitions of Religion by theologian philosophers Paul Tillich and John Dewey], Geisler said [Religion] does not always involve the idea of a personal god or God in the traditional sense, nor does belief that a god or God exists necessarily involve religion, for one can make things other than a "god" one's object of ultimate concern, or one can believe that a god exists without making that god the object of one's ultimate concern.

Geisler explained the idea of transcendence by giving the example of [instances] when empirical objects suddenly take on "disclosure power" for some scientists. Those scientists have said that empirical objects have suddenly lent them a "flash of creative insight" and led to an effort on the part of those scientists to "go beyond empirical data to a comprehensive, unifying principle of life." In so doing the scientist "transcends" the merely empirical.

If the transcendent unifying principle the scientist "discovers" or makes up from the flash of insight becomes an object of ultimate concern for the scientist and he commits himself to it personally, he takes up a religious relationship with it and from that moment until he no longer is committed to it as an object of ultimate concern, his endeavors in relation to it are both scientific and religious.

Geisler testified that a "humanistic" religion centers its ultimate commitment on mankind. He gave as an example of such religious commitment the beliefs of Thomas and Julian Huxley, both great evolutionists, and other members of the American Humanist Society. Geisler quoted statements in the *Humanist Manifesto I* and *II* which declare evolutionism a central doctrine in humanism's belief, and which speak openly of humanism as a religion.

Geisler said the first line of the preface to a combined publication of *Humanist Manifesto I* and *II* describes humanism as a "philosophical, moral, and religious view," and he said that the word "religion" is used 28 times in the documents, mostly as a description of humanism itself. The publication also refers to humanism as a "quest for transcendent value, and a commitment to abiding values," and later in the documents it says it is "necessary to establish" such a religion.

Geisler also showed the court an article by Julian Huxley titled "The Coming New Religion of Humanism," in which Huxley says the framework of humanism is evolutionary and its "gods are made by men." Geisler said one of the central tenets of humanism is either no God or a god who is not involved in the world, that it is based on the "revelation" of science, and that it is religiously "naturalistic" rather than "supernaturalistic."

Geisler explained that there is a difference between speaking of "nature" and believing in "naturalism." "Naturalism" is a philosophical/religious system, Geisler said, which claims that there is nothing outside of nature, nothing other than what is physical, nothing but matter and energy. Such a position, Geisler said, is clearly atheistic, not merely neutral on the question of existence of a god. Evolutionism as commonly held by scientists, and especially as believed in by the humanistic religion, is expressly naturalistic and therefore non-neutral toward the existence of a god or God.

Asked by defense attorney Rick Campbell for examples of evolutionary religions, Geisler described the philosophy of Herbert Spencer, who made "evolutionary process itself become the transcendent." On that basis Geisler said, many scientists of the late 19th and 20th centuries used evolution to attack theism. Darwin, he said, applying the theory consistently, became increasingly skeptical toward Christian belief and eventually referred to "my deity Natural Selection."

To show the belief that acknowledging a supreme being or creator is not necessarily religious, Geisler referred to the teaching of the Greek philosophers Aristotle and Plato.

Aristotle believed [that] there was a "first cause" or "unmoved mover," but did not worship or commit himself to the being, and did not posit any moral attributes to it. Plato believed in a "demiurgos" which served as a creator in his philosophical system, but again did not think of the being in a religious way as something deserving of his commitment.

"Belief that there is a Creator," Geisler said, "has no religious significance. Belief in that Creator does." He explained that belief "that" a Creator exists is merely intellectual and requires no personal commitment, whereas belief "in" implies a commitment of oneself to that Creator. In the same way, Geisler said, belief that there is such a thing as biological evolution is not religious, but belief in that concept is religious.

[Geisler said that you cannot reject the Creator just because He is an object of religious worship for some. He illustrated this in two ways: (1) Jesus is an object of religious worship. It is historically verifiable that He lived. Do we reject His historicity just because He is an object of religious worship? (2) Some people have made rocks the object of their religious worship. Do we reject the existence of rocks because they are an object of religious worship? Then he said you cannot reject a creator just because some have made him the object of religious worship.]

Geisler also testified that the modern scientific ideas of regularity of the world, which are the foundation of the scientific method, sprang from the Christian belief that the world is ordered by an intelligent Creator who has made it regular. He also said the Christian commitment of many early scientists, such as John Newton, Lord Kelvin, and Sir Francis Bacon, had led them to do their scientific studies as a way of learning more about their Creator through His creation. Bacon for instance, wrote his *Novum Organum,* that the command to "subdue the world" in Genesis was the motivating force behind his scientific studies.

Geisler said the Christian motivation and sometimes even source for early scientific ideas was never and is not now considered a reason to doubt their legitimacy as a science, because scientists distinguish between the source of a theory and its scientific justification. Kekulé, discoverer of the model for the complex benzene molecule, got the idea while dreaming about a snake biting its tail; Tesla, inventor of the alternating current electric motor, got the idea from a vision he had while reading the German mystical poet Goethe; other scientific discoveries, he said, had equally unscientific sources or motivations behind them, but they were not rejected from science for that reason; rather, since they stood the tests of scientific justification, they were accepted. [Geisler also referred to Spencer who, while meditating on a beach, derived his theory of cosmic evolution by watching the motion of the waves of the sea. Judge Overton at this point stopped Geisler from giving more examples, saying, "I have your point."]

In the same way, Geisler said, one need not reject evolutionism as unscientific just because some evolutionists have a religious motivation for believing that it occurs, nor need one reject creationism as unscientific simply because some creationists have religious motivation for believing it occurred. Rather, Geisler said, each needs to be judged on its ability to stand the rigors of scientific testing.

Geisler said there are narrow and broad definitions of science, and that an ambiguity in the controversy over creation science being taught in public schools often stems from the ambiguity between the two definitions. In the narrow definition, nothing is scientific unless it is observable, repeatable, and directly testable. In the broad definition, however, something may not be directly observable, testable, or repeatable, but one can make predictions based on a logical construct designed to explain the world around us, and then test the prediction themselves.

Evolutionism, he said, does not fit the narrow definition of science, and neither does creationism. For evolutionism, Geisler illustrated, "We can't say to fossils, 'Would you repeat that death for me?' or to the Big Bang, 'Would you repeat that for me?' " while for creationism, we cannot go back in time and ask the creator to do it all over for us again and let us watch.

Therefore, Geisler said, both views are built by scientists as "models" or logical constructs designed to give unifying meaning to the data in the world around us. Predictions are made based on these models, and the predictions are compared with the real world.

Asked how many views of origins there were, Geisler replied that in religion there are many views, but that philosophically all can be put in one of two contrasting categories: (1) a supernatural, intelligent creator designed and created the world, or (2) the world is not the result of intelligent intervention, but came about through random, mechanistic processes.

Geisler said although the authors of Act 590 probably got their "inspiration" for the bill from Genesis, the source of the bill was irrelevant, and what is important is the scientific and legal justification. Asked if it is legitimate to derive a scientific model from a religious source, Geisler said it was "perfectly legitimate, it's done many times."

Under cross examination, Geisler was asked by ACLU attorney Anthony Siano if he would "consider it absurd to talk about creation science without a creator," and responded, "Yes, and I would consider Webster's Dictionary coming from an explosion in a print shop absurd, too."

Asked if he believed in the "inerrancy of Scripture," Geisler replied that he believes that "everything the Bible affirms is true is true." Siano then asked him about his beliefs about Satan, and Geisler responded that he believes Satan is a personal, supernatural being who is a fallen angel, that other angels fell with him in rebellion against God, that he is a deceiver, and that some satanic phenomena are demon possession, exorcism, parapsychology, and UFOs. When asked about the purpose of UFO encounters he said he believes they are "Satanic manifestations in the world for the purpose of deception."

Monday, 14 December 1981
Defense Witnesses Parker, Morrow, Townley

Dr. Larry R. Parker

At the beginning of Monday's hearings, the defense called Dr. Larry Ray Parker, former teacher of the fifth, sixth, seventh, and ninth grades and currently associate professor of curriculum and instruction at Georgia State University, a specialist in curriculum principles, curriculum trends, and curriculum development, and often a consultant to public school districts in curriculum development.

Parker said he was not a scientist, but that he believed in

teaching two models on scientific views of origins of life because it is sound educational practice to allow students to see two sides of such issues and examine the arguments for themselves.

Parker described five major principles which lie at the basis of curriculum development: the nature and character of the learner, the nature of the learning process, the nature of society, the nature of knowledge and the sources of knowledge, and the role of the schools in society. He said teaching two sides of a controversy like this is consistent with all those principles, because the students (the learners) are capable of handling controversy rationally and learn better when they have the opportunity to examine contrasting points of view, because learning functions best when opposing ideas compete for the respect of learners, because for students to function well in a society in which many members believe in either of the two contrasting points of view demands that the students understand both, because knowledge and the sources of knowledge are interrelated with opportunities learners have to make evaluations and decisions of their own, and because the schools, since they are "creatures of society," supported by taxpayers' money, ought to be responsive to the needs and demands of society. [He said the nature and character of the learner are found in the general area of educational psychology and specifically in the topic "human growth and development." Parker stated that the best expression of this is found in the French psychologist Piaget who proposed that "thinking is innate to the learner."]

Parker said that an especially important element in the quality of a learning experience [or learning process] is the "extent of inquiry" that is involved. "If the learner can be an active part of the learning process . . . the learning is greatly strengthened," he said. The extent of inquiry and the activeness of the student are greatly increased if the educational process asks the student divergent questions, questions which demand that the student consider alternative possible answers. Education works best, he said, when it challenges the students to "comparative analysis," asking students to "compare and analyze divergent questions leads to a great increase in divergent answers and learning."

Asked what he thought would be the impact of Act 590, Parker said, "I believe that implementation of Act 590 would allow the classrooms to be stimulating, thought-provoking" places where "students can be involved in analyzing." "Schools should be places where students are taught how to think, not told what to think," Parker said.

Asked about the relationship of the schools to the society, Parker said the schools "belong to the people, the students belong to the people, and the schools must be responsive to society and its changing needs." [Parker said, the role of the school is that of "passing on the culture and heritage of our civilization." Because education takes place within a culture, whenever a law is passed it is "the voice of the people" who represent that culture and heritage.] He said the very fact that Act 590 was passed by the legislature "demonstrates that the constituency of the curriculum in this state has not been served or satisfied with that curriculum." He said several polls showed a strong favor in society as a whole for teaching both evolution science and creation science in the public schools. He mentioned one in which 9% said evolution only should be taught in the schools, 16% said creation only, 70% said both, and 5% said neither should be taught in the public schools. Most others, he said, gave similar results.

Parker referred to a movement in education called "accountability-based education," which says curriculum should be tightened to meet the demands of the constituency, and shows that society wants its schools to be more responsible for producing students capable of certain skills. He said examples of new programs in education which resulted in educational responsiveness to society were law-related education in the state of Georgia, consumer education, multi-cultural education in areas which have many cultural groups, bi-lingual education, sex education, metric education, personal finance education (which was made a requirement by the Georgia state legislature), career education, drug education, and, most recently, computer literacy. [Parker also said that sources of knowledge were the responsibility of the state, thus it is the state that develops criteria for facilitating knowledge and developing textbooks based upon the desires of its constituency.]

Parker said he thinks one message the state is giving to the educational establishment in Arkansas with the passage of Act 590 is that society wants its students to graduate from high school with a certificate that shows they're "capable of thinking" critically about competing ideas.

Asked what "balanced treatment" would mean, Parker said it is normally used in curriculum development to refer to treating all materials from an unbiased perspective. He said the creation/evolution problem is not unique as a balance problem in education, but rather that discussion of balance in other areas is common in curriculum texts and courses. He said in most teaching on curriculum development, it is stressed that "balance needs to be constantly monitored."

Asked if he thought that required "equal time" for competing ideas, he said that was not the case, because of the nature of the content of the competing ideas. "Time is not necessarily of the essence," he said.

Asked whether he thought Act 590 violated academic freedom, Parker said, "In a public school context, my understanding is that academic freedom relates more to the student than to the teacher." [He said the teacher conforms the state's views to the students regardless of what those views are.] The main point of academic freedom, he said, is allowing the student to be exposed to a wide range of materials and ideas.

He said in actuality, a law like Act 590 was necessary to protect teachers who might want to teach things normally outside the curriculum in many science courses. He said many teachers had come to him asking him whether it were "safe" to teach certain things, and added that because of the climate of the scientific community and educational establishment, presenting creation science as an option is a "professional risk."

Asked if Act 590 were consistent with sound curriculum principles, he said it was, not only for the reasons given earlier, but also because one of the main functions of curriculum is to "transmit the culture," and "depriving students of learning creationism is actually violating the culture and the tradition of western civilization," putting students out of touch with their cultural roots.

Under cross examination, Parker was asked if he would advocate teaching two views on a controversial subject even if there were "not a shred" of evidence for one of them. Parker responded that was not quite his view, and gave as an example the "flat earth" theory. Although the theory is clearly wrong, it could be helpful for learning scientific principles of testing for students to examine the arguments used for the "flat earth" theory and see how those arguments are treated by sound scientific principles.

Attorney Kaplan of the ACLU asked Parker whether one principle for determining course content were the question, "What can the subject contribute to the general education of the law-abiding citizen?" and Parker responded that that was a valid principle, and that it was also one reason he supported Act 590, since it "helps students to think and analyze," and added that any bias in the controversy is on the part of the evolutionists, since they want to teach only one view. Teaching only one view, he said, is "tantamount to indoctrination."

Dr. William Scot Morrow

The defense then called Dr. William Scot Morrow, professor of biochemistry at Wofford College, South Carolina. Asked about his religious beliefs, Morrow said he is an "agnostic," " . . . a person who holds the middle ground and hasn't made his mind up on the existence of a divine being or god." He also said he is "an evolutionist."

Morrow defined science as "learning the nature of nature," [or an effort to determine the nature of nature] and the scientific process as consisting of the elements of curiosity, observations of data, hypothesis, and experimentations. He said the principles of experimental repeatability, testability, and falsifiability are essential to science. [Morrow explained that you must have a correct operating model to affirm or falsify an experiment. He said that creation and evolution have no such model available.]

Morrow said evolution is not falsifiable, and therefore does not fit a strict definition of science. Neither, he said, does creation. He said he thinks the main reason many scientists believe in evolution is that they have "wanted to believe in it, they looked at evidence and saw it one way, and didn't consider alternatives."

He said new ideas are not easily accepted in the scientific community unless they are "linear extrapolations" from existing scientific theories. He described two camps in the scientific community, the "conservative and defensive," in which people try to preserve the status quo, and the "revolutionary," which focuses on "anomalies," the unexplained in science, and uses those as step-off points to new discoveries. "These people (the revolutionaries) frequently have a problem getting published because they can shake cherished ideas" because their new theories don't fit an established worldview or philosophy. Often, he said, they're either not given the slightest consideration and are treated with "plain silence," or the scientific community refuses to publish their work, even though it's good science. Then, he said, as is the case with creation scientists, lack of publication in the scientific community is used as a reason for saying it's "not scientifically respectable."

He put creationist scientists in the "revolutionary" camp in science, saying they were "on the cutting edge of science." He compared the closed-minded rejection of their work with earlier closed-mindedness toward the theory of continental drift, the work of the earliest molecular biologists, and the explanations of early biochemists of biological problems "conservative biologists" had been unable to solve.

Morrow explained there is a difference between data and interpretation in science. Data are the evidences collected, the accumulated "facts" scientists study, while interpretations are an "intelligent analysis of data." He said the data creationists look at are the same as the data evolutionists look at, but that creationists have a different interpretation for the data. He also said creationists generally are willing to "look at more of the data," and that evolutionists often "refuse to look at it."

Asked what he thought the prohibition of religious teaching in Act 590 meant, Morrow said he thought it meant a prohibition of trying to persuade students toward any particular religious point of view. He said balanced treatment was something that might often confront teachers, and that the fact a teacher might not like one view was no excuse for not teaching about it. He compared the responsibility of teachers to teach opposing views with that of a doctor to treat a patient even though he doesn't like the patient.

He said both evolution and creation should be taught, and that both can be as "scientific or non-scientific, as religious or non-religious, as the teacher is capable of making them."

He said multiple-model teaching, even in science, is quite common and works well. He added that he was surprised that Dr. Mayer of the Biological Sciences Curriculum Study would oppose a multi-model approach, since one of the textbooks the BSCS developed actually encouraged multi-model approaches to scientific controversies, and Morrow himself had used that textbook as the basis for a multi-model approach to origins in a course he taught at Concord College. He said the approach emphasized helping students think about evidence and fostered open minds as a learning device. He said the point of a multi-model approach is "to teach how to learn and how to think" more than simply teaching the facts of biology.

He said in preparing that multi-model approach to origins, he had to do most of the preparation of the evidences for creationism himself, but that by using the principles for seeing various interpretations of data shown in the BSCS textbook, he had found it easy to see how creationists could legitimately understand the same data in different ways from evolutionists.

He said he supported Act 590 because it "makes for good science" by giving balance to two models, neither of which "lends itself easily to scientific testing and both of which are held by good scientists" [Morrow said that it forces the student to test other views]; because as an educator he believes the inquiry and multiple view ideas are good educational principles [he said that they "cause the student to have a deliberate introduction to contrasting ideas"]; and because as a parent and citizen he thinks the schools should be responsive to the citizenry. He said refusal to present two models on origins was "intellectual arrogance."

Asked for evidences for the creationist model, Morrow said they were the same data as were used by evolutionists, but interpreted differently. Creationists, he said, use fossils, ex-periments on synthesis of life, geology, study of living creatures, and all the other areas of science, just as the evolutionists do. He added that the creation model was just as intriguing to him as a scientist as the evolution model, and that it had a "lot more potential for explaining things."

Asked why distinguished scientists who witnessed for the ACLU had said that evidences used by creationists simply are not science, Morrow said, "They're wrong. They're lousy in their interpretations on this case." He added that the fact that "heavy-weights favor evolution is of no great matter." He said he thought the reason witnesses like Stephen Gould, Harold Morowitz, and Francisco Ayala had ridiculed creationism was that they "don't like it's conclusion," they don't want it to be considered, and they're "closedminded."

He said one of the best evidences for creation as the explanation for the origin of life was the fact that the statistical probability of the random formation of life from non-life was "negligible—even for a piece of DNA, let alone a living cell." He said, for example, that the statistical probability of getting one histone by chance was about $1/20^{100}$, or about like trying to find a single certain grain of sand in all the deserts of the earth—basically impossible. "And that's just one polypeptide, not life!" he said.

Under cross examination, Morrow was asked if he knew of evidences for some of the specific points in creation science. Morrow said some examples were the statistical "impossibility" of life coming from non-life by chance, absence of transitions in the fossil record, insufficiency of mutation to bring about large changes in populations of organisms, and the work of Robert Gentry, another of the defense witnesses, on radiochronology (radioactive decay measurements for dating the earth). [Morrow repeated his previous statement that those who held to diverse opinions on scientific issues were shunned by the scientific community. When asked for specific examples Morrow said that he could not immediately think of any. It was here that Judge Overton stopped the cross examination and vehemently lashed out at Morrow. Overton said, "Something bothers me about you, Dr.

Morrow. Do you mean to tell me that you make that statement and cannot give one reference?" Overton continued, "We have been sitting here since 10:30 (time now: 12:10); you have made numerous various opinions, but you have not given any reason for creation except the improbability of the evolutionary position. Can you site anything in support of the creationist position?" In response Morrow said, "Yes, the fossil record." Overton again questioned Morrow: "Are you saying the scientific community is engaged in some sort of conspiracy?" Morrow replied that he "would not be surprised to find systematic censorship."*

Jim Townley

The defense then called Jim Townley, a chemistry teacher in Fort Smith Southside High School.

Townley said he understood balanced treatment of two views on origins as requiring that each be taught sufficiently for students to understand them, but that this would not require equal time. He explained that as a chemistry and physics teacher, he would like to be able to teach his students some of the statistical improbabilities of evolution that point toward creationism, and some of the invalidities of radiometric dating which call into question the extremely old ages given by evolutionists for the earth.

However, Townley said, he had not taught these, and would feel liable for "discipline" from his administrators if he taught them without the backing of Act 590. He said he felt confident that under Act 590, he could research both sides and teach each competently and with balance. He added that he is sure he could teach creation science without its being religious. He

---

* Morrow told reporters after his testimony: "Closedmindedness is something which we have no room for in the courtroom and I think the judge is closedminded." He later said, while in an interview with United Press International, that Overton's interruption of his testimony was "inappropriate and represents bias."

said he thought it would be good for his students because it would generate greater interest and the students would therefore try harder to understand the ideas on both sides.

Under cross examination, Judge William R. Overton, the judge hearing the case, interrupted ACLU attorney Robert Cearley to ask Townley why he felt like he couldn't teach about statistical improbabilities of evolution and problems in radiometric dating without teaching creationism. Townley said that it was because questioning one side of mutually opposed options would imply support for the opposite. [In this case, support for creationism. During this exchange between Townley and Overton, Overton warned him the classroom "is not Sunday School.* You're trying to teach about science!" Townley added that in order to teach creation science the concept of a creator must be included. He said, based upon the untestable character of either model, a creator is "not a scientific concept," yet when spoken of in the realm of origins is as certainly a viable option as evolution.]

After hearing the actual accounts of the philosophical, religious, and educational witnesses, the media represented those accounts as follows:

Sample Media Coverage

Washington Post, Friday—December 11, 1981:

Creationist Tells of Belief
In UFOs, Satan, Occult

LITTLE ROCK, Dec. 11—The defense of the Arkansas creation law opened today with a spectacular courtroom fireworks display as the opening creationist witness described, under cross-examination his belief in unidentified flying objects, demon possession and the occult, which he said he sees as actual satanic attacks in the world.

---

* See Chapter Two for word-for-word official court transcript of this discussion.

Dallas Times Herald, Saturday—December 12, 1981:

Theologian Testifies UFOs Work of Satan
LITTLE ROCK, Ark.—A theology professor testifying
Friday in a court test of how creation should be taught in
public schools said he believes UFOs exist and are the
work of Satan.

St. Petersburg Times, Saturday—December 12, 1981:

Defense in Arkansas Creation Trial
Opens With Fiery Cross-Examination
LITTLE ROCK, Ark.—The defense of the Arkansas creation law opened Friday with a spectacular courtroom
fireworks display as the first witness described under
cross-examination his belief in unidentified flying objects,
demon possession, and the occult, which he sees as actual
satanic attacks in the world.

The Saturday Herald and Leader, Lexington, KY, December 12,
1981:

Theology Teacher Says He Believes
UFOs Satan's Work
LITTLE ROCK, Ark.—A theology professor testifying
yesterday in a court test of how creation should be taught
in public schools said he believes UFOs exist and are the
work of Satan.
Norman Geisler, professor of theology and philosophy
at Dallas Theological Seminary in Dallas, who testified as
the state's first witness, said unidentified flying objects are
"a satanic manifestation in the world for the purpose of
deception."

Jackson Clarion Ledger, Jackson, Miss., December 12, 1981:

Creationism Defense Witness Describes
Belief in UFOs, Occult
LITTLE ROCK, Arkansas—The defense of the Arkansas
creation law opened Friday with a spectacular courtroom
fireworks display as the opening creationist witness
described under cross-examination his belief in unidentified flying objects, demon possession, and the occult,
which he sees as actual satanic attacks in the world.

Arkansas Gazette, Little Rock, Saturday—December 12, 1981:

Theologian Contends UFOs Work of Satan

The final witness for the plaintiffs and the first witness for the state agreed Friday that Act 590 of 1981, the state creation-science law, was inspired by Genesis, but disagreed on whether the law should stand.

In his testimony, Dr. Norman Geisler, a professor of theology and philosophy at Dallas Theological Seminary, who was the first witness called by the state in the trial of the law's constitutionality, also said, "I believe in UFOs—I believe they are a satanic manifestation in the world for the purpose of deception.

Los Angeles Herald Examiner, Saturday—December 12, 1981:

Witness in Creation Trial Links UFOs to Satan

LITTLE ROCK, Ark. (AP)—A theology professor testifying yesterday in a court test of how creation should be taught in public schools said he believes UFOs exist and are the work of Satan.

Norman Geisler, professor of theology and philosophy at Dallas Theological Seminary in Dallas, who testified as the state's first witness, said unidentified flying objects are "a satanic manifestation in the world for the purpose of deception."

Arkansas Gazette, Little Rock, Saturday—December 12, 1981:

Highlights of Trial

A Dallas theologian, the first witness for the state in the creation-science trial, said Friday that he believed "UFOs exist—I believe they are a satanic manifestation in the world for the purpose of deception."

The witness was Dr. Norman Geisler, professor of theology and philosophy at Dallas Theological Seminary, who also said that he believed that Act 590 reflected the book of Genesis, but that the Bible served as the inspiration for many legitimate scientific inquiries.

Detroit News, Saturday—December 12, 1981:

Creationist Takes Stand, Calls UFOs Work of Devil

LITTLE ROCK, Ark.—UFOs are the work of the devil, says the first witness called to defend an Arkansas law that allows teaching creationism in public schools.

"They're a satanic manifestation in the world for the
purposes of deception," said Norman Geisler, a professor
of theology called to help defend the law against a federal
suit by the American Civil Liberties Union.

Geisler, who said he believes everything in the Bible is
true, made his comments under a grueling cross-
examination by Anthony Siano, a New York attorney, who
with Little Rock attorney Robert Cearley Jr., is assisting
the ACLU in the case.

The Tampa Tribune-Times, Sunday—December 13, 1981:

Creative Testimony At Creationism Trial
LITTLE ROCK, Ark. (AP)—Testimony in the trial of a
state law requiring balanced presentations of evolution
and creation-science has so far encompassed UFOs, the
devil and fears about student vigilantes.

The Miami Herald, Sunday—December 13, 1981:

UFOs Are Caused by Satan, Witness
At Creation Trial Says
LITTLE ROCK, Ark. (AP)—A witness who supports
teaching creationism in Arkansas public schools says he
finds evidence in the Bible for UFOs, which he called "a
satanic manifestation in the world for the purpose of
deception."

"I believe everything the Bible affirms is true," Norman
Geisler of Dallas Theological Seminary in Dallas testified
Friday.

The Daily Democrat, Woodland-Davis, CA, Sunday—December 14, 1981:

Key ACLU attorney Phillip Kaplan catches up on his
phone messages during a break in the creation science
trial in Little Rock, Ark. this week. Dr. Norman L. Geisler,
a professor at Dallas Theological Seminary led off the
defense by saying "UFOs are a satanic manifestation."

Arkansas Gazette, Little Rock, Monday—December 14, 1981:

Satan's UFOs
Considering all the testimony that had preceded creationism's first witness, it could hardly be surprising that
Satan has now been introduced in the constitutional test
before Federal Judge William R. Overton of Arkansas'

"creation-science" law, Act 590 of 1981.

Introducing this fresh element into the trial on Friday was Dr. Norman Geisler, a professor of theology and philosophy at Dallas Theological Seminary, as he began the testimony of defense witnesses called by Attorney General Steve Clark. It was interesting testimony, not only on direct examination but also on cross examination by the attorneys for the American Civil Liberties Union, which represents the plaintiffs, half of them religious leaders themselves.

The West Australian, Tuesday—December 15, 1981:

Fiery Start to Trial on Creation Law

LITTLE ROCK, Mon: The defense of the Arkansas creation law has opened with a spectacular courtroom fireworks display as the opening creationist witness said he believed in unidentified flying objects, demon possession and the occult, which he sees as satanic attacks in the world.

Chemical Engineering News, December 21, 1981:

Creationists Expected to Lose Arkansas Fight

There have been some strange moments as the trial has unfolded. For instance, in cross-examination, Norman Geisler, of the Dallas Theological Seminary in Texas, testified that unidentified flying objects are "Satanic manifestations in the world for the purpose of deception."

Discover, February 1982:

Judgment Day for Creationism

Siano pounced on the Satan reference, pressing Geisler to recall any personal experience that confirmed his belief in the Devil . . . . Geisler declared, "I believe UFOs exist." He explained that "they are a satanic manifestation in this world for the purposes of deception." Siano: "No further questions."

The New York Times, Tuesday—December 15, 1981:

Professor Defends Teaching of
Creation as "Stimulating"

LITTLE ROCK, Ark., Dec. 14 (AP)—Teaching evolution in the public schools without also teaching "creationism" is tantamount to indoctrination, an educator testified today in defense of Arkansas' new creation science law.

Larry Parker, a professor of education at Georgia State University in Atlanta, also said that teaching creationism as well as evolution in public schools would make classes "stimulating and thought-provoking."

Arkansas Gazette, Little Rock, Tuesday—December 15, 1981:

Perceives Benefits

The other witness Monday was Dr. Larry Parker of Dunwoody, Ga., a professor of education at Georgia State College, who said that students would benefit from being taught both concepts. He said educational psychologists had established that children who were given divergent questions showed an increased divergence of ideas.

Arkansas Gazette, Little Rock, Tuesday—December 15, 1981:

Highlight of Trial

Dr. Larry Parker of Dunwoody, Ga., an education professor at Georgia State College, said both creation-science and evolution should be taught in the public schools because people wanted them taught and because students would learn more.

Commercial Appeal, Memphis, Tuesday—December 15, 1981:

Creationism Defenders Trip Over
Question From Judge

The first witness to testify Monday cited local and national polls that indicate most people want both theories taught in public schools. Students should learn how to think in schools, not what to think, said Dr. Larry E. Parker, associate professor in the department of curriculum and instruction at Georgia State University.

Arkansas Democrat, Little Rock, Tuesday—December 15, 1981:

State Witness Calls Overton Closed-minded

Dr. Larry E. Parker, a Georgia State University specialist in curriculum development, said the introduction of creation science into the classroom would create "stimulating, interacting, thought-provoking sessions" and should be taught because of public demand.

"This bill would simply be responsive to society," he said of Act 590.

Arkansas Democrat, Little Rock, Tuesday—December 15, 1981:

State Witness Calls Overton Closed-minded
A biochemist called U.S. District Judge William R. Overton "closed-minded" on Monday, saying the judge was paying no attention to state Attorney General Steve Clark's defense of Arkansas' creation-science law.

Arkansas Gazette, Little Rock, Tuesday—December 15, 1981:

Censorship Charge Not
Supported, Judge Complains
Federal Judge William R. Overton showed frustration and exasperation several times Monday during the state's first full day of testimony in the creationism trial and rained consternation on one witness for sniping at the scientific community without citing evidence.

The Commercial Appeal, Memphis, Tuesday—December 15, 1981:

Creationism Defenders Trip Over
Questions From Judge
LITTLE ROCK—Defenders of an Arkansas law that would force creationism into public schools faltered on the witness stand Monday from an apparent lack of homework.

Dr. William Scott Morrow, professor of biochemistry at Wofford College at Spartanburg, SC, testified Monday that most scientists won't even consider new theories that "shake cherished concepts." He identified himself as an evolutionist but said the creationism theory was "more exciting" and that, "I think the creationists look at more information than my fellow evolutionists."

In the face of tough cross-examination by attorney Robert M. Cearley Jr., Dr. Morrow continued leaning back on his chair and said, "I know enough of my fellow evolutionists to know closed minds when I see them."

But Dr. Morrow received a start when Overton interrupted to ask whether he claimed there is "some sort of conspiracy to keep scientific evidence that will support the Genesis version of the Bible out of publication."

Morrow replied that "it has nothing to do with the Bible," but that he wouldn't be surprised to find "systematic censorship" of creationism.

Arkansas Gazette, Little Rock, Tuesday—December 15, 1981:

Highlights of Trial

Federal Judge William R. Overton critically questioned a scientist Monday in the sixth day of the trial of Act 590 for making allegations against other scientists without citing proof.

The scientist, Dr. W. Scott Morrow, a chemistry professor at Wofford College, had said scientists who believed in evolution were "closed-minded" and appeared to exercise "systematic censorship" of creationist views.

Dallas Times Herald, Tuesday—December 15, 1981:

Judge Scolds Professor in Creation-Science Trial

LITTLE ROCK, Ark.—A red-faced federal judge Monday scolded a South Carolina biochemist for inadequately supporting his statement that the scientific community has systematically censored creation-science.

Commercial Appeal, Memphis, Tuesday—December 15, 1981:

Creation Defenders Trip Over Question From Judge

Another witness, Jim Townley, a chemistry teacher at Southside High School in Fort Smith, said he needed Act 590 of 1981 so he could teach creationism and criticize evolution. He had difficulty explaining to Overton why he couldn't criticize evolution without the law, however.

Arkansas Gazette, Little Rock, Tuesday—December 15, 1981:

Highlights of Trial

Jimmy Don Townley, a chemistry teacher at Fort Smith Southside High School, said he wanted to teach certain aspects of creationism that raised questions about the credibility of evolution.

Arkansas Democrat, Little Rock, Tuesday—December 15, 1981:

State Witness Calls Overton Closed-minded

Jim Townley, a Fort Smith chemistry teacher, told Overton he wanted to supplement his science classes with creation-science theory, but did not because of his uncertainty about Arkansas law.

Chemical & Engineering News—December 24, 1981:

Creationists Expected to
Lose Arkansas Fight

Another witness, James Townley, a chemistry teacher in Ft. Smith, Ark., testified that he could not teach evidence that questions the accuracy of radiometric dating methods without the protection of Act 590. When pressed by Judge Overton on why he couldn't, Townley said he wanted to use the evidence to teach creation-science and that, "I don't see why I can't." In response Overton snapped, "Because it isn't Sunday School."

Frequently those holding creationist ideas could plead ignorance of the means and affirm only the facts. That seems to summarize the feeling I get in talking to evolutionists today.

—**Dr. Colin Patterson**
British Paleontologist
In lecture delivered
November 5, 1981

Chapter Seven

Record of Defense's Science Testimonies

Summary of Defense Testimony
Monday, 14 December 1981
Defense Witness Frair

Dr. Wayne Frair

The defense then called Dr. Wayne Frair, professor of biology at The King's College, Briarcliff Manor, N.Y.

Frair testified that through his work in biochemical taxonomy (classifying forms of life by the chemicals they contain), he has become convinced that a "limited change" model—essentially like the creation science model—is the best explanation of living things. This model would be described as a "forest of trees" in which individual kinds of life are the trees, with the branches representing variations within limits of the individual kinds of life. The trees themselves are not connected with each other.

Evolutionism, he said, could be described as the view that all of life forms only one tree, rather than a forest of trees; and the various kinds of life are the branches, and variations of the kinds are the twigs and leaves on the branches. In this model, every kind of life is related genetically to every other kind of life.

He said that within the creation science model, one could hold to the "special theory" of evolution, which says that variation has taken place within certain limits among the types of life, but that one would oppose the "general theory" of evolution, which says that all forms of life developed from a single early form and that they are therefore all genetically related.

Frair said he considered the "State of Arkansas to be on the very cutting edge of an educational movement" which promised to improve education around the country by focusing on teaching students how to think and analyze alternative views not only in science, but in other areas as well.

Frair quoted from several scientific writings that have been in circulation for as many as fifty years which called into question the general theory of evolution on purely scientific grounds, but which, he said, had been ignored by the scientific community. He also referred to scientific writers who said it is important to present "scientific heresies" to students so they'll learn to examine points of view and judge them intelligently.

Overton interrupted the examination by state's attorney Williams to ask whether Frair could show positive evidence for creation science, not just negative evidence against evolution science. Williams responded that since the two are mutually exclusive, whatever is evidence against one is automatically evidence for the other.

When Williams asked how creation science could be presented without religious instruction, Frair replied that teachers could present evidences for the two views that life is either all related on a single tree (the evolutionist view) or that life is on many unconnected trees and therefore genetically unrelated. "There wouldn't even [need to be reference to] a creator," he said. "They're just saying, 'There they [the evidences] are.' And maybe some people would infer a creator [from that]." He said people could be non-religious and be creationists. [When asked about the meaning of balanced treatment, Frair said that it meant the teacher should give enough information to make the basic positions "clear and fair." When asked by Williams how his view of creation effects his teaching methodology he said, "It basically doesn't."]

Frair said most evolutionists seem to misunderstand the creation model. He said they don't understand the value of having the option of viewing various kinds of life as genetically unrelated, an option he said had made him able to do more objective biochemical research in his own laboratories. Instead, he said, evolutionists feel constrained to fit all life into a single tree, and that can put heavy pressures on their research.

He said the assertion that removal of evolutionary theory from biology would leave scientists with nothing but confusing, unconnected facts, an assertion made by witnesses for the ACLU, was "patently false," and that his own studies [Frair here made reference to his studies in proteins and DNA] showed how creationism could be an equally good unifying principle in biology.

Under cross examination by ACLU attorney Bruce Ennis, Frair acknowledged that as a professor at The King's College he had to sign a doctrinal statement which said the Bible is without error, and that he is on the board of director of the Creation Research Society, which has a similar doctrinal statement.

Ennis asked Frair if he could give a clear definition of a "kind," as referred to in the act, and Frair said a "kind" would "constitute a group of organisms genetically unrelated to other organisms." He said there was considerable discussion within the evolutionist community about groupings of types of life, and that there was the same kind of discussion going on in creationist circles. He added that "kind" is not necessarily equivalent to "species."

Ennis asked Frair if he had Biblical reasons for rejecting evolution, and Frair asked for reference to a particular part of Scripture. Ennis said he was referring to a part of Frair's own book, *The Case for Creation,* p. 81, where he said that there were Biblical reasons for rejecting evolution. Frair responded that that statement occurred in a footnote to the book and was a quotation from a Biblical commentator, not his own words.

Tuesday, 15 December 1981
Defense Witnesses Helder, Chittick, Roth, Coffin

Dr. Margaret G. Helder

The defense then called Dr. Margaret G. Helder, retired professor of biology at Brock University, St. Catherial, Ontario, Canada, a specialist in the biological study of algae and other areas of botany.

Helder testified that her research showed that the green algaes could not be, as evolutionists had long thought, ancestral to all the types of plant life, but rather that the various types of plants had to have genetically unrelated ancestors, a view which she said supports creation science.

Helder also testified that there are two groups in the world of science, one of which says that there are some things that cannot be explained by purely mechanistic, naturalistic processes, and another group which says there aren't. She said an assumed *sine qua non* of much scientific endeavor has been the belief in an ability to explain all phenomena in mechanistic terms. "I want to challenge that definition of science," she said. She said, though, that her own religious faith had nothing to do with her studies in plant biology which indicated that creationism was a better explanation of origins than evolutionism.

Helder said that she had often discussed evidences for separate ancestry for plants in her botany classes, showing that while certain characteristics might indicate a relationship between two kinds of plants, other characteristics contradicted the idea of relationship. She had never had to introduce any religious literature to discuss her creationist views. She said her studies indicated that many biologists, especially among botanists, are "becoming more and more aware of the differences in forms of life. They are tending more and more toward the position of creationism of separate origins of life."

Dr. Donald Chittick

The defense then called Dr. Donald Chittick, former professor of chemistry at the University of Puget Sound and George Fox College, and currently director of research and development of Pyneuco, Inc., a business which converts biological waste materials into usable fuel.

Chittick said he was an evolutionist while in graduate school, but that by reading literature on origins from both sides when he was a graduate student he "was convinced that the creation model was a better explanation of the data."

Chittick pointed out that science works by beginning with certain assumptions, which it uses to interpret data, and then arrives at conclusions which are consistent with both the assumptions and the data. However, if one begins with different assumptions, he can interpret the same data and come to different conclusions. This, he said, is what happens in the controversy over evolution and creation—evolutionists begin with certain assumptions about reality and natural processes, interpret the data in accord with those assumptions, and arrive at evolutionary conclusions. The important thing to realize, he said, is that both groups look at the same data, and the different conclusions are necessitated by the different assumptions.

He said he believes, even though he is a creationist, that evolutionism should be taught, but that it should be balanced with teaching creationism. He said he has taught creationism often, and that he has done so without making it religious. Balance, he said, need not mean equal time for the two, but simply mentioning both and giving evidences for both. Each view, he said, should be taught by starting with an examination of the assumptions behind each view, then seeing how those assumptions bear on the interpretation of the data, then examining the data themselves, and then viewing the conclusions.

He said his own preference for the creation model had assisted him in making discoveries about converting biological wastes into synthetic "fossil" fuels. Evolutionists, he said, assume that the earth is extremely old and that "biomass" was converted to oil and coal through millions of years by biochemical processes.

However, he said, if one assumed that the earth were young,

he could look for another way of forming "fossils fuels" like oil
and coal. When Chittick did this, he found that geochemical
processes could convert biomass into fuels much more quickly than biochemical processes, quickly enough to do it within
thousands of years, thus consistent with a creation model
assumption of a relatively young earth.

Experiments he performed based on this assumption resulted in the development of a process for converting biomass
into fuels which he has already shown workable by using that
fuel to power a cross-country trip.

He said actual studies showed that because of geochemical
processes, wood used as mine supports had in some cases
been known to convert to the level of anthracite coal in as little
as ten years, implying that a geochemical explanation for the
formation of coal and oil was better than the traditional
biochemical explanation. The studies showed that coal and oil
actually resulted from having large amounts of biomass buried
rapidly, heated and pressurized rapidly. This, he said, supported a young age for the earth and also the creationist idea
that a universal flood was responsible for much of the
geological structure of the earth's crust.

Chittick also testified that his research had shown traditional radioactive decay dating systems to be unreliable for
dating the age of rocks, and therefore of the earth. [The rocks
Chittick referred to were actually moon samples. He said that
when examining moon rocks by isotope methodology re-
searchers concluded with three different ages for the same
rock.] Instead, he said, those systems were an indicator of the
type of geologic forces which acted on the rocks when they
were formed, and were not indicative of age at all. This meant,
he said, that the most highly-relied-upon method for dating the
earth to the about 4.5 billion years assumed by evolutionists
could not be used, and other methods, which indicated a
young age for the earth, should be used instead.

[When asked if it was fair to challenge the evolutionary
theory Chittick said yes, that refusal to teach creationism
"dulls education—teaching only evolution is bad science and
bad education."]

Under cross-examination, Chittick was asked whether he

held certain religious beliefs. Defense attorney Williams objected to that line of questioning, as the defense had done several times before, on the basis that a person's religious beliefs had nothing to do with his reliability as a scientific witness and were therefore irrelevant unless it could be proved that "in fact one's religious beliefs have caused one to compromise one's profession as a scientist," and referred to a ruling in another court which said the religious beliefs or opinions of a witness could not be used to discredit him. Judge Overton overruled the objection. [When asked whether he agreed with the contents of a Bible Science Association newsletter about putting "Christ and the Bible . . . back into science is one of the most powerful methods of witnessing," he said no.]

Dr. Ariel Roth

The defense then called Dr. Ariel Roth, director of the Geoscience Research Institute at Loma Linda University, California. Roth is a former professor of biology at the University of Michigan, Andrews University, and former chairman of the biology department at Loma Linda University. [Roth testified that when the creation and evolution models were compared, creation best fit the available data. He said that since both use the same data, interpretation is the real issue.]

[When asked if both were theories, he said yes, based on the fact that each view was an extrapolation from available information. The issue of origins cannot be tested but can be theorized. When asked if both views should be taught, Roth answered in the affirmative yet asserted that both should be carefully scrutinized.]

Roth testified that his research on coral reefs in the Pacific Ocean showed that the reefs probably grow much faster than evolutionists had thought, and explained that this supported the creation model. He said the reefs grow 1-4000 times as fast as the speed at which the ocean floors are dropping, yet there are many reefs which are "drowned," which are now so deep in the ocean that they get too little sunlight to continue growing. This means, he said, that the ocean floors must have dropped very quickly at one time, a fact which is consistent with the creationist belief that a worldwide geological/hydrological catastrophe helped shape the earth's geology.

According to the evolutionist assumption of the speed at which the ocean floor drops, Roth said, the reefs should never have gotten "drowned" because, according to his studies, they would have been growing so fast they would have kept their tops right at the surface.

Asked about other evidences for creation science, Roth mentioned a number of "serious problems" with the evolution model: high improbability of random formation of life; difficulty of evolving complex integrated structures since each part of the integrated structure alone would be useless to the organism in which it first appeared and therefore would be weeded out by natural selection; the near impossibility of the random formation of chromosomes, genes ordered to fit together both by internal components of genes and the ordering of the genes to fit each other. Roth explained that while these problems can't be explained by the evolution model, they fit perfectly into the predictions of the creation model and therefore support creationism.

As examples of the difficulty of evolving "complex integrated structures," Roth noted the relationship of "the ear, the brain, and the auricular nerve," and the respiratory system. Of the respiratory system, he said, "This system would not be functional until all the parts were there . . . . How did these parts survive during evolution as useless parts under natural selection?"

Roth said evolutionists usually have not fairly evaluated creation science, but simply reject it without proper scientific investigation because it is a "paradigm" that conflicts with the "paradigm" of evolution. He said a paradigm is an "interpretive grid" through which scientists examine data. Roth said it is difficult for scientists to question their paradigms, but that in the history of science, many paradigms have been adopted and used for awhile, and then questioned and replaced by others. With their commitment to the evolutionary paradigm, Roth said, it is not surprising that evolutionists should "object so strongly" to a balanced presentation of creation science and evolution science.

Asked if creation science could be taught only on scientific grounds without religious references, Roth said it could, since "origin by design" is a scientific idea and since "knowledge is separate from commitment." "I don't have to join a church to learn about it," Roth said.

Dr. Harold G. Coffin

Dr. Harold G. Coffin, senior research scientist at the Geoscience Research Institute, Loma Linda, Calif., testified next for the defense.

Coffin began by saying that both evolution science and creation science are assumptive constructs through which data is interpreted. "We are dealing with something that we have to accept by assuming, by assumption, in both cases." He said evolution has to assume spontaneous generation of life, because it has never observed it, and creation science has to assume the existence of a creator, because it cannot prove the creator's existence. [Coffin said that in either case "faith" is necessary for acceptance.]

He said his own work in biology supported the creation science model and opposed the evolution science model because he had found four important factors: (1) the "uniqueness of life" ["We cannot define what life is; we can tell what it does, but we can't define it."]; (2) sudden appearance of life in the "Cambrian" rocks of the geologic column indicates sudden creation instead of slow evolution, since on the evolutionary assumption, the complex life forms found there should be preceded by millions of years of less complex life forms, but are not; (3) the absence of "connecting links" between basic kinds of animals and plants in the fossil record; (4) the inability of scientists to cause or observe in modern life forms changes from one basic kind of life to another.

He said he estimates that about 95% of the material he reads on evolution he would have no quarrel with, because it deals with minor changes within basic kinds of life, while the rest of evolutionary theory "is speculation."

Coffin said many examples of fossils supported the creationist model which says fossils are primarily the result of a worldwide flood. [He said that according to present processes, an expired fish decays in one week. In order to get the perfect shapes available in the fossil record, the fish would have to be covered within a period of five hours. This rapid burial could only have been caused by a catastrophic flood.] He showed a picture of a fossil fish which was completely intact when it was buried and which had its mouth open at the time, showing it suffocated. This, he said, was one of thousands of fossils around the world which support the idea that a flood buried most life forms and resulted in the present fossil record.

Other examples of fossils which he said would require rapid burial in a flood are animal footprints in sand and fossilized animal dung, either of which would have been obliterated if they had to wait for slow burial as predicated by the evolution model. He said such fossils suggest "rapid geological activity" similar to what would be expected in a worldwide flood.

He said modern research on coal beds indicates that they are not the result of slow, stationary burial of biomass but rather of enormous amounts of biomass being transported in liquid and deposited quickly into depressions, and then buried quickly by sediments. This, he said, was the earlier understanding of coal beds, but when George Lyell and others postulated a slow buildup for geology in accord with evolutionary assumptions, many coal geologists abandoned this understanding, but now the geological community is returning to it. Such formation of coal beds would indicate enormous flooding.

Under cross-examination by Ennis of the ACLU, Coffin said that the term "kinds" should probably be understood as broader than the term "species," and in some instances could include all the organisms in a given order in standard taxonomy.

Wednesday, 16 December 1981
Defense Witnesses Wickramasinghe, Gentry

Dr. N. Chandra Wickramasinghe

The defense then called Dr. N. Chandra Wickramasinghe, professor and head of the department of applied mathematics and astronomy at University College, Cardiff, Wales, in Great

Britain. Wickramasinghe is a Buddhist.

Wickramasinghe testified that his research in partnership with Sir Frederick Hoyle at University College in astronomy and astrophysics proved beyond doubt that "interstellar dust," the tiny dust particles which form immense clouds in space and filter the light from some stars, are actually bits of biological material similar to the bacterium E. coli, a bacterium which aids in digesting food in animal colons. This discovery led Wickramasinghe and Hoyle to examine modern theories of the origin of life.

They found on examination of the traditional Darwinian idea of the random formation of life through mechanistic processes that the statistical probability of forming even a single enzyme, which is a building block of genes, which in turn are building blocks of cells, is 1 in every $10^{40,000}$ tries, or in other words, statistically impossible. That would require more tries for the formation of one enzyme, he said, than there are atoms in all the stars of all the galaxies in the entire known universe.

These statistical improbabilities caused Hoyle and Wickramasinghe to decide that there must be some intelligent creator, either within the universe or outside it. Wickramasinghe testified that his Buddhist background drove him to the belief that the creator was a part of the universe, but that it would be equally possible to think the creator was supernatural.

Hoyle and Wickramasinghe theorize that this creator designed and formed life in the cosmos, and that life came to earth during its early periods through influxes of this interstellar dust. They said they do not believe that spontaneous generation of life is possible, but that they do believe life evolved on earth.

They added a twist to evolutionary thinking, however, by saying that the new genetic material needed for upward development of life forms is added to earth life forms by the addition of new bacteria from space, carried sometimes on meteorites. These new bacteria, Wickramasinghe said, would combine with the genetic material in a given organism and would cause upward changes.

Wickramasinghe said, though, that the probabilities of upward change by chance combination of the new bacteria with current life forms was so infinitely tiny that he and Hoyle had to postulate the idea that the "intelligent designer" arranged the times and places at which the interstellar bacteria would arrive on earth so that it would cause upward change.

Wickramasinghe explained that he and Hoyle came to their conclusion about the nature of interstellar dust through minute astrophysical examination, and that the scientific community, while skeptical of their findings because they militate against traditional ideas, has not been able to show any flaws in their research. He said they measured the light spectrum given by interstellar dust and compared it with the spectrums of known chemicals on earth. They first found that the dust particles had to contain large amounts of carbon, hydrogen, and oxygen; in other words, that they had to be organic. Then they realized that the spectrum was that of a highly complex organic substance. Then one day while searching through an atlas of light spectrums, Wickramasinghe stumbled on a spectrum that was exactly like the one given by interstellar dust. The amazing thing, he said, was that the spectrum was one for cellulose, a sugar which is the basis for most fibrous plants. Further research led them to the conclusion that the chemical makeup of the dust is most like that of the bacterium E. coli.

Wickramasinghe said he and Hoyle were both surprised at their findings, and described the experience as "traumatic" because it called into question age-old assumptions about life having been limited primarily to earth. They delayed publishing their findings for nearly a year because they wanted to test the findings thoroughly and rule out all other possible interpretations of the data. "We tried, in the true spirit of science, to remain as conservative as possible, until it finally became impossible to remain conservative."

Wickramasinghe said the scientific community had responded primarily with silence, and that this was common when research challenged basic scientific assumption. However, he said, another scientist studying meteorites had found corroborating evidence in the form of fossilized bacteria in the meteorites, bacteria which he said had to have come from space before the meteorites came into the earth's atmosphere.

He said he and Hoyle had encountered a bias from the scientific community against anything which questioned traditional neo-Darwinian ideas, and that was the reason for his support of Act 590. He said the best spirit of science is an open mind. While he did not accept all of the ideas of the creation model, he said that as a scientist he would not reject any of them until he had examined the scientific arguments pro and con, and said examination of competing views in science would be beneficial to students.

Wickramasinghe said that contrary to the popular notion that only creationism relies on the supernatural, evolutionism must as well, since the probabilities of random formation of life (spontaneous generation) are so tiny as to require a "miracle" for spontaneous generation to have occurred, making belief in spontaneous generation "tantamount to a theological argument." [Wickramasinghe said that to believe life came from spontaneous generation was about as plausible as "a tornado blowing through a junkyard and assembling a Boeing 747."]*

He said his research drove him to believe that an intelligent creator exists because of the impossibility of the chance formation and development of life anywhere in the universe. He said this conclusion was despite his agnostic Buddhist beliefs. It was a difficult position for him to take emotionally because it differed from all his earlier thought.

His research, however, left him two possible conclusions:

---

*   "I think that these scientists have been incredibly perverse," Wickramasinghe said in an exclusive interview with the [Pea Ridge, Arkansas] TIMES after the trial. "I believe that they have made all manner of ridiculous statements. In fact, [they] sort of imply that some kind of scientific miracle occurred. They are quite vehement in denying the possibility of miracles in the theological or religious way, but they have involved miracles all along in this chain of argument—processes that are so improbable that to postulate that it happened really is tantamount to saying that a miracle happened."

either life and the universe were the result of a deliberate act of a creator, or they are eternal. For those who accept the modern cosmological ideas which hold the universe to be about 15 billion years old, he said, the idea that it and life are eternal is impossible.

"I think one is driven, almost inescapably, to accept the fact, or rather the possibility, that there is a creator, . . . and this brings the creator's existence into the realm of empirical science." He concluded that denial of some form of creation implies "blindness to fact" and "absolute arrogance."

He said such denial of a creator and creation in the scientific community generally comes from an "anti-religious bias" in the scientific community. He said there was an implied rejection of theological views in the rise of Darwinism at the beginning of the industrial revolution. He said the "strong instinctive reaction of scientists" against creationism stems from their "belief in the supremacy and centrality of man and earth," and added, " . . . the human ego has been pushed right into an insignificant corner," and humanistic evolutionary ideas are a way of saving that ego. He said evolutionists view man as a god.

Wickramasinghe said he and Hoyle had not published their research in standard scientific journals because the editors of those journals generally are closed-minded to anything which questions Darwinian ideas on the origin and development of life. Instead, they chose to publish it in book form so their critics and they would be free to have exchange of ideas on the matter. He said the general commitment of the scientific community to the "conventional wisdom" about biology made it nearly impossible for most people to objectively analyze ideas that called the "conventional wisdom" into question, and added that his own lack of training in biology since he graduated from college was an advantage to him because he would have been "hamstrung" by the "conventional wisdom." [He stated that you cannot accommodate the conventional wisdom in a rational framework. He said that creationism "so profoundly and so deeply" challenges the main line thinking in biology. He asserted that children who are made to accept the evolutionary model in the classroom are "brainwashed." He added "it is the biggest travesty of all that a society would close its mind to the biggest question of all, the origins of life."]

When asked to compare evolution and creation as to their religious overtones, Wickramasinghe said they were both "deeply religious," and that if he had to choose between the two, he thinks evolution is religiously "more insidious and has more evil implications" than creationism.

Under cross-examination, the ACLU lawyer argued with Wickramasinghe that probability arguments are really illegitimate, since highly improbable things happen all the time. He gave as an example the chance attendance of any given 50,000 people at a football game. He said the chances for that would be $50,000^{50,000}$, a probability far less than that Wickramasinghe had estimated for the random formation of an enzyme. But, he said, the attendance of a given 50,000 people at a football game occurred regularly nearly every week through football season. This, he said, showed that probability statistics are not relevant.

Wickramasinghe responded under redirect examination by the state that the ACLU's argument on probability misunderstood probability theory. First, he said, the 50,000 people attending a football game don't get there by chance—they decide to go, buy tickets, and travel there. Second, the arrangement in which 50,000 people sit at a football game is unimportant, since any order is fine enough for a football crowd. However, with enzymes, arrangement is of utmost importance, there being at least 15 positions in a chain of amino acids in any given enzyme which must be "present." Since people go to football games by intelligent choice, Wickramasinghe said, the ACLU attorney's argument actually supported the creation model, not the evolution model.

Robert Gentry

The final witness called by the state was Robert Gentry, a research scientist at the Oak Ridge National Laboratory in Tennessee. Gentry specialized in the study of the breakdown of radioactive materials in rocks.

Gentry testified for nearly five hours regarding research he had done on "haloes" formed by radioactive decay of polonium in granite rocks and in coalified wood (wood that has turned to coal). The "haloes" are circles around the decaying atoms of the radioactive material, circles which are etched into the rock by escaping alpha or beta particles that result from the decay.

These circles, Gentry explained, can be identified with certainty through examination under an electron microscope, and are made by all decaying radioactive materials in solidified rocks. The circles given by different radioactive materials are different from each other.

Gentry said one isotope of polonium has a half life of only about three-and-a-half minutes. This means that the rock has to be solidified before or within seconds of the time the polonium isotope gets into it, or there will be no halo in the rock.

In some instances, this isotope of polonium can be given by the decay of uranium, of which the polonium isotope is one byproduct. However, sometimes polonium decay haloes are found in rocks without any possible uranium source for the polonium. This, Gentry explained, means the polonium had to be present in the rocks at the moment they solidified.

This in turn, Gentry said, means the rocks had to solidify extremely rapidly, under conditions unknown to science today. This indicates the likelihood of a creation of the earth and its primordial rocks and elements by a supernatural creator, and cannot be explained on the basis of evolutionary assumptions.

Evolutionary assumptions about geology insist that "basement granites," the granites which underlie the sedimentary layers of the earth, and the type in which Gentry often finds polonium haloes without uranium sources for the polonium, were formed by slow cooling and compaction over periods of two or three billion years. Since Gentry's research shows that they must have cooled almost instantly, Gentry said his research calls into serious doubt the traditional scientific idea that the earth must be 4.5 billion years old.

Similar experiments on polonium haloes found in coalified wood led Gentry to postulate that the wood had been buried during a huge deluge and had turned rapidly to coal rather than very slowly, as evolutionary assumptions would predict. This, he said, supported the idea of the creation model that the earth's geology is best explained on the basis of a flood.

Gentry also testified and showed letters substantiating his testimony regarding what he called a bias in the scientific community once it realized the implications of his research. Before the implications became clear, he was able to get his studies published quickly in the leading scientific journals, because his work was recognized around the world as the leading work on radioactive haloes in rocks. However, when it became clear that his work was calling into question the whole of traditional "geochronology," the assumptions about dating the age of the earth and its rocks, and would support a belief in a young earth, the journals suddenly became closed to him, and it took repeated efforts, and threats to tell the press about the bias, for Gentry to be allowed to publish the papers in the journals again.

He said the general reaction of the evolutionist community was to discount the research, even though they could show no errors in it. He gave several examples of geologists who responded to his research simply by saying it must be wrong because if it were right it would require them to rethink all their theories about the age of the earth and the formation of the earth's geology—a hard task!

Thursday, 17 December 1981

Responding to one critic who said Gentry's research called into question the whole of modern theories of geologic time and who said that should not be done since so much data had been shown to fit into those theories, Gentry said, "While I can appreciate York's desire to emphasize internal consistency, it should be evident that irrespective of how much data has been or yet can be fitted into the present model, the question of its ultimate reliability hinges on whether there exist any observations which falsify the theory." He said his data on radiohaloes were such data, and that therefore the theories of an old earth and slow formation of earth's basement rocks should be abandoned in favor of a theory of a young earth and rapid formation of the basement rocks.

Gentry concluded with a challenge to the scientific community to try to falsify his theory. He said if they could simply synthesize one piece of granite the size of a fist under ordinary physical processes, he would abandon his theory and become an evolutionist.

Under cross-examination by Ennis, Gentry acknowledged that he does subscribe to the statement of belief of the Creation Research Society, of which he is a member, but added that if the scientific evidence leads him to believe that the Bible is in error, he will certainly abandon his current belief that the Bible is without error in matters of science.

Judge Overton's Closing Statements

At the close of the cross-examination of Gentry, the defense rested its case, and Judge William R. Overton gave a concluding statement. He told people not to write to him with suggestions for how to decide the case because he does not consider mail about cases, and told reporters not to make collect phone calls to his office because he wouldn't accept them.

"I will not undertake to decide the validity of the Biblical version of the creation of the earth and life, or the theory of evolution," Overton said, but rather he will decide whether Act 590 itself is constitutional—in other words, whether it violates the separation of church and state guaranteed under the First Amendment, whether it violated academic freedom, and whether it is unconstitutionally vague.

He said he would try to make a decision before Christmas. [The decision was not announced by the judge until January 5, 1982.]

Sample Media Coverage

Commercial Appeal, Memphis, Tuesday—December 15, 1981;

Creationism Defenders Trip
Over Questions From Judge

Another scientist who testified Monday referred to Charles Darwin, the father of evolutionary theory, and said, "I feel if Darwin were alive today he'd be a creation-scientist." Dr. Wayne Frair, professor of biology at The King's College in New York, said Arkansas was on the "cutting edge of a progressive movement" that is cutting through "decades of ignorance" to let students consider creationism in public schools.

Arkansas Gazette, Little Rock, Tuesday—December 15, 1981:

Doubts Suppositions
Dr. Frair also questioned the basic suppositions of evolution and said that "evolution just doesn't hold up; if evolution science doesn't hold up what do we have left? We have creation-science."

Dr. Frair, who said he believed that if Charles Darwin were alive today "he would be a creation-scientist," said that "time has been wasted constructing an evolution science model—if we had had the creation-science model earlier, we'd be further ahead today."

Arkansas Gazette, Little Rock, Tuesday—December 15, 1981:

Highlights of Trial
Dr. Wayne Frair, a biochemist at The King's College in Briarcliff Manor, N.Y., said that if Charles Darwin, considered the father of modern evolution, "were alive today he would be a creation-scientist." He also called creation-science "a wave . . . moving across this nation . . . [and] around the world."

Arkansas Democrat—December 16, 1981:

Educators Say Plant Ancestry Proves Creation
Scientific evidence on the ancestries of plants and minerals challenge accepted principles of evolution, creation scientists said Tuesday in defense of Arkansas' creation-science law.

But one witness confirmed he was a member of the Bible Science Association, which says putting "Christ and the Bible and the power of the Holy Spirit back into science is one of the most powerful methods of witnessing in the church today."

Discover—February 1982:

Judgment Day for Creationism
Little scientific research to support creation had been done by the state's witnesses. Frair's testimony, for example, was essentially negative. He explained that, according to evolutionists' predictions, red blood cells should be

smaller in advanced vertebrates. But he had found that some amphibians, although higher on the evolutionary scale than fish, had larger blood cells.

New York Times, Wednesday—December 16, 1981:

Evolutionary Theory Attacked At Trial

The first witness, Margaret Helder, a botanist from Alberta, Canada, told the court that contrary to the theory of evolution, which holds that living things have a common ancestry, scientists have found "tremendous variation" in the structure and processes of algae and protozoa.

"This should be viewed as rejection of evolution theory," she said, adding that she believed botanists were moving "closer and closer toward the creationist theory of separate ancestry."

Dallas Times Herald, Wednesday—December 16, 1981:

Zoologist Bases Belief of Origins on Bible

Donald Chittick of Newberg, Ore., explained one way creation-scientists had arrived at the 10,000 year figure for the Earth's age. He said uranium releases helium as it turns into lead, and the amount of helium now in the earth's atmosphere could have been reached in about 10,000 years.

Chittick, a Quaker, is a member of the Bible Science Association, Inc. of Minneapolis, Minn., which refers in its creed to evolution as a "pagan religion."

Dallas Times Herald, Wednesday—December 16, 1981:

Zoologist Bases Belief of Origins on Bible

Little Rock, Ark.—A zoologist testifying in support of Arkansas' creation-science law admitted some of his ideas about the beginning of life are based on biblical scripture.

Harold Coffin of Loma Linda University, a Seventh-day adventist school in California, said Tuesday the earth was only about 5,000 years old—contrary to most scientists' opinions—and that life was once wiped out by a massive flood.

His belief, he testified, was based "mostly on scripture."

Coffin said the fossils found from the Cambrian period are "fully formed, complex creatures" much like animals that exist today. Most geologists say the Cambrian period, when the first organisms appeared, was about 500 million years ago. But Coffin said it was 5,000 to 7,000 years ago—not long before a worldwide flood wiped out most animals and left their fossils.

"My data for that is religious and not really scientific," Coffin said.

He said the genealogical record in Genesis is one basis for his belief in a young Earth. "Based on the scientific evidence alone," Coffin said, he could not argue with evolutionists.

Chemical and Engineering News—December 21, 1981:

Creationists Expected to Lose Arkansas Fight

Robert Cearley, a Little Rock lawyer working with the ACLU summed up the state's case for creationism in a post-trial press conference. "I think you saw in the courtroom," he said, "the best effort that could be made on the part of the creation movement to demonstrate the legitimacy of their science and there is no legitimacy."

Dallas Times Herald, Wednesday—December 16, 1981:

Estimates of Earth's Age Called Unreliable

LITTLE ROCK, Ark.—The reliability of dating systems which indicate the world is very old should be re-examined because they have proved inaccurate in some cases a scientist testified Tuesday.

Donald Chittick testified for the defense in an American Civil Liberties Union Challenge to a new state law requiring balanced treatment for evolution and creationism in public schools.

Arkansas Gazette, Little Rock, Thursday—December 17, 1981:

Life Brought to Earth From Space, Witness For Defense Testifies

Life arose on earth as a result of organic molecules brought from space by comets, an astronomer testified Wednesday in federal court during the eighth day of the creationism trial.

Dr. N. C. Wickramasinghe, head of the applied mathematics and astronomy department of University College of Wales University at Cardiff, said that "terrestrial life had its origins in the dust clouds of space."

He also said that his theory—developed in collaboration with Sir Fred Hoyle, a noted British astronomer . . . .

Arkansas Gazette, Little Rock, Thursday—December 17, 1981:

Highlights of Trial

Life on earth arose from "seeding" by organic materials brought from space by meteors, a noted astronomer said Wednesday in testimony in the eighth day of the federal court trial testing the constitutionality of Act 590 of 1981, the state's creation-science law.

Dr. N. C. Wickramasinghe, head of the mathematics and astronomy department at the University of Wales and a collaborator on several books with Sir Fred Hoyle, the noted British astronomer, also said viruses "rained" on the earth from space, causing flu epidemics.

The Commercial Appeal, Memphis, Thursday—December 17, 1981:

Comet Brought Life to Earth, Witness Claims

LITLE ROCK—Organisms from space created life on Earth and the planet is still being bombarded with material that causes changes in species and viruses in humans, an astronomer testified in the Arkansas creationism trial Wednesday.

"The facts as we have them now clearly point to life being derived from . . . an allpervasive, galaxy-wide living system," said N. C. Wickramasinghe of University College in Wales. "It's the comets that brought life to Earth."

Arkansas Democrat, Little Rock, Thursday—December 17, 1981:

Welsh Astronomer Says Life Reached
Earth Via Comets

Life was brought to Earth from the far reaches of the galaxy on comets, a Welsh astronomer said Wednesday during the trial of Arkansas' creation-science law.

Arkansas Gazette, Little Rock, Thursday—December 17, 1981:

Highlights of Trial

Robert Gentry of Oak Ridge, Tenn., testified that radiation damage to rocks indicated the earth might be only a few thousand years old, rather than the 4.5 billion years usually accepted by geologists.

Chemical & Engineering News—December 21, 1981:

Creationists Expected To Lose Arkansas Fight

The scientists who testified on behalf of creationism maintain that it and evolution are mutually exclusive. Therefore, any evidence against evolution counts as evidence for creationism. The research they testified about, much of it done in a library, is directed at showing that what they call evolution cannot have happened and that, therefore, creation must have happened. Much of the rest of their testimony concerned theories purporting to prove that the Earth is only 10,000 years old and that the Earth's geology can be explained by Noah's flood.

*. . . God save the United States
and this honorable court.*

—U.S. Marshal
opening each day of
the Arkansas Trial

Chapter Eight

The Judge's Decision Against the Creation-Evolution Act

MEMORANDUM OPINION

Introduction

On March 19, 1981, the Governor of Arkansas signed into law Act 590 of 1981, entitled the "Balanced Treatment for Creation-Science and Evolution-Science Act." The Act is codified as Ark. Stat. Ann. §80-1663, *et seq.*, (1981 Supp). Its essential mandate is stated in its first sentence: "Public schools within this state shall give balanced treatment to creation-science and to evolution-science." On May 27, 1981, this suit was filed challenging the constitutional validity of Act 590 on three distinct grounds.

First, it is contended that Act 590 constitutes an establishment of religion prohibited by the First Amendment to the Constitution, which is made applicable to the states by the Fourteenth Amendment. Second, the plaintiffs argue the Act violates a right to academic freedom which they say is guaranteed to students and teachers by the Free Speech

Clause of the First Amendment. Third, plaintiffs allege the Act is impermissibly vague and thereby violates the Due Process Clause of the Fourteenth Amendment.

The individual plaintiffs include the resident Arkansas Bishops of the United Methodist, Episcopal, Roman Catholic, and African Methodist Episcopal Churches, a principal official of the Presbyterian Churches in Arkansas, other United Methodist, Southern Baptist, and Presbyterian clergy, as well as several persons who sue as parents and next friends of minor children attending Arkansas public schools. One plaintiff is a high school biology teacher. All are also Arkansas taxpayers. Among the organizational plaintiffs are The American Jewish Congress, the Union of American Hebrew Congregations, the American Jewish Committee, The Arkansas Education Association, the National Association of Biology Teachers and the National Coalition for Public Education and Religious Liberty, all of which sue on behalf of members living in Arkansas.

The defendants include the Arkansas Board of Education and its members, the Director of the Department of Education, and the State Textbooks and Instructional Materials Selecting Committee. The Pulaski County Special School District and its Directors and Superintendent were voluntarily dismissed by the plaintiffs at the pre-trial conference held October 1, 1981.

The trial commenced December 7, 1981, and continued through December 17, 1981. This Memorandum Opinion constitutes the Court's findings of fact and conclusions of law. Further orders and judgment will be in conformity with this opinion.

I.

There is no controversy over the legal standards under which the Establishment Clause portion of this case must be judged. The Supreme Court has on a number of occasions expounded on the meaning of the clause, and the pronouncements are clear. Often the issue has arisen in the context of public education, as it has here. In *Everson v. Board of Education,* 330 U.S. 1, 15-16 (1947), Justice Black stated:

> The "establishment of religion" clause of the First Amendment means at least this: Neither a state nor the Federal Government can set up a church. Neither can pass laws which aid one religion, aid all religions, or prefer one religion over another. Neither can force nor influence a person to go to or to remain away from church against his will or force him to profess a belief or disbelief in any religion. No person can be punished for entertaining or professing religious beliefs or disbeliefs, for church-attendance or non-attendance. No tax, large or small, can be levied to support any religious activities or institutions, whatever they may be called, or whatever form they may adopt to teach or practice religion. Neither a state nor the Federal Government can, openly or secretly, participate in the affairs of any religious organizations or groups and *vice versa*. In the words of Jefferson, the clause . . . was intended to erect "a wall of separation between church and State."

The Establishment Clause thus enshrines two central values: voluntarism and pluralism. And it is in the area of the public schools that these values must be guarded most vigilantly.

> Designed to serve as perhaps the most powerful agency for promoting cohesion among a heterogeneous democratic people, the public school must keep scrupulously free from entanglement in the strife of sects. The preservation of the community from devisive conflicts, of Government from irreconcilable pressures by religious groups, of religion from censorship and coercion however subtly exercised, requires strict confinement of the State to instruction other than religious, leaving to the individual's church and home, indoctrination in the faith of his choice.

McCollum v. Board of Education, 333 U.S. 203, 216-217 (1948), (Opinion of Frankfurter, J., joined by Jackson, Burton and Rutledge, J.J.).

The specific formulation of the establishment prohibition has been refined over the years, but its meaning has not varied from the principles articulated by Justice Black in *Everson.* In *Abington School District v. Schempp,* 374 U.S. 203, 222 (1963), Justice Clark stated that "to withstand the strictures of the Establishment Clause there must be a secular legislative purpose and a primary effect that neither advances nor inhibits religion." The Court found it quite clear that the First Amendment does not permit a state to require the daily reading of the Bible in public schools, for "[s]urely the place of the Bible as an instrument of religion cannot be gainsaid." *Id.* at 224. Similarly, in *Engel v. Vitale*, 370 U.S. 421 (1962), the Court held that the First Amendment prohibited the New York Board of Regents from requiring the daily recitation of a certain prayer in the schools. With characteristic succinctness, Justice Black wrote, "Under [the First] Amendment's prohibition against governmental establishment of religion, as reinforced by the provisions of the Fourteenth Amendment, government in this country, be it state or federal, is without power to prescribe by law any particular form of prayer which is to be used as an official prayer in carrying on any program of governmentally sponsored religious activity." *Id.* at 430. Black also identified the objective at which the Establishment Clause was aimed: "Its first and most immediate purpose rested on the belief that a union of government and religion tends to destroy government and to degrade religion." *Id.* at 431.

Most recently, the Supreme Court has held that the clause prohibits a state from requiring the posting of the Ten Commandments in public school classrooms for the same reasons that officially imposed daily Bible reading is prohibited. *Stone v. Graham*, 449 U.S. 39 (1980). The opinion in *Stone* relies on the most recent formulation of the Establishment Clause test, that of *Lemon v. Kurtzman*, 403 U.S. 602, 612-613 (1971):

> First, the statute must have a secular legislative purpose; second, its principal or primary effect must be one that neither advances nor inhibits religion . . . ; finally, the statute must not foster "an excessive government entanglement with religion."

Stone v. Graham, 449 U.S. at 40.

It is under this three part test that the evidence in this case must be judged. Failure on any of these grounds is fatal to the enactment.

II.

The religious movement known as Fundamentalism began in nineteenth century America as part of evangelical Protestantism's response to social changes, new religious thought and Darwinism. Fundamentalists viewed these developments as attacks on the Bible and as responsible for a decline in traditional values.

The various manifestations of Fundamentalism had a number of common characteristics, but a central premise was always a literal interpretation of the Bible and a belief in the inerrancy of the Scriptures. Following World War I, there was again a perceived decline in traditional morality, and Fundamentalism focused on evolution as responsible for the decine. One aspect of their efforts, particularly in the South, was the passage of statutes prohibiting the teaching of evolution in public schools. In Arkansas, this resulted in the adoption of Initiated Act 1 of 1929.

Between the 1920's and early 1960's, anti-evolutionary sentiment had a subtle but pervasive influence on the teaching of biology in public schools. Generally, textbooks avoided the topic of evolution and did not mention the name of Darwin. Following the launch of the Sputnik satellite by the Soviet Union in 1957, the National Science Foundation funded several programs designed to modernize the teaching of science in the nation's schools. The Biological Sciences Curriculum Study (BSCS), a nonprofit organization, was among those receiving grants for curriculum study and revision. Working with scientists and teachers, BSCS developed a series of biology texts which, although emphasizing different aspects of biology, incorporated the theory of evolution as a major theme. The success of the BSCS effort is shown by the fact that fifty percent of American school children currently use BSCS books directly and the curriculum is incorporated indirectly in virtually all biology texts. (Testimony of Mayer; Nelkin, Px 1)

In the early 1960's, there was again a resurgence of concern among Fundamentalists about the loss of traditional values and a fear of growing secularism in society. The Fundamentalist movement became more active and has steadily grown in numbers and political influence. There is an emphasis among current Fundamentalists on the literal interpretation of the Bible and the Book of Genesis as the sole source of knowledge about origins.

The term "scientific creationism" first gained currency around 1965 following publication of *The Genesis Flood* in 1961 by Whitcomb and Morris. There is undoubtedly some connection between the appearance of the BSCS texts emphasizing evolutionary thought and efforts by Fundamentalists to attack the theory. (Mayer)

In the 1960's and early 1970's, several Fundamentalist organizations were formed to promote the idea that the Book of Genesis was supported by scientific data. The terms "creation science" and "scientific creationism" have been adopted by these Fundamentalists as descriptive of their study of creation and the origins of man. Perhaps the leading creationist organization is the Institute for Creation Research (ICR), which is affiliated with the Christian Heritage College and supported by the Scott Memorial Baptist Church in San Diego, California. The ICR, through the Creation-Life Publishing Company, is the leading publisher of creation science material. Other creation science organizations include the Creation Science Research Center (CSRC) of San Diego and the Bible Science Association of Minneapolis, Minnesota. In 1963, the Creation Research Society (CRS) was formed from a schism in the American Scientific Affiliation (ASA). It is an organization of literal Fundamentalists who have the equivalent of a master's degree in some recognized area of science. A purpose of the organization is "to reach all people with the vital message of the scientific and historic truth about creation." Nelkin, *The Science Textbook Controversies and the Politics of Equal Time*, 66. Similarly, the CSRC was formed in 1970 from a split in the CRS. Its aim has been "to reach the 63 million children of the United States with the scientific teaching of Biblical creationism." *Id.* at 69.*

It is true, as defendants argue, that courts should look to legislative statements of a statute's purpose in Establishment Clause cases and accord such pronouncements great deference. See, e.g., *Committee for Public Education & Religious Liberty v. Nyquist,* 413 U.S. 756, 773 (1973) and *McGowan v. Maryland,* 366 U.S. 420, 445 (1961). Defendants also correctly state the principle that remarks by the sponsor or author of a bill are not considered controlling in analyzing legislative intent. See, e.g., *United States v. Emmons,* 410 U.S. 396 (1973) and *Chrysler Corp. v. Brown,* 441 U.S. 281 (1979).

Courts are not bound, however, by legislative statements of purpose or legislative disclaimers. *Stone v. Graham,* 449 U.S. 39 (1980); *Abington School Dist. v. Schempp,* 344 U.S. 203 (1963). In determining the legislative purpose of a statute, courts may consider evidence of the historical context of the Act, *Epperson v. Arkansas,* 393 U.S. 97 (1968), the specific sequence of events leading up to passage of the Act, departures from normal procedural sequences, substantive departures from the normal, *Village of Arlington Heights v. Metropolitan Housing Corp.,* 429 U.S. 252 (1977), and contemporaneous statements of the legislative sponsor, *Fed. Energy Admin. v. Algonquin SNG, Inc.,* 426 U.S. 548, 564 (1976).

The unusual circumstances surrounding the passage of Act 590, as well as the substantive law of the First Amendment, warrant an inquiry into the stated legislative purposes. The author of the Act had publicly proclaimed the sectarian purpose of the proposal. The Arkansas residents who sought legislative sponsorship of the bill did so for a purely sectarian purpose. These circumstances alone may not be particularly persuasive, but when considered with the publicly announced motives of the legislative sponsor made contemporaneously

---

*   A section elaborating the judge's views of the religious motivation of those in favor of creation science follows here. It and the footnotes of the ruling are omitted to align it in size with the other chapters.

with the legislative process; the lack of any legislative investigation, debate, or consultation with any educators or
scientists; the unprecedented intrusion in school curriculum;
and official history of the State of Arkansas on the subject, it is
obvious that the statement of purposes has little, if any, support in fact. The State failed to produce any evidence which
would warrant an inference or conclusion that at any point in
the process anyone considered the legitimate educational
value of the Act. It was simply and purely an effort to introduce
the Biblical version of creation into the public school curricula. The only inference which can be drawn from these circumstances is that the Act was passed with the specific purpose by the General Assembly of advancing religion. The Act
therefore fails the first prong of the three-pronged test, that of
secular legislative purpose, as articulated in *Lemon v. Kurtzman, supra,* and *Stone v. Graham, supra.*

III.

If the defendants are correct and the Court is limited to an
examination of the language of the Act, the evidence is overwhelming that both the purpose and effect of Act 590 is the advancement of religion in the public schools.

Section 4 of the Act provides:

> Definitions. As used in this Act:
>
> (a) "Creation-science" means the scientific evidences for
> creation and inferences from those scientific evidences.
> Creation-science includes the scientific evidences and
> related inferences that indicate: (1) Sudden creation of the
> universe, energy, and life from nothing; (2) The insuffi-
> ciency of mutation and natural selection in bringing about
> development of all living kinds from a single organism; (3)
> Changes only within fixed limits of originally created
> kinds of plants and animals; (4) Separate ancestry for man
> and apes; (5) Explanation of the earth's geology by
> catastrophism, including the occurrence of a worldwide
> flood; and (6) A relatively recent inception of the earth and
> living kinds.
>
> (b) "Evolution-science" means the scientific evidences for
> evolution and inferences from those scientific evidences.
> Evolution-science includes the scientific evidences and

related inferences that indicate: (1) Emergence by naturalistic processes of the universe from disordered matter and emergence of life from nonlife; (2) The sufficiency of mutation and natural selection in bringing about development of present living kinds from simple earlier kinds; (3) Emergence by mutation and natural selection of present living kinds from simple earlier kinds; (4) Emergence of man from a common ancestor with apes; (5) Explanation of the earth's geology and the evolutionary sequence by uniformitarianism; and (6) An inception several billion years ago of the earth and somewhat later of life.

(c) "Public schools" means public secondary and elementary schools.

The evidence establishes that the definition of "creation science" contained in 4(a) has as its unmentioned reference the first 11 chapters of the Book of Genesis. Among the many creation epics in human history, the account of sudden creation from nothing, or *creatio ex nihilo,* and subsequent destruction of the world by flood is unique to Genesis. The concepts of 4(a) are the literal Fundamentalists' view of Genesis. Section 4(a) is unquestionably a statement of religion, with the exception of 4(a)(2) which is a negative thrust aimed at what the creationists understand to be the theory of evolution.

Both the concepts and wording of Section 4(a) convey an inescapable religiosity. Section 4(a)(1) describes "sudden creation of the universe, energy and life from nothing." Every theologian who testified, including defense witnesses, expressed the opinion that the statement referred to a supernatural creation which was performed by God.

Defendants argue that: (1) the fact that 4(a) conveys ideas similar to the literal interpretation of Genesis does not make it conclusively a statement of religion; (2) that reference to a creation from nothing is not necessarily a religious concept since the Act only suggests a creator who has power, intelligence, and a sense of design and not necessarily the attributes of love, compassion, and justice; and (3) that simply teaching about the concept of a creator is not a religious exercise unless the student is required to make a commitment to the concept of a creator.

The evidence fully answers these arguments. The ideas of 4(a)(1) are not merely similar to the literal interpretation of Genesis; they are identical and parallel to no other story of creation.

The argument that creation from nothing in 4(a)(1) does not involve a supernatural deity has no evidentiary or rational support. To the contrary, "creation out of nothing" is a concept unique to Western religions. In traditional Western religious thought, the conception of a creator of the world is a conception of God. Indeed, creation of the world "out of nothing" is the ultimate religious statement because God is the only actor. As Dr. Langdon Gilkey noted, the Act refers to one who has the power to bring all the universe into existence from nothing. The only "one" who has this power is God.

The leading creationist writers, Morris and Gish, acknowledge that the idea of creation described in 4(a)(1) is the concept of creation by God and make no pretense to the contrary. The idea of sudden creation from nothing, or creatio ex nihilo, is an inherently religious concept. (Vawter, Gilkey, Geisler, Ayala, Blount, Hicks.)

The argument advanced by defendants' witness, Dr. Norman Geisler, that teaching the existence of God is not religious unless the teaching seeks a commitment, is contrary to common understanding and contradicts settled case law. Stone v. Graham, 449 U.S. 39 (1980); Abington School District v. Schempp, 374 U.S. 203 (1963).

The facts that creation science is inspired by the book of Genesis and that Section 4(a) is consistent with a literal interpretation of Genesis leave no doubt that a major effect of the Act is the advancement of particular religious beliefs. The legal impact of this conclusion will be discussed further at the conclusion of the Court's evaluation of the scientific merit of creation science.

IV. (A)

The approach to teaching "creation science" and "evolution science" found in Act 590 is identical to the two-model approach espoused by the Institute for Creation Research and is taken almost verbatim from ICR writings. It is an extension of

Fundamentalists' view that one must either accept the literal interpretation of Genesis or else believe in the godless system of evolution.

The two model approach of the creationists is simply a contrived dualism which has no scientific factual basis or legitimate educational purpose. It assumes only two explanations for the origins of life and existence of man, plants, and animals: It was either the work of a creator or it was not. Application of these two models, according to creationists, and the defendants, dictates that all scientific evidence which fails to support the theory of evolution is necessarily scientific evidence in support of creationism and is, therefore, creation science "evidence" in support of Section 4(a).

IV. (B)

The emphasis on origins as an aspect of the theory of evolution is peculiar to creationist literature. Although the subject of origins of life is within the province of biology, the scientific community does not consider origins of life a part of evolutionary theory. The theory of evolution assumes the existence of life and is directed to an explanation of *how* life evolved. Evolution does not presuppose the absence of a creator or God and the plain inference conveyed by Section 4 is erroneous.

As a statement of the theory of evolution, Section 4(b) is simply a hodgepodge of limited assertions, many of which are factually inaccurate.

For example, although 4(b)(2) asserts, as a tenet of evolutionary theory, "the sufficiency of mutation and natural selection in bringing about the existence of present living kinds from simple earlier kinds," Drs. Ayala and Gould both stated that biologists know that these two processes do not account for all significant evolutionary change. They testified to such phenomena as recombination, the founder effect, genetic drift and the theory of punctuated equilibrium, which are believed to play important evolutionary roles. Section 4(b) omits any reference to these. Moreover, 4(b) utilizes the term "kinds" which all scientists said is not a word of science and has no fixed meaning. Additionally, the Act presents both evolution and creation science as "package deals." Thus, evidence critical of some aspect of what the creationists define as evolution is taken as support for a theory which includes a worldwide flood and a relatively young earth.

IV. (C)

In addition to the fallacious pedagogy of the two model approach, Section 4(a) lacks legitimate educational value because "creation science" as defined in that section is simply not science. Several witnesses suggested definitions of science. A descriptive definition was said to be that science is what is "accepted by the scientific community" and is "what scientists do." The obvious implication of this description is that, in a free society, knowledge does not require the imprimatur of legislation in order to become science.

More precisely, the essential characteristics of science are:
(1) It is guided by natural law;
(2) It has to be explanatory by reference to natural law;
(3) It is testable against the empirical world;
(4) Its conclusions are tentative, i.e., are not necessarily the final word; and
(5) It is falsifiable. (Ruse and other science witnesses.)

Creation science as described in Section 4(a) fails to meet these essential characteristics. First, the section revolves around 4(a)(1) which asserts a sudden creation "from nothing." Such a concept is not science because it depends upon a supernatural intervention which is not guided by natural law. It is not explanatory by reference to natural law, is not testable and is not falsifiable.

If the unifying idea of supernatural creation by God is removed from Section 4, the remaining parts of the section explain nothing and are meaningless assertions.

Section 4(a)(2), relating to the "insufficiency of mutation and natural selection in bringing about development of all living kinds from a single organism," is an incomplete negative generalization directed at the theory of evolution.

Section 4(a)(3) which describes "changes only within fixed limits of originally created kinds of plants and animals" fails to conform to the essential characteristics of science for several reasons. First, there is no scientific definition of "kinds" and none of the witnesses was able to point to any scientific authority which recognized the term or knew how many "kinds" existed. One defense witness suggested there may be 100 to 10,000 different "kinds." Another believes there were "about 10,000, give or take a few thousand." Second, the assertion appears to be an effort to establish outer limits of changes within species. There is no scientific explanation for these limits which is guided by natural law and the limitations, whatever they are, cannot be explained by natural law.

The statement in 4(a)(4) of "separate ancestry of man and apes" is a bald assertion. It explains nothing and refers to no scientific fact or theory.

Section 4(a)(5) refers to "explanation of the earth's geology by catastrophism, including the occurrence of a worldwide flood." This assertion completely fails as science. The Act is referring to the Noachian flood described in the Book of Genesis. The creationist writers concede that *any* kind of Genesis Flood depends upon supernatural intervention. A worldwide flood as an explanation of the world's geology is not the product of natural law, nor can its occurrence be explained by natural law.

Section 4(a)(6) equally fails to meet the standards of science. "Relatively recent inception" has no scientific meaning. It can only be given meaning by reference to creationist writings which place the age at between 6,000 and 20,000 years because of the genealogy of the Old Testament. See, e.g., Px 78, Gish (6,000 to 10,000); Px 87, Segraves (6,000 to 20,000). Such a reasoning process is not the product of natural law; not explainable by natural law; nor is it tentative.

Creation science, as defined in Section 4(a), not only fails to follow the canons defining scientific theory, it also fails to fit the more general descriptions of "what scientists think" and "what scientists do." The scientific community consists of individuals and groups, nationally and internationally, who work independently in such varied fields as biology, paleontology, geology and astronomy. Their work is published and subject to review and testing by their peers. The journals for publication are both numerous and varied. There is, however, not one recognized scientific journal which has published an article espousing the creation science theory described in Section 4(a). Some of the State's witnesses suggested that the scientific community was "closed-minded" on the subject of creationism and that explained the lack of acceptance of the creation science arguments. There was not, however, any witness who produced a scientific article for which publication had been refused. Perhaps some members of the scientific community are resistant to new ideas. It is, however, inconceivable that such a loose knit group of independent thinkers in all the varied fields of science could, or would, so effectively censor new scientific thought.

The creationists have difficulty maintaining among their ranks consistency in the claim that creationism is science. The author of Act 590, Ellwanger, said that neither evolution nor creationism was science. He thinks both are religion. Duane Gish recently responded to an article in *Discover* critical of creationism by stating:

> "Stephen Jay Gould states that creationists claim creation is a scientific theory. This is a false accusation. Creationists have repeatedly stated that neither creation nor evolution is a scientific theory (and each is equally religious)." Gish, letter to editor of *Discover*, July, 1981, App. 30 to Plaintiffs' Pretrial Brief.

The methodology employed by creationists is another factor which is indicative that their work is not science. A scientific theory must be tentative and always subject to revision or abandonment in light of facts that are inconsistent with, or falsify, the theory. A theory that is by its own terms dogmatic, absolutist and never subject to revision is not a scientific theory.

The creationists' methods do not take data, weigh it against the opposing scientific data, and thereafter reach the conclusions stated in Section 4(a). Instead, they take the literal wording of the Book of Genesis and attempt to find scientific support for it. The method is best explained in the language of Morris in his book (Px 31) *Studies in The Bible and Science* at page 114:

> . . . it is . . . quite impossible to determine anything about

> Creation through a study of present processes, because present processes are not creative in character. If man wishes to know anything about Creation (the time of Creation, the duration of Creation, the order of Creation, the methods of Creation, or anything else) his sole source of true information is that of divine revelation. God was there when it happened. We were not there . . . . Therefore, we are completely limited to what God has seen fit to tell us, and this information is in His written Word. This is our textbook on the science of Creation!

The Creation Research Society employs the same unscientific approach to the issue of creationism. Its applicants for membership must subscribe to the belief that the Book of Genesis is "historically and scientifically true in all of the original autographs." The Court would never criticize or discredit any person's testimony based on his or her religious beliefs. While anybody is free to approach a scientific inquiry in any fashion they choose, they cannot properly describe the methodology used as scientific, if they start with a conclusion and refuse to change it regardless of the evidence developed during the course of the investigation.

IV.(D)

In efforts to establish "evidence" in support of creation science, the defendants relied upon the same false premise as the two model approach contained in Section 4, i.e., all evidence which criticized evolutionary theory was proof in support of creation science. For example, the defendants established that the mathematical probability of a chance chemical combination resulting in life from non-life is so remote that such an occurrence is almost beyond imagination. Those mathematical facts, the defendants argue, are scientific evidences that life was the product of a creator. While the statistical figures may be impressive evidence against the theory of chance chemical combinations as an explanation of origins, it requires a leap of faith to interpret those figures so as to support a complex doctrine which includes a sudden creation from nothing, a worldwide flood, separate ancestry of man and apes, and a young earth.

The defendants' argument would be more persuasive if, in fact, there were only two theories or ideas about the origins of life and the world. That there are a number of theories was acknowledged by the State's witnesses, Dr. Wickramasinghe and Dr. Geisler. Dr. Wickramasinghe testified at length in support of a theory that life on earth was "seeded" by comets which delivered genetic material and perhaps organisms to the earth's surface from interstellar dust far outside the solar system. The "seeding" theory further hypothesizes that the earth remains under the continuing influence of genetic material from space which continues to affect life. While Wickramasinghe's theory about the origins of life on earth has not received general acceptance within the scientific community, he has, at least, used scientific methodology to produce a theory of origins which meets the essential characteristics of science.

Perhaps Dr. Wickramasinghe was called as a witness because he was generally critical of the theory of evolution and the scientific community, a tactic consistent with the strategy of the defense. Unfortunately for the defense, he demonstrated that the simplistic approach of the two model analysis of the origins of life is false. Furthermore, he corroborated the plaintiffs' witnesses by concluding that "no rational scientist" would believe the earth's geology could be explained by reference to a worldwide flood or that the earth was less than one million years old.

The proof in support of creation science consisted almost entirely of efforts to discredit the theory of evolution through a rehash of data and theories which have been before the scientific community for decades. The arguments asserted by creationists are not based upon new scientific evidence or laboratory data which has been ignored by the scientific community.

Robert Gentry's discovery of polonium halos in granite and coalified woods is, perhaps, the most recent scientific work which the creationists use as argument for a "relatively recent inception" of the earth and a "worldwide flood." The existence of polonium halos in granite and coalified wood is thought to be inconsistent with radiometric dating methods based upon constant radioactive decay rates. Mr. Gentry's findings were published almost ten years ago and have been the subject of some discussion in the scientific community. The discoveries have not, however, led to the formulation of any scientific hypothesis or theory which would explain a relatively recent inception of the earth or a worldwide flood. Gentry's discovery has been treated as a minor mystery which will eventually be explained. It may deserve further investigation, but the National Science Foundation has not deemed it to be of sufficient import to support further funding.

The testimony of Marianne Wilson was persuasive evidence that creation science is not science. Ms. Wilson is in charge of the science curriculum for Pulaski County Special School District, the largest school district in the State of Arkanksas. Prior to the passage of Act 590, Larry Fisher, a science teacher in the District, using materials from the ICR, convinced the School Board that it should voluntarily adopt creation science as part of its science curriculum. The District Superintendent assigned Ms. Wilson the job of producing a creation science curriculum guide. Ms. Wilson's testimony about the project was particularly convincing because she obviously approached the assignment with an open mind and no preconceived notions about the subject. She had not heard of creation science until about a year ago and did not know its meaning before she began research.

Ms. Wilson worked with a committe of science teachers appointed from the District. They reviewed practically all of the creationist literature. Ms. Wilson and the committee members reached the unanimous conclusion that creationism is not science; it is religion. They so reported to the Board. The Board ignored the recommendation and insisted that a curriculum guide be prepared.

Ms. Wilson researched the subject, sought the assistance of Mr. Fisher who initiated the Board action and asked professors in the science departments of the University of Arkansas at Little Rock and the University of Central Arkansas for reference material and assistance, and attended a workshop conducted at Central Baptist College by Dr. Richard Bliss of the ICR staff. Act 590 became law during the course of her work so she used

Section 4(a) as a format for her curriculum guide.

Ms. Wilson found all available creationists' materials unacceptable because they were permeated with religious references and reliance upon religious beliefs.

It is easy to understand why Ms. Wilson and other educators find the creationists' textbook material and teaching guides unacceptable. The materials misstate the theory of evolution in the same fashion as Section 4(b) of the Act, with emphasis on the alternative mutually exclusive nature of creationism and evolution. Students are constantly encouraged to compare and make a choice between the two models, and the material is not presented in an accurate manner.

A typical example is *Origins* (Px 76) by Richard B. Bliss, Director of Curriculum Development of the ICR. The presentation begins with a chart describing "preconceived ideas about origins" which suggests that some people believe that evolution is atheistic. Concepts of evolution, such as "adaptive radiation," are erroneously presented. At page 11, figure 1.6, of the text, a chart purports to illustrate this "very important" part of the evolution model. The chart conveys the idea that such diverse mammals as a whale, bear, bat, and monkey all evolved from a shrew through the process of adaptive radiation. Such a suggestion is, of course, a totally erroneous and misleading appication of the theory. Even more objectionable, especially when viewed in light of the emphasis on asking the student to elect one of the models, is the chart presentation at page 17, figure 1.6. That chart purports to illustrate the evolutionists' belief that man evolved from bacteria to fish to reptile to mammals and, thereafter, into man. The illustration indicates, however, that the mammal from which man evolved was *a rat*.

Biology, A Search For Order in Complexity is a high school biology text typical of creationists' materials. The following quotations are illustrative:

> "Flowers and roots do not have a mind to have purpose of their own; therefore, this planning must have been done for them by the Creator."
> —at page 12.

> "The exquisite beauty of color and shape in flowers exceeds the skill of poet, artist, and king. Jesus said (from Matthew's gospel), 'Consider the lilies of the field, how they grow; they toil not, neither do they spin . . . ' "
> Px 129 at page 363.

The "public school edition" texts written by creationists simply omit Biblical references but the content and message remain the same. For example, *Evolution-The Fossils Say No!*, contains the following:

> "Creation. By creation we mean the bringing into being by a supernatural Creator of the basic kinds of plants and animals by the process of sudden, or fiat, creation.
>   We do not know how the Creator created, what processes He used, *for He used processes which are not now operating anywhere in the natural universe.* This is why we refer to creation as Special Creation. We cannot discover by scientific investigation anything about the creative processes used by the Creator."—page 40

Gish's book also portrays the large majority of evolutionists as "materialistic atheists or agnostics."

Scientific Creationism (Public School Edition) by Morris, is another text reviewed by Ms. Wilson's committee and rejected as unacceptable. The following quotes illustrate the purpose and theme of the text:

Foreword

> "Parents and youth leaders today, and even many scientists and educators, have become concerned about the prevalence and influence of evolutionary philosophy in modern curriculum. Not only is this system inimical to orthodox Christianity and Judaism, but also, as many are convinced, to a healthy society and true science as well."
> —at page 111

> "The rationalist of course finds the concept of special creation insufferably naive, even 'incredible.' Such a judgment, however, is warranted only if one categorically dismisses the existence of an omnipotent God."
> —at page 17

Without using creationist literature, Ms. Wilson was unable to locate one genuinely scientific article or work which supported Section 4(a). In order to comply with the mandate of the Board she used such materials as an article from *Readers Digest* about "atomic clocks" which inferentially suggested that the earth was less than 4½ billion years old. She was unable to locate any substantive teaching material for some parts of Section 4 such as the worldwide flood. The curriculum guide which she prepared cannot be taught and has no educational value as science. The defendants did not produce any text or writing in response to this evidence which they claimed was usable in the public school classroom.

The conclusion that creation science has no scientific merit or educational value as science has legal significance in light of the Court's previous conclusion that creation science has, as one major effect, the advancement of religion. The second part of the three-pronged test for establishment reaches only those statutes having as their *primary* effect the advancement of religion. Secondary effects which advance religion are not constitutionally fatal. Since creation science is not science, the conclusion is inescapable that the *only* real effect of Act 590 is the advancement of religion. The Act therefore fails both the first and second portions of the test in *Lemon v. Kurtzman,* 403 U.S. 602 (1971).

IV.(E)

Act 590 mandates "balanced treatment" for creation science and evolution science. The Act prohibits instruction in any religious doctrine or references to religious writings. The Act is self-contradictory and compliance is impossible unless the public schools elect to forego significant portions of subjects such as biology, world history, geology, zoology, botany, psychology, anthropology, sociology, philosophy, physics, and chemistry. Presently, the concepts of evolutionary theory as described in 4(b) permeate the public school textbooks. There is no way teachers can teach the Genesis account of creation in a secular manner.

The State Department of Education, through its textbook selection committee, school boards and school administrators will be required to constantly monitor materials to avoid using religious references. The school boards, administrators and teachers face an impossible task. How is the teacher to respond to questions about a creation suddenly and out of nothing? How will a teacher explain the occurrence of a worldwide flood? How will a teacher explain the concept of a relatively recent age of the earth? The answer is obvious because the only source of this information is ultimately contained in the Book of Genesis.

References to the pervasive nature of religious concepts in creation science texts amply demonstrate why State entanglement with religion is inevitable under Act 590. Involvement of the State in screening texts for impermissible religious references will require State officials to make delicate religious judgments. The need to monitor classroom discussion in order to uphold the Act's prohibition against religious instruction will necessarily involve administrators in questions concerning religion. These continuing involvements of State officials in questions and issues of religion create an excessive and prohibited entanglement with religion. *Brandon v. Board of Education*, 487 F.Supp 1219, 1230 (N.D.N.Y.), *aff'd.*, 635 F.2d 971 (2nd Cir. 1980).

V.

These conclusions are dispositive of the case and there is no need to reach legal conclusions with respect to the remaining issues. The plaintiffs raise two other issues questioning the constitutionality of the Act and, insofar as the factual findings relevant to these issues are not covered in the preceding discussion, the Court will address these issues. Additionally, the defendants raised two other issues which warrant discussion.

V.(A)

First, plaintiff teachers argue the Act is unconstitutionally vague to the extent that they cannot comply with its mandate of "balanced" treatment without jeopardizing their employment. The argument centers around the lack of a precise definition in the Act for the word "balanced." Several witnesses expressed opinions that the word has such meanings as equal time, equal weight, or equal legitimacy. Although the

Act could have been more explicit, "balanced" is a word subject to ordinary understanding. The proof is not convincing that a teacher using a reasonable acceptable understanding of the word and making a good faith effort to comply with the Act will be in jeopardy of termination. Other portions of the Act are arguably vague; such as the "relatively recent" inception of the earth and life. The evidence establishes, however, that relatively recent means from 6,000 to 20,000 years, as commonly understood in creation science literature. The meaning of this phrase, like Section 4(a) generally, is, for purposes of the Establishment Clause, all too clear.

V.(B)

The plaintiffs' other argument revolves around the alleged infringement by the defendants upon the academic freedom of teachers and students. It is contended this unprecedented intrusion in the curriculum by the State prohibits teachers from teaching what they believe should be taught or requires them to teach that which they do not believe is proper. The evidence reflects that traditionally the State Department of Education, local school boards and administration officials exercise little, if any, influence upon the subject matter taught by classroom teachers. Teachers have been given freedom to teach and emphasize those portions of subjects the individual teacher considered important. The limits to this discretion have generally be derived from the approval of textbooks by the State Department and preparation of curriculum guides by the school districts.

Several witnesses testified that academic freedom for the teacher means, in substance, that the individual teacher should be permitted unlimited discretion subject only to the bounds of professional ethics. The Court is not prepared to adopt such a broad view of academic freedom in the public schools.

In any event, if Act 590 is implemented, many teachers will be required to teach material in support of creation science which they do not consider academically sound. Many teachers will simply forego teaching subjects which might trigger the "balanced treatment" aspects of Act 590 even though they think the subjects are important to a proper presentation of a course.

Implementation of Act 590 will have serious and untoward consequences for students, particularly those planning to attend college. Evolution is the cornerstone of modern biology, and many courses in public schools contain subject matter relating to such varied topics as the age of the earth, geology, and relationships among living things. Any student who is deprived of instruction as to the prevailing scientific thought on these topics will be denied a significant part of science education. Such a deprivation through the high school level would undoubtedly have an impact upon the quality of education in the State's colleges and universities, especially including the pre-professional and professional programs in the health sciences.

V.(C)

The defendants argue in their brief that evolution is, in effect, a religion, and that by teaching a religion which is contrary to some students' religious views, the State is infringing upon the student's free exercise rights under the First Amendment. Mr. Ellwanger's legislative findings, which were adopted as a finding of fact by the Arkansas Legislature in Act 590, provides:

> "Evolution-science is contrary to the religious convictions or moral values or philosophical beliefs of many students and parents, including individuals of many different religious faiths and with diverse moral and philosophical beliefs." Act 590, §7(d).

The defendants argue that the teaching of evolution alone presents both a free exercise problem and an establishment problem which can only be redressed by giving balanced treatment to creation science, which is admittedly consistent with some religious beliefs. This argument appears to have its genesis in a student note written by Mr. Wendell Bird, "Freedom of Religion and Science Instruction in Public Schools," 87 Yale L.J. 515 (1978). The argument has no legal merit.

If creation science is, in fact, science and not religion, as the defendants claim, it is difficult to see how the teaching of such a science could "neutralize" the religious nature of evolution.

Assuming for the purposes of argument, however, that evolution is a religion or religious tenet, the remedy is to stop the teaching of evolution; not establish another religion in opposition to it. Yet is is clearly established in the case law, and perhaps also in common sense, that evolution is not a religion and that teaching evolution does not violate the Establishment Clause, *Epperson v. Arkansas, supra, Willoughby v. Stever,* No. 15574-75 (D.D.C. May 18, 1973); *aff'd.* 504 F.2d 271 (D.C. Cir. 1974), *cert. denied,* 420 U.S. 924 (1975); *Wright v. Houston Indep. School Dist.,* 366 F.Supp. 1208 (S.D. Tex. 1978), *aff'd.* 486 F.2d 137 (5th Cir. 1973), *cert. denied* 417 U.S. 969 (1974).

V.(D)

The defendants presented Dr. Larry Parker, a specialist in devising curricula for public schools. He testified that the public school's curriculum should reflect the subjects the public wants taught in schools. The witness said that polls indicated a significant majority of the American public thought creation science should be taught if evolution was taught. The point of this testimony was never placed in a legal context. No doubt a sizeable majority of Americans believe in the concept of a Creator or, at least, are not opposed to the concept and see nothing wrong with teaching school children about the idea.

The application and content of First Amendment principles are not determined by public opinion polls or by a majority vote. Whether the proponents of Act 590 constitute the majority or the minority is quite irrelevant under a constitutional system of government. No group, no matter how large or small, may use the organs of government, of which the public schools are the most conspicuous and influential, to foist its religious beliefs on others.

The Court closes this opinion with a thought expressed eloquently by the great Justice Frankfurter:

> "We renew our conviction that 'we have staked the very existence of our country on the faith that complete separation between the state and religion is best for the state and

best for religion.' " *Everson v. Board of Education*, 330 U.S. at 59. If nowhere else, in the relation between Church and State, 'good fences make good neighbors.' " *McCollum v. Board of Education*, 333 U.S. 203, 232 (1948).

An injunction will be entered permanently prohibiting enforcement of Act 590.

It is so ordered this January 5, 1982.

(signed) _____ William Overton _____

UNITED STATES DISTRICT JUDGE

Epilogue

The United States Constitution says nothing about "separation" of church and state. The First Amendment (1791) is against the "establishment" of a church as *the* church by the state. It reads: "Congress shall make no law respecting an establishment of religion, or prohibiting the free exercise thereof; or abridging the freedom of speech, or of the press; or the right of the people peaceably to assemble, and to petition the Government for a redress of grievances." The Declaration of Independence (1776) did not hesitate to acknowledge that creation and the Creator were the very foundations of "Life, Liberty, and the Pursuit of Happiness." It boldly declares: "We hold these truths to be self-evident, that all men are created equal, that they are endowed by their Creator with certain unalienable Rights, that among these are Life, Liberty, and the pursuit of Happiness."

But about the same time Jefferson penned these words, a naturalistic philosophy was taking hold across the Atlantic through the influence of David Hume and Immanuel Kant. This naturalistic outlook was given great encouragement almost a century later when Darwin published his *Origin of Species* (1859). For the following century this anti-supernaturalistic philosophy dominated the scientific community. It had not fully impacted our society, however, until nearly a century after Darwin when the United States Supreme Court, breathing heavily the naturalistic air of Secular Humanism, began to make a series of landmark decisions which effected a separation of religion and government:

1961 *(Torcaso vs. Watkins)*—Secular humanism recognized as a religion protected by the First Amendment.

1962 *(Engel vs. Vitale)*—State required devotional prayers banned from public schools.

1963 *(Abington vs. Schempp)*—State required devotional Bible-reading forbidden in schools.

1968 *(Epperson vs. Arkansas)*—Laws against teaching evolution declared unconstitutional.

1980 *(Stone vs. Graham)*—Posting Ten Commandments in classroom is banned.

Finally, in a federal court decision *(McLean vs. Arkansas, 1982)*, a law mandating the teaching of creation (with evolution) was struck down in Arkansas. It is the last of these decisions which is the most radical. Thankfully, it is only the opinion of one lower court federal judge and is not the law of the land. If, however, the United States Supreme Court should ratify such a ruling it would signal the official estabishment in this country of a secular humanistic religion in our public schools. Anticipating this trend, some highly respected religious leaders have already called for Americans to engage in protesting secularistic court decisions and to emulate, if necessary, the original American revolution (see Francis Schaeffer, *A Christian Manifesto*, Westchester, IL: Crossway Bks., 1981). While we do not endorse this reaction, one thing seems clear: we have come a long way from a country which based its freedom in the Creator to one which used that freedom to bar the Creator from its schools.

Defense Rationale For Not Appealing

In a news conference February 4, 1982, one day before the deadline to appeal, attorney General Steve Clark announced his reasons for declining to appeal. In his professional opinion, there were insufficient grounds for anticipating a reversal by the Eighth Circuit Court of Appeals. The reasons for this were not detailed by the attorney General, but we later obtained them from a highly placed source.

First, it was believed that the bias of the judge was too subtle to be clearly reversible.

Second, they believed that there was also bias in the panel of three judges to which they would have to appeal. One such judge had already been quoted by the media to the effect that the people behind the creation-evolution Bill were "right wing kooks and freaks."

Third, in order to gain a reversal they would have to prove that the judge was wrong on all counts. They did not believe they could do this. It seemed to them that the judge was more clearly wrong on some points than others.

Fourth, they believed there were some problems with the actual wording of the Act which gave it the unjustified appearance of looking too much like the book of Genesis. Phrases like "worldwide flood," "creation from nothing," and "kind" were, for course, troublesome.

Fifth, Judge Overton had overruled their objections about

allowing irrelevant religious material in the record. This left the record to be reviewed by the higher court cluttered with the impression that there was a strong religious association with the desire to teach creation science.

What the media failed to report, however, was that Attorney General Steve Clark also said at this news conference that he personally favored the two-model approach in the schools and that he predicted in the near future that Arkansas would have such a system in effect.

Few creationists were ultimately disappointed that the decision was not appealed. Most felt that a better-worded Act would have a better chance in the Supreme Court and were waiting to see what would happen in upcoming Louisiana litigation or elsewhere. In fact, one creationist group, "The Foundation for Thought and Ethics" (of Dallas, Texas), made a special personal plea to Steve Clark *not* to appeal the decision on these grounds.

Appendix Two

Testimony of Religious Beliefs

The defense attorneys protested on several occasions the ACLU references to religious beliefs of creationists and defense witnesses.

First, it was done during the pre-trial depositions (preliminary statement of testimony). For example, here is the section from the deposition of one witness.

"Mr. Campbell: For the record, I object to these questions on the occult, as to their relevance.

"Mr. Siano [ACLU attorney]: Your objection is noted."

Second, the defense attorneys made this same objection to the judge during a pre-trial discovery conference on November 16, 1981, but the judge overruled it.

Third, at least twice during the trial defense attorney David Williams objected to using personal religious beliefs of creationists in testimony. He cited federal rule of evidence 610. The judge overruled his objection.

Fourth, David Williams asked for a *continued objection* to be recorded for the rest of the trial, instead of bringing it up each time. In view of these factors, the defense attorneys did not bring it up again later when ACLU lawyers raised the issues of the occult, demons, and UFO's.

Letters to the Editor Wall Street Journal
Thursday, January 14, 1982

World's Beginning Stirs No End of Creative Theorizing

As a witness for the defense in the Arkansas creation-evolution trial, I object to science editor Jerry E. Bishop's mischaracterization of creationism as non-scientific (editorial page, Dec. 28). He concludes that evolution is science because it is "postdictive and predictive" but creaton is not science because it is neither.

As was clearly brought out in testimony at the trial, both creation and evolution are equally scientific (or unscientific). If by "science" one means what is observable or repeatable, then neither creation nor evolution is "science." There were no observers of the origin of the universe or of life, and we can't repeat the original situation in the laboratory.

On the other hand, if by science we mean the construction of a theory that can make testable predictions, then both creation and evolution are scientific. For example, if evolution is true, we can predict that there are missing links to be found in the fossil record. If creationism is true, we can predict there are no missing links in the fossil record. Incidentally, after over 120 years of looking for these links they have not be found. Thus evolution's prediction is falsified.

Further, according to evolution, life arose spontaneously from non-living matter. If this is so then according to evolution one can predict (as many evolutionists did), that this will happen again. However, Louis Pasteur proved that spontaneous generation does not occur. In view of these and other falsifications, one wonders whether evolution as held by many evolutionists has not left the ranks of a falsifiable scientific theory and become an unfalsifiable "religious" belief.

NORMAN L. GEISLER

Dallas

*   *   *

In the semantic games with the words "predictive" and "postdictive," the argument was so arranged that when a cause is catastrophic and non-recurring it is labeled "unscientific." I'm sure that several thousand of my colleagues in astrophysics will be happy to know that their theories on the origin of the universe are unscientific, by decree of the lawyers at ACLU!

The big bang theory is neither predictive nor postdictive, and it can't be falsified. None of us will get the chance to see it fail the next time the universe starts up. The best you can say is that it doesn't violate known laws of physics.

Not so with evolution. It postulates the spontaneous generation of order from disorder, complex forms from simple forms, and higher information content from lower, all in violation of the second law of thermodynamics (systems tend toward disorder when left alone).

BERNARD VANCIL
Portland, Ore.

Appendix Four

Letters to the Editor *Discover* Magazine

Dear Editor:

Your article on the Arkansas Creation-Evolution trial gave me new insights into how evolution has maintained itself in the absence of substantial evidence for over a century.

First, you *emphasized the irrelevant*. The judge said "the court would never criticize or discredit any person's testimony based on his or her religious beliefs." Yet you made sure that the *irrelevant* personal religious beliefs of the creationist witnesses were clearly noted. There was, on the other hand, a conspicuous absence of the radical liberal, agnostic, and atheistic and even Marxistic beliefs of the evolution witnesses.

Second, you *omitted the essential*. Creationism was judged wrong because of its religious *source*. Yet you omitted all of the crucial testimony that *source* has nothing to do with the scientific *justifiability* (as evolution witness Dr. Ruse said). You also failed to inform your readers of my testimony about the source of Kekulé's model for the Benzene molecule—a vision of a snake biting its tail! Or of Tesla (whom you heralded in the same issue) whose source for the alternating current motor was a vision while reading a pantheistic poet (Goethe)! What about Socrates, whose inspiration for philosophy came from a religious prophetess, the Oracle of Delphi. Has anyone ever rejected their scientific theories simply because of their odd religious-like source?

Finally, have you told your readers what the ACLU lawyer, Clarence Darrow, said at the Scopes trial (1925), that it "is bigotry for public schools to teach only one theory of origins"? Oh yes, my insight into evolution.* When you emphasize the irrelevant, omit the essential, and forbid the opposing view a hearing, it is easy for a theory to long outlive its evidence. Myths die hard.

Sincerely,

(Signed)

Norman L. Geisler

---

* This whole sentence was omitted by *Discover* magazine without indicating it (3/82). They also omitted the emphasis placed on the words.

Appendix Five

Christianity Today Article

BETWEEN DECEMBER 7 and 17 of last year, a historic trial took place in Little Rock, Arkansas. The American Civil Liberties Union charged that the recently enacted Arkansas Act 590 (of 1981), which mandated a balanced treatment of creation-science and evolution-science, was a violation of First Amendment guarantees of the separation of church and state. I was asked to be a religious witness for the state in defense of the constitutionality of the law.

The Essence of Act 590

The preamble to the act states well its purposes:

An Act to require balanced treatment of creation-science and evolution-science in public schools; to protect academic freedom by providing student choice; to ensure freedom of religious exercise; to guarantee freedom of belief and speech; to prevent establishment of religion; to prohibit religious instruction concerning origins; to bar discrimination on the basis of creationist or evolutionist belief; to provide definitions and clarifications . . . .

The crucial section of Act 590 is the fourth, which defines the meaning of "creation-science" and "evolution-science":

Section 4. Definitions. As used in this act:

(a) "Creation-science" means the scientific evidences for creation and inferences from those scientific evidences. Creation-science includes the scientific evidences and related inferences that indicate: (1) Sudden creation of the universe, energy, and life from nothing; (2) The insufficiency of mutation and natural selection in bringing about development of all living kinds from a single organism; (3) Changes only within fixed limits of originally created kinds of plants and animals; (4) Separate ancestry for man and apes; (5) Explanation of the earth's geology by catastrophism, including the occurrence of a worldwide flood; and (6) A relatively recent inception of the earth and living kinds.

(b) "Evolution-science" means the scientific evidences for evolution and inferences from those scientific evidences. Evolution-science includes the scientific evidences and related inferences that indicate: (1) Emergence by naturalistic processes of the universe from disordered matter and emergence of life from nonlife; (2) The sufficiency of mutation and natural selection in bringing about development of present living kinds from simple earlier kinds; (3) Emergence by mutation and natural selection of present living kinds from simple earlier kinds; (4) Emergence of man from a common ancestor with apes; (5) Explanation of the earth's geology and the evolutionary sequence by uniformitarianism; and (6) An inception several billion years ago of the earth and somewhat later of life.

(c) "Public schools" mean public secondary and elementary schools.

Several things should be noted about these "definitions." First, the lists are parallel and opposing views, point by point. Second, the lists are suggestive, not exhaustive. The key word is "includes," which does not mean "limited to." Third, not only are these series of six factors opposing, they are in fact logically opposite.

For example, the universe and life either arose spontaneously, or they were created; there is no third alter-native. Also, all living things either have one common ancestry, or they have separate ancestries. The same is true of man (4). Further, either there were changes between fixed kinds or there are not. And the world is either billions of years old, or it is more recent (6). The same contrast is true between "uniformitarianism" and "catastrophism" as explanations of earth's geology (5). Both cannot be true, since one involves millions of years and the other a very short worldwide flood.

It should also be noted that the Act does *not* imply that no combinations of choices can be taught. For example, someone holding to points 1 through 4 of "creation-science" might also opt for 5 and 6 of "evolution-science," or many other combinations. (In fact, I testified in defense of the Act even though for years I have been inclined against "catastrophism" and a "recent" earth. These are viable views, held by credible people who have a right to be heard even if I don't believe them.) What the Act does ensure is that both sides of *each* issue will be presented.

Another important point is brought out in Section 5:

This Act does not require each individual classroom lecture in a course to give such balanced treatment, but simply requires the lectures as a whole to give balanced treatment; it permits some lectures to present evolution-science and other lectures to present creation-science.

One final point is important (from

Section 5):

This Act does not require any instruction in the subject of origins, but simply requires instruction in both scientific models . . . if public schools choose to teach either.

There is thus always the option of avoiding either evolution or creation and sticking to the observable and repeatable areas of science.

Some Misconceptions About Act 590

An informed reader of Act 590 can see that many of the popular misconceptions of what the Act intends are obviously false. Among these false ideas are beliefs that:

1. It mandates teaching of the biblical account of creation. (It actually forbids that.)

2. It is opposed to teaching of evolution. (It actually mandates teaching evolution alongside creation.)

3. It refers to God or religious concepts. (There is no reference to God and it opposes teaching religion.)

4. It forces teachers who are opposed to creation to teach it anyway. (Actually, teachers do not have to teach anything about origins and/or they can have someone else teach and give the lectures they do not want to give.)

5. It is a "fundamentalist" act. (Actually, the "fundamentalists" of the 1920s were categorically opposed to teaching evolution and wanted only the Genesis account of Creation taught. This Act is contrary to both attitudes.)

Why I Supported Act 590

My first reason for supporting Act 590 is one uttered by Clarence Darrow, the famous ACLU lawyer for the 1925 Scopes trial. He called it "bigotry for public schools to teach only one theory of origins." I found it a strange irony to hear the same ACLU 56 years later argue that, in effect, it would be religious bigotry to allow two models of origins to be taught.

This same inconsistency can be seen in the most recent statement of "A Secular Humanist Declaration" (Winter 1980/81, *Free Inquiry*). It declares admirably:

"The lessons of history are clear: wherever one religion or ideology is established and given a dominant position in the state, minority opinions are in jeopardy. A pluralistic, open democratic society allows all points of view to be heard. Any effort to impose an exclusive conception of Truth, Piety, Virtue, or Justice upon the whole of society is a violation of free inquiry" (p. 4).

And yet only two pages later, in an inconceivable inconsistency, the same declaration says:

"We deplore the efforts by fundamentalists (especially in the United States) to invade the science classroom, requiring that creationist theory be taught to students and requiring that it be included in biology textbooks. This is a serious threat both to academic freedom and to the integrity of the educational process" (p. 6).

For the same reason therefore that I regret the narrow-mindedness of some Christian religionists in the 1920s who opposed the teaching of evolution as a scientific theory, I now deplore a similar narrowness on the part of those holding a humanistic religious perspective (and their sympathizers), who would exclude the teaching of creation as a scientific theory in public schools.

Second, I favor Act 590 in the interest of openness of scientific inquiry. As anyone who has studied the history of Copernicus and Galileo knows, minority scientific opinions are often the cutting edge of progress. Suppression of the "loyal opposition" is seldom if ever good politically, and never scientifically. Academic freedom entails hearing opposing points of view. Many times during the trial I was reminded of the value of the adversary relationship of the courtroom. When only one side of an issue is presented (without cross-examination or rebuttal), a judge or jury would often come to an invalid conclusion.

The same is true when only one view is presented in the classroom: it is a trial without opposing witnesses. Since there are serious religious implications when origins are taught from only one perspective—one that favors humanistic religion—it is necessary as a guarantee to religious neutrality that the opposing view also be taught.

Third, teaching creation is no more teaching religion than is teaching evolution. Creation and evolution are both beliefs that belong to religions, but teaching creationism is no more teaching the Christian religion than is teaching evolution teaching the humanist religion. If teaching a part of a religion is automatically teaching that religion, then teaching values (such as freedom and tolerance) are also teaching religion. But the courts have ruled that values can be taught apart from religion, which may hold the same values. Likewise, creationism can be taught apart from the religious systems of which it may be a part.

The fact that "creation" may imply a Creator while "evolution" does not is no proof that the former is religious and the latter is not. Believing that there is no God can be just as religious as believing that there is a God. Humanists hold, and the Supreme Court has ruled, that belief in God is not essential to religion *(U.S. v. Seeger,* 1964).

Fourth, scientific progress depends on teaching alternative models. There would be little progress in science if it were not for minority scientific opinions. Copernicus's view that the earth revolves around the sun was once a minority scientific view. So was the view that the earth is spherical, not flat. If no alternative models to Newton's law of gravitation were allowed, then Einstein's insights (and space travel) would have been rejected and scientific progress retarded.

That creationism may be a minority view among scientists today does not make it wrong, and certainly does not mean it should not be heard in science classes. (Arguing that it should be taught only in social studies classes is like telling someone running for the Senate that he can present his views only to sociologists' groups, but not to political gatherings.) One of the most despicable examples of intellectual prejudice I have ever witnessed was when evolution scientists at the Arkansas trial claimed that creationism was not science and that creationists were not scientists. It reminded me of Voltaire's famous satire in which he described ants on one anthill looking at different colored ants on another anthill and declaring that they were not really ants and that what they were on was not really an anthill.

John Scopes summed up well when he said, "If you limit a teacher to only one side of anything the whole country will eventually have only one thought, be one individual." I believe it would be (is) a gross injustice for the court to rule it unconstitutional to teach both sides of any issue. Although I would not go as far as some in these matters, one can understand why Francis Schaeffer in his recent book, *A Christian Manifesto* (Crossway, 1981), has called upon Christians to engage in civil disobedience and even use force to overcome the tyranny he sees implied in a negative decision in the Arkansas creation-evolution issue. □

—Norman L. Geisler

This article was first printed in *Christianity Today* (March 19, 1982).

Appendix Six

Arkansas Attorney General

First Allegation—Clark's Refusal of Expert Legal Help

"Defense needs no outsiders, Clark insists" was the headline used by *The Arkansas Democrat*, Thursday, December 17, 1981. It was reported that according to Attorney General Steve Clark: "The people of Arkansas did not want an outsider to defend the creation-science law . . . . " Clark said, "It would be a violation of my oath of office to cede responsibility for the trial to the Creation Science Legal Defense Fund. They didn't take an oath to uphold the laws of the state . . . . " Clark was referring to Wendell R. Bird and John W. Whitehead, whom the Defense Fund said he had "summarily rejected" because of their desire to be "counsels of record" in the suit. *The Democrat* said, "There was nothing summary about his dealings with the lawyers . . . . " and quoted Clark as saying, "I met Bird two or three times and each meeting lasted a minimum of an hour." There was a great deal of discussion . . . . " *The Democrat* stated that "Clark said he had offered to let Bird write the pretrial brief, but Bird declined to participate." Clark was quoted in *The Commercial Appeal* of Memphis, Thursday, December 17, 1981, as saying that Bird had told him, "If I can't be counsel of record, then I'm not going to participate."

When asked by *The Appeal*, "What he stood to lose by accepting the help of the two, Clark said, that was the 'wrong question.' The question is what did I stand to gain?' "

Second Allegation—Clark's Preparation

The Arkansas Democrat, Thursday, December 17, 1981, reported the Defense Fund as alleging that Clark "did nothing for two months after the ACLU filed suit."

Clark was quoted by The Democrat as saying, "Unless they were in my office, they don't know how much preparation we did . . . . " According to The Democrat, Clark "was especially angry about suggestions that his assistants had not worked hard on the trial preparations," and said that members of his staff "had turned their office inside out" and even allegedly worked on holidays. According to The Commercial Appeal, Memphis, Thursday, December 17, 1981, Clark said, "Since the lawsuit was filed, . . . we have worked on it earnestly; we have worked on it zealously."

Third Allegation—Clark's Commitment and Alleged Participation with the ACLU

The Arkansas Gazette, Friday, December 11, 1981, reported that Clark had been slandered by Pat Robertson, President of the Christian Broadcasting Network, of whom The Gazette said, "Robertson implied that Clark would deliberately lose the 'Creation Science' suit." Robertson was quoted as saying that "it appeared that the ACLU had 'hand picked' Arkansas as the place to challenge the law because of Clark's alleged friendliness with the ACLU."

The Arkansas Gazette, Saturday, December 12, 1981, reported that Robertson accused "Clark of being 'crooked' and 'biased' because he participated in a fund-raising auction to benefit the American Civil Liberties Union . . . . " The Gazette said, The ACLU had auctioned the opportunity for two persons to have lunch with Clark which cost $25."

The Gazette reported Robertson as comparing "Clark's action to bribing a jury or an athlete throwing a game."

In again another article in The Arkansas Gazette, December 11, 1981, Robertson was reported as saying, "There appeared to be collusion and the collusion is crooked. 'It's a gross impropriety for an attorney to give money' to support a cause he is opposing in court."

According to *The Gazette,* the apparent misunderstanding of Clark's position resulted in an invitation for Clark to explain matters and "to appear on the preacher's nationwide cable television program, 'The 700 Club.' "

In yet another attack on Clark, *The Arkansas Democrat,* December 16, 1981, headlined "Another Blast at Clark." The caption under the statement read: "Zapped again—Attorney General Steve Clark took another jab for his handling of the Creation-Science trial Sunday, this time from Moral Majority leader Jerry Falwell . . . . "

In a related article, "Moral Majority Backs Clark, but has Qualms," in the same issue, Falwell was reported as accusing Clark of "collusion" in a sermon delivered on a Lynchburg radio station.

According to *The Democrat,* Rev. Roy McLaughlin, president of Moral Majority in Arkansas, "had defended Clark after Robertson had made his initial charges, and he expressed surprise Monday when he learned of Falwell's similar comments."

Although there is "at least an appearance of a conflict of interest," *The Democrat* reported Falwell's top-ranking aid, Cal Thomas, as saying, "The Moral Majority supports Attorney General Steve Clark in his handling of the defense of the state's creation-science law . . . . "

Appendix Seven

Creation Science Legal Defense Fund

CREATION SCIENCE LEGAL DEFENSE FUND

P. O. Box 1238 • Little Rock, Arkansas 72203

(501) 562-3754

LEGAL COUNSEL

WENDELL R. BIRD
El Cajon, California

JOHN W. WHITEHEAD
Manassas, Virginia

CARTER & WOODS
Little Rock, Arkansas

For Immediate Release
December 16, 1981

The prospects are indeed dim for a victory by the State of Arkansas in its defense of the Balanced Treatment Act 590. This is not a surprise to the Creation Science Legal Defense Fund. A poor defense was anticipated. On November 1, 1981, the attached news release was prepared but never issued for fear that it might prejudice the trial in some manner. However, it is now time for the public to know the facts behind the scenes regarding the Arkansas Attorney General's lack of adequate preparation to defend this Arkansas Law. That inadequate defense may now cost the Arkansas taxpayers in excess of a million dollars in ACLU legal fees. Those facts are included in this November 1, 1981, news release—which is now made public.

ARKANSAS LAWSUIT PROSPECTS DIMMED

(November 1, 1981.) The prospects have been dimmed for a court ruling in favor of balanced treatment for creation-science and evolution-science, because of the Arkansas attorney general, Steve Clark, and his mishandling of the defense against the ACLU lawsuit.

The prospects look very bright, by contrast, in the Louisiana battle against the forthcoming ACLU attack. There attorneys Wendell R. Bird and John W. Whitehead will assist in defending the Louisiana Balanced Treatment of Creation-Science and Evolution-Science Act.

After the ACLU filed suit in Arkansas on May 27, Clark asked for an unusual 2-month extension to file the defense's answer, and did nothing on the case during those 2 months before August 15 even though the trial date was soon set for late September, just 1½ months after the answer was due. Clark summarily rejected any formal assistance by Bird and Whitehead, who are generally recognized as the legal experts on the subject.

Attorney general Clark publicly expressed "personal qualms" about the constitutionality of the Arkansas bill, an extraordinary action for the state officer charged with its defense, soon after the bill's passage.

Clark strenuously opposed intervention as co-defendants by the science professionals, public school teachers, and parents of public school students that Bird and Whitehead represented, even though they would have done much of the defense work for the attorney general's office. His opposition was in indefensibly strident tones in arguing that these intervenors represented "special interest groups" who would "open the floodgates to innumerable interventions." In fact, this opposition to intervention in July was the only significant action taken by Clark during the first 4 months of the lawsuit, and Clark's office lept in just a couple of days to file documents opposing intervention. The attorney general's opposition was doubtless the primary reason for the district court judge's denial of intervention.

Clark's subordinates have given the deceitful and spurious argument that the intervention efforts called his defense "incompetent" so that he had to oppose intervention. One of the three requirements for intervention of right is "inadequate representation" by existing parties in the sense of their divergent interests—not inadequate representation by existing attorneys in the sense of their legal incompetence—and the intervenors merely alleged inadequate representation by existing parties who are educational bureaucrats rather than teachers and scientists. In fact, the intervenors intentionally omitted mentioning Clark's "personal qualms" about the very act he was defending, at that stage, in order to avoid attacking him in any way, even though the intervenors were extremely dubious about his ability or willingness to give an adequate defense to the act. They only raised the "personal qualms" argument a month after Clark opposed intervention.

Nearly 4 months after the suit was filed, the attorney general's office said that it had "done nothing" on the case yet to Professor William E. Gran, leader of the intervenors. By contrast, the ACLU was actively carrying on research and depositions during that time.

In a late September meeting, Bird summarized for the attorney general and his two assistants the vast amount of discovery and trial preparation necessary for adequate defense of the case, which could not possibly be done even if Clark's office worked full-time on it until the then-October trial date or the possible December trial date. Expertise is needed in the 4 complex fields of constitutional law, science, religion, and education, to which Bird and Whitehead have devoted several years of study, and Clark's office has never handled a major First Amendment or science case. (In a recent antitrust case,

Clark retained a private law firm of experts in the field and paid about $750,000 in legal fees, yet he has been unwilling formally to use even cost-free expertise in this case.) Several dozen depositions are needed on the trial issues, each requiring a day for the deposition and travel and at least a second day for preparation, to substantiate the defense claims in the record because of the shortness of the scheduled trial, and to impeach or contradict the ACLU claims. Bird and Whitehead recommended that the defense take deposition testimony of 7-15 creationist scientists on the scientific evidence for creation, of 2-5 expert witnesses on religions having evolutionist doctrines, of 5-10 legislators and educators, and of all ACLU clergy plaintiffs and expert witnesses.

Clark and his staff have simply refused to do this extensive discovery of creationist and evolutionist scientists, religious experts, educators, and legislators, and to do the extensive research needed. Bird and Whitehead estimate that "Clark's office is putting less than 20% of the necessary time into the case, and less than 10% of the time the ACLU and its 7 or more attorneys are spending on it."

Clark rejected a second time the legal assistance of Bird and Whitehead, the generally recognized experts in the area, as counsel of record in the case, at the end of September. He knew that the ACLU had accepted the free full-time assistance of 3-4 attorneys in a 200-member New York firm along with the existing 4 ACLU attorneys; the ACLU recognizes the complexity of the case. (If Clark loses, Arkansas will have to pay massive attorneys fees to the ACLU lawyers that easily could exceed $1 million.) The Creation Science Legal Defense Fund had made an exceedingly generous offer in providing cost-free legal assistance and underwriting expert witness costs.

At the pretrial conference on October 1, the judge asked for an example of the scientific evidence for creation, and the deputy attorney general was so unprepared on the case that he could not give one. The judge asked whether creation-science is not inherently religious because it assumes a creator, and the deputy denied that creation-science involves a creator—"only a force." He forced himself into this foolish argument by refusal to make several crucial arguments and unpreparedness on the unquestionable constitutionality of mentioning a creator in public schools under cases involving the pledge to the flag and the national anthem.

Attorney general Clark has refused thus far to make several legal arguments that the CSLDF attorneys deem crucial: that evolution is a doctrine of numerous religions and that evolution science presupposes that there is no creator (although many evolutionists modify this presupposition).

In depositions taken by the ACLU, the attorney general's office has refused to press an objection to ACLU questions about the religious beliefs of the legislative sponsor, the model bill's draftsman, a science teacher, and others in order to prevent the questions. The CSLDF attorneys urged the attorney general's staff in the first few depositions to take the issue to the judge so that irrelevant religious issues would not prejudice the trial on balanced treatment of scientific explanations. The cross-examination questions by the attorney general's office in the crucial deposition of the legislative sponsor and in other depositions were "woefully inadequate," in the opinion of Bird and Whitehead, to counter the misleading impressions created by numerous ACLU questions. The approach of the attorney general's office has been to shoot from the hip rather than to prepare carefully weeks ahead for depositions.

Clark's nonfeasance has created needless headaches for 5 creationist organizations against whom the ACLU served wide-ranging subpoenas asking for a large portion of their files. The district court judge expressed disapproval of many of the 24 subpoena points, and instructed Clark's office to enter an agreement with the ACLU narrowing the subpoena. The attorney general's office did not seek the protective order that it should have sought, and did not even narrow the subpoena in its agreement with the ACLU; it merely protected its own hide by getting copies of all documents turned over and limited the scope of the depositions (which was what the ACLU already had proposed). This shifted the burden to the 5 creationist organizations to retain attorneys and to fight the subpoenas in court themselves; 4 called on attorney Wendell R. Bird who provided advice and consulted with 3 local attorneys. The Creation Social Science & Humanities Society recently succeeded in quashing the entire subpoena, and the Institute for Creation Research and the Creation Research Society are currently litigating the issue.

Bird and Whitehead have given and remain willing to give advice to the attorney general when requested, such as the names of possible expert witnesses and of useful sources, but are not in any way representing Arkansas. They had made arrangements to represent half of the existing defendants including the largest Arkansas school district, but those defendants were subsequently dismissed from the case.

In summary, attorneys Bird and Whitehead believe that attorney general Clark's defense of the Arkansas Balanced Treatment Act is "totally inadequate." They are "pessimistic" about the chances for a victory for balanced treatment of creation-science; although the legal and scientific arguments are strong they are not being adequately presented. For this reason, several noted creationist scientists have declined to serve as expert witnesses in the Arkansas trial.

Attorneys Bird and Whitehead are now focusing their efforts on constitutional defense of creation-science in Louisiana, and are not taking part in the Arkansas litigation.

APPALLING EVENTS FROM NOVEMBER 1 TO DECEMBER 16, 1981

During the discovery phase of the case, the Attorney General refused to stop depositions in order to challenge religious questions and answers, contrary to the strong advice of numerous individuals. The consequence was that many of the key depositions of creationist scientists focused almost entirely on religious issues. The Attorney General's staff did almost no consultation with the creationists before the depositions and did almost no rehabilitation by questions at the end of the depositions, contrary to universal legal practice.

The 5 creationist organizations that received the ACLU's subpoenas incurred many thousands of dollars in unnecessary legal expenses, because of the Attorney General's failure to seek a protective order, in fighting the subpoenas in court. The Institute for Creation Research won and the Creation Research Society lost after court battles against the ACLU's attorneys (flown in from New York and Los Angeles).

The Attorney General refused to assist 5 creationist leaders in Arkansas when the ACLU served subpoenas for virtually all of their private papers. These individuals offered to pay private attorneys to draft the necessary legal documents if the Attorney General's office would merely file them and seek a protective order. Because of the Attorney General's refusal even to do that, these individuals incurred over a thousand dollars of legal expenses for work that the Attorney General should have done for the trial he is handling.

During the first week of the trial the Attorney General's staff asked shockingly few questions on cross-examinations, which caused the Judge to berate Clark for inept cross-examination. Clark found it necessary to begin his argument by referring to God as "he or she." During the first week of the trial, it was evident to those in the courtroom that the Attorney General's staff failed to ask many obvious questions and obviously had not prepared adequately for the trial. The Attorney General made his vital objection to the admissibility of personal religious beliefs without even submitting a brief or citing a case* and the Judge ruled against him with devastating consequences.

During the second week of trial, the Attorney General's staff reflected a total lack of research or preparation in shooting questions from the hip at the creationist witnesses. One witness was publicly humiliated when the Judge cut him off with the exasperated comment that he had not presented one shred of scientific evidence for creation. This reflected a lack of consultation or adequate questions from the Attorney General. A Dallas newspaper that editorially supported the creation cause described the Attorney General's performance as the most "bumbling" and inadequate courtroom defense that its reporters had ever seen.

---

* See Chapter Four for legal grounds given by defense attorneys for their objections.

There are many strong constitutional and scientific arguments that can be made for public school instruction in creation-science but the Attorney General is either refusing to make them or is inadequately presenting them. The one encouraging note is that the constitutional question is being litigated on a second front, because the Creation Science Legal Defense attorneys are fighting the Louisiana lawsuit on the constitutionality of creation-science in public schools.

— — — — — — — — — — —

Authors' Comments

The Attorney General's office chose not to respond to these allegations. But when asked about them we were told by one staff member that they considered them misleading or false. In fact, some of them they believed to be grounds for legal action against Wendell Bird. They also noted that, if true, the report that Bird had discouraged witnesses from testifying could be obstructing justice.

Many objective observers close to the facts believed that a serious shadow was cast over the validity of Bird's allegations because he had been denied his desire to handle the Arkansas case. Regardless of whatever merit any of the charges may (or may not) have, it is our opinion that given the total Arkansas situation (especially with that judge) that no attorneys could have won the case in defense of the Act.

Appendix Eight

The Two Models Of Origins

The judge (and others) claimed that there were more than two views of origin because the views of creation and evolution are not mutually exclusive. This is based on a misunderstanding. First of all, the two models present a series of six points of origins, each of which is mutually exclusive with the opposing view in its category. The following chart summarizes the two mutually exclusive approaches spelled out in Section 4 of Act 590.

	Creation Model	**Evolution Model**
Life	supernatural origin	natural origin
Kinds	mutations insufficient	mutations sufficient
Change	only within kinds	also between kinds
Man	separate ancestry from apes	same ancestry as apes
Geo	sediments formed rapidly	sediments formed slowly
Age	young earth	very old earth

Even without explanation anyone can readily see that in each column the contrasts are of logical opposites; there is no third alternative. So one either holds a "creation" model or an "evolution" model on each of these six points of origin. There are two and only two views. Of course one may choose to believe the first four points from the "creation" model and the last two from the "evolution" model (which is what one defense witness testified to holding), or any other combination from opposite sides of the chart. But no one can logically hold both "evolution" and "creation" models on one and the same point.

This logically apparent contrast between these mutually exclusive views as outlined in the various points of the Act is widely recognized even by evolutionists. Many admit, for example, that there are only two views on the origin of life. The evolutionist, George Wald *(Scientific American,* August, 1954) wrote:

> The reasonable viewpoint was to believe in spontaneous generation; the only alternative, to believe in a single, primary act of supernatural creation. *There is no third position* [emphasis added].

Also, the famous astrophysicist, Robert Jastrow *(When the Sun Dies,* New York: W. W. Norton and Co., 1977, p. 62), noted:

> *Either* life was created on the earth by the will of a being outside the grasp of scientific understanding, *or* it evolved on our planet spontaneously, through chemical reactions occurring in non-living matter lying on the surface of the planet [emphasis added].

Even Charles Darwin *(Origin of Species,* Great Books, pp. 234, 235) speaks of two opposing views he calls "the theory of evolution" and "the theory of creation."

The same kind of dichotomy is recognized in an article in *Nature* (2-10-29):

> . . . the theory of evolution itself, a theory universally accepted not because it can be proved by logically coherent evidence to be true but because *the only alternative,* special creation, is clearly incredible [emphasis added].

Davis and Solomon in their college biology text write:

> Such explanations tend to fall into one or the other of two broad categories: special creation or evolution. Various admixtures and modifications of these two concepts exist, but it seems impossible to imagine an explanation of origins that lies completely outside the two ideas. *(The World of Biology,* McGraw Hill, 1974, p. 395)

So, then, the language of the Act, simple logic, and even the testimony of evolutionists, all combine to support the thesis (against the judge) that "creation" and "evolution" are mutually exclusive explanations of origins.

Appendix Nine

Louisiana Creation- Evolution Act

Regular Session, 1981

SENATE BILL NO. 86

BY MESSRS. KEITH AND RICHEY AND REPRESENTATIVES F. THOMPSON AND CAIN

AN ACT

To amend Part III of Chapter I of Title 17 of the Louisiana Revised Statutes of 1950 by adding thereto a new Sub-Part, to be designated as Sub-Part D-2 thereof, comprised of Sections 286.1 through 286.7, both inclusive, relative to balanced treatment of creation-science and evolution-science in public schools, to require such balanced treatment, to bar discrimination on the basis of creationist or evolutionist belief, to provide definitions and clarifications, to declare the legislative purpose, to provide relative to inservice teacher training and materials acquisition, to provide relative to curriculum development, and otherwise to provide with respect thereto.

Be it enacted by the Legislature of Louisiana:

Section 1. Sub-Part D-2 of Part III of Chapter I of Title 17 of the Louisiana Revised Statutes of 1950, comprised of Sections 286.1 through 286.7, both inclusive, is hereby enacted to read as follows:

CHAPTER I. GENERAL SCHOOL LAW

* * * **

PART III. PUBLIC SCHOOLS AND SCHOOL CHILDREN

* * * * *

SUB-PART D-2. BALANCED TREATMENT FOR CREATION-SCIENCE AND EVOLUTION SCIENCE IN PUBLIC SCHOOL INSTRUCTION

§286.1. Short Title

This Subpart shall be known as the "Balanced Treatment for Creation-Science and Evolution-Science Act."

§286.2. Purpose

This Subpart is enacted for the purposes of protecting academic freedom.

§286.3. Definitions

As used in this Subpart, unless otherwise clearly indicated, these terms have the following meanings:

(1) "Balanced treatment" means providing whatever information and instruction in both creation and evolution models the classroom teacher determines is necessary and appropriate to provide insight into both theories in view of the textbooks and other instructional materials available for use in his classroom.

(2) "Creation-science" means the scientific evidences for creation and inferences from those scientific evidences.

(3) "Evolution-science" means the scientific evidences for evolution and inferences from those scientific evidences.

(4) "Public schools" means public secondary and elementary schools.

§286.4 Authorization for balanced treatment; requirement for nondiscrimination

A. Commencing with the 1982-1983 school year, public schools within this state shall give balanced treatment to creation-science and to evolution-science. Balanced treatment of these two models shall be given in classroom lectures taken as a whole for each course, in textbook materials taken as a whole for each course, in library materials taken as a whole for the sciences and taken as a whole for the humanities, and in other educational programs in public schools, to the extent that such lectures, textbooks, library materials, or educational programs deal in any way with the subject of the origin of man, life, the earth, or the universe. When creation or evolution is taught, each shall be taught as a theory, rather than as proven scientific fact.

B. Public schools within this state and their personnel shall not discriminate by reducing a grade of a student or by singling out and publicly criticizing any student who demonstrates a satisfactory understanding of both evolution-science or creation-science and who accepts or rejects either model in whole or part.

C. No teacher in public elementary or secondary school or instructor in any state-supported university in Louisiana, who chooses to be a creation-scientist or to teach scientific data which points to creationism shall, for that reason, be discriminated against in any way by any school board, college board, or administrator.

§286.5 Clarifications

This Subpart does not require any instruction in the subject of origins but simply permits instruction in both scientific models (of evolution-science and creation-science) if public schools choose to teach either. This Subpart does not require each individual textbook or library book to give balanced treatment to the models of evolution-science and creation-science; it does not require any school books to be discarded. This Subpart does not require each individual classroom lecture in a course to give such balanced treatment but simply permits the lectures as a whole to give balanced treatment; it permits some lectures to present evolution-science and other lectures to present creation-science.

§286.6 Funding of inservice training and materials acquisition

Any public school that elects to present any model of origins shall use existing teacher inservice training funds to prepare teachers of public school courses presenting any model of origins to give balanced treatment to the creation-science model and the evolution-science model. Existing library acquisition funds shall be used to purchase nonreligious library books as are necessary to give balanced treatment to the creation-science model and the evolution-science model.

§286.7 Curriculum Development

A. Each city and parish school board shall develop and provide to each public school classroom teacher in the system a curriculum guide on presentation of creation-science.

B. The governor shall designate seven creation-scientists who shall provide resource services in the development of curriculum guides to any city or parish school board upon request. Each such creation-scientist shall be designated from among the full-time faculty members teaching in any college and university in Louisiana. These creation-scientists shall serve at the pleasure of the governor and without compensation.

Section 2. If any provision or item of this Act or the application thereof is held invalid, such invalidity shall not affect other provisions, items, or applications of this Act which can be given effect without the invalid provisions, items, or applications, and to this end the provisions of this Act are hereby declared severable.

Section 3. All laws or parts of laws in conflict herewith are hereby repealed.

— — — — — — — — — — —

Authors' Comments

There are several reasons that the prospects for victory in the Louisiana case are better. First, the Law is not as specific, detail-

ed and controversial. Second, the history of the Louisiana Act is less tainted with partisan religious associations. Third, the creationists are plaintiffs which provides a momentum advantage (creationists were defendants in Arkansas). Fourth, Judge Frank Polozula (Louisiana) has not shown the bias manifested by Judge William Overton (Arkansas). Fifth, there is more favorable climate of cooperation and a wider basis of support for the Louisiana law. Sixth, the leading creationist attorneys in the Louisiana litigation, Wendell Bird and John Whitehead, are specialists in First Amendment issues, and Thomas T. Anderson is a top-notch trial lawyer.

Is Evolution Scientific?

The answer to the above question depends on what one means by "evolution" and by "science." The ACLU attorneys used the ambiguity of these terms to their advantage at the trial.

Evolution: General or Special Theory?

The first ambiguity is between the "general theory" of evolution and the "special theory." The noted evolutionist, Kerkut, wrote: "There is a theory which states that many living animals can be observed over the course of time to undergo changes so that new species are formed. This can be called the 'Special Theory of Evolution' and can be demonstrated in certain cases by experiments. On the other hand there is the theory that all the living forms in the world have arisen from a single source which itself came from an inorganic form. This theory can be called the 'General Theory of Evolution' and the evidence that supports it is not sufficiently strong to allow us to consider it as anything more than a working hypothesis." *(Implications of Evolution,* 1960, p. 157.)

These small variations or changes are admitted by creationists to occur, so there is no real dispute about the "special theory." These changes (such as Darwin noted in finches) are observable and testable. The "special theory" then is truly scientific. So when evolutionists refer to "evolution" as testable (or falsifiable) this rightly includes evolution as a "special theory." However, "evolution" in the sense of a "general theory" of change from particles to people, or molecule to man, has not been observed and is not testable (or falsifiable) in the sense that the "special theory" is.

The fact that evolution as a general theory is not strictly falsifiable is recognized by evolutionists. One of the greatest living philosophers of science, Sir Karl Popper wrote, "Darwinism is not a testable scientific theory, but a metaphysical research programme." *(Unended Quest, P. 151.)* Two evolutionists writing in the science journal *Nature* (April 22, 1967) added, "Our theory of evolution has become, as Popper described, one which cannot be refuted by any possible observations. Every conceivable observation can be fitted into it. It is thus 'outside of empirical science' but not necessarily false. No one can think of ways in which to test it. Ideas, either without basis or based on a few laboratory experiments carried out in extremely simplified systems, have attained currency far beyond their validity. They have become part of an evolutionary dogma accepted by most of us as part of our training." (L. C. Birch and P. R. Ehrlich, p. 351.)

Nobel lauereate Harold C. Urey said, "All of us who study the origin of life find that the more we look into it, the more we feel that it is too complex to have evolved anywhere. *We all believe as an article of faith* that life evolved from dead matter on this planet." *(The Christian Science Monitor,* Jan. 4, 1962, p. 4.) Professor Murray Eden of MIT stated, "During the course of development of neo-Darwinian evolution as a theory, a variety of suggested universal postulates with empirical content have been invalidated. In consequence the theory has been modified to the point that virtually every formulation of the principles of evolution is a tautology." *(Mathematical Challenges to Neo-Darwinian Interpretation of Evolution,* eds. Paul Moorhead and Martin Kaplan, 1967, p. 109.)

Loren Eisley contended that evolution as a general theory functions like a religious myth. He wrote, "With the failure of these many efforts science was left in the somewhat embarrassing position of having to postulate theories of living origins which it could not demonstrate. After having chided the theologian for his reliance on myth and miracle, science found itself in the unenviable position of having to create a mythology of its own: namely, the assumption that what, after long effort, could not be proved to take place today had, in truth, taken place in the primeval past." (The Immense Journey, 1957, p. 199.) Speaking of the origin of first life, a member of the army radiation faculty wrote, "One must conclude that, contrary to the established and current wisdom a scenario describing the genesis of life on earth by chance and natural causes which can be accepted on the basis of fact and not faith has not yet been written." (Journal of Theoretical Biology, 1977, 67, p. 346.)

Many evolutionists consider the Darwinian theory of evolution to be an untestable tautology. Robert H. Peters wrote, "Although Darwinian evolution remains one of the greatest unifying concepts in biology, its utility has been questioned. Difficulties in defining 'fittest' in the phrase 'survival of the fittest' have led some authors to conclude that the Darwinian theory is a meaningless formulation because fitness is apparently equivalent to survival (Waddington 1957; Coffin, cited in Scriven 1959) . . . .Birch and Ehrlich (1967) maintain that our theory of evolution is 'not necessarily false' but 'outside of empirical science' . . . . The essence of the argument is that these 'theories' are actually tautologies and, as such, cannot make empirically testable predictions. They are not scientific theories at all." (The American Naturalist, Vol. 110, No. 971, Jan. - Feb., 1976, p. 1.)

So in the strict sense of the word, "science," that is something observable, repeatable and/or falsifiable, cannot be used to describe evolution, for evolution as a general theory is not a science. But the Arkansas judge ruled creationism not to be a science on the grounds that it isn't falsifiable. Logically, on this ground, the general theory of evolution should have been judged non-scientific, too. But since evolution as a general theory is considered "science" by the court, it must be concluded that the judge made an error in judgment.

Evolution: Fact or Means

Evolution can be understood in two ways. These must be

kept separate.
1. The "fact" of evolution—*that* it happened.
2. The "mechanism" of evolution—*how* it happened.
Most evolutionists do not question "evolution" in the first sense. They simply assume evolution happened. But evolution in this sense is not falsifiable. It is only the mechanism of evolution which evolutionists seriously question. Many mechanisms have been suggested such as Lamarckianism (inheritance of acquired characteristics), Darwinism (natural selection), random mutations with natural selection (neo-Darwinism), and more recently, punctuated equilibria. These are all tentative and debatable for evolutionists. In this sense "evolution" understood as a *specific means* by which these changes between different types of animals took place is truly tentative, for the various mechanisms are discussed and sometimes discarded by evolutionists. But the fact that most evolutionists do not give up evolution as a happening when their specific mechanism has been discarded indicates the strength of their faith commitment to the fact of evolution. In short, evolution is assumed to be a *fact;* the only thing that is "tentative" or seriously debated is the means by which the fact of evolution occurred.

This came out clearly at the trial when one ACLU scientist was being cross-examined. He had claimed that evolution was a "fact" and yet that it is "scientific" because it is "falsifiable" and "tentative." He found it very difficult to explain what a "tentative fact" could possible mean! (See Chapter Four.) And how can a fact be falsified?

Science: Broad and Narrow

The other ambiguity which emerged in the trial is what is meant by "science." In the normal (strict) sense of the word something must be observable and repeatable to be subject to scientific tests. But in this sense evolution (as a general theory) is not "science." The origin of life and new life forms were singular, unobservable events of the past. No observers were there and the original events are not repeatable. So even general evolution must be understood in some "special" (broader) sense, if it is to be considered science, for scientists do not have the original events (of origins) against which they can test their theories. Hence, their ideas about origins are not based on *observations* (as an evolution witness admitted, Chapter Four); they are *speculations*.

Science in the narrow sense involves some observable or repeatable event against which we can measure our theories. But when there is no direct access to the original event, the best scientists can do is to offer speculative reconstructions of the past. These imaginative reconstructions cannot be either verified or falsified in a strict scientific way. They may be plausible or implausible, but they are not scientifically provable. They can be tested for consistency and comprehensiveness, but they cannot be scientifically tested because *they cannot be checked over against the original event.* Thus all "theories" or models about unrepeatable origins can at best be "science" only in some broad sense of the term. They are science in the sense that we speak of "forensic science." What happens in court is that attorneys offer plausible or implausible reconstructions of the crime based on the available clues. But if there were no eyewitnesses, then we can never be certain what actually happened. They can, however, offer a speculative model of what *might have happened.*

Now in this broad speculative sense of the word "science," a creationist's view is just as scientific as an evolutionist's view. Unfortunately, what happened in Arkansas was the application of a double-standard. Evolution as a general theory was considered science on a broad definition of "science," and creation was considered unscientific on a narrow definition of science. If the courts are ever to recognize the scientific character of creationism, then this kind of "double-dealing" must be avoided, for creationism is no less scientific than is evolutionism. To be fair the courts must either rule both theories in or both out of the science classroom.

Christian Media Coverage of the Trial

The evangelical media coverage of the trial was generally scant, poor, and second-hand. No magazine or paper assigned anyone to attend the trial daily. *Christianity Today* hired a freelance reporter who attended a short time on one day. Though he was living in the Little Rock area, when we asked him why he didn't attend the trial daily, he told us he was going to write a contemporary "historical account" based largely on the newspaper reports. It was no surprise that the CT report (1-22-82) reflected the typical irrelevant, sensational, and distorted picture presented in the secular press.

The Moral Majority and the "700 Club" (Pat Robertson) concentrated on the Attorney General (see Appendix Six). They gave little substantive reporting on the actual trial proceedings. *Moral Majority Reports* (2-22-82) did publish one eyewitness evaluation of the trial (on page 15).

Eternity Magazine (May, 1982) published a strongly negative article on the trial by someone who didn't attend. They gave only limited space to an article by a trial witness at his request.

Moody Monthly (May, 1982) strongly supports the creationists' cause but strangely enough attacked the creation witnesses and defense of the trial. In an article entitled,

"Arkansas: Where Creationism Lost Its Shirt," they asked: "Why did creationism lose?" They answered in large bold print: "Its defenders simply would not fight science with science" (p. 11). Like many others they joined the chorus of criticism of the defense handling of the trial, especially on the matter of questioning the witnesses religious beliefs. *Moody Monthly* says, "Geisler stood behind the state and explained that Clark's staff had objected to this type of question earlier in the trial to no avail and that it would have been futile to have done so again. But Clark's spokesman did not agree with Geisler, and he told *Moody Monthly,* 'It was just part of our strategy not to. We didn't plan to win the case on cross-examination. We planned to win it under direct testimony.' " These false charges were apparently due to some misquotes and misimplications drawn by a Washington free-lance reporter Moody hired to give his account of the trial. The *Moody* article drew the following response.

Letter From Attorney General's Office

May 10, 1982

The Editor
Moody Monthly
c/o Moody Press
2101 West Howard Street
Chicago, Illinois 60645

Dear Editor:

The article entitled "Arkansas: Where Creationism Lost Its Shirt", which appeared in the May, 1982 issue of your magazine, suffers from numerous and substantial inaccuracies. While space would not allow an exhaustive cataloging of all errors which the author, Mr. Martin Mawyer, made, it is important that your readers be informed of some of the more serious errors, lest they be lulled into accepting Mawyer's comments as a fair and accurate representation of the trial that actually occurred in Little Rock. Please permit us to bring to your attention the following inaccuracies:

1. Paul Ellwanger did not "help Arkansas legislators and at-

torneys construct'' Act 590, as your article states. (Page 10.) Ellwanger and other individuals (including Wendell Bird) were solely responsible for drafting the bill which eventually became Act 590. No changes were made in his draft by the Arkansas Legislature, nor was the Attorney General's Office ever consulted prior to passage of the legislation. If we had been consulted prior to the bill becoming law, the result would have been a sounder, more defensible act.

2. Act 590 did not require teachers "to spend as much time on creation-science as they spend teaching evolution science." (Page 10.) The bill mandated "balanced treatment," not "equal time." Throughout our defense of the Act, we stressed that balanced treatment did not necessarily mean equal time. Our reading of "balanced treatment" (and the testimony of defense witnesses) was to the effect that giving balanced treatment would require spending a sufficient amount of time on both creation-science and evolution-science so that students could fully understand both theories. The amount of time devoted to each would necessarily vary, depending upon the perceptiveness of the students, the ability of the teachers, and the available scientific evidence for both theories.

3. Mr. Mawyer's characterization of the attempted participation by attorneys Wendell Bird and John Whitehead similarly is inaccurate in several respects. First, Mawyer labeled Bird and White [sic] as "constitutional attorneys" and as "experienced creationist attorneys." To the degree that either attorney is called a "constitutional expert," they are only self-appointed experts. Since graduation from law school, most of Bird's employment has been as a law clerk to federal judges, a job which consists of reading trial transcripts and doing research. As a law clerk, there is no opportunity to try cases. The difference between reading trial transcripts and actually trying cases is analogous to the difference between reading medical textbooks on the human heart and performing open heart surgery. The second error by Mawyer lies in his editorializing that we offered Bird "only a minor role." In fact, Bird was offered the opportunity to participate in all aspects of the case, but as one member of a team. (This is the same role which expert attorneys have had in other cases with our office in the past.) Not content to merely serve as an integral part of a team, Bird

stated in no uncertain terms that if he could not run the team, he would not play at all. It need only be pointed out that it is Steve Clark—not Wendell Bird—who is elected by the people of Arkansas as the State's chief legal officer. Steve Clark never has nor will he ever abdicate the duties and responsibilities entrusted to him by the people of Arkansas.

4. The article states that the Attorney General became "extremely upset when, out of 16 witnesses scheduled to witness, only 8 appeared. One, a Dr. Dean Kenyon, flew into Little Rock and left the next morning." (Page 11.) It is correct that Kenyon left Little Rock abruptly. (We accept as accurate the statement in Mawyer's article that Kenyon left at the urging of Bird. Tampering with witnesses is not looked upon with favor in the legal profession!) Beyond the departure of Kenyon, it is a falsehood to say that the Attorney General was "extremely upset" when only eight witnesses appeared. The fact is that we made a conscious decision not to call several witnesses whom we had previously listed as potential witnesses. The individuals were not called because we did not need their testimony or they presented various strategic problems for the defense which would have hurt our case more than it could have helped.

5. Perhaps the most serious of Mawyer's many errors is found on page 12, where he states: "Virtually all defendants [witnesses] admitted that they were only familiar with creation in the context of the Bible, not scientific study. This admission laid bare the essential weakness of the entire defense." First, this statement is patently false. The defense expert witnesses said that in thier opinion the scientific evidence fit the creation-science model better than that of evolution. All of the defense expert witnesses had done work which in their professional opinion supported creation-science. Almost all of the defense science witnesses have had articles published in scientific journals. Thus, there is no basis in fact for the author's quoted statement. Perhaps Mawyer was attempting—in his own inarticulate, imprecise way—to allude to another aspect of our defense. Some (but not all) of our witnesses did admit that their initial interest into delving into the scientific evidence for creation had been spurred by their study of Genesis. The testimony at trial was uniform that this fact was not relevant to the scientific

validity of creation-science. The source of a scientific theory is absolutely irrelevant if the facts justify or support the theory. Witnesses for both the plaintiffs and defendants agreed on this point. (For example, Dr. Michael Ruse, one of the plaintiffs' experts in the philosophy of science, testified under cross-examination that Marxism is a religion, and that Harvard Professor Stephen J. Gould is motivated by Marxism in espousing a variant on evolution known as "punctuated equilibrium." Nonetheless, Ruse said, the fact that Gould's source is religion does not require dismissal of the theory.)

6. Illustrative of Mawyer's slanted postmortem is the slight mention of Dr. Robert Gentry of Oak Ridge, Tennessee, who testified on behalf of the defendants. Gentry's work is the most compelling evidence within the scientific community for a relatively recent age of the earth. His work, which centers on the age of the granites which underlie the continents, strongly indicates that these granites had to have cooled in a matter of minutes, rather than over millions of years as evolutionary theory presupposes. Mawyer neglected to point out that Gentry is acknowledged as the leading expert in the world on this theory and has provided a test to falsify his theory. To date, his theory has not been falsified.

7. Another glaring error was the statement attributed to a spokesman for the Arkansas Attorney General concerning the testimony of Dr. Norman L. Geisler, a Professor of Theology at Dallas Theological Seminary. (Page 13.) In the context of the article, Mawyer quotes a spokesman for the Attorney General's Office as disagreeing with Dr. Geisler's statement on the reasons why no objection was made to Geisler's testimony on UFOs. Quite the contrary is, in fact, true. Dr. Geisler was the State's leading expert witness on philosophy and religion. The substance of his testimony was never challenged by attorneys for the ACLU on cross-examination. Rather, they chose to question Dr. Geisler about a totally unrelated matter, *i.e.*, his belief in the existence of Satan.

Throughout the first several days of the trial the Attorney General strenuously objected to all questions concerning the religious beliefs of witnesses. These objections were consistently overruled by the Court. Indeed, we told the Judge that we had a continuing objection to any question concerning a witness' religious beliefs, and this objection was noted in the official court record. Inasmuch as Dr. Geisler testified on the fifth day of trial (and after the entry of our continuing objection), it would have been mere folly to again object to this line of questioning.

The article further implies that we did not object to the cross-examination of Dr. Geisler because, "[i]t was just a part of our strategy not to. We didn't plan to win the case on cross-examination. We planned to win it under direct testimony." (Page 13.) In actuality, what Mr. Mawyer has done is construct what lawyers term a classic non sequitur *(i.e.,* an inference that does not follow from the premises). The quoted statement deals solely with our cross-examination of ACLU witnesses, not the ACLU's cross-examination of our witnesses. The decision not to object to the cross-examination of our own witness (Dr. Geisler) had nothing whatsoever to do with our plan not to win the case on cross-examination of the witnesses for the ACLU. In other words, we felt that witnesses for the State could, on direct examination, offer convincing evidence in support of the creation model of origins. We certainly never expected witnesses for the ACLU, who were irrevocably committed to the evolution model of origins, to offer any evidence favorable to our position during cross-examination. Thus, in view of the Court's previous rulings on the admissibility of witnesses' religious beliefs, absolutely no useful purpose would have been served by again objecting during Dr. Geisler's cross-examination. To have done so would have only served to emphasize an inconsequential detail.

In conclusion, Mawyer's article is a misleading and inaccurate attempt to utilize the Office of Attorney General and the defense witnesses as convenient scapegoats for the failure of Act 590. The issue of creation-science and evolution-science is a complex one, and will continue to be debated for years to come. Mr. Mawyer's article hurts, rather than helps, that debate. But, perhaps we expected too much of him. On page 12 of the article, Mawyer identified Dr. Ariel Roth as a woman (referring to "her deposition"). In all our meetings with Dr. Roth both before and during the trial, he was a man. Someone who cannot accurately report the sex of one individual should not be entrusted with the responsibility of reporting the origin of all mankind.

Yours truly,

STEVE CLARK
Attorney General

DAVID L. WILLIAMS
Deputy Attorney General

RICK CAMPBELL
Assistant Attorney General

SC/DW/RC/pa

Letter From a Witness

Dear Editor:

Your article on the Arkansas creation trial was a colossal disappointment and a gross distortion of the truth. By mimicking the secular media's focus on the out-of-context, irrelevant, and sensational, you held up the creation witnesses and defense attorneys to public scorn. You also misrepresented a spokesman for the Attorney General, thereby casting aspersions on the credibility of another witness. Further, you distorted the testimony of the valiant science witnesses, many of whom risked their professional reputations to testify.* And contrary to your uninformed claim that they did not fight "science with science," these scientists gave three solid days of scientific evidence for creationism! If your "reporter" had attended the trial he would have known this. Duane Gish, Cal Beisner, Mark Keough, and myself were all evangelical writers present for the whole science testimony, and we all disagree with your gross misrepresentation. Why didn't you get someone who knew what they were talking about? Why did you hire an absentee, free-lance writer from Washington, D.C.? And why did you refuse to print a first-hand account offered you by an evangelical writer who did attend the trial? Why didn't your "reporter" even telephone any of the above mentioned eye-witness writers to get the

---

* Robert Gentry has been informed since the trial that his contract at the Oak Ridge National Laboratory (Tenn.) will not be renewed.

facts? And why didn't he use the first-hand material of the pre-publication manuscript on the trial *(The Creator in the Courtroom,* Mott Media) sent to him?

To cap it all off, you printed an interview with Dr. W. T. Brown in which you proudly paraded the scientific evidence you believe should have been given at the trial. Well, a little first-hand knowledge would have told you that *this very same scientific evidence was presented at the trial!* In brief, your report was woefully ignorant, grossly distorted, and potentially libelous. This is the kind of thing we expect from the world, but not from fellow Christians.

> Sincerely,
> Norman L. Geisler

The *Institute for Creation Research* (ICR) has an accurate but brief (2-page) report in their "Impact" (March, 1982, No. 105) on the trial by Dr. Duane Gish who was an observer at the trial. He spoke of the defense testimony as "brilliant," "excellent" and concluded: "From his decision it is obvious that Judge Overton (as well as most of the news media) completely ignored the scientific evidence presented by the defense witnesses while accepting without question evidence offered by the plaintiffs' witnesses. Many remarks made by Judge Overton during the trial revealed his bias against the creationist side." (p. iii.)

A few other evangelicals took time to talk to eye-witnesses of the trial. Their reports were more insightful. The national magazine of the "Jesus People," *Cornerstone* (March-April, 1982, Vol. 10, Issue 59) is an example. The article concludes: "The religion of humanism has such a stranglehold on the courts and on the public school system that if we're going to survive with our religious liberty, we're going to have to stand up and be counted."

Unfortunately however, most of the good reports were brief and/or not the main fountain-heads of evangelical public opinion. The second-hand reports, taken largely from secular sources, are to date the dominant influence from the Christian media.

PRAISE FOR THE NOVELS OF RACHAEL HERRON

Splinters of Light

"A poignant, profound ode to the enduring and redemptive power of love. Very much like Lisa Genova's *Still Alice* (although the writing here is better!), this title is sure to resonate with fans of . . . Jodi Picoult and Genova and will have the book clubs lining up." —*Library Journal*

"Beautifully written and heartbreakingly real . . . a compelling examination of how the bonds between women—sisters, mothers, daughters—are tested by tragedy. The Glass family women will have you smiling in recognition and then grieving, laughing, and (consider yourself warned) sobbing along with them right up to the heartfelt ending."

—L. Alison Heller, author of *The Never Never Sisters*

"An awesome book that grabs the reader by the heartstrings and wrings emotions from the soul."

—Carolyn Brown, *New York Times* bestselling author of *Long, Hot Texas Summer*

"This story will be with me for a very long time."

—Kritters Ramblings

"A beautiful story." —ABCD Diaries

continued . . .

Written by today's freshest new talents and selected by New American Library, NAL Accent novels touch on subjects close to a woman's heart, from friendship to family to finding our place in the world. The Conversation Guides included in each book are intended to enrich the individual reading experience, as well as encourage us to explore these topics together—because books, and life, are meant for sharing.

Visit us online at penguin.com.

"Herron has written a tenderly crafted story, compelling the reader to examine some difficult issues—single parenthood, family dynamics, and the heartbreaking realities of early-onset Alzheimer's—and handles each one with sensitivity and compassion. But the beauty of this novel lies in the strength and resilience of the love between two sisters."

—Kimberly Brock, author of *The River Witch*

"With this profoundly moving, compelling tale of a woman who is on the verge of losing everything, Rachael Herron will break your heart and then mend it again, leaving you stronger than before."

—Holly Robinson, author of *Haven Lake*

Pack Up the Moon

"The perfect vacation or staycation read. It's filled with fiercely honest emotion, a celebration of the power of love to heal even the most broken of hearts."

—Susan Wiggs, #1 *New York Times* bestselling author of
The Beekeeper's Ball

"A superlative architect of story, Rachael Herron never steers away from wrenching events, and yet even moments of deepest despair are laced with threads of hope. It's impossible to stop turning the pages, breathless to discover the fate of beautifully drawn characters who are ravaged by loss and rescued by their devotion to each other. Herron is an inexhaustible champion of the healing power of love."

—Sophie Littlefield, national bestselling author of
House of Glass

"A heartbreaking story of loss and family that achieves an optimistic feel in the end. . . . The language [is] poetic and moving at many points."

—*RT Book Reviews*

ALSO BY RACHAEL HERRON

Pack Up the Moon
Splinters of Light

the ones who
matter most

RACHAEL HERRON

NAL ACCENT
Published by New American Library,
an imprint of Penguin Random House LLC
375 Hudson Street, New York, New York 10014

This book is an original publication of New American Library.

First Printing, April 2016

For more information about Penguin Random House, visit penguin.com.

LIBRARY OF CONGRESS CATALOGING-IN-PUBLICATION DATA:

Names: Herron, Rachael, author.
Title: The ones who matter most/Rachael Herron.
Description: New York, New York: New American Library, [2016]
Identifiers: LCCN 2015043882 | ISBN 9780451476760 (paperback)
Subjects: LCSH: Domestic fiction. | BISAC: FICTION/Contemporary Women. |
FICTION/Family Life. | FICTION/Literary.
Classification: LCC PS3608.E7765 O54 2016 | DDC 813/.6—dc23
LC record available at http://lccn.gov/2015043882

Printed in the United States of America
10 9 8 7 6 5 4 3 2

Designed by Kelly Lipovich

Penguin
Random
House

This one's for Dad and Lola, with love

the ones who
matter most

chapter *one*

Abby Roberts tucked a sachet of allspice and thyme—
for healing and courage—into her jeans pocket and
mouthed again the words she'd thought she'd never say to
her husband.

She'd practiced them all day. "I want a divorce," Abby had
whispered to the overwintering kale, her knuckles darkened
with dirt. "It's not you; it's me," she tried on the bag of bone
meal. Poking her fingers into the ground around the baby broccoli starts, she said, "No, wait. This *is* about you. How *dare* you?"

Divorce.

Unthinkable.

Not that she was against it for others, of course. There were
seasons where divorce seemed to be contagious, roaring through
couples they knew like wildfire, burning up carefully decorated
homes and meticulously wrought child-care plans. And even
though it was commonplace, the word was always a shock of

ice water to the face. No one was ever casual about that kind of gossip. "The Quinceys are getting divorced? Well, they never seemed to be that happy. Want to get a coffee?" No, the response was always abject horror. "You're *kidding*. I can't *believe* it." Seventy years after feminism made divorce something that could be both borne and afforded, it was still mentioned in a dropped voice, with a moment of silence, an invisible crossing of the body, a warding off.

The fact that Abby needed a divorce was flattening. She was a bruised pansy pressed between the pages of a book she never thought she would have to read.

Scott's truck pulled into the driveway. His quick footfalls came up the porch steps. The door opened—he was often late, but he was always cheerful and apologetic. "Look! Yellow roses! It's not Valentine's Day yet, but I thought I'd surprise you early."

Had he felt her anger across town? While he was rounding up his gardening crew, buying his latte, settling in at the office, and putting his dirt-worn fingers on the Mac keyboard, had he somehow known what the doctor had told her? Had he thought then of buying her flowers?

No. They'd never had that kind of connection. So many other kinds of connection, yes. Humor, sex, fun. But he'd never been able to read her mind.

"Thank you." Ten years together—she was thirty-six; how the hell had that happened so quickly?—and he'd never seemed to remember that she didn't like roses. She loved their hips, for their myriad uses, but not the flowers themselves. "I want a divorce." Her voice was loud. Too loud.

Scott froze, one arm out of his jacket, one arm still in. His face went carefully blank, as if she were a difficult client, one who wanted the newly laid sod ripped out and Astroturf put in. "Sorry?"

It was exponentially harder to say it a second time. "I want a divorce."

There was a stillness after that, a muting of the sounds that usually traveled through their big old house. She couldn't hear the whirring of the ceiling fan or the rumble of traffic that drifted down from Solano Avenue. The house was as numb as Abby.

Scott squinted at her. His mouth moved strangely, twisting sideways.

She wanted to reach forward and take her words back. *I was kidding. Never mind. Bad joke, I'm sorry.*

But she didn't.

Scott finished taking off his jacket and hung it on the coat-tree. The knot in Abby's throat moved up until her jaw was clenched so tightly she wondered whether she would break a tooth waiting for him to say something.

"Honey," he finally said. "What?"

"I want a divorce."

His face was red. "No."

Fear bit at her hands, gnawing at the last bit of bravery she had clinging to her fingers. "Yes." She wouldn't tell him why. Not now. He deserved to sweat. To hurt.

Scott walked out of the living room and into the hall bathroom. He shut the door gently behind him. The exit was his statement, and Abby had no idea what to do next. She'd spent hours trying to predict which way tonight would go, but she hadn't ever wondered what she would do if he left the room altogether.

She stood in the hallway, leaning against the wall. She listened to her husband—the man who would soon be her ex-husband—urinate. He would make sure not to drip, as usual. He'd put the seat down afterward, because he'd always been considerate that way.

Then there was a crash.

Had he thrown the framed picture of Vernazza? Scott wasn't a thrower when he was mad, but Abby didn't know what else it could be—the sound was loud enough that it traveled under the door and through the hardwood, up into the soles of her bare feet, into her knees, through her empty stomach, traveling to her chest, where the sound waves battered her heart.

Or—had he fallen? That wasn't likely, though. You didn't just trip in your own bathroom, did you? But Abby froze at the thought, terrified into solid ice. She was glaciate, the frost in her blood too thick to allow motion. Instead, she listened as hard as she could for any sound at all.

There was nothing.

Bastard. Was he messing with her? Again?

She pressed her ear to the door.

Still nothing.

She knocked. "Scott?"

The house, all of it, was silent. The only thing Abby could hear was her own heart pounding and tripping over itself.

She smelled lemon balm, sharp and pungent, and only then did her brain finally—*finally*—allow her feet to move, her hands to hit at the door, beat at it (why had he locked it? who did that in their own home?). Eventually, at the urging of the 911 dispatcher, she knocked the door open with her shoulder.

He was on the floor, his red face now green-gray. His eyes opened and closed slowly. He looked vaguely pleased to see her. *"Scott."* She scrabbled at his arm, which was twisted under his body at an awful angle—he must have broken it as he fell, as he partially wedged himself between the toilet and the sink. "Scott, get *up*." She tugged at his shirt, patting at his face, scrubbing his skin with the tips of her fingers as if she could bring the redness back. There was no anger in his eyes, none at all. There was no fear. He only gazed at her, blinking with an interested look of confusion.

Then he closed his eyes. For good.

chapter *two*

"Found anything yet?" Kathryn called from the kitchen. "Only keep the good memories, remember."

Abby jumped. She stared at the living room bookshelf as if she'd never seen it before. "Almost!" She was supposed to be finding something to give away. Kathryn said it would help her. She wasn't sure how. She wasn't sure about anything.

Every time Abby thought of her husband lying in the funeral home, the twisted mass of manzanita lodged in her chest sprouted three or four more sharp red branches. At some point, she was pretty sure it would grow up and through her esophagus, and she'd die.

Good memories.

Memories were sharp, a razor blade dipped in cayenne powder. It had been only two days since she'd dialed 911, since the ambulance had called the coroner, since her husband's body had been rolled out of the house on a gurney, a dark cloth over his face as if they'd been suddenly transported into an extremely boring episode of *CSI*, one in which the person died just because he died. Just because Scott's heart—his large and loving and careless heart—had decided to shut down like a computer monitor. He'd been only thirty-eight. If his heart *had* been a computer monitor, it would have still been under warranty.

Scott's handkerchief in her hand, a can of Pledge in her other, she looked for things to dust in the living room, but their housecleaner—*her* housecleaner now—was too efficient. Dust didn't settle for long.

"Are you sure it's going okay in there, girlie?" Kathryn poked her head out of the kitchen.

"Great!" Lies were ready in her larynx, eager to spring out. She had agreed with Kathryn that decluttering might help. One of many recent lies, it just stacked on top of the assertions she'd made to the funeral home (*I'm fine, thank you*) and to her next-door neighbor (*Yes, I actually did sleep okay last night*). Yesterday, the day after Scott had died, her entire house had been full of friends. Brook, with her almost-painful hugs laced with the smell of the soap she made; Therese, with that way of listening that made you want to tell her the truth; Vivian, with the wine; Simone, with the Scotch. Abby had lied to each one of them, one after another. *I'll make it through this. I'll be all right. You're making all the difference in the world, just being here.* And Kathryn, of course. Kathryn was always there, in the background, holding things together. Abby didn't lie to Kathryn. Much.

What Abby wanted she couldn't say to anyone, not even to Kathryn.

She wanted to get the fuck *out*. To move. To leave through the front door empty-handed and not even bother to lock it behind her. No looking back. If Abby's garden hadn't been

RACHAEL HERRON

behind the house, if she could have slipped it into her pocket whole—onion sets and perfect compost (such *gorgeous*, sweet-earth-smelling dirt) and all—she thought she might actually have done it.

Today, though, Kathryn had arrived with a plan of action instead of another kind of tea. She'd reached forward and taken Abby's hands in hers. "Darling girlie. Let's look at clutter today."

It was an excuse, Abby knew it was. The house was tidy. There wasn't much clutter anyway (except in her potting shed, and she loved that just the way it was). This was Kathryn helping her *do* something instead of letting her lie in bed in shock.

"Okay."

"So, let's get rid of a few of the extraneous things."

"Wait—"

"Not throwing his things away. Nothing like that. This will just make you feel lighter, give you another place to store a little of your sadness."

Maybe it would work. Darling old hippie Kathryn, with her perma-scent of Nag Champa and weed, often knew what was best.

"You go work in the living room, my girlie. Get rid of a few things that are just pretty, a couple of things you're not passionate about. Keep the good memories only. Don't you worry about me—we'll go through everything I think you can get rid of. I'm only looking for things like fondue sets and heated ice cream scoops. Things you don't use, that you don't care about."

Funny, thought Abby, they (no, *she*) owned both those things. Wedding gifts, as useless as emoticons in a voice mail.

She ran the handkerchief over the mantel clock. Scott had

always wound it. It had stopped at one twenty-three. She hadn't even noticed the chiming stop.

Everyone *said* Abby hadn't actually been the cause of Scott's demise, everyone from Scott's GP to the priest she'd confessed to yesterday. (Abby wasn't Catholic and the priest had seemed irritated behind the red wood panel. She'd left feeling very small and even sadder than when she'd garnered the courage to pull open the confessional door.)

And while in the smart, sensible forefront of her mind, she knew she hadn't killed Scott, in the back of her mind— the part that held old bits of Latin from college and an exact memory of the first time she'd ever smelled wisteria—she knew she had killed him.

But he'd started it.

He'd gotten a vasectomy. In secret. She'd gone in to talk about her fertility, and the doctor had looked so confused. *But I assumed you knew.* Then there had been a terrible, awkward few sentences while the doctor explained he'd just violated medical privacy rules, and he shouldn't have accidentally told her.

She was his *wife.* She wasn't supposed to *know*? The whole last year of hope (silent, secret hope), the whole time she'd been clocking her ovulation, making sure they had sex, living in hope that turned to familiar disappointment again and again, almost (incredibly) missing the miscarriages (at least she'd been pregnant a few times, life inside for weeks at a time), the whole last year of non-conception wasn't her fault. It was *his*.

So she'd killed him by asking for a divorce. His damaged heart had just stopped beating.

Her fault. All hers.

"Um." Kathryn cleared her throat behind Abby. "Is that a handkerchief? You don't have a rag somewhere?"

Abby held up the light blue striped linen. She'd bought them, classic and soft, for Scott to keep in his pocket. She thought he'd like the old-fashionedness of them. But after folding the first one with a smile and shoving it into the pocket of his chinos, he'd never used one. She'd taken to keeping one in her purse, or in the pocket of her sweater. They came in surprisingly handy. She'd used one just the other day to wipe off the inside of her car's window. The heater had been spitting that invisible film that obscured the world, and the expensive handkerchief of Scott's was just right to make it clear again. They were nice to wash, too. They came out clean and ready to go. The opposite of a Kleenex gone through the wash—handkerchiefs were there for you after the dry cycle ended. Intact. Still strong.

"Abby?"

She'd been staring again. "Laundry," she said, and moved around Kathryn, dodging her concerned gaze. "I love laundry. You know?"

Kathryn just nodded, her long, mismatched crystal earrings jangling.

Abby dropped the handkerchief into the washer with satisfaction. She wished she could keep the feeling, wring it between her hands and smash it into her thighs, push it into her cheeks, keeping it for later when she'd really need it, when she was alone. Alone. *Shit.* The breath went out of her again. Scott was gone. She'd lost him.

But she'd wanted him to leave.

Where did that put her? What was she supposed to feel?

Abby turned on the washer, adding the still-clean kitchen rug to make the cycle worth it. She choked, and swallowed what felt like a mouthful of dryer lint.

Kathryn said, "It's grief, honey. Let yourself feel it."

Feel it? Oh, no. No, thank you. She wasn't strong enough for that. When her grandparents died, the grief had been terrible. When her parents died, it had been so much worse, ripping her out at the roots.

This new grief was different. Unexpected. This was bodily, enormous, too big for her. It was grief for Scott, and also, secondarily but just as monumentally, for the children she would never have with him. The names she'd never use. The grief was the monster in the washing machine when the cycle went off-balance, that house-jarring thudding that made her feel like the walls were about to come down around her ears.

Abby propped her hip against the washing machine.

Kathryn said something behind her, words that didn't add up to a sentence in her brain. Then, "Abby?"

Against Abby's thigh, the washing machine gave a warning grumble.

She turned to face the machine, and put one hand on either side of it. She would damn well try to hold it in place if she had to. She would figure out how to be strong enough. For once. If the machine started to judder and thump across the floor, she would sink her fingers right through the metal, ignoring the blood that mixed with the wash water. If the house rocked on its base, she would try to hold it—all of it—in place.

"Abby. I'm right here."

What she wanted to do was turn and grab Kathryn by the shoulders. *I can't do this. I can't do any of this.* The sharp, breath-taking pain of grief warred with something else, a feeling she wouldn't—couldn't—acknowledge.

My fault, my fault. My fault.

The other feeling, the one she could never admit to, was the slip of relief—a newly bloomed silver lupine—vulnerable to air itself. Abby knew if she brushed her fingertips against it even once, it would die.

So she stood and held the washer as it shook the way she wanted to so badly.

chapter *three*

Abby had believed in *Till death us do part*. She had believed in it so *hard*.

For two years before they died, Abby's mother (ovarian) and father (prostate) had made chemo appointments together, each refusing to let the poison drip into only one of them. They held hands while the nurses wiped away furious tears at the injustice of it. Hospice took over. The volunteers couldn't stop crying. Their doctors conferred and agreed: neither of them had much time left. Abby's parents had gotten dispensation from the mortuary on Green Avenue in Berkeley to be buried together in a coffin custom-made to fit them both. Abby's mother died first, and her body was held at the mortuary, cold and chemically prepared, until Abby's father finally let go nine days later. The inside of their joint coffin was lined with blue silk the exact same shade as their bedroom walls. A faux head-board matched the one they'd commissioned from a Santa Cruz woodworker for their first anniversary. At the funeral, the twenty-two-year-old Abby would have crawled in bed with them as she had so many times before if Kathryn, her mother's best friend, hadn't slipped her a limb-dulling Ativan just before they walked into the church.

When her parents died, she was left with only Kathryn for family. In the billions of people on the planet, she had no one related to her by blood at all. She'd had a sister, once. Well, that wasn't exactly the way she thought of it. Her mother had given birth to a baby girl who'd lived just one day, a year before Abby came along. She'd been raised knowing she was missing something she couldn't understand. Her sister, Meg. Gone before she really existed. She'd always thought the loss didn't really count.

(Now, of course, she understood the loss better.)

Scott had been her landscape architect. As a trained botanist, she shouldn't have needed one, but while good—no, excellent—with plants, she'd never had a knack for lawns. The house she'd bought in Berkeley with her inheritance had a vast expanse of green velvet that came with an equally vast set of neighborhood expectations.

The first time Scott kissed her, they'd been talking. Just talking. About . . . she could hardly remember now. Something about a problem with Bermuda grass? Whatever it was, it had just been an excuse, for both of them. He'd smelled like the lawn itself, strongly green, like herbal tea made from an apple Jolly Rancher. He was smart (so much smarter than she would have guessed, just from watching him ride the riding mower like it was a long-legged horse). He was carefree. Self-effacing. And when he kissed her, she lost all knowledge of where her feet were—she was floating, they were together, and that was all that mattered.

They started dating.

He wanted to know everything about her, but he hid parts of himself from her, which only made her more interested in what she couldn't see. He said his apartment was too small for her to visit, that he'd be embarrassed if she saw it. He wanted to do so much, change the world to a brighter, greener place. *Roberts and Sons,* he'd say, looking at her, as if she could help with the last word. And god, she wanted to. She could practically feel the eggs in her womb lining up, readying themselves. He had no family, and seemed ashamed of that, too.

"I have no family, either," Abby whispered to him, the old loneliness of the words choking her. "Not anymore."

Three months into their relationship, he couldn't afford a ring, so he made her one out of red clover stems. She wound one for him out of six braided pine needles, and then they lost the rings in the sheets.

Marriage meant family. *Her* family.

When Abby and Scott married, Kathryn walked Abby down the short aisle at St. Edward's Episcopal. Abby wore a mermaid-style pale cream, raw silk dress with just a few carefully placed beads. She felt her mother smiling down at her from somewhere above the transept.

Till death us do part. Abby's voice shook as she said the words, but Scott's confident voice rang all the way up to the rafters.

chapter *four*

Abby lifted out the load of dry clothes and put them into the laundry basket. So much less of it now. She wished she wore more clothes, more often, just so she'd have more to fold.

"Have you eaten today?" From behind her, in the kitchen, Kathryn opened the fridge and then tsked. "Even one thing? You haven't touched the roast chicken I left you."

"I think I ate some of it." Abby brought the basket out of the laundry room and set it on the kitchen table so she could fold it. "Yesterday."

"Today, sweet girl? Tell me what you've eaten." Kathryn's hair was falling out of the braid she'd put it in. Her T-shirt was black, and torn right above the Grateful Dead bear's eye. It might have been ripped lower, too, but Kathryn's favorite overalls covered the worst damage. A few years more than sixty, she always looked like a hurricane survivor. If anything, though, she was the force of the hurricane itself. Kathryn had been Abby's mother's best friend, and she was the rock to which Abby had clung when her parents died. After the joint funeral, Kathryn had moved into Abby's spare room for two weeks, saying only, "Your mother was my best friend for most of my life. Let's work our way through this together. Come with me to the nursery tomorrow. I'll teach you how to garden." Abby's pale blond thumb had been vibrantly jade by the time Kathryn had gone back to the house she shared with her wife, Rebecca. Abby had gone back to school for biological science, and the day Abby was hired at the Berkeley Arboretum, Kathryn had been thrilled. *I'm only in it for the free plants you'll give me, my girlie,* Kathryn had said, but Abby had felt her own mother's pride coming through Kathryn's radiant smile, too.

Right after she and Scott had married, the arboretum had a major budget crunch and they had to let half their staff go. Abby didn't need the money, thanks to her parents' property investments. Instead of going after another job, she'd fallen in love with the patch of dirt behind the house. There, with her hands in the soil and the sun on her face, she could forget for hours how much she missed her parents. Her full-time obsession became her carefully tended beds. Every year that passed, her plants became as important to her as Scott's clients did to him. As Scott's business thrived, so did Abby's garden. Her bear's-foot hellebore was so precious to her she would have counted it among her friends, and while she knew she needed to pinch off the lime basil's flowers to keep it from getting leggy, she did it gently so the plant knew it was appreciated.

Then she started infusing oils with herbs, selling them in small batches to herbalists and soap makers locally. Kathryn sold them from a countertop at her nursery. Abby knew she could do more with it, but the business end of things made her cranky. She didn't *want* to invest time in a Web site or marketing. What was the point of a Facebook page, the upkeep of which would keep her out of the garden? She just wanted to grow things, to transform them into oils and tinctures that brought out their healing properties. Rue flower for headache and arthritis. Ginger for PMS and joint pain. It made Abby happy to see the oils darkening in their bottles. Her potting shed, where she worked, smelled like heaven: dirt and spice and dried burdock and calendula.

Scott had been dead for only two days.

She wondered idly if there was an herb for loneliness. Water violet, maybe, since it encouraged warmer relationships.

She wondered if there was an herb for penance.

Now Kathryn's silver eyebrow jumped. "Will you answer me, please? Or are you just going to do fake laundry all day?"

"No."

"Okay, then, what about sleep?" Kathryn put a hand on her hip, an unstoppable loving force, an embrace wrapped in a train crash. "Huh?"

Abby twisted a dryer-warm washcloth in her fingers and cast her thoughts back to her afternoon nap. Unable to stay awake after two phone calls from the mortuary, she'd gone back to bed and pulled the covers over her head, dropping into a heavy slumber. Hours later, she'd rolled over in bed and had felt for a moment, before she came back to full consciousness, a burst of pure happiness. That feeling—an unforgivable lightness in the center of her chest—kept hitting her out of the blue. She'd forgotten, again, that she was a new widow. All she'd known was that the bed was empty, and that sun spilled over the windowsill and onto the new duvet she'd found herself buying at Nordstrom. Before Scott died—the word was still so foreign to her as it pertained to him, *died*, *dead*, *deceased*—she'd kept the bedroom well-appointed with gender-neutral grays and taupes, highlighted by eggshell and dove accents. At the department store, shopping for something appropriate to wear for the memorial service, she'd shocked herself by spontaneously buying a lemon and pink duvet cover.

It felt like a new bed.

"I slept. I napped today."

"And food?"

Did thirty drops of Saint-John's-wort tincture in a cup of ginger tea count as eating? "I think I had a yogurt."

Kathryn, never one to avoid confrontation, kicked the foot lever of the garbage compactor and slid it open. "Really?"

"Really."

"Where's the container, sugarplum?"

"Are you calling me a liar?" She was one, of course. "It was mango peach."

"Aren't you allergic to mango?"

Abby pulled open the drawer that held her napkins and touched them, enjoying their flat green smoothness. Last night she'd washed a whole load of clean ones, just so she could justify washing her bathroom towel, used only once. "I'm not. I don't know why you always say that."

"Mango made your mouth itch that one time."

"Once. I was six. Thirty *years* ago."

"Oral allergies are nothing to mess with. They can change quickly. Do you have an EpiPen?"

"Of course I don't."

"Have one of mine." Kathryn dove into her huge jute purse and came up with a yellow tube.

"Come on."

"I have two spares at home and one in the car even though the doctor warned me they shouldn't get too hot."

"But . . . what are you allergic to?"

"Nothin'. But I swear to the goddess, every customer who walks through the asters and marigolds seems to be deathly allergic to bees, so I keep them handy. One guy bought a bare-root lemon tree last week and then came running back in with his hands swelled up like fat little balloons. He knew he was allergic to citrus, but he didn't think the tree would hurt him."

"You would stick a person with one of those without knowing if they had a prescription?"

"Sure. I'd probably save their lives."

"Wait, how did *you* get a prescription?"

Kathryn shrugged. "Lied."

"Don't they test you for that?"

"With what, a lie detector? Nah. Powers of persuasion."

"Well, maybe your dream will come true and you'll save a life someday. Be the hero." Scott had needed a hero. When she'd dialed 911, the dispatcher had talked her through CPR. Abby hadn't done it well enough, or fast enough, or something. She hadn't been enough to save him.

Kathryn slid the still-open garbage bin closed quietly, the opposite of the way she usually slammed it. "Not the hero," she said. "Just a helper." She held out the EpiPen.

"Fine." Abby put it into the junk drawer next to the scissors with the broken handle that she kept forgetting to throw out.

Kathryn moved back to the refrigerator. "Here." She held up a raspberry yogurt.

"No, thank you."

Kathryn peeled off the foil top and plucked a spoon from the drawer. "Eat, please? Make me happy?"

"I hate raspberry."

"No, you don't. It's in your fridge. Why would you have it if you didn't like it?"

Abby didn't feel like pulling the punch. "That was Scott's."

"Oh. Shit." Kathryn blinked hard. "I'm so sorry, girlie."

Abby shook her head, ignoring the silver sparks that swam at the edge of her vision. "It's fine. I ate his disgusting pistachio ice cream last night just because it was the only sweet thing in the whole house. Except for that yogurt, apparently, but I'd forgotten about that." Tears thickened the back of her throat. *Scott.* Scott and his stupid taste in disgusting ice cream. He liked rum raisin, too, and no one in the whole world liked rum raisin.

Kathryn pitched the yogurt into the garbage. "Fuck raspberry. I'm sorry."

Abby said, "It's fine." And it was. Grief as thick as mold coated her soul, but at the very bottom of it, if she had scraped off the greenness, she knew she would find a bit of light.

She'd find a bit of relief. She'd find a bit of desperate and totally unforgivable hope.

chapter *five*

Abby's phone buzzed with a text while she was crouched over, fighting with the lowest drawer on Scott's desk. She was *sure* she had the right key—it matched the patina on the brass drawer pulls. And it almost fit. She jiggled it harder.

Her phone buzzed again.

Abby fell backward onto the Berber carpet. "Damn."

The text was from Kathryn. *Don't get too carried away. Take your time. You don't need to go through everything now.*

Abby snorted. Too late. Kathryn's decluttering encouragement had stuck a windup key in Abby's back. She was wound to the edge of snapping, but if she kept moving, she'd be able to soldier her way right through this. It was *good* to get rid of things. It felt great. His stuff—that would be easy to pitch, right?

Abby jiggled the key again, then turned it upside down and tried for the fourth time. Stupid key.

Stupid *desk*. It was the size of a small cow, and—Abby was just guessing—probably just as unwieldy. She'd always thought the huge rolltop would look better a foot to the left, closer to the light of the window, but once the deliverymen had dropped it into place (a gift from her to Scott on their third anniversary, when he was busy enough with the business to have to work from home some nights), she and Scott couldn't move it, not even a millimeter.

Abby had never opened even one drawer of it. She'd never had a reason to. She had her own desk, upstairs, in her bright office, where she researched gladiolus and spearmint varieties. She didn't need to go through his files. She didn't care about his clients' needs for drip irrigation or the perfect succulent to complete their desert landscape.

So when the key finally persuaded the largest bottom drawer to open, when she was finally staring down into it, she was shocked by what she found. There were no files. No paperwork. Not even a stapler. There was just a pile of *Urban Garden* magazines, a half-eaten bag of white cheddar popcorn, some paper towels, and a white box.

Abby's mouth went dry, her tongue sticking thickly to the roof of her mouth, as if she'd balled up one of the paper towels and placed it on her tongue, a bulky Communion wafer of fear.

She scrabbled at the other, smaller drawers, the ones that hadn't seemed important enough to start with.

He worked in here at night. Often. He would have paperwork somewhere, right? Work stuff.

But the top drawer just held three boxes of Nerds. The wood itself smelled of fake blueberry. What the *hell*? Nerds weren't even a *candy*. Not really. They were just pressed sugar, in the flavors of red and green and yellow. She hadn't had any since she was in her teens, but could still remember exactly how purple (not grape, just purple) felt in her mouth. Abby tried a pink one. The flavor exploded in her mouth, as pink as a little girl's shoe. Nothing about the flavor came from something she would recognize in nature. She held up the small box, twisting it in the insubstantial light. *Double Dipped Lemonade Wild Cherry.*

Abby tossed a palmful more of the pink rocks into her mouth and crunched hard.

Sugar felt amazing. She could practically feel the sugar receptors in her brain light up. She'd been trying to go easy on it recently, keeping it mostly out of the house, eating raisins when she felt the craving. Scott had been trying, too, indulging only in ice cream when he needed a fix, saying it was lower glycemic and therefore okay. Where had he even bought these? When had he sneaked them in the house?

On a hunch, she moved the mouse on his Mac, and the screen lit up obediently. She brought up his Amazon page, his password conveniently autofilling. They had separate accounts, both linked to the joint checking account that Abby had never bothered to pay attention to. She hated to admit it, and wouldn't do so to her friends who shopped responsibly and locally, but in the middle of the night, she'd sometimes remember that they were out of toothpicks, or salsa, or paper towels. It was easier to open the app on her phone and hit one-click-purchase than it was to find a pen to write it down to add to the shopping list the next morning. The boxes would show up, jars of mayo and bottles of white vinegar triple-wrapped in plastic bubbles and multiple layers of cardboard, both of which Abby would carefully recycle to at least be able to pretend that her order, delivered right to her door, had a carbon footprint less than that of a Humvee.

Maybe Scott had done something similar.

And there it was. His last order had been two boxes of MoonPies and a bottle of Jack Daniel's. Sent to his office.

Of course. It wasn't like she checked his work bag when he got home. After a healthy dinner of lean chicken breast and fresh broccoli from her garden, it would have been easy for Scott to squirrel MoonPies into his desk drawers. The meals she made for him with thought and love and the freshest herbs possible, weren't enough for him.

The worst part of the hidden candy was that if Scott had brought a package of MoonPies into the house under his arm, if he'd held them up and announced, "Look what I brought home!" Abby would have laughed. She loved it when he satisfied himself. He bought expensive, locally brewed beer, and liked to talk his way through a bottle, discussing the flavors (cherry! anise! vanilla!) with her. He'd been the one who'd insisted on the raised spa tub in the master bath when they'd done the last renovation, and she'd loved watching him run the taps, adjusting the water, playing with the different buttons, showing her the action of the jets. She'd used the tub itself way more than he did. He loved to sit on the fluffy blue bath mat, laughing at her as she sank under the water and blew bubbles. *I love you,* she told him from underneath the warm weight. *I love you* in bubbles, light as air.

With every miscarriage, they'd moved further apart. Not that either of them had admitted it. They'd moved from lying in bed locked in a love jail of their own making, both of them delightedly fascinated by every tiny facet of each other's bodies and minds, to living separately, so alone that not even their online accounts talked to each other.

Abby unrolled a Tootsie Roll and popped it into her mouth.

Damn. She could eat all this sugar herself if she wanted to (and she kind of did).

The sudden slight thrill that rocketed through her to the tips of her fingers was probably caused by the sugar high. That was all.

She rubbed her eyes and took a deep, shaky breath. Back to the job at hand. She checked the pigeonhole drawers at the top of the desk.

Empty.

How did a person leave drawers *empty*? Jobless? If this had been Abby's desk, she'd have used one of the tiny drawers for the hair bands she was always trying to find while she was working. She'd use one drawer for the orange mechanical pencils she loved. Another drawer for lip balm. These drawers were empty. Wasted.

Her hand went back to the biggest drawer. She hesitated before opening it again, the hairs on the backs of her arms prickling. She shivered once, hard. Then she slid the drawer open again and pushed aside the bag of cheddar popcorn. Scott was lucky they didn't have mice. (No, that wasn't okay to think. He hadn't been lucky in any way at all.)

She pulled out the white box.

Photos.

Relief swamped her as she deliberately exhaled. Just photos.

Abby smiled as she flipped through them. A younger, thinner Scott grinned at the camera. He'd been so *gorgeous* and young and gloriously cocksure. She could almost hear the boom of his laugh, feel the bottomlessness of it. There were shots of him in what looked like a shared house filled with old sofas and bongs propped on coffee tables, him leaning on various girls. Playing beer pong with guys whose faces were frozen in perpetual whoops. Shooting pool in a garage under a garish orange lamp, looking as confident as he had waiting for her to walk down the aisle.

And then there was a short stack of pictures of him with a dark-haired woman.

Abby felt her jaw tense. It was such a small sensation that she almost missed it. She could still dump the pile of photos back into the box, close it, and put the whole thing into the recycling even though photo paper was probably technically too glossy.

But she didn't. She flipped to the next picture.

Scott's arm was around the woman as they stood in front of a large white column. They were dressed up, as if at someone's wedding. Scott was in a suit. The woman was pretty in a simple kind of way with large, wide-set brown eyes, and teeth that looked strong and useful. She might have been Latina. Her long dark hair looked heavy, and though it was straight in the picture, it frizzed into a dark halo around her head, as if it curled naturally, and her skin was a dark olive. She wore a light peach dress and a lacy cream shawl. The setting was familiar, but she couldn't put her finger on it— Abby *knew* that the bay was just out of sight, the Golden Gate close by. . . . The Palace of Fine Arts?

The next picture confirmed it. There was the rotunda and the lagoon, the gorgeous green stretch of lawn flanked by eucalyptus trees.

The funny part, the really *weird* part, was that Scott and the dark-haired woman looked as if they were the center of all the pictures. There were no pictures of the bride and groom, if they were indeed at a wedding. Or had this girlfriend been so important to him that they'd scheduled a real photo shoot?

The most incomprehensible picture of all was the one in which Scott was kneeling on the ground in front of the woman, his hands on her flat belly. They were both laughing into each other's eyes, and neither of them looked at all conscious of the person holding the camera.

Why would they pose like that? It almost looked like one of those cheesy pregnant couple poses. Abby peered into the photograph as if she could get close enough to hear what Scott was saying to the woman.

So odd. Abby shook her head. Another chill ran down her arms.

She should stop going through the box. She should toss it. Right now. It wasn't her business. Scott was gone. She rubbed her bottom lip. Then she looked at the next picture.

Two hands, a man's and a woman's, on top of each other's. With brand-new sparkly rings.

One of the hands was Scott's. She knew his work-worn knuckles like she knew her own. Only his thumb crooked that way. He was almost double-jointed and proud of it.

That peach dress the woman was wearing—it was the woman's wedding dress. The woman and Scott weren't *at* someone's wedding. They *were* the wedding.

Jesus.

Married. He'd been married.

Before her.

Married.

Abby stood, unable to stay in his chair. She walked backward until her calves ran into the low sofa. She stood in place, the photos gripped in her hands.

How . . . how had she never known? How had he never *mentioned* it? Wasn't that something you *had* to tell the person you were engaged to marry? She scanned her memory, searching for some kind of law, something she could have had him arrested for. Back then. Before she married him.

She flipped through the pictures faster, her larynx so tight she coughed.

A photo of them kissing under a colonnade. The woman fit into Scott's arms in a way Abby had once thought only she herself did.

She covered her mouth and stared closer at the picture of Scott and the woman driving away in a shiny black Honda. It was decorated with *Just Married* on the windows and tin cans tied to the bumper. Just like Abby and Scott had. The car decorating had been Scott's idea. Abby had thought it was retro and clever and adorable.

Holy shit.

Then Abby came to the last photo. The color of the paper was different, the feel of it thinner. Less substantial. She let out a low, strangled cry.

A gobsmacked-looking Scott held a ridiculously red newborn. From a narrow hospital bed on the other side of Scott and the baby, the dark-haired woman was radiant, tears in her eyes, hope lighting her face like sunlight.

chapter *six*

Abby didn't sleep, even after half a Benadryl followed by the second half an hour later. Even though the bed still felt new under the pink and lemon (Nerds-colored) duvet, her brain spun, whirring faster and hotter like a disk drive about to die.

Scott had a baby. A *baby*.

A child. Of his own.

Scott had a child of his *own*?

When dawn came, when the clock crept past five, then six, and finally seven—an almost-decent time to call someone—Abby shook the ache from her clenched fingers and reached for her cell. But when she lit the screen and looked at her contacts list, her mind went blank. Kathryn would . . . God, she'd be wrecked. She'd be furious, the spitting mad she got at misogyny and terrorist acts. She'd stage a protest march or something. And then she'd try to take care of Abby. Abby wasn't ready for that. She could call her friend Yvette, but with four kids under the age of five, Yvette was always at her rope's end. She didn't need Abby's problems. Lisa had been around so much already this week, and today she'd been going to her sister's house. . . .

Brook. Brook had problems. Man problems, kid problems, money problems. Brook wouldn't judge. Every time Abby sold Brook a case of herb-infused oils to use in her soapmaking, she ended up staying five hours. They'd met because of Abby's business, but they'd become friends almost instantly.

But she just got Brook's voice mail. "Leave a message and I'll— Oh crap. *Put your sister down, Danny!*" For once, the recorded message didn't make Abby laugh. She hung up without saying anything after the beep.

Abby kept her eyes dry, locked onto the ceiling fan. Waiting.

At eight, Abby let herself rise and dress. She made coffee and toast. Then she went back to Scott's desk. Yesterday, when she'd started going through it, she'd gone slowly, jiggling the key with care so as not to harm the lock. Now she let her body go feral. She was a crime scene in action. She ripped out all the drawers and dumped them upside down, in case he'd taped anything to the wood bottoms. She reached inside, searching for false backs. One drawer was stubborn about lifting from its tracks, so she yanked out the metal with nothing but brute force.

She pulled every single thing out of his office closet, throwing shoes and ski equipment over her shoulder without looking. A snowboard hit the top of the side of the rolltop, driving a deep gouge into the wood. She threw a ski pole at the wall clock, which hit the floor with a satisfying crunch. She moved the sofa away from the wall and banged on the paneling, ignoring the voice in her head that told her she was crazy. She wouldn't even know how to tell whether there was a hidden cache of something. . . . No, Scott would never have a hidden panel.

Not when he had a whole office to himself a ten-minute drive away in South Berkeley.

She was wearing red yoga pants and a pink T-shirt that read, *Is this a garden? All I see are hoes*, a shirt Scott had given her, one that she never would have worn out of the house. She was so very far beyond caring. In the tiny pocket of her pants meant to carry nothing but a car key, she stuffed dried feverfew (for protection) and lilac (for luck). Then Abby was in the car so fast she almost forgot shoes.

At the small office of Roberts and Sons, Scott's assistant, Charmaine, gasped. "Oh, my god." She came out from behind her desk, her hands outstretched. "Abby. I didn't expect to see you here. Not so soon. I was going to call you, but I figured I would be more help just being here. . . ."

"I need to get in his office."

"Oh, no . . . Truth? I haven't put it in order yet. I was going to call you after . . . I'll let you know when I'm done."

Abby walked past her toward Scott's door, feeling her pulse speed up. She was scared of Charmaine, always had been, ever since Scott had hired the brunette with legs that went for days and an attitude to match. Not that she didn't trust Scott. She did. She had. What an idiot.

"That's okay. I don't mind a little mess."

Charmaine moved quickly and put herself between Abby and the door. "No. You have so much to deal with now. I'll let you know when I've handled it."

Abby sucked in a breath. She'd never stood this close to Charmaine before, and the heavy scent of her too-sweet perfume made her dizzy. "I . . ." She faltered.

Putting a hand gently—understandingly—on Abby's arm, Charmaine said, "It's so hard. I know. I feel it, too. He was a good man."

Abby had always vaguely wondered if Scott and Charmaine had ever been attracted to each other. Now, she realized, she didn't care, both a shock and a relief. A potential past wife trumped a possible fling like the sun trumped a flashlight.

Charmaine stood straighter. "There are things I need to handle in there."

"I found out his secret." Five words, five short words, words she didn't even know for sure were true. She hated that she ran out of breath so quickly she could barely finish them.

"Shit." Charmaine stepped to the side. The fact that she moved meant Abby's fear was justified, and terror ran through her blood like frozen acid.

It took Abby fewer than five minutes to scuffle through his hanging file folders to find the one marked *Fern Reyes*. The other files were labeled with addresses, alphabetical by street. Hers was the only name.

Fern? The woman had a specific name now, a name shared with a creeping, invasive, gloriously robust rhizome. Abby had always loved ferns. She'd taken a whole seminar in leptosporangiate ferns at college—they were vascular, reproducing by spores instead of seeds or flowers. Fiddleheads and fronds, fascinating and tropical.

Abby sat heavily in Scott's chair, and then—feeling the way the seat had conformed over the years to his body (his now-dead body)—sprang to standing again. She reached forward to pull up the file and spread it across the top of the desk.

There they were. Divorce papers, naming Fernanda Reyes as his once wife. And the paper that should have howled like

a Hogwarts screamer: a dog-eared photocopy of a birth certificate.

His son. Matias Wyatt Reyes-Roberts.

Fernanda and Matias.

Scott's other family.

"Charmaine!"

The woman popped out around the corner as if she'd been
standing right there, waiting. "Um. Yes?"

Abby would have liked to have yelled and screamed, to
have carried on like a woman freshly scorned, but her moment
of bravery had sunk four inches below the thick mosslike
carpet beneath her feet. "Did you know about Fernanda and
Matias?"

Charmaine's pink-frosted lids dropped for a moment.
Then, "She goes by Fern. And he's called Matty, I think.
That's what Scott called them."

Matty. It was adorable. A sweet name. A name that had
been on her short list (from Matthew) for a while. With a
sickened pang, she remembered passing her list to Scott once,
asking him to cross off names he didn't like. How the hell
had he not struck off Matthew when she'd given him the pen
and made him go through her dreams? *He already had a Matty.*
He'd known that. She hadn't. "I need the address."

Charmaine opened her mouth as if she was going to protest, but then she just nodded. A moment later, she handed
Abby an oversized yellow Post-it.

"Thank you." That was as much as Abby could give her.

"You're welcome." There was a pause as Charmaine watched
Abby putting the file with its contents into the spare fabric
shopping bag she always carried in her purse. "You'll want this,
too, probably." She held out another file, thicker than the first.

Abby's heart sank as she reached to take it. "What is it?"

"Finances."

"Scott's?"

"Um." Charmaine looked down at her peach-colored nails. "Theirs? I guess?"

Abby nodded as if she understood.

Inside was a large stack of business-sized check duplicates. Each was for fifteen hundred dollars. Abby didn't think her legs would hold her much longer. "Monthly support."

"Um. Yes."

"Well." She wanted to curse, but no word was strong enough. She wanted to throw the file, but she wouldn't be able to bear stooping to pick up his shit. She wanted to hurt someone, a very particular someone, but he was assholically dead, and wasn't that the whole problem? She felt like taking Scott around his neck, that deliciously corded and muscled neck of his that used to turn her on just to look at. She felt like choking that same neck until she made him stop breathing. Again. "Well." Such an impotent word.

"Yeah."

Finally Abby found the exact words she wanted. "Son of a bitch motherfucking son of a motherfucker *fuck*."

"Yeah," said Charmaine, and this time it sounded like she meant it.

chapter *seven*

Seven hours later, after digging four holes in the garden for no good reason (yet—she'd put something in them eventually) and a fruitless attempt at a nap that did nothing but amp her up even more, Abby exited the freeway at the Oakland Zoo. The GPS, as if stunned to be out of its everyday zone, stuttered and then blurted to life, telling her to turn left. It sounded doubtful. Abby took a too-quick sip of the passionflower tea she'd bought at Peet's (she'd gotten it for its ability to help with emotional balancing and hysteria relief—she tried to ignore the fact that passionflower also heightened libido).

In the years she'd been with Scott, she'd never seen a single place he'd ever lived. Not one. Now she finally knew why. Her stomach clenched harder than her hand on the wheel did. Rage burned in her stomach like she'd chugged a shot of jet fuel.

Motherfucker.

Scott, of course, had heard about each place she'd lived in over the years. There had been only three, after all, not counting college dorms. He'd known specifics about the Potrero Hill Victorian she'd grown up in, where she'd spent her first eighteen years, where her parents had spent their last. He knew how it creaked in the winter and how those creaks sounded like happy groans in the guest room they'd never used. He knew that her mother had thought it was cheerfully haunted. Abby had sold the house after they died, so Scott hadn't ever been inside it, but they'd once broken into the backyard on a quiet Wednesday afternoon and Abby had cried when she'd seen that the new owners had turned her father's little wood-shop into a yoga space. Her mother's kiln still stood, and Scott had tried valiantly to talk Abby into letting him steal it for her, brick by brick, before the residents turned it into a wood-fired pizza oven or something.

Scott knew all about her first apartment in the Mission, the one she'd moved into after she graduated from State. Her parents had hated that place—its triple locks, the homeless sleeping in the doorway of the lowest unit—but they were too sick that year to fight her much. Every time Abby and Scott had gotten burritos at Taqueria Cancun, she pointed it out. "See it down there?"

He would nod. "You had the room with the broken stained-glass window. The landlord refused to fix anything, and your neighbors wanted to sue. But you loved it and you wouldn't move because you're stubborn as hell."

"I wouldn't move because it was amazing." She'd loved that rattrap apartment with its glorious light and its colder-than-imaginable foggy summer mornings and its clubbing throb on Friday and Saturday nights. She didn't move until after her parents died, until after she found that her bank account was so full it was just plain stupid of her to continue to rent anything, let alone a cheap, run-down studio. The enormous 1914 Craftsman in North Berkeley was the first place her Realtor had taken her. She'd barely noticed the high crown moldings and the built-ins and its proximity to Solano Avenue—she'd just been drawn to the jungle of the backyard. Left untended for at least a dozen years, ancient-looking ferns had tangled with blackberry. Pandanus had encroached on the old pond, and a bamboo stand threatened to take over the entire lower quadrant. The Realtor had been apologetic. *We can stipulate they clean this up. Burn it. Something.* But Kathryn, who had just opened the nursery, had been overjoyed. *I'll make sure you have everything you need. Imagine raspberries right here! Your mother would have loved this.*

Abby turned left on MacArthur and double-checked to make sure the doors had auto locked while she'd been driving. This wasn't anything like her part of Berkeley, where Alice Waters lived around the corner. Abby could walk to three different cafés with fair-trade coffee, and the local schools had on-site gardens that sent organic vegetables to the cafeteria.

This neighborhood, on the other hand, appeared to have only liquor stores and churches bracketing the small wooden houses. Nothing else. She hadn't seen a doctor's office or a grocery store. Not even a bank.

The sun was out, and people were taking advantage of it. A group of older men sat on a stoop and shook something small and white onto a red blanket. A woman wobbled past them on high heels, wearing a long fall of cherry cola–colored hair. The men ignored her, and she kept her eyes on the street. Abby caught her gaze accidentally and then didn't know what to do with it.

She yanked a hard left and winced as the GPS on her phone

caught her mistake. "Rerouting. Rerouting." How did a computerized voice hold that much judgment? Two more left turns and another right at a fork in the road and she was on the correct street, at least.

The houses here were tiny. Most couldn't be more than two or three bedrooms. In Abby's neighborhood, when residents upgraded their homes, they literally dug them up and lifted them skyward, leaving them perched precariously on stilts while they added a story or two below the original body of the house, getting additional bedrooms and garages out of the remodel. If people couldn't go up, they went out. They went out to the very edges of their property lines, out to the back fences, pouring foundations over old lawns, adding loggias and outside barbecue pits, their outside living rooms complete with fountains and wide-screen TVs protected from the elements by environmentally responsible reclaimed lumber.

In this part of Oakland, though, the houses remained small. Narrow side gates led to backyards that, by the signs hanging from almost every one, held guard dogs, not wide screens. Abby felt herself guessing the interior square footage as she slowly drove past. A thousand. Eleven hundred. Eight hundred. Could that one there be any more than six hundred?

She watched address numbers on the sides of houses. The numbers rose in direct proportion to her heart rate. Still, she was startled by the GPS when it announced, "Your destination is on the left."

God. The house she'd been staring at, without realizing that it was the one she'd been looking for, the house she'd automatically slowed in front of.

Of course.

She'd recognized the boy.

chapter *eight*

"Hi."

The boy looked up at her suspiciously and said nothing.

Matty.

His skin was five or six shades darker than Scott's summer tan, but in every other way, he looked like every kid picture she'd ever seen of her husband. He was skinny, with a wide jaw that didn't fit his face. His hair wasn't Scott's red blaze, but the rust was there under the brown. Holy hell. "I . . ." Scott's son was half-Latino. What did that *mean*?

The boy ignored her, dropping his eyes back to the notebook in front of him. Good for him. She was a stranger. He was an eleven-year-old. He shouldn't talk to her.

"Is your mom home?"

The boy didn't even blink.

"Do you mind if I open the gate?"

Now he looked alarmed. His colored pencil stopped moving.

"I'm not—" Not what? If she said *I'm not going to hurt you*, she'd sound like a child predator or something. "You're Matty, right? I'm looking for your mom. Fern." It was the first time Abby had said the woman's name out loud, and the softness of it surprised her. It didn't *look* soft in Scott's file, and it didn't feel soft in her mind. It should sound pointy and dry, a heap of old sticks. But said in the open air, the name felt like the plant itself, light and rounded and brushed.

The boy's face was a mixture of relief and apprehension. His eyebrows stayed close together. "You know my mom?"

"I don't," Abby said, still on the other side of the latched gate. "But I'd like to meet her. Is she home?"

He narrowed his eyes, back to wary.

"I . . ." This was stupid. This was ridiculous. This wasn't respectful, of Scott (although, really, *fuck* Scott) or of his ex-wife or, maybe most important, of his child, the one in front of her right now. "I just have some of your mail." That was true, after all. So it had been returned by the boy's mother. It was still Fern's.

"Oh. We got some of Joe's mail last month."

"Is Joe your neighbor?"

He nodded. "Mom opened it accidentally and it was some kind of crazy big bill, so she said we had to pretend we never saw it. She fixed it with a glue stick and put it in his box." He clamped his mouth shut as if suddenly aware that wasn't for sharing.

"Makes sense."

Matty assessed her, his eyes still. "Did you open it?"

"What?"

"Our mail."

"Well, actually, it was already open. I have quite a bit of it in this bag." Abby looked up at the windows. Dust and spiderwebs danced at the corners of each old pane. She glanced at Matty again. "What are you drawing?"

"Leaf."

"Can I see?"

Suspicion lit his eyes. "Why?"

"I like leaves."

"Do you know how to draw them?"

"Yes," she said. How many veins and petioles and stipules had she drawn in college? "I really do."

Matty stood up and opened the gate. Then he sat back down on the stoop again. Sunlight made the top of his head glow. He scrubbed an eraser over the beat-up page in his notebook.

"Is this for class?"

"Yeah." His tone was miserable.

The blood moved faster in Abby's veins. This was weird—this was much too weird. You didn't just meet a child and sit next to him on a step in the sun; but what were you *supposed* to do when you met your husband's child?

She sat. She looked at the page. He'd drawn a circle in black pencil and then he'd added lines bisecting it in brown. "That's a leaf?" she said.

Around the eraser of his pencil, he said, "Yeah. I guess."

"Because it looks like a dying hedgehog."

He snorted. "You're not supposed to say that."

"Why not? I think it's a very good dying hedgehog. I wouldn't want to run into it in a dark alley."

"I hate art. And this isn't even art—this is for science and that just makes it worse."

"Well, art is one of those hard things. You can't really add it up, you know? Two plus two doesn't always equal four when you're dealing with colors and lines, right?" Abby was proud that her voice didn't shake. She couldn't remember the last time she'd talked to anyone under the age of twenty-one. And she'd never spoken to anyone this important, maybe ever. "Where's your leaf, anyway?"

"Huh?"

"You're out here because this is where the leaves are, right?"

He frowned and jerked his head back as if he'd just remembered he had a shell. "No. I'm out here because Elva baked that curry-lentil thing she makes and it smells dis*gust*ing in there."

Who was Elva? She couldn't ask. *Don't ask.* "So you're not drawing from life?"

Matty just stared at her. His eyes—Jesus, his eyes. Scott's eyes met hers. Brown with dark green on the edges, smart and sweet and holding just that little bit back. He said nothing.

"Well. If you don't have a leaf, you're not going to get it right. Let's find one."

Matty's skeptical look was so clearly written on his face that he didn't need to say anything.

"Come on. Let's do this."

He slouched upward with a sigh and followed her onto the tiny unkempt lawn. "I sure hope you're not an ax murderer."

Abby patted her yoga pants, front and back. "Awfully small ax."

"You never know these days."

It was so unexpected and so *funny* that Abby felt an adrenaline rush spike through her.

Matty's head was down. He scuffed at the overgrown grass with the toe of his sneaker. "What kind of leaf?"

"You're the boss," said Abby. "Pick one you like. No, pick two. Just in case you get mad at the first."

"What do you do then?"

"Rip up the page and then pull the leaf into tiny bitty pieces. Let both of them blow away into the wind."

Matty gave a surprised hoot of laughter.

Abby bent down and picked up an oak leaf that must have blown in from the neighbor's yard. It pricked her finger, and the sharpness of it felt just right. If she were going to draw a leaf, she'd pick this one. Ragged at the edges. Brittle, but still strong. At least for now.

A few minutes later, Matty held five or six leaves in his hands.

"Got some? Okay, I'm going to show you the magic trick now."

"Really?"

Whoops. "I mean, it's not a *magic*-magic trick."

Reasonably, Matty looked confused.

"All I mean is there's something I do when I'm drawing, and it works pretty well. Okay, you like this one?" It was a fat sycamore leaf, bright green with one bug-chewed edge.

He nodded.

"Turn a page in your notebook, that's right. Put the tip of your pencil on the page, yeah, like that. Now, with your other hand, pull that first piece of paper back over your hand."

Matty looked so flummoxed that she wanted to laugh. "Huh?"

"You're trying to hide your hand from yourself with that piece of paper. Get it?"

"No."

Abby held up one finger and traced the top of the leaf's

edge. "Your eyes are talking directly to the tip of your pencil. Move your eyes slowly, *really* slowly, along the edge of the leaf. When it turns, your pencil turns under the page, but you can't see the tip of it. All you can see is the leaf. Look—really look—at the veins of it. Follow each one. Be as detailed as you can."

"But not look *down*?"

Now she did laugh. "Yep. Just try. I'll hold it really still."

Matty nodded once, though his eyes still telegraphed skepticism. Then he plastered his gaze on the leaf.

It was quiet as he drew. Or, at least, it was as quiet as this neighborhood could be. Abby had always thought her neighborhood in North Berkeley could be a little noisy sometimes, with planes taking off from SFO rising overhead and the perpetual whine of lawn mowers in the distance.

But the sound here in Oakland was different. Even though the freeway was on the other side of the low hill, she could feel its rumble in her chest. As soon as one siren died in the distance, another took up the wail. A solid *thoomp-thoomp* beat from a car's bass sound system somewhere close by. She heard two screams. Matty didn't even blink. He kept his eyes on the leaf, his hand moving under the paper. The screams resolved into wild laughter and a group of teenagers on foot loped past the gate. Now that she was really listening, she could hear a hundred other sounds: at least two TVs from the apartment building next door, the rattle of a dryer with spare change caught inside the drum, and, astonishingly, in all that sound, the low throb of a hummingbird's wings as it buzzed them, heading for the early jasmine she'd seen in the yard next door. Its wings flashed green and gold. Matty didn't so much as glance toward it.

After perhaps four minutes, he said, "Can I look now?"

"You're done?"

"Yeah. I think."

"Let's see."

The image on the page was a scribble of intricate pencil marks, woven lines making a fine mesh.

"That's *horrible.*"

"It isn't! Look. It's amazing!"

He jabbed a finger at it. "*This* is not a leaf. *This* is a big old fat pile of dog caca."

"But it is a leaf. Look close." She scooted on the step so she was closer to him. "It's like this wild jungle, and you drew it."

"It's a mess."

"But did you know a leaf looked like that?"

He stopped rolling his eyes and narrowed them, first at her, and then at the paper. After a moment, he said, "No. There's a lot of wiggles. Veins."

"You know what it reminds me of?"

"What?"

"Look at the palm of your hand."

He glanced at her, and then back at his hand. "I guess they're kinda . . . huh. That's weird."

"Isn't that cool? By drawing the leaf, you were sort of drawing your hand, too."

He sighed. "That doesn't make any sense."

"Okay. But was it fun?"

"Yeah. But I don't think my teacher is gonna believe me, that this is the leaf."

"So bring the leaf in, too."

"She's really mean. She didn't say to bring it in."

"Did she say not to?"

He grinned, and Abby's heart suddenly starting beating as rapidly as the hummingbird's wings had thrummed. What would it have been like? If she'd been able to have Scott's child, a boy, a brother to this one? What kind of life would that have been, the one that had passed her by?

"My mom's not home, by the way."

She'd almost forgotten she'd asked. "So . . . Elva?" Was that the housekeeper? His nanny? How old was a child supposed to be before you let him be a latchkey kid? Abby had exactly zero experience with children, and she would have guessed sixteen, but good grief, at that age they could wield two-ton vehicles on the freeway, so, yeah, kids probably got house keys earlier than that.

"Elva's in there. She lives here." He jerked his head backward, toward the front door. "And Grandpa Wyatt."

An abyss yawned in front of Abby and the ground dropped away behind her. *Grandpa Wyatt.* Scott's father had been named Wyatt, but he'd died years before she and Scott met. *I wish you could have met him,* Scott had always said. *He would have loved you.* Abby teetered on the tiny square of solid ground she stood on, unsure whether to step forward or back.

This wasn't right. Everything about this was wrong, so wrong.

She carefully balanced the leaf on the open page of his sketch pad. "It looks good there," she said. "Next to your awesome drawing. Anyway. I should—"

"Hey," Matty exclaimed, making her jump. "My mom's here!"

Behind her, the gate opened.

The woman said, "Holy." Then she said, "Fuck."

chapter *nine*

Fern Reyes had never, ever expected to find Matty talking to the enemy in her own yard. The day's exhaustion fled her bones and if Abby Roberts had flown straight upward like the *bruja* she was, Fern would have been able to follow even without a broom. "Why are you talking to my son?"

"I . . ." Abby's eyes blinked blue innocence.

Fern turned to Matty, trying and failing to keep her voice light. "Did you let her in the gate?"

He hunched forward, a pencil in his hand. "She said she knew you."

Fern's arms had been killing her—three paper bags from the grocery store and her purse—but the pain went away with the burst of adrenaline. "Well, honey, she doesn't."

"Oh, my god," said the woman. "You know who I am."

She would have known Scott's wife, Abby, if she'd boarded her bus wearing a burka. The eminently Google-able Abby Roberts née Crowley, the subject of way too many late-nights-with-red-wine image searches. She was even prettier in person. "Why are you here?"

Abby stepped backward and almost tripped over a broken hose.

"I was just . . ." Her voice trailed off, the way Matty's did when he didn't want to answer a question truthfully.

Sweet baby *Cristo*. Was this really happening to her today? She'd been looking forward to one thing—*one* thing—a hot bath. She was going to let Matty have pizza pockets for dinner after letting him get out of doing homework, because god knew they all needed a break. Tonight she needed to balance her bank account (like, *really* balance it, make sure no stray debit charges were going to sneak through before payday, which wasn't for another four days) and she needed to clean both bathrooms, and there were probably four more loads of laundry waiting for her even though she'd done laundry till eleven the night before. But screw all of it. She'd been planning on taking a bath, bring-ing with her a glass of wine and the latest copy of *People* maga-zine, which someone had left on the bus that afternoon (a regular perk of the job—fresh, read-only-once magazines). Maybe, if she felt really frisky after the bath, she would call Gregory and have phone sex. He was good at it, good at getting her off, listening to her use her vibrator while she laughed and kept her voice as low as possible in her bedroom.

But no.

Tonight was *this* now.

Her.

Scott's wife was still staring at her. A skinny *güera* ghost. She was pale, even paler than she was in her (unlocked) Facebook account. Thinner, too. Bony. There was a blue vein under her chin, and Fern could almost swear she could see it pulsing. Lord.

"Are you planning on passing out on me?"

"Pardon?"

Who said that in real life? Fern sighed, the bags heavy in her tired arms again. "Matty, take one of these, would you?"

Matty and Abby both stepped forward, each putting out a hand.

She gave Matty the lightest of the bags. She kept the other two. "Come on in. Let's do this." Fern felt something like tears form at the back of her tongue, and as she pushed her way inside her house with Scott's wife on her heels, she cleared her throat angrily.

"This way," she said, thankful that Elva drew the curtains at the first sign of afternoon sun. At least it was dark inside, and the woman wouldn't be able to see how many dust bunnies lurked under the TV and in the corners. It had to be three weeks since she'd had time to vacuum. Grandpa Wyatt wasn't in his easy chair, so that meant he was napping, thank god. She couldn't deal with Matty's grandfather right now. "Put that bag in the kitchen and then go to your room."

"But . . ." Matty had that look on his face, the one he still got sometimes when Fern changed the channel on something that was about to go too naked for an eleven-year-old. "What . . . ?"

"Your room. Go play Minecraft."

Matty jolted. "Without finishing my homework?"

"Now." It was her *Off my bus* voice and it worked on her son like it did crackheads. He went.

In the kitchen, Elva was stirring something at the stove. "Oh, there you are! I'm making lentil soup." She peered inside. "Or lentil curry. Or maybe chili."

Fern watched Abby's eyes widen as she took in the elderly woman still in her slippers. Elva was fully dressed, Fern knew that—she dressed every morning as if she were going out even if she wasn't. But in the afternoons, after her nap, she got chilly and she said the ancient blue terry-cloth robe warmed her legs and knees, something a sweater wouldn't do. So, yeah, Elva kind of looked like a homeless person shambling around Fern's kitchen, but that was Fern's business. Besides, very few homeless people had their hair set every Monday morning.

"I was going to give Matty pizza pockets tonight." Way-too-freaking-expensive but blessedly easy pizza pockets.

"Fan*tas*tic. I'll stick this in Tupperware." When Matty got pizza pockets, so did Elva and Grandpa Wyatt. It really was like having three kids. At least Matty's grandfather and his girlfriend didn't eat that much. And they paid her. That was nice. Fern wouldn't make the mortgage without their tiny rent checks. But she wished she knew a polite way to ask Elva to stop helping in the kitchen. A couple of years ago, when Fern hadn't been able to get much overtime, she'd tasked Elva with cooking on the cheap a few nights a week. It made her boarder feel good to be needed. Elva, though, took a bit too much liberty with the sale bin at the back of Safeway. Fern had pointed out, more than once, that there might be a very good reason that particular brand of oysters had been discounted to nineteen cents a can, but Elva adored making something brand-new. "Getting honey from wax," she called it. Sometimes Fern was pretty sure she'd rather eat the wax and leave the oyster-flavored honey alone.

Elva looked interestedly at Abby. "Hello. I'm Elva Schwartz. I'm a dancer." She didn't mention she hadn't been a dancer since the fifties. "And you are?"

Scott's wife put out her hand. "Abby Roberts."

"So nice to meet you. I'll put away the curry later, and let you two have some time together in here."

"Thanks," said Fern.

"You're welcome. You probably have quite a bit of"— Elva looked from one woman to the other—"catching up to do?"

Huh. Elva might be getting forgetful, but she was no dummy.

Fern sighed and heaved her purse onto the table next to the shopping bags. This morning she hadn't minded that the tabletop was covered by mail and mostly empty boxes of cereal, but now the whole kitchen looked cluttered. The clock on the wall was an hour fast—she hadn't changed it since they fell back, months ago. Soon they'd spring forward and it would be on time again, and she wouldn't have to bother. She made a halfhearted swipe at some crumbs with her hand. She hoped Abby just wouldn't see the dirt. It was dark in the room, after all—only two of the three overhead bulbs were working. She was going to buy some more, just as soon as there were a few dollars in the grocery budget, as soon as the bulbs were more important than pizza pockets and a single bottle of three-dollar wine. She pushed the hair back out of her face. She hadn't had time to dye the roots in more than a month, and she had at least a quarter inch of salt-and-pepper showing at her part. The cheap incandescent bulbs did her no favors.

Abby said, "Matty. He's lovely."

She didn't have the right to say that. "Mmm."

"I know this is weird."

"Weird? You think this might be *weird*?" Her voice was so sharp she reminded herself painfully of her mother, which wasn't normal or at all comfortable. Fern was known for being chipper, not strident. At work she was the funny one. Always cheerful. Well, fuck that right now. Fuck that right off. Fern put the bottle of sale wine on the door of the refrigerator. The freezer might still be broken, but at least the wine would be cold. And no, she wasn't going to offer this woman any of it.

"So, Fernanda? Or Fern?"

Fern wanted to say *Ms. Reyes to you*, but she'd never liked her last name. For that matter, she wasn't that fond of her first. "Fern is fine."

Abby bit her bottom lip. "Fernanda is so pretty."

Was she criticizing Fern's choice of preferred name?

"Is it, um . . . Spanish?"

"Mexican," said Fern bluntly. Is that what she wanted to hear?

"Ah."

Fern could almost see the thought bubble over Abby's head as the woman wondered if she was illegal. She couldn't decide whether to laugh at the woman or cuss her out, so she just went with simple. "I was born here."

Abby flinched. "I didn't know anything about you until yesterday. Fernanda and Matias. That's all I knew. And your picture."

"My picture?"

"Of you and Scott getting married. And in the hospital. I found them yesterday. You looked . . ."

Fern thought her heart might pound right out of her skin. She took a deep breath and tried to rid her mind of the image of pushing this woman bodily out of the kitchen and—preferably—into traffic. "Seriously, what the fuck is Scott trying to pull, sending you here?"

Abby looked over her shoulder. "Is Wyatt . . ."

"*Wyatt?* Is he what?"

"He's . . . alive?"

Fern laughed, even though humor was the last thing she was feeling in the tight band across her chest. "He told you he was dead, huh? That's rich. Of course he did. His father's fine. Probably napping in his room." *He chose us.* She wanted to say it. She wanted to say it *so* badly. "What else don't you know about us?"

"I don't know anything."

Fern weighed the words, balancing them against the woman's paleness, the way her fingers opened and closed on empty air. "You're serious."

Abby nodded.

"You know nothing."

Abby shook her head, still wordless.

"Did you know Scott and I bought this house together before we got married? Did you know he got me to put just my name on the deed because of his credit score? Did you know I was stuck with it when he left? Did you know I'm still driving the piece-of-shit car I had just bought when we met? Did you know I've worked overtime every week since I can remember just to make the house payment, to keep a roof over his son's head, to keep peanut butter on his bread? I don't even know what my regular salary looks like on a check—it's been that long since I worked a forty-hour week."

"I—I don't even know what you do."

"Driver." Fern crossed her arms. Did she actually feel *shame* admitting her profession? Bullshit. "AC Transit."

"You're . . . a bus driver?" Scott's wife bit her lip.

Fern kept her arms crossed and squared her body to face her. Screw this woman and whatever she came here to find out. "What do you want from me?"

"I'm so sorry. I didn't mean to . . . I'm doing this all wrong. Can I help you put away the groceries?"

"No!" Fern surprised herself by following the question with a sharp laugh. Nerves. They were about to kill her.

Abby looked frightened, her light blue eyes so wide Fern could see the whites all the way around.

Fantastic.

Feeling a level of exhaustion so deep that her very bones wanted to lie down and sleep with or without the rest of her, Fern said, "Look. Can we skip the niceties and just get to the point?"

"The point? The point is . . ." Abby's eyes went to the ceiling as she bit her lip.

Fern leaned against the sink, willing Abby not to notice that it was dripping as usual.

Abby bit her lip harder, as if she wanted her teeth to go right through her bottom lip.

Fern really didn't feel like dealing with blood. "Okay." She used the softer voice she used on the ancient tweakers, the ones who didn't look like they'd make it through another night. "Let me guess. He's cheating on you. Possibly with someone you know. And you want advice."

Abby shook her head. Tears swam in the lower half of her eyes, threatening to spill but somehow staying in place, like clear mercury.

"He hit you?" He had never laid a hand on Fern—didn't seem the type—but who knew how he'd changed?

"No!"

"Spent all that money of yours." Whoops, that came out a little cold, but after all, if Scott had gone for Abby *because* of the money, he'd probably skate when the well ran dry.

Abby stepped forward and raised her hands as if ready to catch Fern if she fell forward. "He's dead."

The inside of Fern's head went fuzzy and dark. "Excuse me?"

"God, I'm so sorry to tell you this."

"Holy . . ." Fern couldn't find an expletive good enough. Big enough.

Dead.

Scott was *dead*?

She'd imagined Scott dead so many times. In the worst months, she'd lain in bed and put herself to sleep with cheery images of him strapped to railroad tracks, screaming for her to let him loose. She'd imagined his parachute not opening, his hot-air balloon burning up, his car crashing through a guardrail. She thought she'd be happy to hear the news. Thrilled, even. She thought she'd throw a party and invite everyone she'd ever complained about him to, and her small rooms would overflow with good friends congratulating her.

Instead, Fern burst into tears in front of Scott's goddamned skinny little wife.

chapter *ten*

Abby had no idea what to do.

If she were at home, she would have brought Fern a box of tissues. She would've opened a bottle of sparkling water and brought it to her with a straw. She would have moved her to the couch and put a pillow on her lap. Everyone needed a pillow to hold when they cried.

Instead, she was in the kitchen of a woman she'd never met—a woman she hadn't known existed until the night before—and though there was a six-pack of paper towels still in plastic sitting on the floor next to the refrigerator, she saw no tissue box in the clutter that rested on every flat surface.

Still, every house had cushions.

"Here." Without stopping to worry about whether what she was doing was wrong or right, she took Fern's hand and led her to a kitchen chair. "Sit for a minute." She placed Fern's hand on the top of the table, because if she let it go, it would just smack down into Fern's lap. Tears rolled from Fern's closed eyes, and she was making a terrible small noise, a tiny mewling.

Abby ripped open the plastic that encased the paper towels and tore off a sheet. "Take this."

Fern groped for it, her eyes barely opening.

"I'll be right back. Don't move."

Abby darted into the living room and grabbed a cushion at random from the sofa. Back in the kitchen, she thrust it into Fern's hands. She took a clean-looking glass from the dish drainer and filled it with tap water before setting it next to Fern's purse on the table. Then she paused, putting her hands on her knotted stomach. She wished she had a pillow, too.

Fern gave a sob that ended on a strangled intake of breath. She clutched the pillow. In a constricted voice, she said, "Fuck."

Abby sat in the chair next to Fern. She carefully looked forward. Sometimes the best thing you could do for someone was to look away.

Fern cried almost soundlessly for another minute. Maybe two. The only sounds were from outside: a radio blaring something in Spanish and a woman yelling something about how a kid better come in or else. The inside of the house, except for Fern's choked breath and a faucet's drip, was almost completely silent.

Abby sat next to her and waited.

When Fern stopped crying, she stopped abruptly. She gasped another half sob and then, to Abby's surprise, broke into what sounded like a laugh. "What an *asshole*." Fern glanced sideways at Abby, her face wet from the eyelids down. "Sorry. But, you know. I'm not sorry. What a totally shitty thing for him to go and do."

"I think so, too," said Abby, and it felt good to say even through the wave of guilt.

"How did he die?"

"Coronary. Massive."

"Where?"

"In the bathroom."

"Oh." Fern sat back, still hugging the pillow. It was brown, decorated with a yellow stitched giraffe. It looked hand embroidered.

"Did you make that?" Abby reached a finger forward to touch it.

"This? Are you crazy? No. Goodwill."

Abby wanted to run right out the door, hit the sidewalk running, and not slow down till she was back in her car and on 580 headed home. Scott's ex still had feelings for him. Obviously. Why had Abby thought this might be easy? That she could come over and get a simple explanation, something like, *Married to him? Oh, that. It was annulled; the baby was mine from someone else. I'm sure he just didn't want to upset you with something that was really nothing.*

Instead, Fern seemed demolished, the eleven-year-old was definitely Scott's, and Scott was just the biggest asshole that had ever lived (or died) for keeping such a devastating secret for so long.

"You said in the bathroom?"

Startled, Abby said, "Yeah."

"Taking a shit?"

"Would it help to know that?"

Fern closed her eyes as if she was thinking for a minute about the correct answer. "Yeah," she said slowly. "I think it might."

"He was done with whatever he'd been doing in there. He was buckled up. Standing when he fell."

"Were you home?"

Abby nodded.

"Did you . . ." Fern's voice trailed off.

Abby had no idea what Fern's next words might be. *Did you try to save him? Did you run? Did you cheer? Did you cry? Did you love him?*

But Fern didn't finish her sentence. She just looked at Abby.

"I called 911. The dispatcher talked me through CPR."

"God."

"I'm not sure how much . . ."

Fern sat straighter. "Tell me all of it."

"I don't need to—"

"But I need to hear it," Fern interrupted. Her fingers dug into the giraffe's neck.

"We'd had a fight. No. A disagreement." About the end of their relationship. "I thought he'd thrown something. I thought he'd taken the heavy picture off the wall and thrown it to the floor." Later that night, she'd wondered why she'd ever thought that. When Scott got angry, he raised his voice, but she'd never felt physically threatened by him. Why she thought he would take down the huge framed photo of the Vernazza terrace, the photo she'd taken on their honeymoon and spent seven hundred dollars getting framed, she'd never know. It was what she'd heard.

But then she'd heard nothing else.

Fern stared. "You heard him fall—"

"No. Like I said, I thought he threw—"

"There's a difference between something falling and a body hitting the floor."

There was. Abby didn't want to know how Fern knew. "After a few minutes—"

"How many?"

Abby paused. An urge filled her, an urge she hadn't predicted. She wanted to tell this woman. "Three. Or maybe four."

"Wow."

"Yeah."

"So . . . you heard him hit the floor and didn't go to him for four minutes?"

"I was listening. The picture—I thought—maybe . . ."

Fern just looked at her. "I don't blame you."

Abby's throat was tight. "Maybe you should."

"I would have waited an hour."

The air left Abby's lungs in a rush. Was Fern kidding? Was she supposed to laugh? But Fern just made a go-on motion with her hands.

"I knocked on the door. He didn't answer. I didn't know what to do." She tightened hold of her fingers in her lap and wished Fern would pass her the pillow to hold. "I swear I didn't do it on purpose. I don't know why I waited. I thought—"

"I know." Fern's voice was soft. And then, as if she'd read Abby's mind, she passed over the cushion.

It was warm from Fern's lap. Abby dug her thumbs into it. "I pounded on the door. I was terrified. I yelled through the door at him—" She cleared her throat. "I yelled that I was going to call the cops. The dispatcher asked me if I thought he was okay, and first I said yes. Then I realized I didn't know. I told her so, and she asked if I thought I could break down the door. I didn't think I could, but I had all this . . . fear, I guess. It only took one hit with my shoulder, and the door broke in." The corner of it had struck Scott in the leg with such a sick thud that she'd wondered at first if breaking down the door was what had knocked him down. Nothing had made sense to her. Nothing at all. The dispatcher's words, *Place the heel of your hand on his breastbone in the center of his chest, right between the nipples.* For a wild second of disbelief, while she knelt next to him, she'd thought the dispatcher had made a mistake. *No, it's my husband.* Only women had breasts with nipples, she'd thought, literally forgetting basic anatomy. Nothing had made sense.

"I did CPR for a long time. It felt like forever." They'd already e-mailed her the medical report for her insurance company. When she'd read the terrible words, it showed she'd been on the phone with the dispatcher for just six minutes total. A couple of those had probably been spent not understanding what the dispatcher was saying, another one spent breaking down the door and rolling him from his side onto his back. "I heard his ribs crack. She told me that meant I was doing it right, but it was—there was air going in and out of his lungs, I could hear it, but—god. I should stop. This is terrible."

Fern's eyes were twin blackened marks of heat. "No. Go on."

"His lungs wheezed. No, that's not it. His lungs sounded wet, like something old and damp peeling apart. The operator kept telling me that was what was supposed to happen, that I was keeping the oxygen moving around in his blood, but I *knew* it wasn't helping. Maybe that's just what they say—maybe it helps some people to hear that. . . ."

Fern nodded.

"But I knew it was a lie. I wanted her to tell me that I should stop. That he was beyond help. That I was just making it worse."

"You weren't, though. You were doing everything you could."

"No. I was doing everything I could to guarantee that I'd have nightmares every night since."

"Then what?" Fern seemed impatient now, the tears almost dry on her cheeks.

"The ambulance came. They took over. They used their defibrillator. Shocked him." The real shock had been hers. If they'd been able to hook him up the way her own heart had pounded in her chest, they could have brought him back. Instead, they'd pushed her out of the way, two of the men barking questions at her that she couldn't seem to follow. *When did you last see him, what are his medical conditions, does he have an advance directive?* She'd stood in the hallway, and some-how, even though she knew he was dead, she was surprised when they'd stopped pumping. They'd peeled the sticky paddles off Scott's chest gently. (Why gently? Why didn't they just rip them off? Scott was gone. Everyone there knew he was gone by then.) They'd put away their gear, and then one of them, a very young man with not even one single crease on his face, not even a laugh line, sat her down on the couch in the living room and asked her if they could call anyone for her. She'd given them Kathryn's phone number, and she'd sat in numb silence. Pre-grief. Pre-everything.

Now she said to Fern, "It was my fault."

"Bull." Fern rubbed the back of her neck as if it ached. "You can't tell yourself that. It's not true. When I was with him, he had blood pressure that was sky-high, and he was practically a kid then. Did he ever get that treated?"

Of course he hadn't. All the blood pressure medicine the

doctor threatened him with would have jeopardized his ability to function sexually. Abby had—ridiculously—taken this as a strange kind of compliment. Her husband wanted to make love to her so badly that he'd risk his health.

I asked him for a divorce. She wanted to say it, wanted to see the look that would cross Fern's face.

"God. It's been so long. . . . I don't remember what he wanted. Burial?"

"Memorial service. Then cremation." The words didn't apply to Scott. They couldn't. "Sunday."

"*This* Sunday?"

"Oh, damn." Abby had no idea how bus drivers' schedules worked. Of course they drove on weekends, too. "It's . . . maybe we can—"

"I'm off." Fern wiped her face with both hands. "I work tomorrow and Saturday, but I'm off on Sunday. Oh, god, I have to tell his father. And . . . Matty. My poor Matty." Her voice broke on the last word.

Scott's father. This was worse, so much worse than she'd thought it could possibly be. If she'd known what it would feel like to be in this small, dark house with the people Scott had once loved, would she still have come? "Let me know if I can help. With anything."

Fern stared at her as if she'd just appeared in the kitchen. "Do people keep saying that to you?"

"Yes."

"Does it help?"

"No."

Fern tore out a piece of paper from a battered notebook she pulled out from under a pile of place mats. "Here." She wrote something. "My e-mail. Send me the time and place. I'll try . . . I'll see if we can be there. Can you please . . ."

"Yeah." Abby knew how the sentence ended. It was fine. She couldn't breathe in this small kitchen, which was literally the size of her pantry at home. She felt like the asshole Fern obviously saw her as. A sob was crawling up her esophagus, but she managed to say, "I'll go."

There was gratefulness tangled with something else— anger? grief?—in Fern's gaze. "E-mail me."

"Yes."

Abby left. The old woman, Elva, silently raised the remote at her as she made her way through the living room and out the front door. There was no sign of Matty or his grandfather. The front door opened with a creak and closed with a snap that Abby felt somewhere near the bottom of her soul.

chapter *eleven*

F ern predicted the stop request and was already pulling over at Fortieth when the ding ran through the line, singing up from the back along the wire. The sound went into her seat and up her spine. It was her song, her jam, her holy bell, the one she heard ring in her sleep. She pulled her coach over smoothly, just another wide ripple in traffic.

But the guy in the back row yanked it again. And then again. "Hey!" he yelled. "I gotta get off!"

Why did so many people not believe that she was going to pull over when they rang the bell? A good twenty percent of people yelled at her to stop, even after they'd pulled the request, even after she was actively pulling to the curb. That was about nineteen percent too many.

But she called, "You got it, pal!" That was her shtick. She was the nice one. You couldn't piss off Fern. Even when she had to physically put hands on people, "encouraging" them off the bus, she could make them think she was being polite. *No. Hell, no. Put that away—grab your pipe and go. You have to get off my bus, but you have a nice day, now, okay? Gorgeous day out there.* Some people, the ones who boarded wasted, the ones furious with their lives in general and her in specific, would call her names—"*pendeja fea*," "you fuckin' fat cow," "stupid cunt"—but it wasn't like that was anything new. Some tried to fake-swing at her occasionally, but the guys riding her line were usually too tired to swing at her for real.

"Hey!" the man in the back yelled again as her front right tire kissed the curb with a whisper.

"No problem, my friend," she said in a loud voice over her shoulder as he disembarked at the middle doors. "You have a nice day, now."

Four more stops till she picked up Matty from the skate park. Fern smiled at the older woman who climbed on board with her even more ancient mother. "Afternoon," she said. "Good to see you again." Sixteen more stops before she finished driving for the day and told Matty his father—his shit-tastic, absent father—was dead.

Back on the road, she dodged a silver kamikaze Honda while keeping her eyes on a guy in the fourth row who seemed like he was about twenty years too old to try to be hitting on the girl behind him who couldn't have been more than thirteen. At the next stop, a bicyclist loaded his bike, obviously for the first time. He pulled down the front bar awkwardly and struggled to get his wheels in line. Three more stops.

Patience was just counting. Up or down, it didn't matter. You were going to something or away from something else. She'd been counting routes till she got this one, the one she needed, the one that ran in front of Matty's middle school, right in time for him to start. Grade school had been fine—they'd lived so close that she'd trusted him to walk the four doors home and then text her as he spread peanut butter on saltines—but his middle school was too far from home, too many blocks across an urban wasteland where bullets flew too fast and too often for her to let Matty walk home alone. It had taken years to work this out, years of counting trades and tallying favors for other drivers, getting to the point where she could hold this route. It was hers now. *Hers.* Now she picked him up every school day she drove.

There was more math to be done, and soon, but it wasn't the kind of counting she could do while driving. She'd need to pick up more overtime to make up for the lost fifteen hundred a month in child support. And since the winter hiring, when they'd finally trained enough drivers for the first time since she'd worked for the agency, overtime was in short supply.

She could do it, though. She could make it work. Worst case, she could double-bunk with Matty and rent out her own room to another boarder. No, that wasn't fair to Matty. She could sleep on the couch.

Her bell's ding brought her out of imagining the slimness of her bank account and back into the driver's seat. Later. She could figure that part out later.

Three stops left, the same number of Canadian dimes that had gone into the fare box today. Then two stops left. Fern made herself unclench her grip on the wheel. That was the way Shirley Broadmore had gotten her carpal tunnel. No one was going to take care of her if she didn't, and if she couldn't drive, who would take care of Matty? Relaxed fingers were key. Her epilepsy was under control. She always took her meds. Her hands were strong. She could be more physically active, but her blood work always came back great. There was nothing that could take this job away from her. Fern breathed as deeply as she could, given that the man in the first row hadn't taken a bath in a year that began with the number two.

The smell didn't matter. The closer she got to Matty every day, the lighter her heart got. It was that simple. It didn't matter if she had a load of loud, swearing teenagers, the kind that littered as she drove, trailing bits of candy wrappers and soda cups out the cracked windows like they were leaving a line of bread crumbs behind them to find their way home. It didn't matter if, like today, the only person at the penultimate stop before Matty's was a thirty-something guy, jittery and jumpy, obviously strung out, the kind of guy who was going to argue with her about how much he should have to pay.

And of course he did. "Fifty percent?" he said.

She shook her head. "Sorry, buddy."

"A dollar?"

Oh, that was good. He was going down, not up. The fare was $2.10. It had been for years. "Sorry, friend. Two ten it is."

"But I got a dollar."

Fern drew her sigh back into her chest. This was the problem with bending the rules sometimes. The information spread. You let an old lady get on board for a dollar once, and everyone in five miles knew about it. Ralph, he never had these problems. He'd been driving for AC Transit for longer than God had been making light, and he never let a single person skip fare, not once. Most drivers didn't worry about that stupid extra dime. Who had two dollars *and* a dime? People stuck two dollars in the machine and then moved along, giving Fern that look, the one that made her feel the pain they obviously had in their feet, in their backs, in their necks. She let them slide. It wasn't fair, anyway, that the Clipper card gave that ten-cent discount to people rich enough to have computers at home, people who had enough money to *have* a bank account that issued them a debit card and direct withdrawal. *They* didn't need those two-dollar rides, not like her regulars, who could use the slim weight of those dimes resting at the bottom of their threadbare, repaired pockets.

"A dollar?"

He was a repeater. If she let him on board, that was probably all he would say. A dollar, a dollar, a dollar. She was going to stick with no. This time, she would hold out. She would respond in the negative and mean it.

Then she looked in his eyes. Most people met her eyes, if they did so at all, with just a flicker. Just a half second of connection. That's all anyone had time for, not including little kids and the seriously ancient ones.

Fern met the guy's eyes, and they were empty. Under his wrecked, ruined skin, above the slit of a mouth that wobbled, his gaze held hers, and the awful thing was that there was nothing in it. No one should be able to hold a look that long without communicating something—anything—and this man had nothing left to give. Probably hadn't for years and years.

"All right, buddy. Come on." He didn't give her a dollar, and she didn't ask him to.

Matty was the next stop. That was all that mattered. Then she was there, the door opened, and the jittery no-dollar man swung himself off, jangling down the sidewalk.

Fern scanned the flock of kids waiting to board. Three boys, two with skateboards, and one girl dressed in black, carrying a longboard. Matty was behind them. She could tell he was trying to fit in, to eavesdrop. He wanted to be a skater—it just wasn't ideal that he fell off his thirdhand skateboard more times than he stayed on it. He wanted to listen to them, to think of something cool to say—she could see it in the way he kept his shoulders high and tense. The kids paid no attention to him. They climbed on board the coach without glancing over their shoulders once at her boy.

Matty swung himself into the seat that Fern always kept for him by putting her coat over it. Funny, how there was obviously no one *sitting* in the seat. It wasn't like a passenger had nipped to the bathroom or something. This wasn't like a café, where someone might lay claim to a chair by leaving a sweater on it, by putting her sunglasses on the table. If a seat on a bus was empty, for sure there was no one coming back to claim it. But when Fern put her coat on the seat, no one ever touched it. Over the last two years she'd been picking up Matty on her route, only one elderly man had pointed out that someone had left a jacket behind, and in thanks, she'd given him a coupon for three free rides that she was supposed to save for people who gave up their seats.

The rumble of the bus ran up her legs to her seat. She glanced over her right shoulder. Matty held his skateboard on his lap, absentmindedly spinning a wheel with his thumb.

"Pizza when I finish my shift?"

He frowned. For about a month at the beginning of middle school, when everything had changed, he hadn't wanted her to speak to him at all when he got on the bus. *You can't,* he said. *You're the bus driver. The* other *bus drivers don't drive their kids around.*

The other drivers weren't as lucky as she was, that's what Fern always told him. *What other job,* she'd ask Matty, *would let me hang out with my best kid for the last hour or two of my shift every day?*

I'm your only kid, he'd say back.

Best kid, she'd repeat.

Free day care. That's what Fern never told him.

Once, Matty had admitted he didn't actually totally hate riding her bus. She hadn't planned on eavesdropping, but she'd been putting towels away in the hall closet and she'd eavesdropped on what her son and his friends were talking about while they played Minecraft. "Your mom seriously drives a bus?" River had said scornfully. That was rich. Even though River was white as a Safeway receipt, even though his family lived on the north side of 580, River's mom, Heather, was a night waitress at a diner that got regularly raided for having a cardroom in the back.

"Yeah," said Matty.

"You *have* to ride her bus home from school?"

Fern's heart had lodged uncomfortably right underneath her tonsils.

"Yeah. It's cool, though."

"Yeah?" River hadn't sounded convinced.

"I get to see her fight with people."

"Whoa. Like with weapons?"

"Nah." Matty had paused for effect. "Not that often. Only sometimes."

"What kind?"

"A guy had a knife once." Matty had made a squeak then, as something went wrong in the game. "And once maybe a gun."

"You saw her use a gun?"

"No. She told me, though. She didn't use it, though. The guy had one."

"A real one?"

Fern, even though she couldn't see into his room from the hallway, could almost see his small shoulders lift and fall. "She told him to get the eff off her bus. That's all." Hearing that had made Fern feel like she'd won something huge. Something better than the lottery, maybe.

A bike darted in front of her left wheel. She swerved and gave a long blare of the horn, making sure the bicyclist would live another day.

"Hey, kiddo. You didn't answer. Only twelve stops left. Wanna get pizza with me?" *So I can break your perfect hopeful heart.* While keeping her eyes on the road and her left hand on the wheel, she stuck her right fist out behind her.

"Okay." Matty leaned forward and fist-bumped her. He'd picked it up from Fern's brother, Diego, and on these streets, it was as good as a kiss. Matty, her baby boy who wasn't a baby anymore. He was eleven, and someday he'd be a man, and he'd want to go by "Matias" instead of "darling Matty" or *"mijo,"* and then he probably wouldn't let her kiss him good night, but Fern had this idea that she'd sneak up into his house on a ladder like the mother did in *I'll Love You Forever* and kiss him good night. Grown-up Matias would never know she'd been there, but maybe he'd sleep better because she had been.

But all she had right now was this minute, and that's just about all she had, so with her boy tucked safely in his corner seat, Fern made her coach dance.

chapter *twelve*

The first time, Abby had been fourteen weeks along.

Fourteen weeks was long enough to have had the colors for the nursery picked out (a yellow that reminded her of thinned sunshine, as if they'd put it in the can and mixed it with unclouded well water and then added the warmth of a light blanket).

Fourteen weeks was long enough to have a short list of names. Hannah, Timothy, Mabel—old names, and all of them probably too trendy, but she couldn't help it—they were sweet and warm and round, exactly the way she felt about the sweet, warm, round thing she was growing. She was better than a plant. She was stronger than a tree. She was growing a *human*. Someone had cast a magical spell on her, liquid and preternatural. At night, lying next to Scott, she felt sorry for him, and that made her generous. She would share as much as she could of this with him. He would never know what it was like to feel like a mystical being. While he slept, she pressed the low bulge of her stomach against his back, trying to share the glorious warmth of her skin, the strength of her bones.

After all, the miracle had all started right there, in that bed. The embryo had begun to grow inside her one night, as she slept. Her body had made it happen, and she hadn't had to think about it. Abby—who had to make notes on her calendar to remind herself to change the filter in the water jug and when to fertilize the tomatoes—hadn't had to think about making a *person*.

It had ended there, too. She'd felt a cramp in her sleep, and had twisted once. Then twice. Three times, she'd stretched her legs out straight in the bed, pushing her toes against the top sheet. Cramps. She'd have to get up and take an Aleve, or she'd be miserable for the rest of the day.

It wasn't until she tried to stretch out the pain a fourth time that she remembered, still wrapped in slumber, that she wasn't getting her period—she was pregnant.

During any earthquake, big or small, Abby had always found herself in a doorway so fast she couldn't remember getting there, couldn't remember making the conscious decision to move. It was like that then, the first tremor of her body's betrayal. She was in the bathroom before she knew she was moving, before she'd even totally worked through what might be happening.

"No, no, no, no." If she said it enough, it would be true. "No, no, no, no, no." If she'd imagined a miscarriage (which she carefully hadn't, not once letting it slide through her hopeful mind, not even reading that section of her pregnancy book), it would have been bloodier than this. It would have been a hemorrhage, a red war, a sea of blood that would rush through her bathroom, carrying her out of the house and straight to hell.

Not this. There was just a streak of blood on her panties. Not enough to terrify her. Definitely not enough. Thank god. The pain was low and dull. She wiped, the blood bright on the tissue, and left the bathroom to get the book. She took it back into the bathroom and sat on the toilet again to read. She didn't have to pee, just felt that solid ache, but she wanted her legs bare, parted, open. She wanted to be able to reach down to feel, to push it all back inside, if she needed to.

It had stopped, though. The tissue was clean.

She sat, and found the sentences she needed. "Spotting is normal—as many as one in five mothers-to-be experience it in their first trimester." She clung to the words, memorizing them.

Then the cramp twisted, moving to pain. Real, actual pain. Pain that would have required more than Aleve to fix, if she'd been willing to actually admit that it was happening. *NO* wasn't a strong enough word, but as flimsy as it was, it was all she had. It was a shout in her head, but only a whisper in her mouth, and it slid sideways, *ohhnn-ohhnn-ohhnn*, the beginning of the word bleeding into the end of it as the blood trickled again, this time increasing to a rush that nothing could have stemmed.

And even though Scott said she would be okay, even though the nurse who'd checked her in had said she'd be just fine (she'd been such a *pretty* liar with eyes the color of blue borage), Abby had known.

Scott held her hand. He'd looked upset. So sad. And no matter how sad he'd looked or felt or said he was, it wouldn't have been enough to match her grief.

Abby hadn't been strong enough to hold all that life inside her.

Abby, who could unroll chicken wire without wearing gloves, who could carry two large bags of Black Gold potting mix at once, who had always had small biceps curled under her skin, wasn't strong enough.

She'd always thought Meg, the lost sister who'd lived only one day, was a bit of an exaggeration. Her mother cried every time she thought about the (nonexistent) baby. They celebrated her birthday every year with as many strawberry cupcakes as she would have been turning in age. As a child, Abby had always thought if they *had* to celebrate an intangible birthday, they should have at least done it with chocolate cupcakes. She didn't like strawberry. She never had.

But then, with her first miscarriage, still twenty-six weeks shy of how long her mother had carried Meg, she understood. How had her mother ever stood up again?

And even though she'd gone home that night (that *night*, they hadn't even kept her overnight to see if Abby would live, which, obviously, she probably wouldn't), even though she still had sensation in her limbs and familiar air in her lungs, there was a part of her that had never gotten up off that bloody soil. She'd felt the shot to her gut, she'd lain down in the battlefield, she'd closed her eyes, and she'd died. Then she'd had to leave that part of her behind, harder than petrified wood, useless even for composting.

chapter *thirteen*

Matty should have been more suspicious.

When Zingo, their old Siamese, needed to be put down, Fern had brought Matty to Itza Pizza to tell him. When his first-grade best friend, Hawk, was moving to Chicago, she'd brought them here on their last playdate. Not pizza pockets on sale, not frozen pizza from Target's sale section, not even takeout. The real stuff, eaten in the parlor.

Soon her poor kid would equate pizza with pain. *Dios.* She should have thought about it harder. Next time she had something bad to tell him, she'd take him to the dentist. At least that kind of association would make sense.

"You want quarters for the video games?" If they were really smart about their business, they'd put in both an ATM and a coin changer. They had neither, and Fern knew that the person at the counter never had enough quarters in her till, either. You had to remember to bring them in with you, and what about the parents who didn't know that? They had the *cool* games here, the old-fashioned ones, the ones she'd grown up with—Frogger and Battlezone and Tron—the ones that made a holy racket of blips and beeps that you thought would drive you out of your mind until you realized that they'd been pinging behind you for a half hour and you hadn't heard a thing. Their noise was awful and soothing at the same time. Exactly like the noise of an eleven-year-old boy.

Matty took the quarters and raced off. He didn't ask her to play with him like he did with Diego. Fern ordered the pizza and took a picnic table in a corner. It was deserted this afternoon, just them and another mother with two children that she was keeping close to her side. Maybe that woman was sharing bad news, too. Maybe those children's grandfather had just died in his sleep. Maybe the woman lost her job and this was their last pizza until she graduated night school and got a better job. Oh, god, maybe her oldest had been killed by a stray bullet—but as Fern watched, the woman put her head back and laughed, twisting in her seat and rubbing her very pregnant belly. No, that woman wasn't telling bad news—she was hoarding all the good news in the room. Maybe on this side of town.

That was okay.

Fern could do this.

She could probably do this.

The stuffed Roadkill came, with its five different kinds of cured meat. Even though it gave Fern heartburn, she got it because the name made Matty laugh. He sat across from her, saying something about a new board someone had had at the park. She should be listening to him—she should be completely engrossed in whatever it was he was saying about Raul's new wheels, Santa Cruz somethings.

"Yeah?" she said. Fern didn't know crap about skateboard wheels. She put another slice of pizza on his plate. Inside her mind, she practiced the words she would say in her head, slipping them like abacus beads across a string, counting them, one by one.

"You're not listening to me," accused Matty.

Fern jumped. "I *totally* am."

"Tell me what I just said."

Quickly, she rewound what she'd just heard. Something he wanted her to buy for him. "You need a new pair of . . . shorts."

"Nice try," he said.

"Gym socks."

"Nope."

"Jockstrap?"

Rewardingly, Matty fell sideways laughing. A jockstrap was always, always funny to him, along with farts and diar-rhea and wet burps.

"Hey, *mijo*."

In response, Matty straightened and took a bite of pizza. Around his mouthful, he said, "Yeah?"

She chickened out at the last second, swerving hard. "Mrs. Hutch wants to see me."

He hunched his shoulders. "I hate her."

"It's just life science."

"It's *stupid*. And she's mean. She hates me, too."

"You don't know what it's about? What she wants?"

A shrug. He didn't meet her eyes. "Maybe she's talking to all the parents."

That's not what the e-mail had implied. *Matias might need help more specialized than we have discussed in the past.* Fern hadn't been able to help the knee-jerk thought: *Bullshit.*

But then again, that's not why they were having pizza. It

was so much worse than a difficult teacher who didn't like kids to talk in any voice above a whisper.

"Okay. Anyway. Your dad . . ." Oh, god. She'd meant to be strong about it. *Your father died. Let's talk about what that means.*

Matty's jaw slowed. "Huh? Is he coming *back*?"

As if Scott were Jesus or Santa Claus or some other perfect and completely mythical white guy.

"Sorry," Fern said. "No. It's just really hard to say. Your father died."

Matty swallowed his bite of pizza, his small Adam's apple working hard, as if it had the whole job of pushing the food downward. Then, instead of asking anything, he took another large, deliberate bite.

"It was a heart attack. It was no one's fault." Of course that wasn't true. It was Scott's fault for not eating right and keeping his arteries clear. It was Abby's fault for not making him exercise with her. It was Grandpa Wyatt's fault for giving him faulty genes. Something. There had to be a reason. "It happened four days ago."

Matty swallowed. Then he took another bite.

Fern accepted this. "I'm feeling really sad about this. Your dad and I split up, but he gave me the best gift I've ever gotten."

Matty blinked and then frowned as if confused.

"You. He gave me you."

Matty chewed harder. Behind him, a video game sounded like it was going to come to life and hop across the crooked wooden floor, shooting lasers at them. The two children with the pregnant mother laughed and laughed.

This was so much more difficult than she'd thought it would be.

"You can ask me anything. Anything at all."

Instead, Matty took yet another bite, as if eating were a new video game fight combo and he was going to get it right. He choked for a brief second, and Fern's whole body froze—Heimlich. Did she remember it? Sheer, naked terror flooded her limbs and she couldn't remember how to breathe. Then he coughed a little and cleared his throat and the world came back to her. The picnic-table top was rough under her fingertips, and she pressed harder, hoping for a splinter. Something to feel, something immediate.

A thin muscle jumped in Matty's jaw, the echo of his father's. Scott got that jump in his cheek when he was upset, just like that.

Then his eyes filled with tears.

"Oh, baby . . ." Fern didn't get up. She didn't move around the table to hold him. That would have made it worse. Something in her son's watery eyes told her that.

He leaned forward and spit out the mouthful that had defeated him. "Why?"

"A heart attack." She'd tell him as many times as it took him to understand, even though every time she thought the words, her chest pulled with the tightness of the irony surrounding the circumstances. A heart attack. That implied Scott *had* a heart, and if Fern had come to doubt anything about her ex, it was that. "You know how my car used to stall sometimes before I got it fixed?"

Matty nodded.

"A heart attack is like that. The engine just stalls." She paused. Matty's jaw still worked even though his mouth was empty now. His face was so thin. Was that new? Was that to go along with his growth spurt?

"They can jump-start a heart," he said finally. "Like a car.

With jumper cables. They showed us in health. There's one in the cafeteria. It's a blue box and once Simone pulled it out and an alarm went off and she got in trouble."

Fern imagined the stocky metal clips attached to Scott's heart, red and black leads clipped to a Honda battery. "You're right. A defibrillator."

"They didn't have one?"

"They did. They put the thingies on his chest and they gave him a jump start, just like Mr. Hayes used to do to the car. But you remember that morning it didn't work even with his cables? That morning we had to call a cab to get you to school on time?" She remembered that morning, the panicked wings beating in her lungs, Matty's small worried face, the phone call to Friendly Cab, the searching for her emergency twenty-dollar bill that she *knew* she'd stashed somewhere once, after a strangely flush payday. After ripping apart her address book and her calendar, she'd found it behind the small stack of business cards she'd been collecting from speakers in her night business classes.

"Does Grandpa know?"

That had been bad last night. Fern had woken him from his nap. He'd laughed at first. *Thought you were coming to tell me I was late for work!* The man hadn't been behind the wheel of a tow truck in seven years.

Scott died.

Wyatt had sat on the edge of his small bed, already in his pajamas even though it was barely eight at night, his hands on his lap, palms up. He'd looked over Fern's shoulder, his gaze blank.

I thought he'd come around. I really did. I thought he'd come around. Tears had dripped down the old man's face as if the loss was new.

Fern bit the end of her straw and tasted plastic. She spoke around it. "I told Grandpa last night."

"You didn't tell *me* last night."

"That's because you were harder to tell."

"Why?"

Because Grandpa gave up hope a long time ago. You lived in it. "Because."

"Is there . . ." Matty pushed away his plate, his second slice uneaten.

"Yeah?"

"Is there gonna be a funeral?"

Fern bit the inside of her lip. "A memorial, yes."

"Are they going to put him in the ground?"

She took a breath to try to slow her racing heart. It didn't work. "Cremation."

He scowled and picked up a fork. He poked at the crust, then stabbed it. "When?"

"Day after tomorrow. Sunday."

"*Sunday?* Can we go?"

"Do you want to?"

"No."

"Okay."

"Wait. Maybe."

"It's okay not to know what you want to do. Grandpa is going. You and I can decide later. We can stop at the store to get some clothes, if you want." She meant the thrift store. She meant funeral-appropriate clothes.

Matty was still catching up. "He'll *burn*?"

Fern wanted to reach out and stroke his hair, but she knew he would just bat away her hand. "When you think about it, it's kind of the same as being buried. It's just your atoms rearranging. . . ." The church used to think you shouldn't be cremated, but Vatican II said it was okay, like God suddenly figured out how to pull the dust back together in the atomic age. God got smarter as man did, apparently. What a crock. Matty was eleven. He shouldn't have to think about this. Ever. He was bad at science already. He shouldn't have to—

"No, that part is okay. Would we get to watch?"

Fern stared. "What?"

"Burying people is disgusting. Maggots and worms and stuff. And stinky. Like when we found that possum under the house. Cremation is just like . . ." He held the blackened end of his crust in front of his eyes. "At school, Asman was talking about it. For his uncle. He thought it was cool."

Fern wanted to parrot the last word incredulously but stopped herself just short of uttering it. He was eleven. He didn't know his father, didn't know that the shape of Scott's wrists was identical to his bony ones, and after he burned, the comparison would be impossible. Forever. She'd bet Asman Singh had made cremation sound macabre and amazing—that kid could talk the rest of them into doing or wanting anything. He was the reason Matty had wanted a skateboard, come to think of it.

Matty started to say something else, then stopped.

She waited.

"I just . . ."

Fern felt fear spike at the back of her head, right where a headache was starting.

Matty's voice was tiny. "I just thought I'd get to . . . that he would come back for—"

Back for me.

"I know, baby."

"*I* would have." He started to say something else, but the noise stuck in his throat like the pizza had.

Fern's breath juddered. "You are nothing like him." Except for those wristbones.

"Grandpa says I look like him. Sometimes he says I act like him, too, but that's usually when he's mad at me."

Last spring, Fern couldn't completely get the toxic green abandoned-vehicle sticker off the front of her car window (it had *not* been abandoned—she'd just left it in the same spot for three days and it wasn't like she had time to wash the old beater). She'd been chipping and peeling at that sticker for almost a year now. The cheap paper stuck forever and ever. It would go to the junkyard with traces of it left on the glass. But Scott could erase a whole family from his life without ever getting in trouble for it. He hadn't even told his new wife he had a *kid*. He'd sent them money, which was *not* being a father. (God, the money. She should have gotten a smaller pizza.)

"Trust me, Matty. You're not like him."

Deep down inside, Fern had known Scott would someday get his comeuppance. She'd yearned for it in a way that wasn't right—anything that hurt him might end up hurting Matty somehow, so she was wrong for wanting it. But she imagined it sometimes. How he'd come to the door and Fern would slam it in his face. She could almost hear his voice sobbing on the other side of the wood. Or later, years down the road: he would want to be near his son, and Matty wouldn't meet him. He'd be denied. He would hear he had a grandchild, maybe, and wouldn't be allowed to meet her.

But no. Scott had gotten away with it. He'd gotten away with all of it. She picked a flake of red chili off her plate and put it in her mouth. She bit it in half, and let the heat spread over her tongue.

Matty's gaze turned suspicious, his chin angling southward. "Is this about that lady who came over last night?"

"Abby. Yeah. It is."

Matty nodded and stabbed his pizza again—it was oozing bloody tomato sauce all over his plate. Then his hand stilled. He looked up. "She *said* she knew you." His voice was fractious, like he was a feverish toddler.

"She's your dad's wife." Was. Damn it, Fern should have said *was*.

"Oh."

So much in that one word. Fern's heart, already small and weak, shriveled even more inside her chest. "Did you like her?"

He shrugged. His default move.

"She thought you were nice." *Lovely* had been her word. Fern had to admit, it was a good word for her boy. He was lovely.

Matty frowned, but his pizza jabbing slowed.

Fern waited.

More jabbing. He sprinkled chili flakes from the shaker on top of the perforated pizza crust and then used a tine to shove them more deeply into the bread.

"I don't get it."

"She . . . she loved your dad."

"So what does that mean to me?"

"Nothing." Why had she told him that? Scott couldn't even manage to love his only child. "It doesn't mean anything, *mi pollito*."

Matty groaned and leaned backward. "I *hate* it when you call me that. I've *told* you that a *million* times."

"Sorry. *Hijo*—"

"I don't want to talk."

She swallowed the words she wanted to say, all of them, one by one. "Okay. Eat some more."

Another stab of his fork. "Mom?"

"Yeah." She swallowed the endearments, all of them, that rose in the back of her throat.

"I'm pretty mad at him."

"Me, too. Matty—"

"Can I have some more quarters?"

"Honey, we should . . ."

"God." Matty threw himself over the bench to standing. "If I knew we were coming here just to *talk* and *talk*, I would have said I didn't want pizza. I still have a dollar anyway. I don't *need* any more quarters." He stomped away, dragging his heels on the wood like he did at home.

Fern felt the happy-looking woman looking at her. At her son who yelled, at her table now empty of anyone else. She wrapped her hands around the pint glass of root beer she'd ordered because it sounded like fun when Matty had said he wanted one. It was still half-full, now warm and flat. It was sickly sweet, too sweet for an adult to tolerate.

Kind of like that Abby, with her pillow pressing, her big eyes, her damned concern. *Lovely.*

Fern tipped the glass, slowly. The edge of the liquid slid toward the lip. She let a little fall onto the picnic table. It ran through the crack and dripped to the already sticky floor.

There.

She'd poured one out for Scott.

That's all he would get from her. He deserved no more.

chapter *fourteen*

Abby was being handled. If she hadn't been so aware of it, she might have welcomed it more. But from the woman at the front desk who greeted her with a soft handshake and an even softer gaze, to Isaac, the "memorialist" in charge of the service, everyone was ushering her around like she was in danger of bolting.

She wasn't.

She *might* have run, another day. Two weeks ago? She would have bolted like her intransigent arugula had last month, shooting up spikes of green and white flowers faster than stars streaked across the night sky.

But today, her skeleton had been replaced by wood. Teak, probably, strong and fast-growing. The wood was twisting under her skin, moving through her veins, replacing the calcium in her bones. It would take more than a lightning strike to weaken her.

"Here you go," said the woman named Perla. Her voice was ready to empathize. "There's a box of tissues here, under the registry. And there's a box at the end of each row of chairs."

Now that they'd been pointed out to her, Abby couldn't see anything but the ubiquitous pale blue boxes. They jumped into her vision like bunting at weddings, gaudy and ready to do their job.

She'd cried for days, on and off. At first, she thought she'd swallowed the sea. She would never run out of water, out of salt. But since her drive to Oakland on Thursday, since meeting Scott's son and his son's mother, she'd run totally dry. Even when she tried to make herself cry, she hadn't been able to conjure up so much as a sniffle. It was numbness, she knew that. There would be more tears where they'd come from. That's what Kathryn had said, "Normal. Sometimes we don't feel things all the way through till we grow smack into 'em. Like a tree root, you know? It doesn't hurt the plumbing till it tears out a pipe."

Normal.

Abby knew one thing: normal was *not* a room like this. Dark wooden chairs lined perfectly along a deep maroon, plush carpet. The vacuum lines were so straight at first Abby had thought they were a pattern on the carpet. Who pushed the vacuum that carefully? A young man, she imagined, some stoner kid who couldn't find a better job than cleaning a funeral home at night. Did he take pride in his straight lines? Or were they something he had to do so he didn't get fired? Did he listen to heavy metal on his iPhone as he worked? Did he have to clean the back rooms, too? Were spilled fluids his responsibility?

What about the burning machine? (Abby had Googled it: it was called a cremulator, which made it sound like something to be used while baking. *Use the stand mixer to beat the dough, then use the cremulator until desired texture is reached.*) Whose responsibility was getting all the ash out of it and into the boxes or urns? What if they didn't get it all? Was that even policed? Abby felt a burst of nerves—oh! decidedly not numb—in the pit of her stomach. At least with burying bodies, like she'd done with her parents, there was a comfortable level of deniability as to what was going to happen to the people. They were made to look pretty. They were put in a solid box that would take a long time to degrade. No one had to imagine what they would go through when you turned and walked away.

Burning, though.

Scott would be gone, physically, within a couple of hours, according to the tasteful pamphlet Isaac had given her when he'd run her credit card. It would take two to four hours. Nothing left but smoke and ash. She didn't ask about metal fillings. The screw placed in his wrist after he'd broken it right after they'd met. She didn't want to know.

Abby went to the bathroom (Perla ushered her carefully to the private one marked FAMILY—so thoughtful of them to provide a private place for a widow to sob and scream and wail, Abby thought dispassionately). She didn't have to use the restroom—it was just someplace to be that wasn't out there, standing with Kathryn. Kathryn—wonderful Kathryn—who would have taken all the pain for her if she could have. She'd even put on a dress and makeup for the event, her lipstick chalky and her foundation unevenly applied. She was trying so hard to help, and it almost physically hurt Abby to stand next to all that love.

Abby sat on the closed lid of the toilet and clicked open the small black purse she owned expressly for going to funerals. At home she had at least two more small black purses with equally specific uses: she liked the one with the black-on-black embroidery for night weddings, and the one with sequins was for charity galas.

What *bullshit*. Black, expensively made purses. No one— *no one*—needed to own three. All she had in it was her phone, her credit card, the single pine needle for strength, and one of Scott's handkerchiefs.

Next to her knee was a metal sign that read FOR YOUR SANITARY NEEDS. Perfect. She took out one of the opaque plastic bags and dumped in the handkerchief, the credit card, the pine needle, and her phone. She set her empty purse carefully behind a display of yellow roses next to the sink. If they found it somehow while she was still there, she would deny it was hers. Later, they could donate it to some widow charity, whatever thrift store specialized in ugly black dresses and hats with small black veils.

Clutching the top of the plastic bag, Abby let herself out and followed the vacuum track marks back to the Celebration Room.

The seats were mostly full. It was almost time. Abby knew most of the people. There were Roberts and Sons clients and there were families from their neighborhood. Scott had been active in Berkeley's Small Business Association, and most of them were here. Guys he golfed with stood in a small clump, awkward in suits rather than polo shirts. A tight cluster of her friends sat near the front, a polite two rows back. At the sight of Abby, Lisa waved, and Simone started crying. Even this far away, Abby could tell that Vivian was furious at Simone for starting the waterworks too early, but she also knew that later on, Vivian would be the one who wouldn't be able to stop sobbing.

Then she saw them.

The older woman who'd been at Fern's house, Elva, and an old man wearing a scruffy brown suit. He didn't look like Scott, not exactly, but he held his spine the same way, slightly sideways, as if looking for a wall to lean against.

And next to them, Fern and Matty.

Thank god.

chapter *fifteen*

"All these people knew Dad?" Matty's head was on a swivel and his eyes were huge.

Fern hated it when Matty called him that, like it was a title Scott had earned. "Probably not."

"Huh?"

"Sometimes people just come to funerals to be polite. Even though they didn't know the person."

"That's stupid."

Fern agreed. She didn't point out that's what Matty was doing, too. Goddamn it. What were they doing there? This wasn't the place for them. These weren't people they knew. The plush chapel smelled of the kind of perfume that never got on Fern's coach. All the expensive clothes, the perfect peach lipsticks, the men's gleaming shoes: all of it was freaking her *out*. The last funeral she'd been to had been Earl Stanton's, and that had been at the First Baptist on Adeline. The rollicking service had been followed by a catfish fry-up, his favorite. There had been paper plates and Costco napkins and a keg of Corona that got tapped before the sun went down.

This place probably spent more on furniture polish than the First Baptist paid their pastor.

There was still time to leave, still time to usher Matty to the car. She'd leave Grandpa Wyatt and Elva to pay their respects and take Matty to Fentons, to get him an ice cream sundae bigger than his head and make him forget all this. Like he was five instead of eleven.

Eleven goddamned years Scott had ignored his son and they were *honoring* him by being here? A sudden punch of fury made the inside of Fern's head feel as if it were made of tin— lightweight and hollow. She looked at her watch, counted backward. Had she taken her Carbatrol? God, she didn't remember taking it, didn't remember swallowing the glass of milk she took it with. . . . Was the tingling in her arms from anger or part of a seizure aura? Because if she fell down and started seizing right here, in front of Scott's people? Oh, *hell*, no. When she came out of it, when she looked up at these terrified faces staring down at her like she was an animal in the zoo, she would just have to kill herself, and wouldn't that be something for Matty's therapist in twenty years, watching his mother stab herself to death with a ballpoint Bic at his father's funeral?

She put her hand on Matty's shoulder.

And there she was. Abby.

She looked so relieved, so happy, as if she'd been waiting for no one but them. It was just weird. Fern couldn't help looking over her shoulder as if there was someone behind her who'd made Abby's face light up like that. But no. Abby was coming to them, to Fern and Matty, like they were the reason everyone was there, like they were the ones she'd been waiting for.

Fern decidedly did *not* want to hug Scott's widow. She took one protective step backward, but it was too late—Abby swept in and went high. Surprisingly, it was a good hug. Tight but not uncomfortable. Fast, but not a hit-and-run. It felt like a friend hug.

"I'm a hugger," Abby said, as she released her. "I hope that was okay."

Fern was a hugger, too. She just didn't quite want to admit it.

But Abby must have felt Fern's hesitation, and she didn't fold Matty into a hug. Thank god. Matty's eyes were wide, the way they got when he was nervous about where to put his feet next. She nudged his shoulder. "Say hi to Abby. You remember her."

"Hi," he mumbled.

"Hi. Oh, hello. I'm so glad you're here. All of you." Abby folded her hands under her chin, and in the black dress that was a little too big for her, and her hair pulled back simply with a black ribbon, she looked like she was a child from a picture book. A confused, clueless child with dark circles under her blue eyes. "Hello again, Elva. And you must be . . ."

Grandpa Wyatt stepped forward and held out his hand. "I'm his father."

"I'm sorry I didn't know about you before."

"I'm sorry my son was a jackass. And I don't give a shit about talking ill of the dead. I loved him. But he was a jackass."

Abby's shrug was graceful. "I'm glad you're here now. Will you all sit with me?"

"Sit?" Fern looked around, as if a chair would suddenly

materialize next to her knees. The back of Matty's hand brushed hers, and if she didn't know him so well, she would have thought he wanted to hold her hand. He was eleven. He didn't.

Abby gestured to the front of the room. "Up there."

"Oh, no."

"Please."

The room was already full of people who looked like they belonged there. Fern could feel their curious gazes crawl over her softly, like spiders' legs, ticklish and unwelcome. She could feel them wondering. Judging. Who was the brown woman and the light brown boy? Their maid and her son, perhaps? Why was Abby standing so close to them? Was the boy a charity case of the family's? That would explain the black sneakers instead of the expensive, shined black shoes everyone else wore. Fern stood straighter, wishing again that she could have afforded to buy Matty a whole new outfit from Kohl's—even Macy's— instead of scrounging for a black button-down and black twill pants at the thrift store. She had bought herself a black blouse that she'd thought was nice, but it wasn't until they were leaving the house that she'd noticed the buttons on the front gapped. She hadn't been able to find a safety pin, and had finally decided it wouldn't matter.

Now it felt like it mattered.

No. Fuck that. She was here because the man who donated half Matty's genes had up and died, letting her son down for the very last time. There was an unexpected relief in the thought.

"Okay. We'll sit with you."

The tiny lines at the corners of Abby's eyes creased happily. "Thank god. Kathryn's here. I'll introduce you. But I have no . . . no other . . ." She paused, and it seemed as if all the low, polite chatter in the room just stopped.

No other family. That was obviously what Abby had almost said.

The unspoken—the *incorrect*—words hung in the air and Fern brushed past them as she walked up the aisle.

She raised her chin. Hell, yes, they'd sit in the front. She whisked invisible dust off the back of the chair before she sat, making pointed eye contact with the old white lady sitting behind her.

Hell, yeah. She'd make them all wonder about the maid.

The service was nice. Nicer than Scott deserved, Fern knew, but hey, whatever.

Kathryn, who was apparently Abby's deceased mother's best friend (a maternal stand-in? Fern felt jealous for one brief, unpleasant moment before giving her a California nice-to-meet-you hug), seemed kind and concerned. She sat on the end of the aisle and passed things down throughout the service. Mints. Gum. Tissues, drawn from a pale blue box. At one point, she'd handed down a ziplock bag containing granola, as if they all needed sustenance. Fern let Matty have a little and Grandpa Wyatt wolfed down two handfuls.

The casket was closed in that strange Protestant way. The wood was ruby red and gleaming, decorated with gold accents. Fern would bet it was the nicest one the place sold. In the same way she used to wonder what would happen if she stood up and yelled *Curse God* during Mass when she was a kid, she wondered what would happen if she ran to the coffin and shoved the hideous floral arrangement off the top of it and opened it. What would she do next? Spit in Scott's cold, waxen face? Kiss his stiff lips? She shivered and wrapped her arm around Matty, who couldn't take his eyes off the casket, either. Later tonight, she'd call Gregory, see if he could meet her on Wednesday afternoon, her early day. She needed warmth. She was cold inside, chilled to the bone, and she wasn't sure if even Gregory would be able to warm her up, but she'd let him try. Three days away. *Three.*

Fern, Matty, Abby, Wyatt. All of them Scott's people at one point, all of them in one place. *Four.*

Counting helped. *Five.*

Five people spoke after the minister's generic address: two men who had worked for Scott and had good things to say about his entrepreneurial spirit, one guy who had apparently golfed with him (golf!), a man from a board he'd sat on (Fern's mind boggled), and Abby.

Abby said only a few things, her words rapid-fire, as if she'd memorized the sentences a few minutes before and was trying to spit them all out before she forgot them again. *A good man. A loving companion. A thoughtful husband. Funny. Sweet.* Her voice didn't shake. It didn't break in that way guaranteed to choke everyone else up. She told a story of a time he'd taken an elderly woman back to her care home after she'd gotten lost—he'd lied to the staff, pretending to be her nephew, so the woman wouldn't get in trouble for wandering away. He'd stayed with her till she slept, holding her hand. He'd gone to visit her twice a week until she died three months later. In a rare lucid moment, the woman had rewritten her will, leaving Scott her storage locker, which was full of nothing but junk: useless lamps, old newspapers, and school yearbooks. He'd kept the unit for an extra year, paying the fees while looking for a relative who might want her old, broken things. Abby laughed, self-deprecatory, as she confessed the worst lamp of all, the pink one with the shredded gold shade, was still in pride of place in her husband's office.

She sat down again. For a second, Fern wondered if Grandpa Wyatt was going to stand and take the podium. He stirred as if he might. Then he sighed slowly, and the pain of it compressed a part of her own lungs.

Damn Scott. It would have been so much easier for Fern to *truly* hate him if he hadn't been loving when he'd been around. If he'd screamed at his father when he'd left. If he'd shouted epithets at Fern. In a hidden spot in her belly, just behind her navel, she wished—really wished—that he had hit her. That he'd thumped her just once. If he'd screamed at her in the middle of the night—the way her mother used to scream in Spanish at Diego and her in a voice thick with emotion and tequila—she could hate him from now until forever. Fern knew how to handle an enraged drunk and poorly aimed curses—it was easy. All you had to do was get out of the way so if they needed to hit something, it wasn't you or your brother. Fern's mother had spent a lot of time hitting the door of the refrigerator with a flyswatter because Fern learned to put it into her hand and suggest it. Not once had Fern's mother said, "Why? What good does this do me?" She'd just done it. She'd broken three flyswatters one bad winter, and luckily, she never protested when Fern put another one in the basket at the corner store. "Flies are bad this year," was all she'd say. Fern never knew if she remembered how they broke.

But Scott. He'd come into her life happy, and if he'd been sure he could have left them without hurting them, he would have departed happy, too. At the end of the service, the overhead speakers played "What a Wonderful World" and a series of photos scrolled across a tastefully framed screen. In every picture, Scott was smiling. He didn't know how to take one straight-faced. He'd been delighted with the world, but somehow he'd managed to let go of his only child, the boy who sat next to Fern, his eyes glued to the rotating photos, a child just as susceptible to delight as his father had been.

Matty blinked hard and jerked his neck backward. A noise rose among the people behind them—not so much a gasp as a collective sound of surprise. Of curiosity.

Fern looked away from Matty's face to see a picture of herself up on the screen. She was in the hospital. She was red, her face sweating. Scott was smiling with tears in his eyes. (T-minus one hour to liftoff—had he had a plan then? Or had he just run, spontaneously? She'd never found out. Now she never would.) Matty, wrapped in a thin blue hospital blanket, had just been placed in Fern's arms. It had been, literally, the happiest moment in her life, up to that point.

"Mama, that's me!" Matty's voice filled the room, as clear as if he were wearing a lapel microphone. And in that second, Fern had never been prouder of anyone. She leaned her shoulder against his. "It sure as hell is, *mijo*."

Next to her, Abby said, "I hope you don't mind?"

"No. It's . . ." Fern held a quick breath and then released it. "It's nice to be included." In one million years, she would never have predicted she would say that at Scott's funeral.

"Speaking of included, would you come with me into the back when this is over?" Abby touched her bottom lip and looked at her finger, as if she were checking for lipstick. Or blood. "I mean, not Matty, just . . . Oh, I suppose you can't do that."

And leave her son out here with Grandpa Wyatt and Elva? Not a great idea. At least one was guaranteed to wander off, and it probably wouldn't be Matty. "Why?"

The usher, perfectly suited to his profession with his long, sad face and long, pale fingers, was trying to lead them from their row, but Abby waved her hands at him. "Show everyone else out first, please."

"Ma'am, the widow goes first."

"Sir." Abby's voice was bright. Still friendly but very clear. "The widow pays the bill. Show the others out first."

A low murmur rose again as people gathered their belongings. "What's in the back?" Fern asked again. Next to her, she could feel Matty's ears get bigger.

"Oh. Yeah. They said . . ." The whites showed around the blue of Abby's eyes again. "There's a button."

Fern thought for a moment, scrabbling in her memory for anything about a funeral button. "I don't know what that means."

Matty leaned forward around her. "The button. It starts the fire."

"*Cállate*, Matias!" Why would he say something like that?

But Abby nodded. "It's the ignition button. Or something. To start the cremation."

"You're serious. They want you to . . . Matty, how did you *know* that?"

"I told you. Asman Singh, at school. He told us."

She stared at him. Fern had only ever worried about what blow job myths Matty might pick up on the playground. She'd never thought to worry about funereal horror stories.

"Remember? He said the oldest son in the family gets to push it. He pushed it for his uncle because he didn't have kids."

"*No.*" It was too macabre. Even worse than standing at an open grave.

Abby twisted the handles of a plastic bag. "They said it was an option."

"Well, it's not."

"Mom." Matty looked around the room and then back at her. "I'm the oldest son."

"Holy shit." It was the only thing she could think to say. "No way."

"I'm sorry," said Abby. "I shouldn't have . . ."

No. Abby shouldn't have. "We have to go."

"Mom." Matty used to call her *Mamá* at home. That was a long time ago now. "You're going to make her do it alone?"

Fern tugged her blouse down again, trying to close the gap. "Honey. It's not that easy." But really, it was. That was the problem.

"I . . . of course. That is . . ." Abby seemed to be fumbling for words. "Silly idea."

"Jeez, Mom." And it was that, that grown-up tone in Matty's voice, that told Fern what to do. He knew what was right. "I'll stay here with Grandpa." Wyatt and Elva appeared to be bickering over the last few raisins in the bag of Kathryn's granola.

"You'll be okay? They'll watch you." By that, she meant, *Watch them. Don't let them wander.* Poor Matias.

Solemnly he nodded.

"You're the best." Fern said it all the time. She'd never meant it more.

chapter *sixteen*

Fern had said yes. Abby had hoped she would, but she had automatically walked through every reason she would say no. First, it was creepy. Second, it was weird. Third, it was creepy *and* weird.

But she'd said yes.

Isaac seemed thrilled. "Of course you both may come into the viewing room. No one else?"

Abby watched Fern fold her lips tightly and shake her head.

"Very good."

Isaac in front of them, Perla behind them, Abby and Fern were ushered down a long burgundy corridor. Heavy-looking carved wooden doors hid what was behind them, and Abby fantasized for a moment about pushing one open. Just to see. Was this where they worked on bodies? Would she see a young man using sewing thread to close recalcitrant lips? Would the rooms behind these ornate doors be white and cold, full of medical supplies and liquids meant to stave off decomposition?

Questions battered at her like dark moths. Was this where they'd worked on Scott's skin? Where they'd brought color back to his cheeks? He'd had such natural color when they'd shown him to her—that terrifying green shade had been gone entirely, and while he looked a little too matte and a little too tan, he'd looked so *healthy*. Then they'd closed the casket. Forever. She'd wanted to touch him. Isaac had said she could. But when she'd tried to reach out to brush his face with the tips of her fingers, she'd quailed. (She'd realized too late that she should have slipped the pine needle she'd brought into the casket with him. For strength, pine should burn.)

With a murmured apology, Isaac pushed open the last door on the left. "Just here, to the right."

Fern was completely silent behind her, her footsteps not even making a sound in the deep blue carpet. They were ushered into a small, well-appointed room. A long red sofa was flanked by two burgundy wingback chairs. A pale blue tissue box sat on a glass coffee table next to yet another arrangement of Easter lilies. "Lovely flowers," said Abby.

Isaac beamed. "Aren't they? Locally sourced, of course."

"Of course." A patch of them had popped up in her garden—unasked for, a gift from a previous gardener—every spring since she'd moved into the house. They flourished with no attention, to the point that she'd thinned them the year before, guiltily tossing the bulbs into the green-waste bin.

Perla pulled back a floor-length red drape to display a large picture window facing the seating arrangement. On the other side of the glass stood an enormous machine, silver and industrial and frightening in its appearance of usefulness. That was it, then. The cremulator.

To the left of the window were two square buttons, one green, one red. She'd thought there would be just one.

Isaac gave a jaunty Vanna-like flourish at the window. "State-of-the-art, only a year old. The top of the line in efficiency and automation."

Was that supposed to make them feel better?

Fern made a small noise in the back of her throat. Abby felt her bones strengthen.

"You'll understand, of course, that we are . . ." *Distraught. Confused. Terrified.*

"Of course. I understand. It can be overwhelming, I know. Rest assured, though, that your husband"—he blankly refused to look anywhere near Fern's face, Abby noticed—"is in a better place now. And we'll take excellent care of his remains."

Why didn't they call them cremains? Someone must, right? It would make a good band name. The Cremains of the Day. Horrifyingly, Abby felt a bubble of amusement threaten to rise into her chest. It was just that Isaac's face—he was so *earnest.* He had a huge machine that *burned people to dust* and he was excited and proud of it. Unreal.

"Beyond unreal," murmured Fern, as if she could read Abby's thoughts.

"Now, Mrs. Roberts, the choice of how to proceed is yours." Isaac gestured at the sofa. "You may rest comfortably here while your husband's body is moved to the opening. I am happy to push the button for you, if you'd both prefer not to. Our assistant, Esther, will remain with the body until the operation is fully complete."

The operation. As if they were doctors, fixing Scott. The

same inappropriate urge to laugh rose again. She choked it back. "You said there was a choice?"

"Or, once we load the casket into the machine, you may start the process yourself." He pointed to the red button. "In many cultures, this is a method of honoring the deceased, and it's gaining more mainstream popularity every year." Isaac folded his hands over his belly, one stacked on top of the other. He was settled, his weight resting evenly on both legs. He looked ready to catch either of them, ready to hold out his arms should one of them start to sway. His expression was set to neutral kindness. He reminded Abby of a tax accountant she'd once known. February 1, the start of tax season, was Katie's favorite time of year. As people brought her their worrisome columns of numbers, Katie expanded and grew into the best, most useful version of herself. Isaac had the same look on his face—a deep contentment as he sank into what he knew, what he loved.

As soon as Abby got home, she'd rip out those unasked-for, unwanted lilies. She knew gardens. Easter lilies belonged in a funeral home. Not in her garden.

"What does the green button do?"

Isaac blinked. "It opens the machine. You won't need to push that."

What was it there for, then? "The red one closes it?"

"And starts the process."

Red, like flame. Of course.

"I think we'll do it."

Fern cleared her throat.

Abby turned to her. "That is, unless you can't. I totally understand that. But I'd like to . . . Oh, god."

"Okay."

"Really?"

Fern nodded sharply, as if she was worried she would change her mind. "Can we do it now?"

Isaac inclined his head, and on cue, Perla disappeared out the heavy door.

Abby stared at the red button. It was unlabeled. How many fingers had pushed it? What stories had it swallowed? Her heart clenched again. Was she doing it all wrong, all of this? "I'm—"

Fern said, "Don't worry."

"But—"

"I mean it. Look at me."

Fern's face was strong. So strong, like marble. She was solid stone next to Abby's suddenly flimsy wooden bones. "You haven't done anything wrong."

Isaac said in a voice that was almost a whisper, "I'll be right back, after I escort the casket in."

Abby breathed through her mouth, listening to Isaac's retreating footfalls on the tile. She glanced upward. It felt like a warehouse, not a church. How was this possibly the right thing to do? "We tried for a family. I couldn't keep the babies." Fern could, though. She'd been able to.

"He was just a man." Fern's eyes were furious—blazing— but her expression was still solid. "Simple. He was just a guy. He loved you."

"I should have—"

"No." Fern's hand touched Abby's wrist.

Unable to stop herself, Abby turned her hand, grabbing at Fern's. "But—"

"No but." Fern held both of Abby's hands in hers now. Strong. Solid. "We just push the button."

Behind them, a whirring started, a jerky thudding that

sounded like a luggage conveyor belt at the airport. And then the gleaming casket Abby had so carefully chosen rolled out through a door she hadn't noticed, next to Isaac. Isaac nodded through the glass at them, and a metal door on the machine rolled up. After the casket was pushed all the way into the machine by Isaac and a black-clad young woman with tattooed wrists, the silver door slid down.

Isaac walked out of sight and then back into the viewing room. He stood quietly, with his hands behind him, as if waiting. For what? For them to pray? Wail?

She felt Fern squeeze her hands. Then Fern leaned forward, as if to whisper in her ear. Abby leaned forward to meet her. Whatever Fern would say would be the thing that would get her through this. She knew it.

Almost inaudibly, Fern whispered, "What is it about that guy that makes me want to fart, just to see what his face would do?"

Abby choked on her laugh, pushing it back down into her chest. But the joy rose anyway, tasting sweet in her mouth. It tasted like something she remembered. Something she wanted to grow in her garden.

And then Fern farted. It was the tiniest toot that could have been the squeak of a shoe or a mouse in the wall. Abby bit the inside of her mouth so hard she tasted blood almost immediately. Isaac's face stayed completely straight.

She gave Fern a sideways glance.

"Sorry," Fern mouthed with a tiny wink. *"No hay pedo."*

It should have been wildly inexcusable. It was completely inappropriate that either of them wanted to laugh right now. But Scott had been king of the fart joke, blaming his own on anyone nearby before walking away howling with laughter. Abby knew it, and she knew Fern knew it, and if Scott were here (instead of just being *there*), he would have known it, too. He would have *definitely* made some lighting-his-fart-on-fire-with-the-furnace joke. At the thought, the delighted laughter rocked through her again, silently.

Fern had the same look on her face.

Abby tasted such sweetness in her mouth.

She wasn't alone. In this moment, she wasn't alone.

Isaac motioned to the red button. "Ladies. When you're ready." He sounded like the host on *The Bachelor* and then he faded back like smoke.

Abby stepped forward. Fern moved with her.

The tips of both their fingers (hers wood, Fern's stone) met on the button.

They pushed.

Together they made the machine on the other side of the glass roar.

chapter *seventeen*

Three days later, Fern was naked, listening to Gregory rumble. Fern liked a lot about Gregory, but she *loved* his voice. It was low and dark and thundered as quietly as thunder could—it didn't even sound like it should come out as words. It was just a quiet roar. The fact that he did make words, good ones, was a bonus.

He'd just loosed that voice, loud and strong, a few minutes before. They'd lain on his bed, panting. Fern felt his mattress, so much firmer than her old one at home, hold her up, and she was grateful. "Redneck Woman" played on his stereo— she mocked him mercilessly for his addiction to country (she'd asked him, *You do realize you're black?*), but she loved the way the songs felt in her chest. Warm and familiar.

"You know I'm falling for you," said Gregory, still naked, sweat drying at his hairline. "Right?"

"A la verga," said Fern, and then she laughed. "No."

"You wanna call it Valentine's Day? A little late?" His voice was light, like he was joking. She knew he wasn't.

"More than a week ago. No." She'd been careful not to even text him that day. He couldn't be her Valentine, even belatedly. He knew that. They had *this* time. These few short, deliriously happy hours a week between her early shift ending on Wednesdays and her racing across town to pick up Matty.

The real problem was that she was getting so close to feeling something more for Gregory, and she didn't want to do that. She didn't have time. She didn't want, didn't have, *didn't need.* When she closed her door at night, she dead-bolted it. She counted the people safe under her roof (Matty, Grandpa Wyatt, Elva, and her—always four). She said or whispered or sometimes just thought, *"Estamos completos."* They were complete at four. She didn't need anyone else.

But when she was with Gregory, next to him, skin to skin, she sometimes forgot that. "Oxytocin," she said.

"Bless you."

"No, it's a chemical. A drug."

"I know what it is, Fern. It's a hormone, actually."

"That's what we're feeling. That's all this is." She inhaled. The room smelled of the clove cigarettes he sometimes smoked. It reminded her of the way churches smelled, spice and smoke and hope.

He rolled onto his back. "Call it what you want. It feels really fucking good."

Fern laughed again. She couldn't help it. He was right. It did.

"Tell me I'm right."

She pressed a kiss to the inside of his forearm. "It does feel nice."

"You're adorable."

She snorted. "I am many things, I know." Fern was wide-bottomed. She laughed loudly and broke tension inappropriately (the dirty joke she'd told Matty's principal at Open House, the fart at Scott's funeral). She thought people were fascinating in their sheer *range* of different. Coworkers wanted to pick up buses from her, saying boarding an in-use coach with her leftover and cheerful passengers was always a relief. "Many things. But I'm pretty sure no one has ever called me that. Adorable is for kittens and knitted baby hats."

"What if I say it in Spanish? A-dor-a-blay?"

Fern grinned. "You're fluent! I had no idea!"

"What if one of us changes our mind about getting serious?"

"Mmm. We just won't." It was all she could manage. As surreptitiously as she could, she scoped the room for her clothing. It had come off as fast as usual, and she caught sight of her bra hanging over his exercise bike. Her jeans were at the foot of the bed—she could feel them balled up, right where she'd wriggled out of them. She would give up her panties for lost if she couldn't locate them with her toes. (Gregory loved her wide, white underpants, thinking they were a turn-on. They might not have been as fashionable or sexy as a wiggly thong, but they were practical, the best kind for wearing under the poly uniform pants—they breathed.)

"Fern. Say something."

"Your job," she said. It was all she could come up with. "You would lose your job, and I would never do that to you."

"My job? I get paid seventeen dollars an hour. You think I give a shit?"

He did, though. Some of the teachers at the adult school were just phoning it in, too old or too tired or too jaded to even try to pretend that they wanted to be there, teaching subjects that their students should already know. But Gregory . . . he'd been different. He never stood behind the lectern, for one thing. Most of the male professors held on to it like it was a prosthetic penis, stroking the wood as if they were in charge of keeping it hard.

But Gregory had started off the first night of Business 203: Microeconomic Theory class by having everyone move their seats into a circle. He put his papers and his pen on top of the little desk in front of him, just like they did. He was excited about the allocation and supply of limited resources. When he'd rolled up his shirtsleeves that first night, even with as tired as Fern had been after a nine-hour shift of driving through the rain on a route she didn't normally run, she'd felt something stir inside her. His dark wrists were narrow, but the planes of his hands were wide. She wanted to see more, to see if the hair on his chest matched that on his arms, dark and thick. When he started getting really excited about micro-scarcity models, she decided to try smiling at him. She liked the slight gap between his teeth.

Later he'd told her that when she'd smiled at him that night in class, apropos of nothing at all, he'd been so startled that he'd lost his place in his notes. That had felt good, to watch his eyes slam back down to his desktop, to hear him stammer. On the third night of class, she'd come up with two good questions to ask him after class. The first question had been designed to be boring and to require a long answer: something about the measurement of elasticities. That gave the rest of the students a chance to gather their things and leave.

He'd answered, at length. Fern hadn't listened to a word of what he'd said. She'd just watched his mouth.

"You said you had two questions. What's the other one?" He'd moved his book bag from one shoulder to the next. He smelled like honey, warm and sweet.

Fern had the ability—she knew she did—to act as if she had nothing but confidence. Even when she didn't. "Will you fuck me?"

He hadn't answered for a minute. For the first time all night, he grabbed the lectern. He stroked the wood for a moment, his eyes going darker as he looked at her. "I can't adjust your grade for it."

"I'll get an A anyway," she said, raising her shoulder the slightest bit. She knew she would. Numbers didn't scare her. The way his eyes heated did, a little. In a good way.

"It's against my contract."

She shrugged again, liking the way his gaze followed the movement of her breasts. "I'm thirty-eight. Not eighteen. I won't tell. Besides, do you love this job so much you won't take a little risk?"

Gregory shook his head, slowly. "No. No, I certainly do not love it that much." Then he'd kissed her, and they hadn't even made it to his place that time.

She wished they were back there now, in the classroom. After desk fucking, you just had to stand and pull up your panties and limp your jeans up your legs. It was always just a little too cold, and there was no place to cuddle. She should have kept all of it there, but one night they'd almost been busted by the janitor and it had truly freaked Gregory out, and he'd taken her home to his tiny apartment, to his bed that smelled of spice. Now she'd been there so often she knew where his extra toilet paper was stored. Even though she never stayed the night, or even into the evening, she knew what he sounded like when he slept—heavy breathing that slipped into a soft snore, a sigh as he rewrapped his arms around her body.

"Don't worry."

Fern felt disoriented, as if the mattress below her were floating. "Sorry?"

"There's nothing to worry about. Not here."

Fern wriggled her toes under his soft sheets. For one long second, she let herself imagine what it would be like, not having to leave. Being able to wake with him in the morning. To arise slowly, to make love again, to cook bacon and eat it in bed, to move to the couch with the paper and coffee, to laugh without worrying about waking anyone up. She hadn't had that kind of lazy day for so many, many years.

Gregory wasn't Scott. Not by a long shot. Gregory was a good man.

He might be a really good man.

And god, she didn't want to hurt him. "What about the women you're giving up because I'm keeping you from them?"

Gregory laughed again. "The hordes beating down my door right now, you mean?"

"I can't give you more than two hours on Wednesdays. Sometimes an hour or two on Sundays. That's not fair to you."

"Stop." The laughter was gone from his voice, and he turned to face her. He caught her hand and pressed it against his chest. She could feel his heart beating under his skin. She imagined it: the muscle extra strong from its slow, well-timed percussion set to beat in time with country guitars and fiddles.

A pause. "How did you meet Scott?"

The sudden topic change felt like a splash of cold water. She sat up while Neko Case sang that she was a man-eater. "Did you play this song on purpose?"

Gregory smiled that lazy smile of his. "That's the sweet genius of iTunes, baby. Now tell me about Scott. I don't know the story."

"In a line."

"What kind of line? Club? Starbucks? Bread line?"

"Closer to that last one, I guess. It was a job fair. He was in front of me." It had been at the Cow Palace on a foggy, cold morning. Fern had thought she'd be the first in line, because she was getting there an hour early. Instead, the line was hundreds deep. Yawns spread like the wave at a baseball game. Children ran in and out of the forest of legs, and Fern, still clueless then, wondered why people would be dumb enough to take their kids to a job fair. Now, of course, she understood.

"What were you there to apply for?"

"Anything. Everything."

"What had you been doing?"

Now she needed the pillow. Fern pulled it into her lap and fluffed the top of the case so that her nipples were hidden, too. "Same." She'd bused tables at Ensenada out of high school and moved up to waiting tables. Even though she was good at it and made good tips, it didn't quite cover her rent, so she worked as an artist model in San Francisco. In one hour, she made enough to cover the BART ride there and back and a Subway sandwich to go (veggie six-inch, the cheapest thing on the menu). Every subsequent hour was money she could put right in her pocket, the pocket that even then was lined with dreams. Someday she'd have her own business. She'd sell something that helped people. That made them happy. She just didn't know what that was, back then.

Shit, she still didn't.

But even working seven days a week, she still didn't make enough. God knew she couldn't afford college, even the local JC. She needed a profession. At the job fair, she'd find one. It would be busting at the seams with careers. She would go claim one.

Scott had been in front of her in line. He'd grinned at her, and she'd smiled back even though he wasn't her type. She liked a big, dark, muscled guy, someone who drove too fast and might be familiar with the inside of a jail cell (Fern could admit she'd been more ambitious than smart back then). She wasn't into a skinny white dude with reddish brown hair, a guy who didn't even look like he'd jaywalk without needing to go to confession. He was handsome, yes, but in a pretty-boy way. He probably didn't even *go* to confession—he looked like the kind of man who went to a church with naked walls and a bare, Jesus-free cross. If he went to church at all. But he must. Scott looked so *good*.

"He flirted with me for an hour while we waited for the job fair to open. I thought he was sweet and harmless. I thought he was some kind of college geek, a computer guy. He wouldn't tell me what he was going to apply for when we got inside, kept turning the conversation back around to me instead. It made me curious. I got this idea to follow him around and see if I was right, if he'd go right to the tech area first. So we go inside, and I tell him I have to pee, that I'll see him later. He tried to ask for my number, but I was fast. I saw him when I came out. He was just wandering. Like, aimlessly. Hands in his jeans pockets. Smiling at everyone." Fern dug her fingers into the pillow. "With that charm of his? He could have had any job, I think. But he just walked around and didn't talk to anyone. I followed him up one aisle and down the next, and then he just headed for the front door. I caught him then. I asked him what the hell he was playing at. I accused him of slumming." Fern's face heated. "I think I said something about overprivileged, entitled white boys whose mamas could afford to keep them in gasoline for their late-model muscle cars."

"So you were flirting."

"Basically."

"What did he say?"

Scott had listened to Fern's rant (she'd been a pain in the ass back then, too—excessively fiery for her own good) and then he'd said, all in one breath, "My mother just died of an aneurysm. My dad drives a tow truck. We're losing the house I grew up in because she was the only one who knew how to pay a bill on time. I have no idea what I'm supposed to do now."

Fern had told him that he was an idiot. That he could do anything he wanted. That she would help.

"I fell in love with him," she said, feeling the edge of the pillowcase, worrying the loose thread. "Probably that very second. He followed me back in, and he decided he might like to drive a bus for AC Transit. I applied, too, just to stand nearer to him for a while. Even with the epilepsy, I got the job, but he didn't pass the drug test. Just marijuana," she felt compelled to clarify. "Nothing hard-core. Then, instead, he got a job with a landscape guy out in Livermore. That's where he learned he liked to mow grass, not just smoke it." She shrugged. "I got pregnant. Then he left."

"So you fell in love with him because he needed you?"

She gave Gregory her fiercest look. "Don't you dare. Don't."

"What about your friends? Do they have to need you, too?"

It wasn't like she even needed friends. She had her coworkers. And her family. She didn't need more than that.

He touched her kneecap softly. "I barely know how to boil water, you know."

"Stop it."

"Sometimes I forget to pay the phone bill and I get late charges." He ran his hand up her thigh, nudging the bottom of the pillow.

"Cut it out."

"Mmm. I know what'll get you." Gregory leaned forward and whispered in her ear. "Last week, I couldn't balance my checking account. I was off by a dollar ten, and *I didn't bother to find it.*"

Fern groaned. "I have to go. I've been here too long already."

But then Gregory slipped his hand up her thigh and his hand started doing that thrumming thing that drove her out of her mind every time he did it, and she forgot to protest. That was all she could do, after all. Forget. She could forget what he'd said, she'd forget to worry, and for this long moment of being in this bed that smelled like a church, Fern could do nothing but feel every inch of her skin the way she used to feel it when she was younger and she had a whole lifetime of feeling ahead of her. Martina McBride sang "Let the weak be strong, let the right be wrong," and Fern laughed out loud at the joy of it.

Gregory's mouth, while she came, tasted like leisure, like luxury, like all the time in the world.

chapter *eighteen*

*R*ue oil.

Abby gathered the buds early in the morning, just as they were starting to bloom. She snapped them off with her fingers, taking with them three inches of stem, dropping them into her garden colander.

All the other women who had done this stood behind her as she plucked the flowers, quietly invisible, but there. Centuries of women before her, women of all ages, all body types. Witches, maybe—certainly women who had been *thought* to be witches. Mothers and daughters. Sisters. Probably very few of them had worn a red spandex yoga top and a Title Nine skirt, like Abby was, but they were doing the same thing.

Combating pestilence.

Fighting disease.

Battling pain.

Just by reaching forward and pulling off a few flowers.

She looked up. The sky was a pale, unconvinced blue. It would be the first truly warm day of spring.

Scott wasn't here to see it.

It was the strangest thing, that fact. So fucking strange.

In the potting shed, Abby ran the flowers under the tap and then dried them with a Florida orange tea towel that had been her mother's. She chopped the rue with her garden knife and then used the flat of the blade to bruise it. The broken blooms smelled sharp and acidic, a potent promise.

She combined the rue with olive oil and a little vodka in her biggest nonreactive pot. She heated it, low and slow. *Warm bathwater.* Years before, when she'd first been experimenting with herbal infusions, she'd learned the hard way that when oil got so hot it smoked, the infusion was ruined.

Heat could ruin things fast.

As she stirred, Abby kept her gaze out the small window. Her lower back ached slightly, and she was grateful for the twinge.

Last night, she'd felt nothing at all. Literally nothing. It had been terrifying. Just as she'd been drifting off, she realized she couldn't feel any part of her body. None of it. Her body had been as numb as if she were drunk—no, it had been worse than that. Even when truly, staggeringly drunk, you could still feel the blood pounding in your veins. This was different. It was as if she were a mind suspended in a jar. Nothing but a collection of thoughts, all smoke and no substance.

Terrified, Abby had twitched her arms and legs, to make sure she *could* feel (she could—the sheet was light, the duvet cover heavier; a hair tickled her forehead), and then, as soon as she'd stilled, the numbness had taken over again.

Over and over, she'd twitched to make herself feel. At one point, she'd bitten the inside of her wrist, hard, but the pain had lasted less than a minute.

Was this why people cut themselves? Abby finally understood the motivation.

She'd given up, following the numbness into sleep.

In the morning, she'd stood and stretched, intending to do yoga, to do *something* that would make her feel. But then she'd checked her e-mail—a shop in New Mexico who'd been buying her stuff (who knew how they'd found her? through a Brook soap connection, maybe?) had ordered ten bottles of rue oil. She had only one on the shelf, but rue was just starting to bloom, and it was the right time to harvest it.

Now Abby stood in the shed, stirring. Her back ached. She could feel the spot on her wrist where she'd bitten herself the night before.

And, as the oil warmed, she let herself cry. Slow, thick-feeling tears slid down her face. She didn't stop stirring to wipe them away.

Rue was good for arthritis and headaches. It eased pain. In ten days, the oil would be full-strength. She'd strain it then and pour it into bottles. She'd tie a ribbon around each. She'd mail them to New Mexico while wishing the recipients good health.

But for now, it would sit. The oil would rest.

And even though the potion was weak, Abby took a spoonful and blew on it until it had cooled. She poured it into her left hand, then rubbed her hands together. She pressed the oil into her hair, slid it across her forehead and down her wet cheeks and throat. She ran her fingers down her arms, and then bent, rubbing what was left into her bare legs.

She stood straight.

It was silly. It was just flowers and oil.

But she didn't feel like crying anymore, and she could feel the nerve endings of her skin again. Rue, used for grief. Rue, for regret and remorse. She wasn't surprised.

But she was grateful.

chapter *nineteen*

Fern, just across the threshold and not even all the way out of her uniform jacket, froze in place and stared. "Wait. What? What did you *do*? You broke the couch? Since this morning?"

Elva made a face, pulling her eyebrows together, wrinkling her nose. She looked closer to a guilty eight-year-old than her actual age of eighty-two. "We just ripped it a little." Then she disappeared back into the kitchen.

A jagged flap of blue fabric hung off the front of the couch, exposing a yellow pouf of what looked like wall insulation. It had always been an ugly thirdhand couch, but now it looked like something that should be left on the sidewalk for the garbage truck or an arsonist, whichever came first.

Matty's grandfather had to be involved somehow. He always was. "Grandpa Wyatt?"

Wyatt shook the newspaper in front of his face. "I was showing him how to fence."

"You what?" Fern felt the tension Gregory had untangled with his talented fingers and lips creep back inside her, twisting its way up her spine.

"Every boy needs to know how. Necessary in every trade."

In the sixteenth century, yes, probably. Wyatt had been a tow truck driver before he retired. The only fencing he'd ever done was fixing the barbed wire that ran around the tow yard where they kept the impounded vehicles.

Matty raced into the living room with a whoop. He stuck what looked like a sharpened dowel into a helpless pillow trying to make a run from the newly pathetic sofa. "On guard!"

"Hey!"

Grandpa Wyatt harrumphed and rattled his newspaper, lifting it higher. "My grandson is a natural."

Most days Fern was happy that Scott's father had picked them, but there were the occasional days she wanted to throw Wyatt back.

Fern scooped up Matty's backpack from the floor with her left arm, adding it to the other things hanging there: her purse and her coat and the paper bag from the drugstore. She made her way into the kitchen, sniffing suspiciously.

Tonight was a stew night, apparently, since her largest pot was actively bubbling on the stove. The air in the kitchen had a metallic scent tinged with an undertone of tomatoes and something sickly sweet.

"What are you making, Elva?"

"SpaghettiOs with a surprise protein addition."

"Hoo boy," Fern managed.

"Oh, the washing machine broke, too."

Fern pressed her elbows into her sides. "Broke, like it made that puddle again?"

"Broke, like it blew up. Black smoke."

"Smoke?" Now that she thought about it, maybe the acrid smell was coming from over by the laundry room and not the stove.

Elva pinched the air in front of her face. "*This* much fire. But I put it out! Baking soda worked like a charm, but we need more. Just in case. I unplugged it and cleaned it up best I could, but we're out of paper towels now."

From the living room, Grandpa Wyatt yelled, "Washer's a goner!"

Fern's knees felt shaky. Even a cheap washer was four hundred bucks at the Sears Outlet. The bank account wouldn't be able to cough that up for a while, especially now that she'd lost—she did the math quickly in her head—thirty percent of her income. She brought home thirty-three hundred dollars a month. She had *needed* that fifteen hundred from Scott. She would never have accepted it if she hadn't.

Matty raced through the kitchen, dragging the dowel on the tiles with a clatter. "I am *not* eating whatever that smell is." Then he ran for his bedroom. In a minute, he'd be plugged into Minecraft, his headphones on, his jaw slack as he thumbed the controls.

Grandpa Wyatt kept yelling, "Hey! The fridge isn't staying cool, either!"

Hasta la madre, the fridge, too? The freezer was already on the fritz, but this was new. She needed to get into bed with her Excel budget and make it work, find the money, pull it out from under the rocks she was going to have to start putting in Matty's sandwiches if she didn't figure out a way to come up with some more cash.

Wyatt shouted, "You wanna hear my best one of the day?"

No. She did not want to hear his best one. He made an almost full-time job of writing letters to the editor about how roads could and should be fixed. It didn't matter that he couldn't drive, hadn't been able to drive since he hit a power line and brought it down, draping it across his tow truck, trapping him inside an electrified metal box until PG&E got on scene to save him. He walked now, walked everywhere, noting potholes and fading road paint. He and Fern had that in common.

She yelled, "Maybe later!"

Elva gestured at the huge pot on the stove with her spoon. "This'll feed us for days."

Fern kept the sigh where it started, held tightly at the top of her sternum. *Focus.* She could manipulate the budget and aim for a miracle later, when she was by herself and could allow her face to relax into fear. Maybe this was the time she could finally go through her mother's Mexican coin collection. She could part with a few of them, surely? She had done some research once, and back then the 1959 twenty-centavo piece had been worth like eighty bucks. The 1940 one-peso coins were real silver, her mother had said, and had to be worth even more.

But they were her mother's treasure, the only thing left of her. Playing with the coins her mother had brought with her from Mexico was one of the few good memories Fern had of childhood. She'd learned to count from them, learning the numbers in Spanish first, then English. She got her love of math and talent for numbers from her mother, who'd never used her own talent for anything more than always being able to haggle the lowest rent in town (a not-small skill, truthfully). Fern had used the coins to teach Diego to count, and much later, she'd used them to teach Matty his numbers, too. On really bad nights, when she couldn't sleep for worry (tonight might be one of them), Fern would fold the 1945 fifty-centavo coin into her palm and hold it there while she slept.

Elva gave a mighty sniff and appeared satisfied with the scent of her dinner.

Fern was still suspicious. "Main ingredient? Besides SpaghettiOs?"

"Love."

"Well. How am I supposed to argue with that?" Fern dumped the bags onto the kitchen table and rummaged through Matty's backpack. He'd left half his bologna sandwich in its plastic bag, and the rank smell rose from the depths. Old, warm bologna. No wonder her poor thin kid didn't finish lunch. Well, at least SpaghettiOs were pure sugar—maybe there was a chance he'd eat some of it.

"The inspiration comes from the motherland, Italy." As far as Fern knew, Elva had a German heritage. "I added basil from the garden—"

"Come again?" said Fern. The only things growing in the backyard were weeds, some weird black-and-white tulips, and one artichoke plant that the previous owners must have put in twenty years ago. Fern neglected that plant completely, and every year it came back in the same place, giving them one or two huge artichokes, which she tried to remember to cook before they burst into purple bloom.

Elva rubbed her hands on her apron. "You know."

"You mean the *Silvas'* garden?" Maria Silva's backyard was

perfectly plotted, weeded, and fertilized. Maria was visibly horrified every time spring rains made the weeds on Fern's side wave over the top of their low fence.

Elva folded her lips and gave the pot a mighty stir.

"Elva?" It was like having three kids.

"She has so much basil back there. It's completely overgrown. Kind of a weed, if you ask me."

Nothing in Maria Silva's garden was a weed. "Did you ask her, at least?"

"I knocked." Elva slurped at the wooden spoon and then stuck it back in the pot. Fern turned her mind firmly away from germs. "But she wasn't home. I *would* have asked."

Fern doubted that very much. There was a good chance that Elva had waited until Maria's old Pontiac had pulled away from the curb before she knocked, if she had at all.

"Anyway," Elva continued, "like I was saying, in honor of my heritage, I made meatballs and added some extra spaghetti and some cannellini beans and some oregano. I think you'll love it."

Fern peered over her shoulder, something that was easy to do since Elva seemed to lose an inch with every one that Matty grew. "What are the black things on the surface?"

Elva looked mildly worried and poked one with her spoon. "Croutons."

"Oh, god."

"Scat," said Elva firmly, waving her spoon. Red sauce dripped to the floor. Her eyesight was bad enough now she wouldn't be able to see the carnage to clean it up. That would be Fern's job. It usually was. Grandpa Wyatt always offered to wash the dishes, but every time he did, he broke at least one plate or a glass. It was as if he juggled them while they were still wet for fun. To save money, Fern just did them. Matty helped—his job was to dry and put away, but sometimes, on late nights, he looked so tired with those dark circles under his eyes that it was easier to just send him to bed and do it all herself.

Tonight nothing felt easier at all. Every single knot in her neck that had come undone in Gregory's bed was back, tighter than ever.

While Elva muttered about whether it was right to commingle oregano and thyme in her Italian masterpiece, Fern finished poking inside Matty's backpack. She confirmed he really had done all his homework while they were on the bus—he'd lied about it a few weeks ago, and she hated the mistrust she felt now, but if he didn't stay caught up in science now, he never would. Mrs. Hutch was a nightmare of a teacher, and god knew *she* wouldn't help him.

But there it was—Matty had done it all. He'd put a careful check mark (he loved that part of his homework, that heavy black doneness of it) next to each of his assignments in his homework folder. Good kid.

She pushed the mail around on the table. Junk, junk, three bills, more junk. She had no idea how she was on so many catalog mailing forms, since she hadn't ordered a piece of clothing online or otherwise in at least four years. Work provided her uniforms, and the thrift store provided both her and Matty their jeans. T-shirts, socks, and underpants were cheap enough at Target. Luckily Oakland rarely got colder than a shrug of frost in the winter, and Fern had learned years ago to shop at Thrift Town in May for sweatshirts and boots a size or two too big for Matty. By the time the weather changed again, she could wrap them up as Christmas presents, and pretend that he hadn't helped pick them out months before.

He was *such* a good kid.

Fern raked through the mail two more times before she realized what she was looking for. The thin envelope from Scott wasn't there. She usually got it on the twentieth, and today was the twenty-second—oh, shit.

Of course it wasn't there.

Fern could practically still feel that red button under her finger, next to Abby's. Scott was ash, like—apparently—the innards of her washing machine.

She'd held out for a year after Scott left, refusing his financial help. The checks he mailed then were smaller. They were whatever he could afford (she'd never taken him to court, never thinking he'd have a real job anyway). When the checks were a hundred bucks, they were easier to send back to him, ripped to small pieces.

That first winter, before Elva and Grandpa Wyatt moved in, she'd used the stove to warm the house, turning on all four gas burners and propping poor coughing Matty up in his car seat on the kitchen table, making sure she never took her eyes off the blue flames, that she never forgot they were on. Gas was so much cheaper than electricity, and all the house had was electric wall heaters. It had taken three years of overtime, but she'd finally been able to put in the central heating. Even now, just hearing the *whoomp* of the gas heater as it kicked on gave her a visceral joy in the pit of her belly.

It wasn't until she didn't have the copay for her seizure meds that she deposited that first check from him. That one had been $537. Such a strangely specific amount. And always in the memo line, always: *Take care.*

The amounts had risen slowly. Once he'd added a Post-it that said, *I finally started my business.*

He'd been married to Abby then. She hadn't been happy for him.

Her phone pinged as an e-mail landed. Probably next week's schedule. She dropped into her seat at the kitchen table and opened the app.

It wasn't work.

It was the mortgage check.

Bouncing.

chapter *twenty*

When the cramps woke Abby in the middle of the night during her second miscarriage, she knew what they meant. She went in the bathroom and called the advice line on her cell phone, keeping her voice low. She could have woken Scott, but she didn't want to. The nurse told her either she could go in then to the ER or she could collect the blood (the "blood," as the nurse called it, was so much more than blood) and bring it to the obstetrics office when they opened at seven. They would determine then whether she needed a D and C like last time.

Abby couldn't face the brightness and noise of the emergency room again, so she let Scott sleep until six forty-five. He drove her to the doctor's office, and she tried to forget— to erase from her mind completely—the quick look he'd had on his face when she'd said, "I need to go to the hospital." On her lap she held a paper grocery bag, folded over at the top. Inside was a kitchen measuring cup that held what she'd been asked to collect. The other two women in the waiting room held their round bellies while they waited. Abby held the paper bag.

Nothing hurt very much, not compared with the shrieking in her head. The D and C removed the rest of the dead tissue and a good chunk of her soul. Pleasantly sedated, Abby wondered if they'd seen that part of her. Small and green, a tendril of curled hope and so much love it shouldn't have fit inside her body, but it had, it really had. The baby, her baby, her perfect boy, had made it to only ten weeks this time. He'd had a name, but she hadn't told it to anyone, not even Scott.

They gave her drugs for the pain. They said they would do genetic testing, just to rule things out. (What things? Things that could change the past?) The medicine made her stupid and slow. Less than eighteen hours after it had started, she was back in bed at home. They told her moving was good. She knew walking to the kitchen to make a cup of tea would make her limbs ache less. She made up her mind and swung her legs to the left, but when she felt the air outside the duvet, she shrank again. She shriveled back into nothingness, into blank space. Blankness required only darkness, not tea.

That night, Scott came to join her in bed, like it was any other night. He brushed his teeth like normal. He changed into his boxers. He slid into bed, slipping his phone into the charger as if it were any other night. He put his arms around her and she could smell his toothpaste. It smelled like relief, and it was unforgivable.

Instead of breaking, Abby felt like moving. Slowly, the drugs making her movements thick and heavy, she stood, taking her pillow with her.

"Where are you going?"

"Spare room."

"Abby." His voice, concerned, and there, she heard it, right at the bottom of the well he dug by saying her name, the slightest tinge of annoyance. Pique.

"I just need to be alone." She hated how her voice broke at the end of the last word.

"Come on. Stay here with me. Honey."

Childish.

He was childish.

She was *childless*. Didn't he see that? She was empty. She was nothing.

She slept alone in the spare bedroom that night. And the next. That bed, the one no one ever slept in, absorbed tears better than her own. It was dry, had never cradled grief. As sterile as she was, the bed was good at holding the pain.

On the third day after her second miscarriage, she heard Scott whistling in the bathroom and she wanted to kill him with her bare hands. She could have done it if she'd been able to make herself move. The rage was better than the grief. The sadness felt like her flesh was being torn by teeth, all rips and snarls and shredding, but the anger was a clean slice of relief.

The fury passed, though, a tornado that left nothing but wreckage and exhaustion in its wake. Twenty-two days after they scraped the hope from her uterus, Abby got into bed with Scott. Still mostly asleep, he reached for her gratefully. His arm curled around her waist, his hand tucking under her (empty) belly.

She allowed it.

. . .

Abby didn't let herself get excited the third time she was pregnant. She wouldn't believe it until the baby socked her in the jaw with a tiny, angry, perfect fist.

Eight weeks into the pregnancy, she was helping Kathryn at the nursery on a busy afternoon when one of Kathryn's employees had called out sick. Abby placed three quarters into the palm of the woman who had just bought a packet of tomato seeds. She felt her body twist, shifting sideways inside her. "Fuck," she exclaimed, and the woman dropped the change.

"Sorry, excuse me. Let me get that."

Abby carefully picked up the change and smiled at her customer. Then she carried her purse into the bathroom and took out the ziplock bag she'd been carrying with her. She pressed two enormous overnight pads into her already spotted underwear, wrapping the wings carefully around to the outer fabric. She slapped her right cheek hard, and that felt good, so she did it again on the left side of her face. Her face flamed, but she didn't feel like crying anymore.

She ignored Kathryn's looks of concern and loaded questions. No, everything wasn't all right. No, she didn't feel well. Of course she didn't. But Abby wouldn't say why. She wouldn't name it. Kathryn had been so upset by the last one. Abby couldn't take care of Kathryn today.

She called her doctor, who had been monitoring her closely—so closely—this time. No genetic problems had been found. They didn't know why it had happened twice before. And now, god, a third.

Her doctor said to come straight in. Maybe it was a false alarm. Abby drove herself to the hospital, knowing it wasn't.

And it barely hurt at all. God knew, she was so scarred by then they could probably do it without any anesthetic at all. It felt like she was a melon, like they were scooping out the flesh, scraping out the seeds. Melons didn't ache inside, so— resolutely—she didn't, either.

The bitchy outtake nurse wouldn't let her drive herself home, though. She had to produce an actual person to take her. She didn't want to call Scott and wouldn't call Kathryn. She presented Pharesh, the cabdriver, to the front desk with a ridiculous amount of sarcasm. She held on to his sleeve. "Here's a person. Can I go *now*?" There at the hospital desk, her insides dripped out onto the winged pads they gave her, the ones big as a diaper. *Diaper.* Everything that could have been was lost. She'd lost it all. Again. She didn't care if she bled through the pads with wings.

Wings held up nothing at all.

From the spare bedroom, she told Scott she had a migraine and that these curtains blocked out the light better than the curtains in their bedroom (they didn't). She said that she'd left the car at the nursery (it was at the hospital), that she'd get it tomorrow (she wouldn't, because she'd never move again).

Scott believed her.

That was the worst part, that he couldn't look into her eyes and know that she was empty. That he couldn't see that she was broken, that she was lost, that she had lost everything again.

He should have been able to tell.

He didn't even look into her eyes, anyway. He just nodded and said quietly, "Let me know if you need anything," before closing the door.

Need?

Need?

She needed rue oil (she hadn't known about it then, hadn't gotten into infused oils yet). She needed a priest to bless her, or a witch to curse her. Or vice versa. She needed help. She needed magic. She needed a map.

Three days later, she told Scott while she poured him a cup of coffee. Her hand didn't shake, which made sense because her blood was made of the same granite they'd just picked out last week for the new countertop. Pulling her to his chest, he said, "You didn't do anything wrong. You did nothing wrong."

Abby wanted to slip the sharpest kitchen knife they owned between his ribs for saying that. For assuming she thought she had done something *wrong*. And all of her, every cell of her failed body, hated herself for needing his arms to stay around her forever.

chapter *twenty~one*

"Shit, shit, *shit*." Fern looked over her shoulder to make sure Matty hadn't come out of his room. He didn't like her swearing. "Damn." Of all things to bounce. Of *all* things. Why not the gas and electric bill? Why not the car insurance? The check she'd written to the grocery store with her fingers crossed behind her back? How could it have happened? She'd counted. She'd counted everything, always. She hadn't bounced anything for years, even though sometimes only a single, careful column of numbers prevented the ricochet.

God, the sheer goddamned *cash* it took to come back from a bounce. The overage fee that could, in itself, bounce. She pulled up her bank account on the phone, her fingers shaking. She bet people with a well-padded savings account didn't have to hand-carry a cashier's check to a mortgage office to pay a late fee. They probably just made a phone call and moved money around.

It *was* that check to Safeway that had done it. A six-dollar check for tampons because she knew her paycheck wouldn't hit her bank till midnight that night. A six-dollar check that had exploded through the barricade, blowing up her home.

"What's wrong?" Elva started to turn in place, the spoon still in her hand.

"Stir. No. Don't drip. *Please.*"

"What's wrong?"

"Bounced a check."

"An important one?"

They were all important, weren't they? Always one step away from losing everything. Fern didn't answer.

"Are we okay?" Elva's voice was thinner than an EBT card. "Do you need help?"

"No. No, sweetheart, we're fine." Fern kissed Elva's cheek quickly with a smack. She drove Elva to the bank the first week of every month. Elva could afford her portion of the rent, her vitamins, and her slow-rumba class. She had just enough left over for her and Wyatt to go gamble quarters one afternoon a month at the Indian casino. That was about it. Because of her perennial eye problems, Elva always asked Fern to look over her bankbook to make sure the teller hadn't stamped the wrong amount. Fern never had the heart to tell her that she was pretty sure that tellers didn't even *use* stamps anymore. The tellers apparently had other pensioners they were used to dealing with, though, because they took the time to handwrite her deposit and withdrawal in her ledger, which they certainly didn't *have* to do anymore. God bless a credit union. When Fern went into her big-name bank, all she got was a printed slip and a fake smile.

Fern would never have asked Elva for money, even if she had money.

Elva still looked worried.

Fern repeated, "No. It's fine. It's nothing. Honestly. Overreaction, that's all. Sorry." She shoved all the mail into her purse. She tossed Matty's half sandwich into the trash can, which was, of course, too full. Could no one in this house see when the bag needed to be taken out? She was the only one with trash superpowers?

The kitchen door opened just as she hit it with her hip.

"Hey!" Diego took the bag out of her hands and chucked it into the outside can for her.

"Why don't you live here?" It was a grumble, not a compliment.

"Because brothers don't live with sisters unless they're total losers."

"But you are a total loser," she said as she followed him back into the house. "Your apartment is the size of my bus."

"I meant the sisters."

"Ass."

"Whiner. Speaking of which," her brother said, "I brought wine."

"In that case, you're amazing and you're my favorite."

"It's cheap. Trader Joe's *and* on sale."

"Just my style."

"Diego!" Elva stood her spoon in the spaghetti-mystery-stew and clapped.

"You're looking spry, young lady."

Elva smoothed her hands down the front of her green

checked apron, which was carefully tied over her bathrobe. "Well, I've been getting my steps in."

"It shows."

Elva turned pink and grabbed the spoon's handle. "Dinner soon."

Diego opened the wine while Fern got out the glasses. She'd found them at the local Salvation Army—a matched set, etched with *Tim's Divorce Bash, 1997*. She'd thought they were hilarious at the time and had happily forked over a quarter each. Now she wished she had plain wineglasses, ones that didn't celebrate Tim, who was probably happily remarried by now—Tim, who'd had to give all those glasses away to the thrift store because he had new wedding glasses to store on high, dusty shelves.

"Do you think Tim got a stripper for the divorce party?"

Diego splashed wine into her glass. "You think too much about that guy is what I think."

She fished out a piece of cork with her thumb. "Probably."

"Outside?"

"Yeah."

The backyard was a jungle, as usual, and the night was cold, but this was what they did unless it was raining. Diego was the kind of guy who didn't talk much about anything indoors. Nothing real, anyway. Get him outside, under his beloved trees, he'd bust open like a parking meter.

She lit the gas fire pit (one of her better Freecycle scores) and then sank into a plastic chair with a sigh.

"Long day?"

Fern nodded.

"How's Matty doing with everything?"

For the last two nights, he'd woken up screaming. Night terrors. Lots of kids had them, Fern knew.

But lots of kids hadn't buried their unknown father the week before. Lots of kids didn't think about their dads burning to ash. Fern wondered for the twentieth time if she should have let Matty come in the back with them to push the button, to see where the coffin had been fed to the fire. Maybe he wouldn't be having the dreams. . . .

"He's okay. Couple of nightmares."

"Damn. Sorry."

"He's tough." Her poor tough little guy. He shouldn't have to be. Last night, when he should have been sleeping, he'd crept out of his bed and stood with her at the front door. As she checked the dead bolt, he'd said it with her like he'd loved to do when he was little: *Estamos completos.* She had wanted to cry. Instead, she'd swallowed the lump in her throat and rubbed the top of his head, sending him back to bed with a kiss.

"It is what it is," she said.

"And you?"

"Fine."

"Hmph." He didn't believe her, she knew. That was okay—she didn't believe herself.

"How's your boyfriend?"

"He's not my boyfriend." Gregory was a fuck buddy. That was all she needed. All she had time for. "And he's fine." She relented. "Okay, he's *really* fine."

Diego laughed.

Overhead, the box elders danced, their still-bare branches making dark silhouettes against the lighter fog. Some nights the city lights were so bright against it that the night sky was white. Tonight, though, it was a pale gray. A car's bass thumped at the end of the cul-de-sac, and the stupid rooster that never knew the time crowed. The noises of the city filtered down, resting in her lap. Fern could almost run her fingers through them, clinking them against one another like their mother's old coins. An impatient horn. Two sirens. A hoot of laughter followed by a mariachi trumpet punch, quickly silenced. The air smelled of dirt and night air and, faintly, of hot plastic.

Diego spread his knees and looked up at the trees. "I gotta get up there."

"No." She didn't want him working in her trees. It was bad enough he was an arborist. She hated thinking about how high he went, the risks he must take.

"The top of that acacia has to go."

"So I'll hire someone."

"People as good as me are expensive."

"I'll get a day laborer over at Home Depot." It was an old joke. Long ago, before he'd gotten certified as an arborist, Diego had stood with the day laborers. He'd helped as a translator when he could, or on really bad days, he'd pretended he couldn't understand a word of English. He and the other men had laughed and waited for work, standing in the parking lot with their eyes hidden under ball caps, never admitting how desperate they were. Grunt labor (house painting, fence repair) paid for kids' lunches and toilet paper, but sometimes the jobs just didn't arrive. The rainy days, Fern remembered, had been the hardest on Diego. What about the men who didn't get out of it like he had? What happened to the ones who were passed over again and again, like the last kids picked at volleyball? What about the man with the scar that ran down his face from the top of his cheek to his collar? Who hired him?

"You put a guy up there who isn't me and I'll show Matty how to hot-wire any car made before 1986."

Fern laughed. The familiar argument was as comforting as

the sound of a Susan B. Anthony dollar rolling into the fare box. "You were lucky you were a kid, that it's not on your record."

"What record?" Diego locked his arms behind his head and peered up at the sky.

"Stars won't be out tonight," she warned him. Too much fog. Smog. Whatever it was that rolled in so often in the flats of Oakland. They got the haunting sound of the trains from the south, but they didn't get the stars that twinkled above Piedmont.

"Can't see 'em if you're not looking."

In her pocket, her phone beeped. She pulled it out—work. Her heart sank. Dispatch never sent an all-page unless something big was happening across the board. When the union needed them for a vote, a text went out. When the main schedule was pulled and adjusted, a page got sent.

Sure enough, *CHECK E-MAIL FOR MAIN SCHEDULE*.

Another text came in, this one from Judy, a woman she'd trained with back in the day. They'd been friends since then, looking out for each other. They traded day care and sob stories. Judy was an extreme couponer, and at least once a week, a ziplock bag of coupons Fern would never get around to sorting ended up in her work mailbox.

Well, that wasn't what you needed.

"What is it?" asked Diego.

"Work." Fern texted back, *Can you just tell me? Matty's on computer inside, I'm outside.* Her stupid crap phone wouldn't ever let her log in to the work schedule.

You got put on the 57. Sorry, friend. I'll do trades if it helps.

"Shit." The word was quiet but no less heartfelt for its softness.

"Tell me."

"I got the 57. I'm off my route."

chapter *twenty~two*

"No more."

That had been Scott's response to her third miscarriage, when she'd finally told him, those long three days afterward. (*Her* miscarriage. Never theirs. He'd never felt involved enough for her to think of it as their loss, only hers. That's when she started to know for sure.)

"What?"

"You can't keep going through this."

"Yes, I can." Abby had been cried out, as dry and thin as the onion skins she collected in a paper bag in the shed.

"I think we should stop trying."

"Oh," Abby said. "You're saying . . ." He was okay with adopting? Years before, she had told him that would be her next step. He'd really listened. She'd asked, back then, and he'd said that when the time came, they could talk about it. He'd said he knew how she felt. He'd held her as she cried.

"Yeah," he said. "It's time."

"Oh." They'd been in the kitchen, sitting at the island. Sun streamed through the glass, over the yellow mugs she'd so carefully chosen when they'd gotten married. She felt the color seep into her skin, into her blood. "Oh, Scott. This makes me so happy. You—*you*—make me so happy."

He'd carefully set his mug of coffee—black in the yellow, a liquid bumblebee—on the countertop. He'd wiped away the drop he'd spilled. "What?"

"You'll see." Abby's thoughts tumbled in her head like a boxful of wildflower seed. All of them—each one—would bloom somewhere unexpected and gorgeous. "It'll be wonderful. How old, do you think?" She had a million ideas. A baby—*an emergency baby*, they called them in the system—would be riskier, since any family member could show up out of the blue (and, from what she'd read, sometimes did) to take the child back. An emergency baby, tiny and squalling and perfect and she hoped theirs to keep. Or they could foster-to-adopt an older child. A little boy with dark eyes and a hopeful lilt to his high-pitched voice. A girl with dark skin and hair that Abby would learn to braid (she would *really* learn—she'd become a pro at it, astonishingly adept at beads and tiny elastics—she wouldn't let strangers laugh at her child's hair).

"How old? I don't know what we're talking about here. I thought we were going to stop."

Abby was confused. That's exactly what they were talking about—stopping trying. "I know we talked about adoption, but the county's fost-adopt program is really wonderful—I know it's a risk, but I've had friends it's worked out for—"

"Abby." He placed a hand on top of hers. "Honey, no."

"What?"

"I don't want to be a father."

One breath of icy air blew down her spine. She drew her hand back. "Don't say that."

"I know I've been putting on a good front with the whole miscarriage thing, but every time it's happened, I've got to admit that I've been relieved."

"That's not true." She could make his feelings up for him like the bed they slept in. She could pull him tight and firm, bounce a coin off what she needed him to do.

"I never would have told you. I knew it was important to you, so I went along with it."

Went along with trying to make a *baby?* "Are you serious?"

"But I just don't think I'm cut out for it. There's a reason that our bodies—together—don't make babies. Your body knows it, that's all, so it doesn't let it happen."

Abby wrapped her arms around her belly and slid off the stool, out of the stream of sunlight. Her bare feet were cold on the tile floor. She knew every millimeter of Scott's face, the way his nose dipped, and the crinkles under his eyes that had deepened in the years they'd been together. She knew the six freckles on his forehead, which turned to fifteen every summer. Last year there had been sixteen, and she'd become more militant about his sunscreen. "Who are you?"

"I'm the man who loves you."

She used to believe that.

He went on, "I know it's hard. You're still recovering from this one. We'll go to Hawaii when you feel up for it. Take some time off."

"Hawaii?" She wouldn't go anywhere with him. Ever. "You said you wouldn't mind adopting."

"I was wrong." His voice was shaking. "I didn't know I didn't want to be a father."

"But—" He'd *always* wanted to be a father. Always.

Oh, god, unless it had just been her saying that, over and over, until it was easier for him just to go along with her? Was that possible? Not only that he could deceive her like that, but that she could delude herself?

"You know the other day when I was two hours late getting home from the office? That Saturday afternoon?" He didn't wait for her nod. "I went to a . . . a friend's house. It was the kid's fifth birthday."

"You spent two hours at a kid's birthday party?"

Scott shook his head. "I didn't stay. They had a raccoon piñata in the front yard. So many kids, just hitting things with sticks. And the idea—just the idea of the kid and all the stuff that came with him, the piñata and the sticks, and all the *shit* that would come with a kid of ours—I left. I spent two hours just driving. I knew I had to tell you, but I haven't known how. Then you told me about this miscarriage. . . . We can't. I just can't, Abby. I'm sorry I told you I could."

Abby had walked out of the room a moment (a lifetime) later. She went up the stairs. She sat at her computer.

She would have to change his mind, because hers never would. Ever. And if she didn't change his mind . . . She would learn actual magic. She was halfway there already, right? She would wish on heliotrope and mugwort. Her healing powers would turn to the dark side, a thing she hadn't believed in an hour before, a thing that had to exist, didn't it? She would *make* him want a child. But . . .

Just as a test, a breathless dare to herself, she typed the words "no-fault divorce California" into a Google search bar.

Pages of divorce results scrolled past her eyes: companies that wanted to make it fast and clean. *No-fault.* Why did the term even exist? Abby needed an at-fault divorce. A full-fault one, as full of fault as anything had ever been before.

Then she closed the window.

Abby didn't need a divorce. She just needed to try again. Even while hating Scott, she knew she could get over that feeling. She just needed to have more sex with him. So much sex. She'd tell him she was on the pill if that's what it took.

And she'd get pregnant one more time. That one would stick because she'd do everything right, and Scott would *see.* He was born to be a father.

Abby made the plan and tried to summon hope from it. But her heart wobbled and tilted slowly, then disintegrated, slanting to dust.

chapter *twenty~three*

Diego stared at Fern, the whites of his eyes bright in the porch light. "Off your *route*? But the 40 is yours. You worked so hard to get it."

"I didn't have enough seniority to hold it, I guess." Fern cleared her throat. "Next time."

"Shit. What are you going to do? About Matty?"

Four hours on his own in the afternoon. She wouldn't be able to pick him up, wouldn't be able to cart him around on her coach. And with the overtime she was going to need, it would be even longer. "We'll be fine."

Diego opened his mouth, but Fern cut him off. "Before you say it, no. You can't help. No more than you're already doing. You need to be working."

He sighed. "I feel like I'm always working. He could come with me. . . ."

"No," snapped Fern. Diego winced, and she felt terrible. He was only trying to help. "He can't be on a jobsite."

"He's good at climbing trees."

"And you have the insurance to cover that?"

"No *way* do I have that insurance," said Diego. "Are you kidding me? There isn't a policy in the world that would cover an eleven-year-old on a tree job."

"I'll work something out," Fern said. Again. It was like her theme song. She needed a dance to go with it. *I'll work something out*, tip of the hat, step-ball-change, jeté into the air, land in the splits for a big finish.

Diego narrowed his eyes but nodded once. "I'm going to help in spite of you. Did the bastard leave you anything?"

"Me? I'm sure he didn't leave anything to me." But what about Matty? Fern suddenly remembered the text that had landed while she was driving home from Gregory's place. "Abby texted me. Earlier. She wants to meet."

"See?" Diego crossed his arms across his chest. "That's what I'm saying. He left you money. I know he did."

Scott was dead. It hit Fern all over again. She'd never again wonder if he'd appear at their door, demanding rights that she might have to give him. She'd never feel that fear, never have to worry about proving to a judge that she—with her epilepsy and crappy work schedule and run-down house in a shitty neighborhood and no money in the bank—was the better parent.

She was free.

"If he weren't dead, I'd kill him." Diego reached forward, drained his wine, and then set the glass down again. He thumped a fist into his palm. Her brother was a big man. He was broad in the same places Fern was, but wide shoulders looked better on a man, especially a tall one. A thick waist just made him look like a lumberjack, which, essentially, he was. "You need a damn break, Fernandita."

The words were unexpected coming from him, the guy who worked as hard as she did. God knew she thought them to herself all the time, but that was her just being weak. Hearing them out loud made those stupid tears rise right to the tops of her cheekbones. She would *not* let them spill, so they sat there, little hot lakes just under her lashes, ready to betray her.

If he hadn't died, she would have gotten his check. It would have covered the fridge, at least. The washer—well, that was what Laundromats were for.

The wine was so strong it was almost thick in her glass. It was her turn to search the pale night sky for a star. Just one simple twinkle, even of a plane's headlight, that would be enough.

It hurt to even think about that check, the same way it had always hurt to get it in the mail. Scott's damn handwriting in the memo box: *Take care.* He'd meant it—she knew him well enough to know that. He probably thought his way through the words each time. *I really hope she's taking care of herself and of Matty.*

Take care. That's all she ever *did*. Of everyone.

All he had to do was write a check while she raised a man.

"Besides the money, he never did *one thing* for that boy." Diego's voice was low.

She wouldn't look at him. "No. He didn't."

Not one damn thing since Matty's birth. Those had been the happiest moments of her whole life, those first ninety minutes while she and Scott held their perfect son, counting and recounting his toes, admiring his astonishingly bald head.

Even the birth bruises on his head caused by the forceps—purple and shocking—seemed somehow gorgeous, like immense storm clouds. Impressive. Something to be proud of.

Then Scott had gone home "real quick." She'd been stupid enough to think Scott had a birth present for her. They'd spent every cent of both of their savings for the down payment on the old house, and then they'd gone into credit card debt to put together the baby's nursery. But still she'd thought maybe he had a surprise for her.

It had been a surprise, all right. When she woke again later that night, Diego sat in the dimness in the too-small chair where she would have expected to see Scott. "He hasn't come back."

"How long have I been sleeping?"

"Almost four hours." Her brother had been vibrating with rage.

She'd checked her phone. Nothing.

Twenty-four hours went by. Enough hours that she'd talked to every hospital and jail in the Bay Area, looking for him. She spoke to the police officer posted to the front of the hospital. "I'm sorry, ma'am. It's not uncommon."

Other women had this happen to them, too? They pushed a human being out their *conchas* and then their men went for a walk and never came back?

Scott's father, Wyatt, sat in the waiting room, flirting with the nurses, bragging about his parking abilities. He pretended he wasn't concerned, but when he bent over to kiss Fern's cheek and brush his fingertips over Matty's warm bald head, she could smell the fear on him. Wyatt knew his son wasn't coming back. They both did.

When the message bounced onto her phone, her hand shook too much to see all the words. Texting was still so new then. A text wasn't casual yet, and Scott had never sent her one before. She knew it would mean something huge. Terrified, she'd asked Diego to read it to her. Her poor brother. They weren't kids anymore. Fern had always protected him from their mother's drunk rages against whatever she was out to get—the blinds that rattled too much, or the sofa that needed to be dragged out to the curb—fury spit in Spanish they could barely understand, fury that too often turned on them. Fern had shielded him as much as she could, and when Diego became a broad tree of a teenager, he returned the favor, threatening the boys she dated by looming in the dark near the Dumpsters as they dropped her off, by showing up at the same parties and just *being* there in the dark background. Being him.

But he couldn't protect her from the first and last text Scott would ever send her. Every word Diego spoke was a punch. *I'm sorry. I thought I could be a father. I can't. Let me know what I should do.*

Fern started to cry and tiny Matty, resting on her chest, gave a startled whimper. Wyatt, who'd been shifting from foot to foot by the door, said, "That little fucker." Wyatt hadn't wanted Scott to date her, not at first. *I tow a lot of Mexican cars, son. You think maybe there's a reason for that?* When Scott had admitted what his father had said, Fern had said she would never meet the man. Then she was pregnant, and Wyatt's whiskered chin had trembled the first time he'd asked to touch her belly.

"He'll come back," said Wyatt. "Or he's no son of mine."

"He'll come back," said Diego. "And I'll beat the living shit out of him, but I won't kill him."

"No son of mine would abandon his child. His child's *mother*." Wyatt had fat tears rolling over the gray sand of stubble on his cheeks. It looked like his face would crack apart, his skin a ceiling, a leaking faucet on the floor above— soon the plaster of his skin might disintegrate and crumble. "I'll choose you," he choked. "I swear to Christ if he doesn't come back, you'll be my daughter and I'll have no son."

Diego said, "I'll try *really* hard not to kill him."

It had been an unnecessary threat.

"He won't come back." When she'd shown Scott the first ultrasound (she never told him about the pink plus on the pregnancy stick, just like she'd never told him about the first two doctor's visits), Scott had said *"No."* A visceral knee-jerk response. He'd never wanted to be a father, or at least not until he was old, "not till I'm thirty-five or something." They were just twenty-seven then. "I love you, Fernie. Of course I love you. But I don't think I can be a dad. Not ready. I'm *so* not ready."

She'd hoped he'd get over it. He said he would try. They got married outside the Palace of Fine Arts. He wrapped his arms around her at night and sometimes his palms drifted to her belly as it grew. He'd been there for the birth, the whites of his eyes wide the whole time she screamed, but he'd cried— sobbed, really—when they first held tiny Matias. *Ninety minutes.* For that hour and a half Fern had no pain even though the epidural had long worn off. There was nothing inside her but light. Hope. No fear. Just the baby and Scott and her, safe inside a perfect bubble of iridescent joy. She felt sorry for the nurse who checked on them, sorry that she wasn't in the bubble, never would be. How terrible that must have been for her, to witness that kind of happiness and then have to go do her job, snapping on lifeless, loveless rubber gloves.

She'd thought that Scott's tears were of happiness. Of falling in love with his son. She'd never been more wrong.

In that moment as she held Matty with his tiny wrist ID
that matched the wider one on her wrist, as Matty's lips worked
sideways in a brand-new way, as a woman yelled something in
Tagalog out in the hospital corridor, Fern made up her mind.

Scott could be all in or all out.

He'd chosen all out.

All the way out. Fern had always wondered who her father
was—she wasn't even sure she and Diego had the same one.
Every night of her childhood, Fern had fallen asleep listening
for an unfamiliar car door slamming, an unfamiliar tread outside the front door, wondering if he—whoever he was—would
show up one night, open arms, waiting for his daughter to run
into them. Fern's child wouldn't wonder. She wouldn't raise
her son's hopes. Matty would know who his father was, but
he would never expect him to be present in any way. She would
never let Scott change his mind and step back through the
door, even if he wanted to. He'd lost that right.

Now, under the pale night fog, her hair heavy and curled
with moisture stolen from the air, Fern felt something cold
snake into her soul. She held up her wineglass. "More."

Diego said, "What about the child support? You're not
going to get that anymore?"

"Abby shouldn't have to pay for his sins." She gave a hollow laugh. "I bounced the mortgage. It's going to cost ninety
bucks, and that's only if I get the late fee in this week. After
that, it goes to two hundred and ten."

"I'll give you the money."

Diego couldn't afford it any more than she could. "I need
a new washer, apparently. And a fridge."

"Shit." He dropped his head and then raised it. "I got two
grand on a new credit card. You can have it all."

"*Mamón.* You know I'll never take your stupid money."

He grimaced. "Do me a favor, then. Meet his wife. See what she wants."

Fern stayed silent.

"Just do it. Don't be a fucking idiot."

She gave up. "Fine."

He nodded. "Good."

"But if you show up with a washer, I'll kick you so hard in the balls you'll wish you were born with ovaries."

It was the same thing as *I love you.*

Diego smiled and kept his eyes on the ceiling of the sky. That was his way of saying it back.

chapter *twenty~four*

A bby gave a small scream as the blind closest to the bed whipped upward with a clatter.

"Okay, my sleepy girlie. Up and at 'em." Kathryn yanked the cord of the next blind.

Kathryn's habit of stopping by early in the morning had never been a problem before. Scott got up at six to go to the office, and Abby had always been a lark, better in the first hours of the day than she was at night, when she became a yawner. So when Kathryn let herself in, neither of them had minded. (At least Abby hadn't—the corners of Scott's lips had always gone taut, but when asked, he'd said that it was fine. "She's the closest to family you have." She had been unreasonably irritated by this answer.)

Since Scott died, though, Kathryn had caught Abby in bed more than once. For the first time in her life, Abby was good at sleeping. It had been only two and a half weeks of sleeping alone, but her nights were almost dreamless now. She went to bed early and got up later than she ever had, and she sometimes took naps, too. Grief, sure. Everyone told her grief would make her tired. But she didn't feel tired, exactly. She just couldn't keep her brain sparking for as long as she should be able to. She was reading a thriller chock-full of chopped-up people and heart-racing intrigue, and almost every corner was folded over. She could only get one or two pages before the book would drop. Sometimes she didn't even get a whole page, and she'd refold the corner of the page as sleep dragged her under, feeling worthless.

Was it grief that let her sleep? Was that where sadness fit in her body? Was it terrible to admit she loved having the bed to herself? (She knew it was. No one knew she'd asked him for a divorce. She could barely admit it to herself.)

"I made coffee, but you have to come downstairs to get it."

"Hey!" Abby held up her hand to shield her eyes from the sunlight. "My eyes don't adjust that fast." Her words were thick, as if she were hungover.

"Sure they do. Open them wider."

Abby pulled the bright new duvet over her face. "You chirp louder than the damn birds."

"Best time of the day. Come on. I have two azaleas I saved from being put in a wood chipper by some fake gardener over near Point Isabel. They'll look great over by the rhododendron. And Brook called me. She said she left you a message, but you haven't called her back."

Abby groaned. "You're in cahoots. You can't steal my friends. I've told you that."

"I adore your friends. They keep me young. Get me some more. Now up with you! Meet me in the garden! Keep moving! We'll dig holes!" Kathryn left the bedroom door open as she left, clattering down the hall and thumping down the stairs.

Abby dragged a brush through her hair. She'd shower later, after Kathryn made her dig whatever it was she needed to dig. Her limbs felt heavy with grief, her blood thick with concomitant guilt—she knew she wasn't grieving the right way. Her heart should be shrouded in black. She shouldn't have felt the rush of happiness she had when Kathryn yelled at her about digging holes. She didn't deserve it—she had loved Scott less every time she lost a baby, every time that flash of relief shot across his face. How could a woman deserve to mourn a man she was leaving?

And yet she did. She ached with missing him. It wasn't right. But she didn't know if it was wrong, either.

Keep moving.

T-shirt on. Jeans up. Sunscreen slicked. Garden clogs on.

Before Abby put her phone in her pocket, she retrieved the message. Brook, constantly frazzled, sounded even more frantic than usual. "Girl. If I don't get some more of that spearmint bergamot oil from you, I swear to god I will have to make my own from toothpaste. This is not a drill. I repeat, *not* a drill. Can you swing a couple of bottles by this afternoon? I'd come get them myself, but I have two kids down with strep. I promise they won't touch you. Except . . . shit." Abby could almost hear the second Brook remembered about Scott. "Holy *shit*. I forgot. I don't know *how* I did that. Fuck me. You looked beautiful at the service. Everything was beautiful. I'm so sorry Jason started screaming at the end, but Wayne kicked him and I had to fight World War Three as quietly as possible in the back row, but I'm sure you heard them. Germany probably heard them. Sorry about that. So sorry about bugging you. What a dick move." Another pause. "No, wait. I'm not sorry. I love you. I love your oils. I love what they do for my soap business, and I can't fulfill this order to some New York boutique hotel until I get a gorgeous bottle or three from you. So get to work, if that's what will help you feel better. Also, call me back and tell me to fuck off, if that will help you more. Love you."

Abby thumb-typed back. *I'll be there this afternoon. xo.* Brook was right—she needed to *do* something. She had at least four orders that she had to fulfill that had come in from her Etsy site. Thank god Brook had called—thank god she'd sounded so *Brook* about it all. The nicest part was knowing that later she'd go to Brook's house, where no two plates matched and there was usually a cat hair ball or two puked up in a corner. And no matter how much Brook felt sorry for her loss, there would be a moment when they'd be sitting in the living room and Brook would dump all her problems out, unpacking them in front of Abby like a too-full, broken-zippered suitcase. *He says he's got a crush on the receptionist. I told him to try to sleep with her, and he got* all *upset with me, can you believe it? I love him, I swear I do. I just want him to know he's not gonna be able to get in her pants. And lord, if he does, then at least I'll get a little break. And Danny got diagnosed with ADHD, tell me something I don't know already. You know how many bars of soap I gotta ship to make the copay on the Adderall?* Scott had always wanted Abby to be happy—sometimes it had felt like her job. Other friends, too, seemed to need Abby to remain strong and competent. Vivian and Lisa talked about mutual funds and politics over organic, Paleo lunches. They were aggressively cheerful, and needed Abby to be, too. It was a job she was normally good at. But everyone needed a break. With Brook, Abby had always been able to be herself. She could cry when she felt like it and not explain why she was sad if she didn't want to. Brook would pass her peanut-butter cookies in a plastic tray and rub her nose unself-consciously. Then Abby would listen to Brook's complaints and empathize.

Sometimes empathy was all you needed.

Abby looked out the window and saw Kathryn striding across the backyard carrying two shovels.

It was good to be loved. To be supported.

What about Fern? Had she had support when Scott left her?

In the garden, Abby came back into herself. Kathryn was right to bring her out here, to get her in the dirt early. If she could make herself do this every day, maybe she'd be able to figure out her next move. A Brewer's sparrow chirped and bounced from branch to branch of the ironwood. Next to it, the ginkgo tree was just coming into yellow bloom, a month too early. Last year the too-early blooms had made her worry about it and global warming and climate change. This year she was obsessing about other things.

Like how she wanted to see Scott's eleven-year-old son again. Like wondering what the routine was like at Fern's house.

"What is it?" Kathryn's voice was soft.

Abby put her hands to the small of her back and stood straight. Digging holes deep enough for the root balls of the full-grown azaleas normally wouldn't be a problem this time of year, but the six-year drought combined with the fact that Abby hadn't ever put anything in this corner of the huge yard made the dirt as stubborn as Kathryn herself. "Nothing."

"You're not here."

"Hey, I'm shoveling as fast as you are."

"I'm twenty-five years older than you are and I've moved

double the dirt." Kathryn looked pointedly at their respective piles.

"You do this every day at the nursery."

"You kidding me? This is what I pay the boys to do. I don't have to dig *holes*."

"You love it."

"What's on your mind, girlie?"

"Them." Matty. Fern. She didn't have to say their names out loud for Kathryn to know.

Kathryn wiped her face with a green bandanna she pulled from one of the million pockets of her overalls. "What are you going to do about them?"

"What can I do?"

"What do you want to do?"

Be with them. Know them. She wanted to learn what they liked, what their favorite in-jokes were. She wanted to learn what Fern's face looked like when it was relaxed, figure out what made Matty laugh until he toppled over sideways. "Nothing. I guess. None of my business. They don't owe me anything."

"True."

Disappointment shot through Abby's legs, straight down into the dirt at her feet. She picked her shovel back up. It was even heavier than when she'd dropped it two minutes ago.

"But maybe you owe them something."

"The life insurance. I know. I'm going to give her a check." She tugged on the neckline of her T-shirt, suddenly too hot even though the sun hadn't managed to push its way into any part of the garden yet. "A really big fucking check. I texted her to see if we could meet last week, but she hasn't responded."

"Will she *take* a check?"

"Of course she will." It hadn't crossed Abby's mind that

Fern wouldn't. "Without the money from his business, it'll be a little tighter than I'm used to, but one of Mom's investments just exploded. I'll have enough money, and I own the house outright." She looked up at the siding, up to the high window of their bedroom. It was just a shell. A very nice shell with a magic garden in back. But still just a shell. "I honestly don't want to keep his business running on my own. Maybe this will give me the motivation to really get my own business off the ground." Her Etsy site kind of sucked, she knew it. Great ratings, poor photos. She could work on marketing. Promotion. Maybe there was a business class she could take that wouldn't suck the life out of her.

Kathryn rubbed a streak of soil across her nose. "I don't know. From what I saw of her at the funeral, she seemed proud. Strong. I can see her refusing."

"But . . . what do I do then? She has to take the money. For Matty. How would I make her, if she says no?"

Kathryn leaned on her shovel, looking like a cheerful hobo gravedigger. "Offer her something she needs."

"Like I have any clue what that might be."

"She's a single mother. There's only one thing she needs, besides money, I'm guessing, and that's time."

"Um . . ." What step had she missed? "The money will buy her time?"

"Offer to help with Matty." Kathryn leaned down and picked a rock out of the dirt. "Two birds. One of these."

The idea was huge. Presumptive.

Abby suddenly wanted nothing more. "To, like, babysit him? After school?"

"How does she do it now? Does he take care of himself?"

"I have no idea. I don't know where his school is, or how

he gets home. He has his grandfather, and the older woman who lives there, too. Maybe they pick him up? I'm not sure they drive, though." For the first time, Abby wondered if Fern *needed* to have the elderly pair there. Were they paying rent? She looked up at her huge house again. Thirty-one hundred square feet. Five bedrooms (two of which had been made into offices, leaving a room for their workout equipment and only one spare bedroom—she'd always thought of it as a reasonable amount of space, if a little large). Empty except for her.

"What can it hurt to offer?"

"Yes. You're totally right." Abby brushed off her hands as if she would go now, as if she'd track Fern down on her bus right this very second.

"Wanna finish this first?" Kathryn's eyebrow was a sharp upward slant.

Abby nudged the soil with the toe of her garden boot. "Okay. Yes." She smiled. A ray of sun found its way through the ginkgo tree's blooms and landed on the top of her head. She closed her eyes and felt the warmth, letting it soak into her. Just a second or two.

It felt like absolution.

"All right, then." She picked up her shovel, but Kathryn spoke again before she could take another spadeful of dirt.

"Do me one more favor."

Abby felt magnanimous. She had a new plan, a big one, an important one. "Anything."

"Do things that feel good."

"Yes! Look!" She stabbed the side of the hole. "I'm doing that now! With you!"

"When I'm not making you do it, I mean. When I'm at work, when I can't see you."

"I will."

"Eat. Take a bath. Remember your body."

"I know. I'm trying." She'd lost weight—she knew she had.

"Get laid if you can."

Abby blinked and rewound the words in her mind. Kathryn couldn't have just said what she thought she'd heard. "Like, rest more?"

"Like fuck someone."

"What?"

"If you get the chance."

Abby didn't know whether she should laugh or cry—both reactions felt imminent. "I loved him. I know you think I didn't—"

"I know you did, sweetheart. I also know you were desperately unhappy."

Abby had never told her that. She'd been so *careful* to never tell Kathryn that.

"Just remember that your body needs ways to grieve. Different ways. You need to sing and cry and dance and shovel dirt, and maybe get touched by someone else."

Anger spiked, as real and as sharp as the splinter that had just bitten her thumb from the shovel's handle. "Scott and I had *great* sex. *Hot* sex."

"When you had it."

"I should never have talked to you about it. About anything."

"Just remember. If it comes up." Kathryn's upper lip twitched. "As it were. Get it over with."

"Like you would." Kathryn had been married to Rebecca for twenty-seven years.

"Absolutely. Rebecca and I both would, in that situation.

We were talking about it last night. You've lost the one person you could trust to hold you. A bit of holding wouldn't do you wrong."

"No."

"Just keep it in mind. Craigslist has Casual Encounters, you know."

"Kathryn!"

Kathryn raised that eyebrow again. Sunlight winked against her tanned cheek. "Sometimes I read 'em for fun. You never know. Just remember I said it, if it comes up. It's nature's way. Get it over with if you can, and have fun doing it." She pointed downward. "Now, my darling girlie, dig that hole."

chapter *twenty~five*

As Fern entered the café, she kicked herself for feeling so nervous. She felt like she'd shot a can of Mountain Dew and then jumped up and down, like Matty used to do to feel the fizz in his stomach (before that throwing-up-at-the-movies incident). After four more texts, two e-mails, and one very long phone message from the suddenly quite-pushy Abby, Fern had finally agreed to meet Abby: *Okay.*

The response had come almost immediately. *Great. Zocalo Cafe, 1 p.m., Friday?*

Who in the whole world got to go hang out at a café at one on a weekday? Women who didn't have jobs, that was who. And, more worryingly, women who had a newly fluctuating work schedule. Fern was free at that time, and she hated that she was. *Zócalo.* It meant public square in Spanish, but she'd only ever heard it used casually, as an interjection of surprise. *Oh, my god.* It seemed appropriate.

The café was quiet. A few scattered men sat at dark wooden tables, tapping on computers. One man with a beard to his chest was sketching, casting quick non-subtle glances at the pretty blond barista. The art on the walls had changed since Fern had last been there, and showcased an artist who apparently liked blue skies and the small San Leandro bungalows that surrounded the café.

Abby was there already, papers spread in front of her on a larger round table. As if she felt Fern's gaze, she looked up and waved. *Dios*, she was too eager. Fern wanted to pull her internal e-brake and U-turn out the way she'd come in, but instead, she took a breath and made a gesture toward the counter. "Coffee," she mouthed.

In line, Fern looked up at the café's board, staring blankly. A coffee. She just wanted coffee. Why couldn't she see how much that was? If she'd been in charge of writing out that chalkboard, she would have kept it clean and simple. The names of the simple drinks with clear prices next to them. Instead, all she could make out on the busy signboard were things like Paraguayan mochas, low-fat caramel steamers, and Mexican Borgias, whatever the hell they were. She had a dollar seventy-five in quarters. That had to be enough for a cup, didn't it? She'd be damned if she had to put a four-dollar latte on her debit card.

She ordered. A dollar sixty-five, just a dime for a tip. They used a point-of-sales unit that looked ten years old. If she'd been running the café, she would have put in an iPad Square system. Easy. Cheap.

Fern stepped to the side to wait, ignoring Abby's smiling face half a room away. She pulled her shirt away from her body and flapped the edges of her cardigan as surreptitiously as she could. She'd had to park three blocks away, and the sun, for spring, was hot as hell.

She stole another quick glance at Abby, who was looking down at her phone.

God, she looked so *sweet*. Abby had the kind of face that half the mothers in the PTA had. Matty's school straddled an Oakland zone that was smack-dab in the middle of a gentrification sweep (a fancy word for whites discovering things that weren't theirs). So the mothers who came to the PTA meetings were split right down the middle—half stay-at-homes, half work-all-the-motherfucking-timers.

Those stay-at-homes. It was funny, they always looked the most worn-out. From what? All the driving they did for their children? A rough day was a day they volunteered *and* had to drive their kids to soccer. One of the rich moms had once thanked the mothers who donated the most time to the PTA because "stay-at-home mothers are the hardest-working mothers in the world."

Such bullshit. Fern had wanted to scream, but instead she dug her embarrassingly non-manicured fingernails into the palms of her hands and didn't say a word, just went along with the group on the vote for gluten-free nut-free (flavor-free) cupcakes for the bake sale. Single mothers who worked full-time, *those* were the goddamned hardest-working people in the whole world, and Fern would bet her house on the fact that this was true the world over. In India, single mothers lost sleep trying to hold the world together with their bare hands. In Australia, single mothers worked their asses off, just like they did in Japan. In Iceland, single mothers probably had excellent health care and vacation benefits, but when they got off shift, they still had to do the laundry, clean the house, clean the children, and make dinner so they could do it all again, alone, the next day.

Stay-at-home mothers. *Madre.*

But like Grandpa Wyatt always said, being smug was a well-paved two-way street. If she felt smug for working long hours because she was strong enough to do so, that was fine, because stay-at-home mothers got to feel smug about making healthy food choices for their kids, something Fern didn't have the time to do. Homemade bread was a luxury, and yeah, it was probably way better for their growing bodies. And it was *never* going to happen in her house unless Elva decided to embrace a new art. God help them all if that happened.

"Ma'am?"

Fern jumped. "Yeah?"

The barista pointed to the stacks of mugs in front of her. "You can just take a cup and fill it yourself. Right there."

Embarrassment flooded her. She tried to nod like she'd had a plan, standing there, motionless.

Her cup full, she moved to Abby's table. "Hi."

Abby smiled, and Fern swore to god, her eyes sparkled. "Fern! Oh, hi! How are you?"

Fern sat, ripping off her sweater, cursing the fact that she was now sweating at her hairline. She could feel how red her face was.

She ignored the question. "So." She took a sip, carefully not making a face when the liquid, still too hot, burned her. "What did you need?" That was good. Making it clear that she knew Abby was the one who needed something. That this wasn't her idea.

"Okay." Abby looked down at the paperwork in front of her. "Yes. Okay. We'll get right to it." She sounded nervous.

"I've been working on this for days. It's the only answer I can come up with."

Answer? "What's the question?"

"What to do about the money."

Fantastic. Finances, brought up within twenty seconds. "What are you talking about?"

"The money Scott was sending you."

Confusion slowed Fern's synapses. "What?"

"The checks."

"The checks," she repeated. The heat moved from her face down into her chest, and she felt her brain snap to sharper focus, the way it did when a group of the wrong kind of teenage boys got on her bus, the kind that felt threatening in their quietness, the kind of group that didn't bluster harmlessly like the rest did. She settled one hand flat on the table next to her coffee mug. "If I'd taken him to court, he woulda had to pay more."

"Oh. No, that's not . . ."

"He got off easy." Would Abby want the money *back*? Was that possible? Legal? Could they subpoena her bank statements? What would that prove besides the fact that she was broke, that she was always broke? That was fine. It would be humiliating, yes, to have to show off her slim checking account and her empty savings, but she would do it if she needed to prove that she hadn't gotten rich from the checks.

"Fern, slow down. It's okay. I want you to have his life insurance. With just one catch."

chapter *twenty~six*

The only word Fern heard was *catch*. She stilled, conserving her energy. A catch. "Sorry?"

"I'm so nervous. God. I hate this."

Abby looked young, *so* young. Years ago, some embarrassing but inevitable Facebook stalking had revealed to Fern that Abby was only two years younger than she was. Abby was thirty-six now. But Abby looked no more than thirty, while Fern felt like her own bones were in their mid-fifties, at least. "Go on, then." Fern kept her hands carefully wrapped around her mug. She would not agree to a catch, money or no money.

"I want to spend time with Matty."

Fern just stared. The café quieted around them, as if listening. Or maybe it was the roaring in her head that muted the rest of the world. She could hear her own breathing.

Abby—insanely—kept talking. "I mean, not *much* time. Just whatever you say is okay. Like, if you ever need babysitting.

In the afternoons after school, maybe? If there are . . . other times like that? That you might need help? I'd love to—"

"Spend time with *Matias*? No. He's my son. He's not a chess piece."

"No, not like that. Of course not. I thought—in exchange for the life insurance—"

The base of Fern's spine heated as if she were sitting on the plug-in seat warmer she used on the coach in winter. "You thought I'd sell you time with him? With Matty? That you could *buy* him?"

Abby pressed her fingers against her cheeks. "No. God, no." She coughed once and went red. "No, no. I didn't mean it to come out like that."

Fern gritted her back teeth together for a moment. "What you said was that you want to give me money. In return for letting you spend time with my son."

"Shit," said Abby. Her hands dropped from her cheeks, and she laid them, palms up, on the table. "I did. I said that. Exactly. I didn't think it through, not to that conclusion. I thought—I thought—"

Fern stood, the wooden chair clattering backward. She gripped her sweater with damp palms. "I don't need his money." She thought briefly how Abby had been inside her home. She'd seen the broken blinds in the living room. She'd seen the couch, the way it sagged in the middle like an old wooden bench. The scuffed linoleum in the kitchen. The way the wall paint buckled above the sink. "And I sure as shit don't need yours."

Abby shot to her feet. "He owes you. Scott *owes* you."

True. But that would *never* make her beholden to this woman. "He did. But I didn't want it. And you don't owe me a thing." It hurt to say. In her deepest heart, maybe she'd thought that, yeah, this Abby woman, with her perfect brown oversized handbag that looked as light as if it had nothing more than keys and a wallet inside, with her perfectly matching brown boots that didn't have a single scuff, maybe Abby *did* owe her, like Diego said. Maybe the thought had flitted through her mind. Once. Okay, a few times. In her rational mind, the one that controlled what she said, what thoughts were put into words, she had known Scott had owed her. And Scott was dead. So she said it again, to convince herself. "You don't owe me a goddamn thing."

Abby said, "Then I'll just give it to you."

"Did he leave it to his son?"

Abby's face fell. "No. I was the only beneficiary."

Exhaustion made Fern's legs feel weak. "So you want to give me money that belongs to you and then extort me later?"

Abby shook her head. "I promise you, Fern, I never thought it would come out like that. I'll give you the insurance free and clear. I'm sure it will take a while for it to pay out, but I can advance it to you from my own money." She pointed out the window to the credit union across the street. "That's our bank. I mean, *my* bank. That's why I asked you to meet me here. We'll go put your name on that account and take mine off."

Fern hated herself for asking. "How much?"

"Well, okay. It should have been more, but when we bought it, we were only thinking about protecting his business. When we had kids, we were going to up it—we were going to up both of ours. If I'd known about Matty . . . I would have made him buy more." She glanced at a Post-it note. "Five hundred thousand. Plus twenty thousand from an old policy he got online a long time ago."

Abby thought it should be *more*?

A half a million. So much money.

So much fucking *money*. She could pay off the house and still have half left over. No mortgage payment, and a safety net in the bank. All of it for Matty, for his *life*, his extraordinary life, because it could be that, with that kind of cash. College, anywhere he wanted. Her mouth went dry at the astonishing thought. She tried to breathe—she tried to remember why she was saying no. No, no, *no*. No.

Abby glanced down at the floor, and Fern saw a silver hair glinting at her temple. Just one. A promise. She probably had her hair highlighted and dyed every six weeks. She probably happily forked over hundreds of dollars to stay looking as young as she did.

Fern, on the other hand, had Googled her way to learning how to mix her own hair dye when she'd gone prematurely gray at thirty-two. A whole box of dye cost fifteen dollars at CVS. Instead, she bought the color in six-packs meant for professional hairstylists on Amazon. Developer was literally cheaper than bottled water, two bucks for an amount that lasted her two years. Plastic gloves were only pennies if you bought them in bulk at the SavMart on High Street. She used one of Elva's royal wedding shot glasses to measure one ounce of each into a chipped ceramic bowl she kept under the sink for exactly that purpose. Total cost of each touch-up: $5.37.

She *had* this. She knew how to live. What to do.

She didn't need this woman's money. Ever.

But there was . . . Something about Abby was heartbreaking, something other than the fact that her husband had just died, what, three weeks ago? Not just that single gleaming silver hair. It was bigger than that. Fern tried not to look for what it was but couldn't help scanning her face again, one more time.

Abby laced her fingers together at her stomach. "I'm so sorry. I didn't think it all the way through. I wasn't trying to buy time with Matty, I swear. Not like that. I'm ashamed of myself." Her voice was disconsolate.

"I won't take your money." Fern's voice was softer now, but she was still on guard. She could still fight.

"But . . ."

Fern stuck her hand on her hip. "And here it is."

"I promise, no condition. I swear. But I . . . I'd love to ask you as a favor. To let me spend time with Matty."

Fern blew out a breath sharply. "Why?"

Abby's words were rushed, as if she was scared of them. "I asked Scott for a divorce. A few minutes before he died."

Fern couldn't help it—she laughed.

She shouldn't have. The look of sorrow on Abby's face wasn't worth it.

But that, combined with the silver hair she'd just seen. It was . . . time. That was all. Scott's second wife. Leaving him. Finally.

"Why?" Abby's voice was small. "Why would you laugh at that?"

"I'm not laughing at you," Fern said, trying to catch her breath. "I'm sorry. It's just . . . Well. Good job, girl. You should have told me that earlier, don't you think?" Then she sobered. Why, then, if Abby had been going to leave him, would she want to spend any time at all with his son?

As if Abby were reading her mind, she said one word, "Family."

Fern waited.

"It's all I wanted from him. Family." Abby pressed her hands to her stomach again, and now Fern thought she knew why.

"And he never told you about us."

"He *had* one." Abby's fingers were shaking. "And I didn't know that."

If she'd been anyone else, a passenger on the bus, a customer in front of her in a checkout line, Fern would have known what to do. She would have just grabbed her in a hug, wrapped her in her arms, and given her a few reassuring thumps on the back. She would have held on until Abby let go. Then she would have cracked a dirty or otherwise inappropriate joke until Abby's face relaxed.

But this was Abby.

"He had a family," Abby said. "He never told me. He never saw you two even once, am I right about that?"

Well, he'd shown up out of the blue on Matty's fifth birthday, but he'd stayed less than ten minutes. The *pendejillo* hadn't even been able to make himself come in off the sidewalk. He'd clutched the fence and watched the children run around, shrieking. Fern had been pretty sure he wasn't positive which kid was his. "Once. He came by and watched Matty and his friends smack a piñata. He freaked, and left. Didn't even talk to his kid."

Abby gasped.

"What?"

"A raccoon? Was it a raccoon piñata?"

Fern jolted, and her knee knocked the table leg. "Yeah."

"He told me about that. Not about Matty, but that he'd gone to a friend's kid's party. It was his response when I told him I'd just had my third miscarriage. He said he didn't want the . . . the *stuff* that went with a child. I was so shocked I didn't quiz him about who he'd gone to see. It never crossed my mind to wonder."

"Motherfucker."

"He had a *family*. He had the only thing I ever wanted, and he threw it away."

"So you . . ."

"I want to know you. All of you."

"You can't have it." The words were harsh, but this woman needed to hear them. *"You can't have my family."*

"I know. God. I'm so sorry." The words sounded ripped from Abby's throat. "Can we just go to the bank? Can you let me do this for you?"

"No. Never. I won't take the money." Fern was going crazy—she was losing her mind right here in this coffee shop. The money could change everything. She needed more time to wrap her head around it, around the rightness or wrongness of it. She needed to count in her head, up and down, from penury to wealth, with Matty's face at the front of her mind. "But you can babysit him."

"What?"

Fern's stomach leaped. "It turns out . . . that I might need some help. My schedule got changed at work. And I . . ."

"Anytime. I'm free every day." Abby's words tumbled over themselves. "Every single day. I mean, I volunteer with a botany group on Tuesdays, but I was thinking about quitting that anyway. I'm free anytime at all."

Why was Fern even considering this? She shouldn't make any rash decisions. She should go home and think about it. She shouldn't agree to anything concrete. But goddamn it, she felt sorry for Abby. So she said, "Wednesday. Three o'clock?" It was still her early day even on the new route—she could see Gregory a little longer than normal if Abby took Matty. Was that too selfish of her?

"God, yes. Thank you. Yes." Her voice was a gasp.

"Jesus. Breathe, okay?"

Abby gave no sign of hearing. "Where? Where will I go? Where will he be?"

Fern frowned. "Have you ever babysat before?"

"*Oh*, yes."

"When?"

"I was fourteen the last time, but I was *very* good at it. I'm still CPR qualified. I make sure of that. You never know."

Lord have mercy. Matty wasn't that good with exuberance. It made him nervous. "Well, I hope like hell you don't have to use it on him. He's a pretty healthy kid. No epilepsy."

"Oh, *god*. What?"

This was insane. "I have it. It's controlled. He doesn't have it, that's what I'm telling you. He's a healthy kid. Pick him up at the school. I'll put your name down for him, and you'll have to check in the first day so they know you are who you say you are. Bring your ID."

Abby scrabbled at her purse as if she would prove who she was right then, right there. "Yes. Let me write this down. Yes."

Fern told her the name of the school. She gave her the address and told her where Matty would be waiting.

Abby smiled so brightly she could have lit up downtown San Francisco. "This will be amazing. We'll have fun. Wednesday."

Zócalo. "Yeah."

chapter *twenty~seven*

The birdlike woman at the school's front desk who checked Abby's ID didn't even look at her face. She just glanced at her license, and then returned to pecking at her computer. "You can wait outside for him."

"How will the yard monitor know that I'm allowed to take him?"

The woman pursed her beaklike lips and twitched. "She'll know."

"Do I need to show her my ID, too?" Abby wanted to get it perfectly right, from start to finish.

"No."

"But—"

"Outside." The woman flapped the tips of her fingers in the direction of the door.

Abby was half an hour early. The school yard filled and emptied twice already while she leaned against the fence trying her best not to look suspicious, trying to look like a mother. Or, okay, at least a babysitter. She kept her face relaxed, a nonthreatening smile affixed.

There was an ebb and a flow to the yard, a tide of traffic and running feet. Cars pulled up, behind and next to hers, double-parking with assured nonchalance. The city buses wheezed up, doors flapping open. Women (and the occasional man) filed into the playground. There was some chitchat, but less than Abby would have thought. Most of the women kept their eyes on their phones, thumbs scrolling. As classes were dismissed, children launched themselves at their adults. They all hugged, as if on cue, and then the women ferried them away. The buses pulled out. The playground emptied. Then, five minutes later, the next classroom—or grade, or whatever it was—would let out and it started all over again. The waves of the tide were women, the ocean breeze was car emissions, and the sand dollars left behind were worried-looking kids whose mothers were late.

The bell rang again, and even from half a playground away, Abby could hear doors slamming. She could practically hear the backpack zippers, recalling the feeling of freedom that came with pencils sliding into cases, math books shoved into desks. She remembered the feeling of hair perma-tangled from hanging off the parallel bars during lunch. Abby had loved school, doing better in class than out. She'd hated summer break after the first two weeks, and within a day or two of a new school year, she was always deeply smitten with whatever teacher she had, bringing her bright cherries and the best caterpillars and construction-paper love letters.

She checked her compact mirror as subtly as she could and quickly reapplied a layer of gloss. It was armor. The playground monitor would see it and know she was well put together. More trustworthy. Where *was* the monitor? A harried-looking woman with frizzy black hair had patrolled the playground twice without saying a word, but Abby hadn't seen her in at least twenty minutes. Abby could be *anyone*.

Then Matty was there.

Even at a distance, she recognized him. He had Scott's walk, that steady rhythm, little pistonlike legs, regimented arms. The similarity was unexpected, and it took her breath away.

She waved.

Shyly, he waved back. He didn't smile. The distance between them felt like a mile though it was less than the interior of her regular Starbucks.

When he was close enough, Abby said, "Hi." Original. She should have had something planned. *Hi, tiger. Hi, cutie pie.* She added, "Matty," and then felt like an idiot.

"Hey," said Matty. He hitched his backpack higher on his shoulder.

"That looks heavy," Abby said, grateful to have something to say. "Can I take it for you?"

Matty's eyebrows slammed upward. "No!"

"Sorry."

Matty didn't answer, just trudged toward the open gate.

"I checked in at the office—do I need to check out with you?" Like he was a library book.

"Mrs. Perez saw you." He gestured at the harried woman near the double yellow doors.

"But she doesn't know me."

"It's fine."

Abby felt her driver's license burning through the wallet in her purse as they walked. It was the one thing she had to get right, she knew that.

RACHAEL HERRON

Or she'd *known* that. Turned out what she had to get right might end up being much harder.

Just outside the gate, Abby stopped and Matty, two steps behind her, did, too. "This is *so* weird," she said.

Matty nodded.

"That's my car over there." She pointed at the champagne Lexus RX.

"Okay."

"Are you nervous, too?"

Matty shrugged. He didn't answer.

"I'm super nervous and I think it's because I want this to go right." She started walking again, and just behind her, he followed.

"Why?"

The question startled Abby, and she wondered if the rest of the afternoon would go like this: them startling each other until one of them fell over in surprised exhaustion. *Because you're more important than I ever knew you would be. Because I have no idea what to do with you.* "Because I've never had an eleven-year-old friend."

"Aren't you, like . . . babysitting me?"

Abby hit the unlock button on her car. The familiar chirp was reassuring. "Well. You're not a baby."

Matty looked at the sidewalk, apparently fascinated with the way the concrete cracked and buckled. He didn't move to open the passenger door, so Abby did it for him. He jumped up, tossing his backpack on the floor in front of him.

Abby got in on her side and started the car. "So."

Matty blinked.

"What should we do?"

He turned his head to look at her, and something about his unblinking gaze reminded her of an owl. "You're asking me?"

"Yep. What do you normally do?"

"Mom used to pick me up, but she's on a new route this week, so Diego has been doing it."

"He's your uncle, right? What do you do when Diego picks you up?"

"He takes me home and then goes out to work again."

"What does he do?"

"He climbs trees."

"Sorry?"

"He cuts them down. From the top."

"He's an arborist?"

"Yeah. He's cool."

Abby longed for Matty to say that about her someday. *She's cool.* "What do you do then? When you're alone?"

"Not usually *alone*. Usually my grandpa and Elva are there."

"So they watch you?"

Matty didn't answer. He unzipped his backpack and poked into it as if he was looking for something. He came up empty-handed, leaving the mouth of the pack open. "I'm supposed to do my science homework."

"What's the assignment?"

"Stupid."

"Ah." Abby didn't know what to ask next.

"It's for, like, a stupid science fair. We have to change something into something else."

All Abby could think of was Harry Potter. "Like magic?"

"I wish. That would probably be easier."

"What are you going to do?"

Matty thumped the back of his head into the headrest. "Die. I'm doomed. That's all. The teacher hates me."

Abby smiled gently. "I'm sure that's not true."

"She told me it was fine, that not everyone can be smart."

"Seriously?"

He nodded grimly.

"That's not cool."

"My mom was pretty mad about that. She had a meeting with the principal and everything."

"Did that help?"

"Made it worse. Now she's out to get me and won't let me use the pencil sharpener more than once a class." His mouth was tight. "But I break a lot of pencils."

"Okay, let's work on it."

"The pencils?"

"The science project." Abby's heart beat faster. "I have a garden. That's practically magic, right there."

He looked at her skeptically. "Carrots? Tomatoes? I think it has to be bigger than turning seeds into vegetables. Anyone can do that."

"You'd be surprised. What about using vegetables to dye something?"

"Like paint?"

"Maybe something that you made?"

"What?"

Abby felt a thrumming of excitement at the base of her throat, an extra pulse. "Let me think about it. I can help you. I want to help you."

Matty's sigh was so heavy it felt like the parked car would tip onto its side.

"We can think more about that later. What's fun for you?"

Matty looked at her seriously. "That's a very big question."

"Yeah. I guess it is."

"The comic book store is fun." He looked sideways out

the front window, and then back at her. He expected her to call him on it. To take him home. To be boring.

"Lead the way."

"Really?" His smile was sudden and dazzling.

"Sure. Tell me how to get there."

Matty blinked again, his smile dimming. "There's one on . . . uh. It's the street where the Safeway is, the one with the stinky fish." He paused and thought. "I'm always the passenger. Not the driver." His *duh* wasn't stated, but it was definitely implied.

Abby got out her cell and tapped at it. "Okay. Comics Unlimited? That one's close. Is that the one you like?"

"I think that's the one." He lifted his shoulders and dropped them. "If it has comics, it's the one I like."

Turning on navigation on her phone, she pulled slowly away from the curb. The shallow fear she'd pushed back into her shoulders rose again, growing into her chest and throat. A red Ford truck came too close to her bumper as it drove around her, and Abby realized that never in her life had she transported more precious cargo. There was no insurance she could take out on her policy that would cover what she was carrying. Why had she offered this? She was driving her husband's *child* around. True, she'd packed dried figs in a ziplock in her purse as a talisman for safe passage. Seriously, though? She'd thought that would be enough? What if a drunk driver came around a corner and smashed into them? What if Matty was hurt? If she didn't die from the impact, she'd have to kill herself. She wanted to pull over, to call an Uber to take them to his house, where she would place him on the couch and then stand over him, making sure nothing with blades or bullets or poison came in the front door until his mother came home.

"Turn left," said the navigator.

"My uncle's GPS sounds like Chef."

"Chef?" All Abby could think of was Julia Child.

"From *South Park*."

"Ah."

Another pause. "Wally thinks I'm a baby," said Matty.

"Sorry?" Abby had missed something, but she wasn't sure what it was.

"You said you weren't babysitting. But he says that I'm a baby every day." His feet didn't reach the floor of the footwell, and he kicked his heels backward into the leather. Abby found she didn't mind at all.

"He's in your class?"

"He's in seventh."

"So he's a year older."

"Yeah. He chases me up the jungle gym sometimes. I hate him."

"Well, I hate him, too, then. He sounds like a bully. Have you told your mom?"

Matty sighed.

"What?" Abby took the right turn so slowly a pedestrian almost outpaced them on the sidewalk.

"Grown-ups are always like that."

"Like what?" Abby felt strangely pleased to be lumped into a group in Matty's mind.

"Like you can do anything about them. You can't."

"I agree."

Matty swiveled, his whole body following his head's motion. "You're not supposed to say that."

Abby started. "I'm not?"

"You're supposed to say something stupid about how I should tell a teacher when he starts or tell my mom when I get home."

"Oh." She thought about it. "Yeah, well. I was bullied when I was a kid, and nothing made it stop."

"I don't think you're supposed to say that, either."

"Sorry." She wished she could see his root structure, like she could a turnip. Study it. Figure out what to say, what to give, what to do to get it all right.

But when she looked sideways, the smile was back on his face.

"Nah." He thumped backward into the seat again. "It's okay." A pause. "You got bullied?"

"Constantly." Abby had grown into her long, thin face, but it had taken a while. "Kids called me horse-face."

"Really?"

"It was true. I did have a horsey face."

Matty said, "Look this way?"

She did, reluctant to take her eyes off the road long enough to do it.

"I can see that," said Matty.

"Thanks."

"Well, now you're really pretty, too." He was matter-of-fact. "But your face is still long. So yeah." His voice changed and she glanced at him again. He was grinning. "Can I call you Mr. Ed?"

"Ow." Abby risked thumping herself in the chest. "That was one of the names. You wound me." But she didn't mind, not even a little bit.

He laughed.

Then a dog as big as a small horse raced into the street and launched itself at her front tire.

Matty screamed.

chapter *twenty-eight*

It wasn't bad, as accidents went. In swerving to miss the dog, Abby had only tapped the back bumper of a parked Scion, which looked like it was used to it. Her air bags hadn't gone off (thank *god*, what if the air bag had blown up and injured Matty?) and her car, sturdily built, barely suffered a scratch. It would probably cost more to fix than the entire Scion bumper, but who cared?

Matty wasn't hurt.

It was like a song in her head. That was the chorus.

Matty's not hurt.

The chorus was nice. The refrain wasn't as good.

I could have killed him.

She could have killed Scott's son. Fern's son. Scott and Fern's son. Matty. *I could have killed him.*

Then the chorus kicked back in.

Matty's not hurt.

He was very *not* hurt, in fact. The enormous dog who'd run in front of her wheels was currently pinning him down on the sidewalk, and the Great Dane—because that's what it was, a *large* black-and-white Great Dane with ears like tent flaps and sticking-out bones—seemed as happy as Matty did with the situation. He was very young, and dirty, and very, very thin, but he grinned at Matty, panting.

Frustratingly, the cops had refused to come. The dispatcher said if no one was hurt and if they weren't blocking traffic, then she had to make the report with DMV, not with them. "But I don't know whose car this is," said Abby.

"Leave a note," said the dispatcher.

"What's to stop me from leaving a bogus name and phone number?"

"Ma'am," said the dispatcher, sounding tired. "If you were the kind to lie about it, then you wouldn't have called us in the first place."

"What about the dog? It's huge."

"Congratulations. Make sure it gets its shots."

Abby wrote a note on the back of an oil change receipt. She left her phone number and insurance policy ID, along with the word *Sorry.*

Matty thumped the dog's side, as if testing a cantaloupe. "What are we going to do about him?"

The dog? No one was around, no one looking for a dog the size of a miniature pony. Abby felt as if, along with the Scion's bumper, she'd hit the wall of her ability to think like the adult. "I have no idea. He has no collar, so . . . What do you think?"

Matty was sure. "We keep him. He's so skinny."

"Um, not an option." She wasn't sure of much, but she was

pretty sure that bringing Matty home with an enormous-pawed puppy would blow what preciously little babysitting credibility she had with Fern.

He only deflated a little. He knew the lay of the land, too. "Then we knock on doors."

"Good idea." Why hadn't she thought of it? "We need a leash." She thought of the inside of her car—nothing. It wasn't like she carried rope around. Her belt? She pulled it off and threaded the end through the buckle. Then she put the loop over the puppy's neck. The dog seemed startled and pulled away, but then relaxed again. His neck was so big the leftover belt had only a few inches to hold on to, but he didn't seem inclined to run.

"He came from that direction," said Matty. He pointed at the nearest apartment building, a run-down block of solid, unmitigated gray. The side parking lot was full of cars in various states of rusted disrepair. Over the main entryway was an incredibly ill-advised iron sculpture, all horns and demonically twisted spikes. It looked like it was waiting for the right curse and a full moon before it uncoiled with a scream and gored someone. A man shambled past, talking to himself, dragging a three-wheeled shopping cart full of cans.

After the first knock got them nothing but a muffled shout, Abby started to doubt the wisdom of what they were doing. This was *not* the kind of place she normally canvassed while volunteering for her favorite local politicians. In Berkeley and Albany, people usually didn't want to talk, but they nodded and took her flyers. There, the sidewalks were clear of dog shit and dime bags (Abby was startled to realize that's what the little cellophane packets were—startled to recognize them as such even though she'd never seen one before).

Here, in front of this building, no one seemed to want to answer a knock. All the doors faced the street, a small relief. They got two more grunted shouts, and one door opened an inch and then slammed shut again. A woman in a very short purple skirt darted out one door and in through the next.

Abby worried about Matty's backpack, which they'd left, probably unwisely, visible on the front floorboard of her car. "Do you want me to hold the leash? Is he pulling?"

"I got him." Matty sounded more grown-up than eleven. "What about those houses, back there?" He pointed to the single-family houses farther down the block. He didn't want to knock on any more of the scary apartment building doors, either.

Too relieved—*she* was supposed to be the adult here—Abby agreed. "Yeah."

The first house had probably once been bright yellow but was now a dirty shade of butter. The porch held two wicker rocking chairs, one with a busted seat. If they got one more grunt in response, they were out of here. Straight to the animal shelter. That was it.

But the door opened. On the other side of the iron door, a tall young man filled the doorway. He didn't look more than seventeen, but his shoulders filled the doorway. "Yeah?"

Abby got nervous again. "We found a dog." Her voice was small.

Matty's voice was bigger. "Do you know him? Can you look at him?"

"Aw. Yeah. That's Snickers."

Abby saw the naked hope on Matty's face only as it ran away with his fallen expression. But valiantly, he rallied in the space of only a few seconds. "He's yours?"

"Nah. Belonged to the dude next door." He pointed to

the house that had four barbecue grills in various states of disrepair littered across the dead lawn.

"Okay. Thanks," said Matty.

"But he don't want it."

Abby turned. Through the iron door, she couldn't see much of the inside of the house, but what she could see looked old-fashioned. A curved upholstered blue chair. Something that looked like a sideboard filled with china. It looked like a place where a grandmother would live. It smelled that way, too. Fresh bread, and laundry detergent. "Excuse me?"

"They threw it out."

"What do you mean?"

"They don't want it. Been running the streets for a week."

The dog's spine poked out his back, his ribs visible. "They just let him go?"

"Yeah."

"You don't want him?"

"Have you seen those feet?"

Well, yeah. Abby looked at the pup's wide head and long ears. "Do you think it's possible he's still *growing*?"

"Sorry, lady. Good luck." The door shut with a polite click.

Abby faced Matty. "So."

His expression remained serious, the corners of his lips tucked in. "So now we knock on that door. Where he came from."

"What if they don't answer?" Why was she asking an eleven-year-old? "You're right. Let's try."

They walked next door and knocked. The door opened, wider this time. A boy not much older than Matty answered. He held half an apple in one hand and his face was blank. "Yeah, he was mine. But my gramma said he barked too much and was too big to fit in here."

"So you put him outside." Abby tried not to let the judgment she felt creep into her voice, but she knew it was there. What kind of an adult-in-charge didn't take a young dog to the shelter? It was less than three miles away. "You know he would have gotten hit by a car if he was just left out here."

Matty stayed where he was, kneeling on the wooden porch, petting the slobbery dog.

An older woman's voice said from behind the boy, "You tell her to get out of here."

Abby and the boy stared at each other through the iron screen.

"Tell her the truth," the woman said. "Tell her I ain't buying food for both you and that damn dog."

The boy's face went even more blank, and he shut the door with a polite but final click.

Abby and Matty didn't look at each other as they filed down the short drive to the sidewalk. They walked together past the scary apartment building and back to where the car was parked. Abby was relieved to see all her windows were intact, and immediately felt shame for feeling surprise.

"So," she said as she hit the unlock button.

"We take him," said Matty. He rested his hand on the puppy's head.

"To the shelter."

"Or to my house."

"No way. Your mother would kill me."

"My dad wanted to get me a dog."

For the first time, Abby understood the phrase *caught flat-footed*. She stood in place on the sidewalk, the dog tugging away from her as he sniffed something in the gutter. She could feel her toes on the ground through her shoes—she spread them so that she could be more grounded, could use whatever the earth wanted to bring up through her legs. Sap rising, and she was the tree.

Scott hadn't even liked dogs. And how would Matty even know *that*, if he'd never seen Scott?

"Did your grandpa tell you that?"

"He always says boys should have dogs. He said he should have let my dad have one. But he never let him." Matty nodded firmly. "My mom, she's been looking for one."

"A dog." Fern hadn't seemed like the type of woman who wanted or needed to bring more chaos into her life.

"She's lonely. She has, like, no friends."

Well. That smacked of truth. What would a boy Matty's age know about loneliness if he hadn't been told?

"What about at work? She has friends there, right?"

"I don't know. I guess. It's not like she hangs out with them. I think she's sad."

The words hit Abby with a thump. "I suppose we could check. With her, I mean."

"Yes." Matty snapped his seat belt with a satisfied click. "Can he sit on my lap?"

Abby looked down at the dog. "No way would he fit up front with you. I think he's grown since we found him."

Matty laughed. "Please?"

"No. Dog goes in the back."

"Can I name him?"

Some remarkable small sense of preservation made Abby say, "Let's hold off on that. I'm sure that if you get to keep him, your mom will let you name him." She opened the back door and heaved the pup inside. As she walked behind the vehicle, she could hear Matty's voice but not his words. She could hear the delight that lit his words, little eruptions of happiness under each syllable.

Abby held her breath when she touched her door's handle and made a wish. A prayer.

May this work.

chapter *twenty~nine*

When Fern got home from an extra hour at Gregory's place—her knees still as shaky as an old articulated bus with a busted suspension—she found a dog the size of a refrigerator in her house.

While she'd been rolling around naked with Gregory, while she'd been biting his shoulder and trying (and succeeding) to forget her son was being watched by her ex's wife, that same wife had given Matias a dog. Not just any dog, but a skinny-ass male *Great Dane*.

Fern's entire household was sitting on the floor in the living room playing with the damn thing. Elva was sitting next to Grandpa Wyatt (god knew how either of them had gotten to the floor) and her brother, Diego, was holding a tennis ball that already looked drippy with saliva. Matty was stretched out on his stomach wrestling with the dog, who rolled ecstatically on his back, flipping his huge paws in the air.

Abby was the only one standing, and Fern didn't blame her. If she were Abby, she'd be poised for a quick getaway, too.

"You did what?" Fern said crisply. She'd heard Abby's words. She wanted to hear them again.

Abby's voice was lower now. "We brought him here. Because . . ."

"Yes?"

Matty, who hadn't appeared as if he'd been paying any attention to them, said, "I told her it was okay."

"To bring a dog *here*?"

"Dad would have—" Matty's voice started out strong but faded almost immediately. "He would have wanted it. Um, Grandpa said?"

"Me?" Instead of protesting his grandson's obvious lie, Wyatt looked pleased. "Yeah! I probably said that!"

The air left Fern's lungs, and she set the paper bag she was still holding down on the ground. The pup immediately righted itself and ambled to her, sticking his head into the bag. Of course he did. She'd bought steak, which had been on sale. It wasn't a huge piece of meat, not one of those twenty-dollar slabs, but it was big enough that when it was cut five ways, each of them would get a little bit.

There wasn't enough for Abby.

And there *really* wasn't enough for Abby's dog.

"Let's get this straight, Matias."

Matty didn't meet her eyes. He knew what was coming. Of course he did. Her son was smart—too smart to try to pull this ridiculous stunt.

"You want me to get mad at Abby, is that right?"

That wasn't what Matty had expected. His head rose. "Huh?"

"Because you better be sure I'm not mad at her." It was a brilliant lie, glowing neon in the air in front of her. "I'm mad at *you*."

"Me?"

Oh, the aggrieved air he could pull off. "Yes, *you*."

Matty ran his hand awkwardly over the angular bones of the dog's thin face. "But, Mom, look. He loves me. He loves me the best already." He made his eyes huge and round. "He's starving."

"He's six feet tall. We can't afford him." She softened. He was a boy. Boys wanted puppies. But puppies grew up into gigantic dogs who wanted steak, dogs who needed shots and collars and walks. "Honey, did you really think I was going to go for this?"

Abby started to speak, but Fern silenced her with her fare-box face.

Matty stopped tugging at the dog's upper lip (which the dog strangely seemed to be enjoying). He stood. He'd grown again—Fern could tell by the way his jeans were too short. One more thing to add to the list.

"No," said Matty. "But I *hoped* that you would want to do something to make me happy." He paused and looked right at her. "For *once*."

"It's not about your happiness. It's just . . . we have so many other things right now with higher priorities. A dog is not going to work. You know that, love. Did you figure out your science project yet?"

Matty scowled.

"You have to start. I don't care what you choose but—"

His tight fists were knots of fury. "I don't care, either! I don't care about anything but the dog, but you don't care about anything at *all*." He stomped past her and then ran down the hallway, his feet thudding heavily on the wooden floorboards.

Even though she'd been expecting the slam of his bedroom door, she jumped. "So dramatic," Fern said. She kept her voice light, but she felt anything but casual.

"I thought—," started Abby.

"You thought he was telling the truth because you had no reason to think he would lie about it."

Elva and Grandpa Wyatt had a brief tug-of-war as they both stood, using each other for assistance. "I'll start dinner," said Elva, pushing a lock of gray frizz out of her face. Wyatt added, "I'll help."

"Chickens," said Diego. Fern's brother had been watching with interest, but this was the first thing he'd said.

"Chicken it is," said Elva as she drifted out of the room, Wyatt on her heels. Fine. If Elva made chicken, then there would be more steak later for Matty and Fern and Diego.

"I'm an idiot," said Abby.

Fern wanted to agree. But instead she said, "Any boy would lie about a dog." This dog, in particular. Fern sank to the floor, trying not to groan with tiredness. "He's cute, I suppose." She touched a long black ear. He looked like he was wearing an even bigger dog's clothes, wrinkles at his shoulders and hips. "His bones look sharp." His skinny black-and-white muzzle hung in velvet folds, giving him an older face than he should have had.

Diego said helpfully, "You should feed him. He's hungry."

"Nice try," she said. "*You* feed him."

"Not a chance. *I'm* no idiot."

How had Abby introduced herself to Diego? *Hi, I ruined your sister's life.* No, that wasn't fair. Scott had done that. Abby hadn't known.

It was hard to remember.

"Can you go help Elva?"

Startled, Diego said, "Me?"

"You."

"I don't cook. Except with the waffle iron."

Fern nodded at the grocery bag. "But you grill. I got steak. Go light the barbecue for me?"

"But this is fascinating."

"*Vete.*"

He shot his grin at Abby—shit, he *better* not—and headed toward the kitchen.

Fern stared after him suspiciously and then gave the dog another scratch. It groaned happily. Probably had fleas. Or worse. "I'll take him to the shelter, I guess." A puppy like him would get adopted, wouldn't he? He wouldn't be put to sleep? Thrown away like so many other dogs in Oakland? He was huge, yes, but cute. He would be saved. Surely.

"Now?" said Abby. "Won't they be closed?"

"They have one-way drop boxes." At work, Bo was always scooping up loose dogs on his shift. They came to him, as if his coach blew the scent of bacon out the biodiesel exhaust pipe.

"No, that's too sad. Would he even fit? Look at him."

Fern was trying very hard not to. "You want to keep him, be my guest."

Abby's face lit up as if a small sun had burst into flames above her head. Then she sobered. "Me? I can't have a horse in my house. He's just getting bigger, I'm sure. I can't keep him."

Fern sighed. "You didn't think this through at all, huh?" Honestly, the woman didn't *seem* dumb, but come on.

"I feel like I did a lot of not thinking today."

Satisfaction prickled her skin. "Says the woman who picked up my child from school."

"I'm so sorry. It crossed my mind that Matty didn't have it quite straight. About the dog, about you wanting one. About Scott . . ."

Fern tugged on the dog's ear and he fell to the floor sideways, landing in a happy thump. "If Matias ever tells you anything about his father, you can be pretty sure he's lying." He'd gotten into that habit when he started school. Everyone else talked about what their dad did, and his best friend in that kindergarten had possessed *two* dads. Of course Matty had wanted to talk about his father, too. Fern had wished so many times that Scott were dead—it would have simplified everything. Then she could have lied her ass off about him. She would have told Matty that Scott had been an award-winning journalist, writing war stories that changed lives. A handsome risk-taking underwater welder, building bridges that would stand a century or more. An accomplished cellist, whose interpretations of Bach made battle-hardened marines cry.

And now she couldn't lie. Matty was too smart, and Fern was too late. "Matty came with hope built right into him. I'm sorry he fibbed."

Abby touched the dog gently on the head. "I'm not. I would have taken him right to the shelter if he hadn't lied. Or if I'd been alone. Instead . . ."

Something protective rose in Fern's chest. Abby was so young-looking, and so thin, and . . . No. Feeling the ridiculous protectiveness pissed Fern off. "You wouldn't have been alone in our neighborhood, though. Not ever. You would have had no reason to come slumming down here."

Abby didn't rise to the bait, further irritating Fern. "I'm glad I was with Matty today. And I'll take the dog."

Fern narrowed her eyes. "For good? Or for the night?"

"I don't know. A normal dog, maybe. But I don't think Great Danes are normal. Are they?"

Fern remembered suddenly the image of a Great Dane she'd seen on the Internet. Standing on his back legs, the dog was taking something off the top of the refrigerator. The *top*. "You should know for sure. Whether or not you're keeping him."

Abby's chin rose. "Should I?"

Fern's irritation left her, leaving her empty. She was hollow without it. "Whatever." Abby could make her own flea-ridden bed.

"Matty named him in the car. I asked him not to, but I don't think he could help it."

"Oh, god. I'm scared to ask."

"Tulip."

Fern craned her neck and looked at the dog's rear end. "That dog has *cojones*. Literally. Big ones."

"I know."

"Tulip isn't the name for a boy dog."

Abby nodded. "Agreed."

"Where did he even get that name?"

"He said it was his favorite flower."

"Oh." They were the only flowers that came up in her yard every year, and only because she didn't have to do anything about them. Matty had always loved them. They'd come with the house, along with the cracked stair rail and the crown molding. They were strange, too—she'd never seen them anywhere else, white and such a dark purple they looked streaked with black-and-white stripes. Just like the dog.

Tulip was chewing Fern's fingers, his teeth sharp but gentle. She shouldn't let him, she knew that. It was teaching him bad habits. But it felt nice—the graze and pinch of it. A love slobber. "Tulip," she said. Then she looked up at Abby. "I guess you have a dog."

chapter *thirty*

Abby punched the button that opened her Lexus. She opened the back door. "Up."

Tulip sat on the sidewalk.

"Wrong command. Get up, dog." She tugged on the makeshift leash, but Tulip sat firmly, as if it were his job.

"Pork medallions," she said to the dog. He stayed in his firm sit and gazed up at her with joyful eyes. "I'll make you pork. That can't hurt you, can it?" When she got home, she would defrost the tenderloin that had been in the freezer since before Scott died. (Would this be the way she classified everything now? Before and after Scott? Would there be a time she wouldn't date-stamp her life this way?) She had leftover jasmine rice from Thai takeout earlier in the week. "Pork and rice. Isn't that what you give dogs with upset stomachs? Or is that chicken?" God. What on earth did you *do* if a Great Dane got diarrhea?

This was crazy.

She had nothing for a dog at home. She didn't have a bowl, or food, or a crate. She didn't even have a collar. She'd have to stop at the pet store on the way home, some place she could get real food that wouldn't upset his stomach. Or . . .

Abby couldn't do this.

Then Tulip pressed his wide, rectangular head into her knee. As if to say she could.

"Looks like you got more than you bargained for today." Behind her, Diego's voice was low. Abby spun.

His shirt was dark green and ripped at the hem, as if he'd caught it on a branch, which he probably had, right? "I guess I did."

"I can help with Tulip. If you want."

Abby stilled. "What do you mean?" Did he want to keep the dog? In the few minutes since Abby had made her decision, she'd gotten attached to the idea of watching Tulip grow into a full-grown zeppelin.

But if Matty's uncle wanted Tulip, he should have him. It was that simple. It didn't matter that the dog had already started chewing companionably on Abby's purse, as if he liked the taste of the leather. She tugged it out of his mouth.

"Like," Diego continued, "when you're not home, I could come by and walk him."

"What do you mean?"

He squatted and leaned forward to touch the pup's huge ears, flapping one back and forth. Tulip closed his eyes and let his tongue flop forward. It was a smile. Clearly a smile. *What* a cute dog.

Abby bit her lower lip. Would it be setting a terrible precedent to allow the big dog to sleep in her bed that night? More than anything else about Scott, she missed his warmth in bed.

She wanted the weight of the bed creaking next to her more than she wanted him. It was an awful thing to know about herself.

No, a crate. She'd have to get a crate. Dogs that size weren't for bed.

Diego looked up at her. His eyes were the deep brown of ground black cardamom. "What do you do all day, anyway?"

"I'm . . ." She cleared her throat. "I'm a biological scientist." Or she had been. A long time ago.

"Seriously? I didn't know that." He spoke as if he knew other things about her. He stood to his full height, which, Abby noticed again, was considerable. "I thought you didn't work."

For the first time in years, she ached to say that she still had her old job. *At the arboretum.* It used to be that people's eyes either glazed over or lit up when she said it. Diego's would have lit, she thought.

Polite. There was something she had to say here to remain polite. "Currently, I just work in my back garden. I sell infused oils, some tinctures. Herbal remedies, that kind of thing. Matty said you swing from trees. Tarzan, right?"

"Arborist, yeah. Same difference."

"What's your favorite tree?" She wasn't sure if she was genuinely interested in what it was, or if she just wanted to see if he had an answer.

He did. Without hesitation, he said, "European beech."

"Why?"

Diego smiled, and she noticed that he had a deep dimple in the stubbled brown skin of his right cheek. "Good branches for climbing. And for logical dismantling."

She winced. "Ah. You like to kill them."

"I hate to kill them. But it's part of the job. Right? Like a vet. You love 'em, you know? But sometimes you have to help put them out of their misery. Before they fall on the house."

Abby reached down and flapped Tulip's ear like he had. The puppy responded by twisting to nibble her fingers. "Tulip can hear you. And he would never fall on a house. Not until he finishes growing up, anyway."

"What's your favorite plant?"

She laughed, the feel of it rusty in her throat. "I don't have one."

"That's like a parent saying they don't have a favorite child."

"They don't!"

"Only child?"

Abby nodded slowly. She felt her dead mother nudge her in the ribs. Meg didn't count. (She did, she knew Meg counted.) She thought of the way her onion bed looked when the bulbs were still young scallions, their vulnerable green tops waving like delicate flags. The way the green was so dense, so full of flavor. Other garden crops—peppers and tomatoes and cucumbers—were full of water and space. But onions, whether harvested as green or globe, were layer upon layer of usable material, a gorgeous bulb. They were aromatic and assertive at the same time. Egyptians had sworn oaths on onions. Onion skins had been dyeing cloth for centuries. But no one would admit they loved onions best. *"Allium cepa,"* she said.

Diego inclined his head. "Ah. Of course. Sweet. But strong."

"Hey." He was smart. This pleased her more than it should have.

"What? I like 'em on my burger, you know?" He stuck his hands into his jeans pockets and then looked over his shoulder at the house. "Seriously, I can help with the dog if you need it. I make my own hours. I run two guys who work for me, but they can do a lot of jobs without supervision."

The polite Abby who jog-walked with the ex-mayor's daughter wouldn't have prodded anymore. The responsible Abby who paid an inordinate amount of property tax wouldn't have pried. But Abby didn't feel like herself. She wasn't sure who she felt like, but it wasn't normal. Not anymore. So she said what she was wondering. "Aren't you supposed to hate me?"

To his credit, he didn't look surprised. Instead, he leaned against the bent white metal mailbox that looked as if it had been clobbered by something. "Nah," he said. "Well. I don't know. I don't think so?"

Abby felt unaccountably flattered by his ambivalence. "Oh. Well. I think I'm good, but I'll let you know if I need help. With walking or . . . something? Thank you."

Diego probably did want to help with Tulip. For Matty's sake. She could feel he meant it.

She felt something else, too. He held her eye for a split second too long and she felt her spine heat. She heard Kathryn's voice in her head. *Get it over with.*

Diego had absolutely every reason to hate her.

And Abby would never even *consider* how hot he was— Diego was her dead husband's ex-brother-in-law. Oh, god, she still had those dried figs for safe passage in her bag. She tried to wipe from her mind the knowledge that they were also used in love spells.

"You bet," he said. "Let me give you my number. To help. If you need it."

Abby said, "Okay."

She took his number, punching it into her phone. Then she gave him hers.

For the dog.

Tulip finally jumped into the backseat.

Abby nodded at Diego. He nodded back. Something in his gaze caught and tangled in her throat, and she felt it there as she drove away through the darkening, unfamiliar streets.

chapter *thirty~one*

Driving into North Berkeley with a carful of boys, Fern realized—for the first time—why people called their upper torsos their chests. Hers was full of things that would have been better stored away. Her feelings—trepidation mixed with confusion mixed with a strange, unfamiliar feeling that she couldn't actually name, but which reminded her of fear—were folded on top of one another, like heavy blankets.

Crammed next to one another on the backseat, the three boys were hopping up and down as much as their seat belts would allow them to. She'd told Matty to ride shotgun, but he'd wanted to be in the backseat with his friends. Neither of the other two boys was interested in sitting next to a mom.

"You guys! Chill! She only said she *might* have a trampo-line." She never should have mentioned that part of Abby's text. How did someone only maybe have a trampoline, anyway? "It's a science afternoon. That's the important part." Abby had said she would teach Matty to dye fabric with plants in the garden. If that worked, then damn. Mrs. Hutch would have to get over her hate-on for Matty. Wouldn't she? The other two boys already had their projects on the go (Jorge was doing a project on how golf balls accelerated on an incline, and Bryson was comparing goldfish heart rates with human ones)—Matty was the last to start his.

From an inch behind her ear, Bryson trumpeted, "I've been on a trampoline before! I was really good at it!" It was such a Bryson thing to say. His mother was one of those touchy-feely women who praised their kids for tying their shoes correctly every day. Bryson got gold stars for saying good morning. He was probably applauded for how interesting his dreams were. "I'm like the best at it ever."

"I'm hecka good at jumping," said Jorge. "There's a place near my dad's house in Sacramento where it's, like, this warehouse? And it's full of bounce houses. You bounce out of one into another like you're Superman."

"Superman doesn't *bounce*."

Jorge didn't care. "It's like you're flying. I can go five feet sideways or something."

Fern glanced in the rearview mirror and caught Matty's skeptical look. "No way."

"So way. There's, like, a hundred trampolines. All next to each other. So you don't fall off. And it's better because you can go higher. Like, you're flying and then you flip? And sometimes you can get a double flip. You're not supposed to, but I did it, and then the guy yelled at me, but I'd already done it."

Matty's voice was worried. "I've never been on a trampoline."

Fern wanted to say, *It'll be all right. You'll be wonderful at it.* But the truth was Matty usually didn't get things on the first try that took coordination. It had taken forever to convince him to take off his bicycle training wheels. The very first time he'd gotten on Diego's old skateboard, Matty had broken his wrist by flying off the board into the Silvas' garbage cans. "Maybe it's like skateboarding. Remember? You got better at it as you went."

She shouldn't have inserted herself into the conversation. In the rearview mirror, she saw Matty's shoulders rise.

"It's not the same," he muttered. "And I'm still not good at it."

The other two boys didn't seem to notice, and the conversation moved to the new deck Angel's brother had gotten with epoxy fiber reinforcement and some kind of new axle they couldn't remember the name of.

Fern stopped looking in the rearview. Instead, she watched the little girl in the Mercedes in front of her contort herself practically inside out, twisting around in her seat to make faces through the back window. It was obvious she was trying to do it without her mother noticing, and her desperate flapping was getting funnier by the second.

Did rich mothers notice less? Fern knew she would have been able to tell if Matty was flipping around in his seat behind her even if she didn't see him do it. She'd be able to feel her old car shake. And if she didn't feel it, she'd still just *know.* Mother's intuition. At the next light, she pulled up next to the sleek, black car. The girl in the backseat looked at them, then plastered herself against her window, her cheeks ballooning as she blew against the glass.

Jorge noticed, then Bryson and Matty. All three hooted and did what they could to match it. Fern would have to clean off their face grease and spittle later, and she didn't mind. That's what Windex was for.

The mother in the car still didn't notice. As they idled at the red, the woman kept talking on her cell phone, holding it to her ear in defiance of the law. A $165 fine probably wouldn't mean the same to her as it did to Fern.

Five hundred thousand dollars. Plus that twenty thousand Abby had mentioned in passing, the amount of the old policy that had seemed to hardly matter to her.

Fern could have all of it sitting in her bank account right now. If she had accepted it. If any part of it had been acceptable to her.

Did stubborn *always* equal poor? It didn't seem fair. Then again, Fern had always believed that people who wasted their time whining about fairness usually just needed more sleep. Fair was something that came and went. It didn't deserve stressing about.

She pulled around the Mercedes only to catch the light at Adeline.

That cash.

It was math she could do in her sleep—she could have done it in rush hour traffic while driving her coach, so it was easy to do while steering the small car around a stalled pickup truck in this early afternoon traffic. *Five hundred and twenty thousand.* Invested in a good S&P 500 index, bringing in a conservative five percent interest, it would earn twenty-six thousand dollars a year. Without doing a damn thing. Just sitting there. Dave Ramsey swore the stock market over the past seventy years had brought in an average of twelve percent, even with volatility. If that was true, the interest could come closer to sixty-two grand. Just *sitting* there.

She breathed through her mouth to slow her heartbeat and ignored the fact that every time Bryson bounced in the seat behind her, he kicked the middle of her seat.

Five hundred and twenty thousand dollars.

Fern had dreamed the numbers last night, the numerals gleaming bright yellow. She'd touched them. They'd been sticky like those plastic gummy decorations you put on windows at holidays.

They were just numbers.

They didn't *mean* anything.

Or, at least, they hadn't meant anything until she'd tried (again) to wring the money for a new washer out of the overtime check that had landed in her bank account on Monday. The life insurance hadn't meant as much until she'd gone to get a flat fixed at the tire shop on Tuesday night after work and found out she needed to buy new brake pads. They were— apparently—imperative, according to Esteban. "Look, *mami*, I told you you could wait the last two times." He'd looked pointedly at Matty. "You can't wait again. You hurt somebody if you do." In order to cover the cost, she'd ignored the second notice on the electricity bill. The new brakes stopped the car smoothly and quickly now, instead of mushing apologetically with a sigh to the floorboards. The car was safe again.

It was funny—she'd always been a grasshopper, believing in the best. She and Scott had that in common once, fiddling for fun instead of working, like the industrious ant. She knew she'd always make it—she used to feel that in her heart. It might be tight, but the money would be there, somewhere, somehow.

She had a job. She'd had child support coming in, exactly enough. She didn't save, but someday she would. Someday she'd be a grown-up, but until then she'd have enough.

Now Fern didn't have enough. She hadn't seen it coming, hadn't planned for this rainy day.

There was an umbrella being offered to her. A huge one. A bright rainbow-colored umbrella, the kind that chased whole storms right out of the sky.

And damned if she couldn't reach for the handle.

"Mom! You missed the turn!"

"No, I didn't."

"It's back there!" Matty wailed as if it were too late, as if they would never be able to turn the car around, as if Abby and the science project and the maybe-trampoline would disappear because she would have to drive an extra three blocks because she'd been thinking of the power a thin piece of bank-issued plastic held. She could have bought a whole *car* with her debit card if she'd taken Abby's money. She could get a used Nissan Juke with that card. She could swipe it, sign somewhere, and drive out of the lot in that boxy clownlike car that made Matty laugh. Not that she ever would have. That money would have been for the house, and college savings, and, god, a tutor for Matty if science kept making him so furiously frustrated.

Fern took two more right turns and pulled into Abby's long driveway. Her brakes stopped firmly, and she tried to lock down her thoughts the same way, tried to fold them the same way she was folding her feelings, storing them in her chest, just above her breath.

It would be fine. She would just pick up a few more hours of OT and pay off the PG&E bill next week. She'd scrape the next mortgage payment out of the next paycheck. She always did. If Abby mentioned the life insurance again, she'd hold up her *Stop* hand, the one that had kept three different would-be robbers from demanding her cell phone in the last few years.

It was just that . . . Fern sighed as the boys threw themselves out of the car like it was full of poison gas.

The people who said money couldn't buy happiness had never thinned mustard with water to make the bottle last another week of ham sandwich lunches.

chapter *thirty~two*

Abby was surprised by the boys' height difference. Matty seemed normal to her, a normal eleven-year-old boy height, coming to just below her shoulder. Bryson, though, had to be six inches taller than Matty, and Jorge was a good eight inches shorter. As if to make up for the disparity, they'd dressed in what seemed to be a uniform—each wore a blue shirt with some comic-book character doing something with a weapon. Matty sported a green man with an ax, Bryson had a red man with a knife, and Jorge wore a yellow man with what looked like a flare gun.

"Are your characters all on the same team?" she asked, earning only blank looks. She pointed to their chests. "Like from the same universe? Is that how you say it?"

Matty looked startled. "Yeah."

"Sweet," said Abby. Then she wondered if that's what boys

said now. Maybe that was the equivalent of "groovy" by now. *Awesome. Dope. Sick.* She had no freaking idea.

Fern looked uncomfortable. She was wearing a black puffy coat that was too long on her—it came almost to her knees and looked like something an old woman would wear to the grocery store. "I parked in the driveway."

"Yay!" said Abby. "That's what it's for." What a dumb thing to say. "Anyway. I'm so glad you're here. Come on in."

She ushered Fern and the boys down the hall into the kitchen. She tried to see it for the first time, the way she had when they'd bought the house. The backyard and its raw potential had been what sold her on the house, but the kitchen's large open expanse of counter and its huge island with its own sink had been what got out her signing pen. She kept three vases full of flowers in the kitchen, always. The blooms varied by season, of course. Now, in March, she had blue statice and dark purple irises.

She pointed at the island. "I set up a taco bar."

The boys said, "Oh, *yeah*," and *"Nice,"* as if they were ogling a girl in a bikini.

Fern frowned, her eyebrows drawn together.

"The salsa is my specialty, made with cilantro from the garden and heirloom garlic, but I'm pretty proud of my guacamole, too."

"Let me guess. Avocado tree?"

Abby felt herself blush. "Yeah. Two."

"Damn. I was kidding. That's just . . . that must be great."

"It is. Yeah. Oh, god. Is a taco bar too weird?"

"Nah. It's great."

Were they still talking about avocados? Abby had no idea. She felt as off-kilter as she had when Hugh had helped her up onto one of the trampolines in the back to try it out.

She blinked in the hopes it would help her feel more focused. "Tulip did *not* help, by the way. He was, in fact, hugely unhelpful."

At his name, the dog nudged her waist with his nose.

"What did he do?" asked a delighted-looking Matty.

"He ate *all* the ground beef. I had to go get another pack. It was *raw*."

It got the effect she was hoping for—the boys chorused, "Ewwww," thrilled and impressed.

Then Matty asked, "Did you get a trampoline?"

Abby clapped. "I did. My neighbor Hugh was getting rid of his. His three girls are in boarding school, and he didn't think it was getting enough use. He helped me set it up this morning. *That* was a chore. You want to try it?"

"Yeah!"

Fern raised a hand. "Don't forget. We're here for your science project."

"Just for a while, Ma. I want to try it." Matty shot Fern a half-excited, half-scared look and raced out the sliding glass door. The other two followed him, stampeding into the yard.

"I'm glad you brought him. Them." There was a polite thing to say, Abby knew, and a right thing. She knew the polite thing. She wasn't sure, though, what would take that look off Fern's face, the look that was throwing Abby off so much she wanted to hold on to the porch rail as they stepped down onto the grass. Tulip had already torn around the lawn twice, and was now trying to lick Matty's face. He didn't even have to jump up to do it. Impolite, poorly trained puppy. Abby wanted to call him back, but knew he wouldn't come, so she didn't even try.

"No problem."

Polite. They were so polite.

"Matty's such a great kid."

"Yes."

Abby's stomach clenched. "We went to the library this last Wednesday, did he tell you? I showed him how to use the Kindle app on his phone to get free e-books."

Fern nodded, her face still.

It wasn't a bad thing, was it? That she'd said *free*? Abby thought Fern would like it, the way Matty had.

"Mom! Look!"

Fern's face changed as Matty called her, her expression going softer, her eyes less guarded. If Abby hadn't been looking right at that second, she would have missed it.

And then Fern said, "Holy shit. *That's* your trampoline?"

"Um. Yeah."

Hugh's trampoline had actually been more of a trampoline complex. He and his wife had had triplets seventeen years before, and had been doing everything bigger than everyone else since. There were six trampolines in total, set up in a large rectangle. There were foam landing pads on all sides. On the farthest side stood a sort of fabric wall, lashed to sturdy posts now sunk deeply into her lawn. Abby had tried jumping earlier. These weren't like the backyard trampolines when she was a kid. These were tighter, bouncier. Better. Or was it that she was heavier now and had the weight to go higher? She wasn't sure, but whatever it was, it had felt wonderful. The falling down toward the trampoline—that had been fast and fun and exciting. But going up had felt like a slow, invisible elevator rise, one that she was making happen herself.

She'd wanted to flip. Maybe later she would dare.

But now worry filled her. "Is it too dangerous?"

Fern squinted.

Abby took a quick step forward. "I knew it. I'll stop them. I knew it was too much. God, the last thing I want to do is hurt them. Kids!"

"No." Fern pulled at Abby's elbow. "They're fine."

The boys launched themselves up without using the small set of steps. Jorge flipped immediately. Bryson flapped his arms and bounced to another surface and did his own flip.

Matty watched, bobbing gently, only his knees moving.

"Are you sure? What if one of them falls off?"

"Kids fall off things all the time."

"What if they *break* something?"

Fern lifted one eyebrow. "You never broke anything as a kid?"

Horrified, Abby said, "No!"

"Overprotected much?"

"Well. Yeah." Abby thought of the way she had had to wear a helmet when she went on the pony ride at Tilden Park, even though no one else but the really little kids had to. The wildly embarrassing way her mother hadn't let her take swimming lessons without arm floats until she was ten.

"Kids bounce. Literally. They're tough." Fern raised her voice to a shout. "You can do it, Matty!"

Encouraged, Abby yelled also. "Yeah! Do it, Matty!"

Matty jumped harder. He went higher. And then higher. Then, almost in slow motion, he raised his arms as he launched upward, tucking his legs and folding forward, sailing into a flip. He didn't quite stick the landing, falling sideways on the second bounce, but it was close.

"Oh, he *did* it," said Fern so quietly Abby almost couldn't hear her.

Matty whooped, stood up, and did it again.

They all did. Like a trio of rubber balls, the boys bounced and leaped. They flew and flipped and glided. Every once in a while, they'd whack themselves into a post, or slap an arm against a side, but they just yelled and started leaping again.

Abby and Fern sat on the lawn in two of the Adirondack chairs Abby had moved down from the porch.

"They're good at it," said Abby.

Fern nodded. "My little Mexican jumping bean."

Abby snorted.

"Not that you could say that," warned Fern.

"Never," said Abby sincerely.

"Okay, then." Fern's face was softer now, the lines that had pulled at her eyes fainter than they'd been. "Yeah. So. Are you trying to throw him a birthday party or something? Because that's not till September. I thought we were here for his homework."

Abby looked at the boys, still flipping. Still flying. Her fingertips tingled, as though she could feel their adrenaline in her own body. "I just wanted to make it fun."

"They're kids. Drinking Coke out of plastic cups and chewing on straws is fun."

"Well." Abby watched Jorge flip himself against the back wall and then chest-bump Matty midair. Tulip watched from the side, barking with excitement. "Now I know."

Fern grinned. "It's pretty fun to watch."

"Fun to do, too. Wanna try?"

"Hell, yes, I do." She didn't hesitate. "Maybe when they're getting tired of it, if we have time." Fern glanced at her watch. "Thirty minutes. Then we work on his project?"

"Yes. Of course."

"Hey." Fern kept her face forward, looking nowhere but at the boys.

"Yeah?"

"Thanks for this."

Bryson sailed in a perfect arc, landed perfectly, and did it all over again. He looked like a tiny astronaut. All three were working on some routine, bumping fists while in the air.

They looked like they were flying. Happiness filled Abby like helium and she felt like she might be the next one floating into the sky. "You're very, very welcome."

chapter *thirty-three*

Taco time was an unholy mess. Fern wanted to keep Matty next to her so she could undo some of the damage as it happened, but every time she reached toward him with a napkin, he laughed and dodged out of her reach. "I'm fine, Mom! Jeesh. It's just taco sauce."

Taco sauce that he could and probably would track out of the kitchen and onto Abby's white carpet (white carpet! who had white carpet except for people in carpet commercials?) if she wasn't actively watching him every second.

The boys mowed through their loaded plates while Fern tried not to show how impressed she was by the guacamole. Ensenada Taqueria had the best guac in the East Bay. But Abby's might come close.

When they were done, after Matty and Bryson had seconds and Jorge took thirds, after Abby had surprisingly let Tulip lick the ground where Bryson had lost half a taco, they went outside again. Abby gave a flourish toward the shed at the bottom of the yard. "Now you get to see my secret lair."

"Is there a dragon? Dragons have lairs." Bryson sounded hopeful.

"I have a dragon tree, and it oozes red resin when you cut it. Does that count?"

The boys made impressed noises.

"That's my potting shed. Well, that's what I call it, but I do most of the repotting out on that table." She pointed to a huge wooden table standing off-kilter next to a redwood with peeling bark. "The potting shed is where I make the magic."

The boys screeched and raced ahead, leaving Fern and Abby to follow.

The shed was painted the same cream as the house, but the paint looked older, peeling in places. It looked, like many of the things in Abby's pretty, pretty home, artfully distressed, only Fern got the feeling that everything else was supposed to match this. This building felt real.

Abby pulled on the wooden door, which opened with a low screech. She reached up and pulled a cord, and a single bare bulb came to life. She tugged back thick canvas curtains, and more light filled the shed. It was about the size of a two-car garage, but it looked like a room where magic potions were made. Long dark tables ran along two walls, and on the other two, shelves upon shelves reached up to the ceiling. Each shelf was full of bottles—cobalt, ruby, and clear glass with cork stoppers. Raffia ties were around their necks, small cards hanging from each.

On two of the tables were stacks of bowls, and underneath the tables were more shelves, full of larger glass jars, gallon-sized or more. These were labeled carefully: *Funnels, Dye pots,*

Mordant. An industrial sink stood in one corner, next to a small stove that held an already-steaming pot.

"Are you a witch?" asked Bryson.

"Do *not* ask that," said Fern quickly. But she wanted to know the answer, too.

"No," said Abby with a smile. "But I feel a lot of sympathy for the women who were called witches, just because they knew things about plants and herbs. Think about it—lots of medicine comes right from plants. Aspirin is made of bark, did you know that? I always wonder who the first person was to chew on a piece of tree bark. And what happened next? Her toothache stopped? So she did it again?"

"What if it had been poisonous and she died?" Matty's eyes were locked onto her.

Abby shrugged. "A lot of people did die, testing things." She appeared to take their measure and then she leaned forward. "Gruesome, *painful* deaths. I hope *we* don't die, getting ready for the science fair."

The boys laughed, falling backward and jabbing one another in delight. Fern leaned back against a shelf, careful not to brush up against anything. You never knew.

"So this is an onion." Abby held up a big red one.

Matty yelled, "I knew that! That's not poisonous!"

Abby grinned. "Wait for it. What's on the outside of the onion?"

"Paper!"

"Skin!"

"Paper skin!"

"Right. You're right! This skin stuff is papery, and it comes right off after the onion has been dried. These are some that I grew last year."

"Ew. So old! Gross!"

Abby suddenly looked a little nervous. She blinked. "Not gross, I promise. I won't make you eat them, but they would be fine if we did. Onions are amazing. Remember when I left the tacos to run out here? I had to turn on the stove so the water would be ready for us. You see this here?" The water was boiling.

"Yeah."

Abby hunched her shoulders and stirred the pot with a long wooden spoon. "Boil, boil, cauldron bubble . . ." Her voice was just a creak. "Science classroom falls to rubble."

The door to the shed banged shut in the wind. Bryson gave a small scream. Matty laughed maniacally. Even Fern jumped. Then Abby straightened and laughed at all of them. "Oh, man, you should see all your faces right now."

She'd gotten them. Fern's spine relaxed.

"Come on, look. I've got boiling water in here. I'm going to add this onion skin, and a whole pile of more skins I've got here in this bag. There. We'll let those cook a little while. Here, Matty, poke at the water."

He stood next to her and swirled the spoon in the pot.

"Do you see what's already happening in there?"

Matty went up on his tiptoes. "Its kind of . . . tan. Like, maybe orange. Why isn't it red?"

"We'll talk about that. Now. What's this?" She held up a cream knitted hat, slipping it over her hair. Her honey-colored hair looked wonderful under it, like a smooth, expensive waterfall. Fern pushed at her own frizzed curls. If she put on a hat like that, she'd look like a homeless person.

"A hat!" they all said.

"Aren't you clever?" Abby grinned at the boys, and Fern saw them all grow at least an inch taller. She had them in the palm of her hand. Tacos and trampolines. The woman wasn't dumb.

"What happens if I put it in the onion water?"

"It'll get dyed!"

"Right! What color?"

Silence.

"Hard to answer, huh? Let's wait and see, and when we're done, we can talk about how Matty can make this magic happen all on his own to wow his teacher at the science fair."

Matty threw his nervous look at Fern. "But . . ."

Fern bit her lip. This was for Abby to handle. And if she couldn't, well, then Fern would come in and figure something out. She couldn't help the small hope that rose in her, the tiny wish that she would *have* to be the rescuer.

"But?" said Abby.

Matty did that quick tiptoe move he used to make when he was nervous. "I don't think it's enough."

A wrinkle creased Abby's forehead. "You don't?"

"Just, like, coloring a hat? Like an Easter egg? Mrs. Hutch hates me. She's not going to say that's enough."

"Not just that. You're gathering the onions, because we'll need more, a lot more, and you're learning how to tell when they're ripe and how to process the skins. Not only that, but you're taking yarn and making it into a hat."

"Huh?"

"You're transforming simple cream yarn into a useful object using just a couple of sharp sticks, and then you're changing that object's color with a natural chemical process. We'll show how it works chemically on paper, and then prove it in the dye pot."

Matty said, "Whoa. Wait. I have to *make* the hat?"

"Simple knitting."

The other two boys hooted with laughter. "Ha! You're going to be a knitter! Yeaaaah, Grandma Matty!"

But Matty looked okay with it. "Shut up, you penis-heads. I'm gonna make a skater hat. Yeah. Cool. I wanna do that."

Abby looked so pleased it almost hurt Fern to look at her bright face. "Good. Oh, good."

Fern's upper chest thumped with a tiny, shameful jolt of disappointment followed immediately by a burst of pride. Those warm blankets of feelings, folded in her chest, rose up again. Muffling her voice. Burying her breath.

"Can you teach me how to knit on Wednesday?" said Matty. "Can we go back on the trampoline now?"

"Yeah," said Abby. Then she shot a quick look at Fern. "If your mom doesn't mind. We can totally start on Wednesday."

"Fine," said Fern. "That's fine."

The boys practically leaped over one another to get out of the small shed, their screams unintelligible and furiously joyous.

"Wow," said Abby.

"I know. They kind of move in and out like a hurricane but with way less warning." Fern looked around. "It's three times bigger in here now that they're out."

Abby picked up a rag from a folded pile and rubbed at the top of the small stove. "I know it's kind of a wreck in here, but . . . I love it more than any other place."

Fern picked up a bottle. *Tulsi Basil*. "You sell this shit?"

Abby blinked.

"I mean stuff," corrected Fern. "It's not shit. Obviously. It's very pretty." Wait, how did she get so off-balance again?

"I sell some of it. But mostly I just like making it. I give a lot away. I never have to worry about birthday presents, you know? I just pick something the person would like." Abby bit her bottom lip. "Like you. I would give you . . ."

Fern shook her head. "Nah. You don't have to."

"I know. Hang on." Abby ran her finger along one shelf of blue bottles, and then up to the next one, where small light blue sachets were tied with dark blue ribbons. "This one. Here."

"I don't need—" But curiosity got the better of her, and she raised it to her nose. "Oh, sweet baby *Cristo*. What the *hell* is that?" It smelled like beer and dirt.

"Sorry. It's not my best smelling. It's hops and mandrake root. I should really put a little lavender in there to even it out." Abby pulled a small notebook out of a drawer and scratched a quick note.

"What is it supposed to do?"

"Hops are for sleep. And mandrake is for protection and prosperity."

Fern snorted. "Well. I'll take it." She looked around again. "I'm surprised this isn't a full-time gig for you. People eat this up." *Right. Abby didn't* need *a full-time job.*

"I want it to be full-time someday. I'm just not that great at the business end of it."

"Do you have a Web site?"

"Just an Etsy shop. It's kind of lost over there, to be honest. There are a lot of people selling this kind of thing. You'd be surprised. I know I always am, every time some stranger randomly orders the lemongrass-basil tincture, or the vetiver oil. And I'm not that great at getting to the post office. I tried to sell some once at a farmers' market, but I kept forgetting to write the money down. Making change and standing upright at the same time is kind of like a miracle."

The way she put herself down grated Fern's nerves the way a broken blinker did. Abby was wicked smart—you could tell just by the way she reacted to things, catlike, with quick, graceful moves. Smart people might miss their stop, but they realized it all in a second, calculating how far they'd gone past it, which line they were going to have to connect with to get back. *I need the 62, or the 41. Where does this line cross?* Dumb people blinked lazily out the window and mumbled, *What the hell?*

"I don't believe you."

"It's true." Abby tapped the side of her head. "Bright but forgetful. That's what my teachers in grade school always said. Matter of fact, I think they said that in college, too."

"You can pay people to do all that for you. Hire a book-keeper, a graphic designer, and a marketing consultant. You can do all that online now, and then you just make the shit." She corrected herself. "The stuff."

"Yeah. I suppose I should look for someone to help, if I'm going to get serious about it. And since Scott died, I'm kind of thinking that I should do it. You have any interest?"

Fern blinked once. Then again. "Sorry?"

A quick, crooked smile. Hopeful. "In helping me? Part-time work?"

"I *have* a job." It was so preposterous—and surprising—that it wasn't even that insulting. Abby was a different breed. A totally different kind of person.

Abby rubbed at her cheeks. "I know. I didn't mean to imply that you didn't. . . . I'm sorry. I was just thinking out loud. Sorry. The most important thing to me is spending time with Matty. That's all."

Abby and Matty—they had a connection. Fern could see it. She could feel it in the air between them. It wasn't too early for Abby to love her son—who *wouldn't* love Matty? But Matias was smitten with her, too.

What if he came to rely on her?

No.

Abby couldn't . . . God, she was lovely. She was gorgeous. She was sweet. No one could argue that. But she couldn't just swoop in and *take* the family that Fern had built, the one that Fern took care of. Her family was her job, the only job that really mattered. Her family was *hers*.

"And that's still okay, right? Us hanging out, me and Matty?" Abby's face was as wide-open as an Oakland street at three in the morning.

Matty thundered into the shed, yelling something about a double flip and how Abby *had* to come watch.

Abby. Not Mom.

No, it's not okay. You can watch him, you can learn about him. You can help. But you can't have him.

Matty will not rely on you.

Matty relies on me.

At least, that's what she tried to say. It came out more as *"Mrpht."*

"Mom?" Matty's voice was worried, and she should reassure him, but the sound faded into the buzz that was inside her head, just behind her teeth somewhere.

"Mom!"

I'm fine, Fern said. She heard the words at least, knocking against the buzzing, but she wasn't quite sure they could hear her.

Didn't matter.

All that mattered was Matty.

"Fern?"

Abby's voice was miles away, in a tunnel. So far down the tracks and in the dark, and she could hear the thumping of the wheels and then Fern forgot to think about anything as she felt herself inside the train, inside the engine itself, rushing toward darkness that was quieter than anything else.

chapter *thirty-four*

A bby watched Fern fall. *Jesus.* She couldn't tell if she'd said the word—a sudden, unexpected prayer—out loud or not.

"It's okay! Move away from her!" Matty rushed at his mother like he could catch her, even though Fern was already down, already lying on the wooden floor of the shed. "Give her space. She needs space." He looked upward at the shelves, as if considering whether things would fall, like it was an earthquake.

Jorge and Bryson, standing in the small bright doorway, stared, frozen.

Fern made a noise that didn't sound human. It was a growl.

Abby felt fear rise from every pore. An ambulance, that's what they needed. *That* was it. "Jorge. Here's my cell, call 911. Matty, help me here."

Jorge took the phone and started dialing.

"Tell them we need an ambulance. Okay?"

Matty screamed, "No! She's fine! Just let her have the seizure."

"Jorge," said Abby, "call."

Fern's face was a rictus, her body a mass of twitches. Abby had never seen a seizure, but she'd had an idea of what they looked like, and this was *not* it. Fern wasn't flailing—instead, she was making the tiniest, tightest motions imaginable, as if every muscle in her body were bound by tight rubber bands. She made that growling noise again, a terrifying low sound that seemed yanked from her throat with every jerk of her body. She lay half sideways on the floor, one arm behind her. Her jaw jutted forward, her lower lip twisting along with her limbs.

"Matty." Abby knelt next to him in the space between the shelf and his body. "What can I do to help?"

"Don't call 911."

Fern's body was spasming now, going rigid, as if she were a woman about to be sawed in half on a stage, and then folding into softness, only to be pulled taut again. One eyelid was halfway open. That horrified Abby most of all. She could see Fern in there, could see her trying to get out. She was almost unrecognizable.

"Honey, we have to." Abby glanced at Jorge. "She's not— oh, *Jesus*—I don't think she's breathing. Are we supposed to do CPR or something?"

"No, just let her come out on her own." Matty's voice was full of tears, and he alternated between holding his arms above Fern and furiously scowling at Jorge. Abby felt a scream build in her lungs, but there was no place for it to go. The only person screaming should be Fern, and she was still a terrifying bundle of jerks and vocal clicks.

He dropped to his knees next to Fern. "Mom says no 911. Never 911."

Fern was softening now, her legs finally stilling. Her right arm was still bent and locked at a forty-five-degree angle, but her head lolled sideways.

Matty held his mother's head. "I got this. She's breathing again, see? We're fine." He pushed his fingers into his mother's hair. "It's just a seizure. *God*. She'll be fine in a minute."

Abby put one hand on Fern's shoulder, the other on her elbow. A fine tremor raced through her fingers, and it took a second to realize it was she who was shaking now, not Fern. "We need to get her—Matty, what do we do now?"

"She's totally *fine*, aren't you *listening*? She's fine. Look!"

Fern gasped. She was blinking and breathing now, but she looked like someone else. Her eyes were slitted, her mouth still open, her body curling like a question mark that had been stretched straight and then released.

She looked feral.

And terrifying.

"How . . ." Abby could hear sirens now. "How long does it take for her to come out of it?"

"She's out of it. Can't you *see* that? She's already out. She'll be fine." Matty didn't look up, keeping his hands on Fern's forehead. "Mom, tell them. Sometimes it takes a minute. That's all. *Mom*. Tell them to stop. Tell them not to come."

"They're just going to check her—"

"*No ambulance*. Cancel it!"

Maybe Abby could change the subject. "What about juice? Would that help her, if we could find some? I think I have some pineapple juice in the kitchen. . . ." It was Scott's—he'd liked it with vodka sometimes. Small cans, she had them somewhere.

Matty's eyes widened. "She's epileptic. Not a *diabetic*." He brushed the hair back from Fern's forehead. "*God*. See? She's fine. Tell them to go away."

"Matty—"

He met her gaze then and his eyes were full of tears. "Please, Abby? Make them go away? It'll make everything worse."

It couldn't. There couldn't be much worse than that half-opened eye, not much worse than watching a woman twitch grotesquely on the floor of her shed.

The siren stopped, and Abby could hear a powerful-sounding engine coming from the front of the house. "Jorge, go get them and bring them back here? Bryson, grab Tulip's collar. Hold on tight to him, okay?"

"Please? Abby?" Matty sat taller and with his shoulders straight, with his jaw set fierce, Abby saw for a split second the man he would become. But his face—his little-boy face broke her heart, the lower lip that was shaking no matter how much he tightened it, the big brown eyes that were swimming.

Behind him, two women in white shirts and black pants hurried across the yard. Bryson, off to one side, tried to make Tulip sit, but the dog was dragging him slowly forward, foot by foot.

"Honey," Abby spoke as softly to Matty as she could, "let them check her."

"How long has she been in seizure?" asked one medic, dropping to her knees.

Another said, "Is she epileptic? On her meds?"

Their voices established them as in command. Relief trickled down the back of Abby's throat. "Matty, come on, let's let them have the space."

Matty hit—whacked—her hand off his shoulder. "Don't *touch* me."

Abby gasped. "I'm sorry." The side of her hand burned. She'd have a bruise there tomorrow.

"What's her name?"

"Don't tell them."

But Abby said, "Fernanda Reyes."

Matty's eyes.

The look of betrayal he gave her just before he turned his back on her was a wretched burn, a pain that seared through her shoulders directly into her heart.

Nothing could erase that look.

"No, no, no," mumbled Fern as the medics, now multiplied to four, loaded her on the gurney. It was all she seemed able to say.

Abby and Matty followed them as they rolled her through the garden and out the side gate. The gurney wobbled on the rocky path.

"Don't let her fall." Matty's voice cracked as they lined the stretcher up with the open back doors of the ambulance.

One of the medics said, "Don't worry, she's strapped in tight. Oh, hey, wait, buddy. You can't get up there."

Matty was in the back of the ambulance before they even slid Fern inside.

The tallest medic pointed at Abby. "Can you grab him?"

Matty's look was ferocious, his eyes narrowed, his top row of teeth bared.

"I . . . I don't think so." Abby's throat was so tight she didn't know how much longer she'd be able to breathe. "Matty, you wanna come with me? We'll meet her . . ."

Matty stayed perfectly still except for his chest, which heaved as he panted.

The medics slid in the gurney, the legs folding below it like magic.

Abby gave up. "I'm not going to be able . . ."

The tall woman addressed Matty again. "Kid, you're *really* not supposed to ride with us."

Matty strapped himself into a side seat and crossed his arms.

"C'mon, now."

"I'm not leaving her."

The medic attaching a blood pressure cuff to Fern's arm said, "Aw, whatever. Let him ride, Cindi."

"Liability."

"Fuck it. This kid's not getting out, and I don't feel like fighting him. My shoulder's still jacked from that dude last night."

"We don't have Mom's permission."

"Yes," said Fern, her voice suddenly clear, ringing through the vehicle.

"All right, then."

As they finished locking the legs of the gurney and moving equipment around her, Abby looked behind her. There on the porch were the other two boys, both of them wide-eyed, tears still streaming down Bryson's face. She would have to get them home. She'd have to do that before she met Matty at the hospital. *Shit.* "Which hospital—?"

"Alta Bates," said the shorter medic, and slammed the doors shut.

The last thing Abby saw was Matty's eyes, so full of anger they almost burned.

chapter *thirty~five*

Fern couldn't remember much, but the sick dread in her abdomen told her everything she needed to know. The vague queasiness and the metallic taste in her mouth meant she'd had a seizure. The noises and smells around her, the thin blanket wrapped around her knees, the ugly blue and white curtain hung high around her tiny bed, meant she was in the hospital.

Those two things combined meant she was fucking *fucked*.

She'd started to come back to consciousness in the ambulance, and she hadn't understood a damn thing at first. She thought there might have been a car crash. Or maybe she'd tripped and hit her head.

God, it had been so *long* since she had gone out. Years, probably. And it had been fifteen years—more—since she'd had a seizure in public. Besides her daily meds, she didn't give her condition a second thought. It was under control.

Fern looked up at the IV pole hanging just to her left. Her heartbeat *bing*ed in time on the machine, right along with the thumping in her chest. Matty sat on a plastic chair, playing some game on his phone, the ER curtain resting on his shoulders. There was never enough room in these emergency room cubicles. He was being sweetly fierce. When the nurses thrust the curtain aside, he watched them carefully, as if he were their boss, evaluating their every move. He'd said Abby was taking the other two boys home. Thank god for that—thank god she wasn't here.

Fuck. Fern was so fucked.

Four years ago, when Matty was seven. That was it—that had been her last seizure. Scott had sent her a registered letter saying he wanted to see his son, and she'd panicked, the letter still in her hands, her fear fanning the flames of her anger. He threatened to take her to court if she didn't let him take Matty on the weekends, knowing, of course, that she'd never have enough saved up to fight him. She'd watched her hands shake, and then her vision had blotched. Luckily, the postman had left as soon as she'd signed for the envelope, and even more luckily, Grandpa Wyatt and Elva had both been home. Wyatt, whose boss at the tow yard had fits, just moved the kitchen table out of the way and let her have the seizure. Elva tucked her up on the couch and put a Band-Aid on the two cuts she'd gotten on her arm, probably from carpet tacks. And best of all, Matty had been at school. He'd missed the whole thing.

Scott had never even followed up on his request. His threat. Didn't care enough, apparently. He'd had a minute of caring followed by his normal apathy. Her terror had been wasted, the seizure pointless.

But bless Grandpa Wyatt and Elva. They'd known what

was imperative they *not* do. They didn't call 911. They knew she didn't need an ambulance.

Matty had known that. Abby—obviously—hadn't listened to him.

Or had they been in on it together? Both of them, caring for her?

It was an intolerable thought, making her head rattle as if her brain were a fare box filled with only change, no paper money to muffle the sound.

A tall man in a gray sweater and jeans pulled the curtain back. He kept his eyes on his iPad, giving it a quick swipe. "I'm Dr. Antes. You're Fern Reyes." Did doctors not wear white coats anymore? What was to say that this wasn't just some guy on the street with an iPad, pretending to be a hospital employee?

"How are you feeling?" Still he didn't look at her, which was enough to convince Fern he was actually a doctor.

Matty glared at him, his phone beeping, the game unplayed.

"Like shit." Fern felt as if she could sleep for a million years.

He laughed. "Most people say fine, for some reason. I like your honesty. Well, I don't see why you shouldn't go home in a little while. I just want you to get a few more fluids in you. There were . . ." He swiped his device again. Fern wondered what would happen if his network went down. Would this man still know how to be a doctor?

He continued. "Ah, here. There were just a couple of questions you weren't able to answer when you came in."

She'd been foggy when they were checking her in. She remembered that she'd gotten impatient with a small, round nurse whose accent she couldn't understand. She was pretty sure the nurse had been even more irritated with her.

"Okay."

"I see your list of meds here. Are you still on all of them?"

"Not the Keppra, it made me too tired. But the carbam-azepine, yes."

Dr. Antes tapped the iPad. "Got it. Could you be pregnant?"

She shot a look at Matty. "No."

Matty, though. Keeping his eyes down. Was that something he ever thought about? *Cristo.* He was too young to worry about her sex life. Wasn't he?

"Is there another adult you want to call to come pick you up?"

It came back to her then, an ice floe shattering, an iceberg cracking in half. What she'd been worried about when she went down.

Abby and her son.

Matty relying on Abby. In any way at all, even small.

Shit, Fern had let this happen.

She pressed her fingers to her top lip.

"Fern?" The doctor looked at her then, his eyes a muddy noncolor color.

"My brother," she whispered. She cleared her throat. "Matty, could you go get me a coffee from the vending machine? Get a dollar out of my wallet."

"No."

She turned her head slowly, deliberately. With the voice she rarely used (it was her mother's voice—she got it out only for extra-special shitty situations), she said, *"Go."*

Matty mumbled something that might have been a curse, but he dug her wallet out of the pocket of her jacket.

When he was gone, the doctor said, "So. Do we have a different answer to that pregnancy question now?"

Pompous prick. "I just finished my period yesterday," she said. She hated admitting even that to him. She flicked the oxygen meter off her left forefinger and yanked off the tape that held the IV needle to the bend of her arm. "Tell your nurse I need to sign out."

"Don't pull that out," he warned her.

"What? I'm not qualified to know what to do with my own body?" She tugged out the needle and pushed her thumb against the bright spurt of red blood.

"If you're pregnant, your medications need to be changed, as soon as possible."

"I'm epileptic. Not pregnant, or stupid." She should have said *nor stupid*. That would have made her sound smarter. "I'm going home."

He shook his head, as if coming back to himself. "You'll need a ride."

Dickbag. What a shithead. "I'm calling my brother."

"And you understand I'm a mandated reporter." He flashed the front of his iPad at her, as if she could read it from four feet away. "Medical-reporting fact sheet."

Why had she bothered to hope anything at all? Hating herself even more than she hated him, she choked back tears. "I understand."

"Your profession is flagged on your chart. I'm sorry."

He wasn't sorry. *His* salary wasn't the one that was going to be immediately frozen. She'd be off the boards for three months, mandatory. If there were no incidents in six months, probation could be lifted with approval. Those were the rules, anyway. But most of the time? Once you were let go for a lapse in consciousness, no matter what kind it was, AC Transit didn't tend to bring you back from purgatory. It didn't matter if someone blacked out from too many tequila sunrises while driving a full coach through rush hour on the Bay Bridge or if it was just a short seizure while inside a private residence on off-time—the agency had been sued too many times, by too many people.

Crying would only make things worse. Crying would only scare Matty when he came back.

But she had no choice left about it. The tears came then, hateful and hot.

She'd be lucky to ever drive again.

chapter *thirty~six*

It took Abby forever to drop off Bryson and Jorge—they lived only nineteen blocks apart, but there had been traffic, and then Jorge's dad hadn't been at home, so she'd had to drive to Hayward to drop him at a place where they were holding some kind of wrestling match. It didn't feel at all acceptable to leave him there, not in the parking lot full of lurching groups of men yelling and drinking out of red plastic cups, but then a short man dressed in black tights and red and blue face paint darted out a side door and lifted Jorge, swinging him around. The man's red cape swirled around his son as they twirled. Just in time for his last match, he'd said, obviously thrilled Jorge was there. *Thank you for bringing him.* Another boy of a similar age waved at Jorge, then both of them yelled abuse that sounded affectionate at an older man dressed in a similar wrestling uniform. Abby figured it was probably okay to leave.

Fern had already checked out of the hospital by the time Abby finally made it there. No one under Fern's name in the ER. That was all the information she'd been told. *No one by that name.* The young woman had actually looked like she felt bad about saying it, but she obviously couldn't say anything else. Rules. Laws. All of it.

Abby drove home. She didn't know what else to do.

Matty wasn't answering his cell phone. Of course he wasn't. He was furious with Abby for calling the ambulance.

She'd had to call 911. Surely he could understand that.

He was eleven.

What had she understood at eleven? She'd had a best friend—Emily—who had a houseful of siblings that fought and laughed and raged and wailed. It was the place she'd loved best to be. She'd pretended she was just one of the kids who lived under Emily's parents' roof, trampled and overlooked and beatifically happy. That was the year she'd decided that no matter what, she'd someday live in a house full of people, instead of a house in which a dead baby's picture took pride of place on top of the grand piano. She loved Meg. Of course she did, as much as she could. But she'd never even met her sister. At eleven, Matty's age, Abby had just started to realize how embarrassed she was by her mother's tears every time they passed the cemetery on the way to soccer practice.

So basically, she'd understood nothing.

The doorbell rang, and Abby dropped the glass she was drying right into the sink, not caring that it shattered. "I'm coming! Coming!"

But it wasn't Matty. It was his uncle.

Diego was curt. No smile. "Matty forgot his backpack."

"Oh, sure. It must be outside. Maybe?"

And there it was, by the foot of the trampoline, lying on its side in the last rays of the setting sun.

"Here." Abby picked it up, surprised by its heaviness. "Thanks for coming to get it. I could have brought it to him."

He nodded and headed toward the house.

"Do you want a drink?"

He paused but didn't turn his head. "Sorry?"

"I feel like I need one." What did that make her sound like? "I mean, I don't . . . oh, fuck it. Yeah, I need a drink."

The back of Diego's neck was dark tan and thick. He dropped his head forward as if checking in with his feet. Then he said, "Okay."

While she poured the wine—a red that Scott had been saving for something special—she watched Diego's wrists. He twisted his wineglass at the stem. His wrists were thick, almost twice as wide as hers. The glass looked smaller than it was. Were his wrists the result of climbing trees all day? Was that where he got the ropes of muscle she could see at the neckline of his T-shirt? Or did he climb trees *because* he had that muscle and had to climb something?

They moved to the back porch. The light had almost left the sky completely, and a ribbon of rose fog unfurled itself, a night-blooming sky flower.

"You're sure she's okay?"

Instead of moving like most people did to the outdoor dining table on the deck, Diego sat on the top step. "Physically, I'm sure she's fine."

"I still don't . . ." She sat next to him and took too big a swallow of the wine. It burned, scratching her throat as if it were cask-strength whiskey. "I don't know why what I did was wrong."

"Doctors are mandated reporters."

"I don't know what that is." But it started to make sense. Slowly.

"She'll lose her job."

"Don't be silly."

Diego shrugged, keeping his gaze steady. Forward.

"She can't."

"Sure. Whatever you say."

Abby felt as if she might throw up. "That's . . ."

"Happens." Diego tilted his head back. "Your palm tree needs help."

She followed his gaze. *Fern*. She couldn't let this happen to Fern. But she said only, "I know."

"True date palms don't belong in North Berkeley. It's too cold. The only one that thrives here is a Bismarck, or maybe a cabbage palm. Poor thing." He sounded honestly sorry for it.

"The fronds are driving me crazy. I was going to try to get up there and do something about it, but I hadn't figured out how to climb it."

"Don't be stupid. Get someone who's trained. Licensed."

"Like you?"

"Yeah. But not me."

Of course not. She pulled at her skirt, tugging the hem toward her knees.

Then their glasses were empty.

Without asking, Diego took her wineglass and walked inside to the sink.

"You don't have to . . ."

Diego didn't answer. He moved as if he'd been in her kitchen a million times, picking the broken glass out of the sink carefully. He washed both wineglasses. Then he dried them. When he folded the tea towel and hung it neatly on the handle of the oven door, the motion nearly brought Abby to her knees with a sudden gut-punch of lust. She hadn't seen it coming. And she didn't know what to do with it.

"Thanks."

"You're welcome." He stood in front of her, tall and steady as a tree himself. Unmovable. Not that she wanted to move him. He was just fine where he was.

Lord, was she this much of an idiot? Was that possible? He needed to go before she made some kind of ridiculous fool of herself. How was it possible that while her skin burned in confusion and fear over what she'd done (what she might have done, what she hadn't *known* she'd been doing) to Fern, that she could also feel this shaft of desire under the burn?

Diego reached out and touched the granite countertop. She had agonized over picking it out, choosing the color of it, the texture. He stroked it with one finger. All the while his black cardamom eyes didn't leave hers.

"Okay, thanks." She'd just said that. She was repeating herself.

"If you hadn't just lost your husband . . ." His voice trailed off, but his eyes stayed steady on hers.

Abby's stomach lurched as if she were on the trampoline. "You'd . . . you'd what?"

"*Quiero besarte toda.*"

"I . . ." She swallowed the rock in her throat and attempted a laugh. "I don't even know what that means." But she knew enough California Spanish to figure out most of it. "I sent your sister to the hospital."

"Yeah. You did."

The words came out before she even thought them through. "After you kissed me. Then what would you do?"

His eyebrows jumped, and she liked that she'd surprised him. "You shouldn't ask what you don't want to know."

"Oh . . ." Her courage quailed. "Were *you* ever married?" she asked.

His surprise only registered in the corners of his mouth, where he relaxed, incrementally. Abby felt relief shoot through her—he was nervous, too.

"Yeah."

"Did you like being married?"

He rested the flat of his palm against the granite. It would warm under his touch. Would she?

"Yeah," he said. "I loved it."

"Why?"

"I liked being with her. I liked going to bed with her. I liked the way she smelled in the morning. I liked the way she laughed at me." Diego glanced down at his bare hand, then back at her. "She laughed at me all the time."

"What happened?" Abby pressed her thumb against the wedding ring she hadn't remembered to take off yet.

He shrugged. "Life."

"What kind of life?" Tulip wandered in the open back door and flopped himself down on the kitchen floor like he'd had an even more exhausting day than they had.

"She fell in love with someone else."

"She cheated on you?"

"No," he said. "She didn't cheat. She told me before she left me. We'd promised we'd never do that, never inflict that upon each other. She told me she loved him, and then, only when I understood, then she left."

"Damn." Was it strange they were being so honest? So transparent? It felt good to listen to him.

"Yeah. Fucking sucked, and that's an understatement. When she said she had something big to tell me, I thought it was that she was finally pregnant. We'd been trying for a long time—I wanted so bad to have a cousin for Matty. A son for me. Or a daughter. I would have been a good dad, I think. Our dad wasn't around, so I guess I don't know that for sure. But I'm a *really* good uncle. When I see what Matty has meant to us, to my family . . . But that wasn't what she wanted to tell me that day."

"I'm sorry." And she was.

Shrugging, he said, "I'm glad we had what we did, for as long as we had it. We were lucky, I guess."

Lucky. That's what he called losing everything?

"She had a kid," he went on. "Within a year of leaving, she was knocked up with his child. I saw her at the café on Bancroft once. She . . ." His voice trailed off. "She broke my heart double, I guess."

"Do you regret the time you spent with her?"

"I don't regret anything I've ever done."

"I've never heard anyone say that."

Diego leveled his gaze on her, clear and steady. "Things I've done I'm okay with. But I've regretted things I've never had."

"Like what?" Abby leaned on the countertop.

"Time and cash to travel. I'd like to see Peru. And the city in Mexico our mom came from, Huatulco. She left when she was little, but we still have an uncle and some distant cousins there."

The intensity of his voice made her skin prickle, as if she'd brushed against a nettle. "What else?"

Diego looked over her head. "Not much. Kids. I still really want kids. Anyway. What about you? Were you in love with him?"

Abby thought of Scott's chin, the almost invisible dimple at the end of it. The way his stubble grew faster and thicker in winter, as if it wanted to warm him. The way he'd laughed affectionately when she got left and right confused, something she'd always done. The way they fit, the way she slept better when she'd been in his arms. The way he listened. "Yeah."

"Yeah," he said.

"He lied, though. In the end." She paused. She could have stepped forward. She could have closed the distance between them, but she didn't, even though she was throbbing now. Finally, she said, "What did you think of him?"

Diego blinked. She could feel him pull back even though he hadn't moved. "Hated him. He hurt Fern and left Matty behind. They both deserved better."

"I tried to give her the life insurance. Or the equivalent, anyway. It'll take a while for it to be distributed, but I offered to give it to her in advance, out of my accounts. I told her she could have all of it."

He laughed, low in his throat. "*Dios.* I would have paid good money to see that. What did she say?"

"What do you think she said?"

"For fuck's sake." Diego rubbed his eyes. "She's an idiot."

"I'll get her to take it."

"Good luck. He really left them nothing? In writing?"

Abby shook her head.

"What a *shit*. Well, it's your money." Diego's brows tucked together. "Not hers. There's no way you'll get her to take it. I know my sister."

"He paid her so little, for so long. If I'd known about it . . . It's not like we didn't have enough." Abby immediately felt shame for saying it out loud. But Diego knew it already. She didn't need to hide it. She didn't have the energy to do so even if she'd wanted to. "It's her money. Not mine."

He pushed his thumbs into his eyebrows, as if to try to smooth them again. "You know? I wanted to kill him for what he did to Fern. For how he left them." Though his face was dark, his eyes shaded, his voice stayed casual. "I've never been more glad that someone was dead."

It was her husband they were talking about. "So fucking me would be a way of fucking him?"

Diego blinked, hard. Shock quickly faded to what looked like simple surprise. Then grudging respect. "I hadn't thought it through, to be honest."

"You should have."

"I guess it would be unforgivable."

Abby's heart stuttered and almost stalled. Then she said, "What if we were both drunk?"

When he smiled, the right corner of his mouth went higher than the left. He said, "I guess it's too fucking bad we're not."

Abby moved then. She went to the liquor cabinet and got out the bottle of Herradura Silver tequila and grabbed two shot glasses. She brought them back, her legs quaking underneath her. She was soft inside, molten. She felt dangerous.

"I'm sorry I don't have any lime left. We used it all on the tacos, I think."

A muscle jumped in Diego's jaw. He reached for the salt-shaker that stood next to the napkins. "Pour it out."

She poured two shots, grateful that her hand wasn't shaking.

"Here," she said.

And then she reached forward and took his hand. She raised the inside of his wrist to her mouth and licked his skin. Then she raised her own wrist to his mouth. His tongue was a slick warmth.

He salted their skin. They drank their shots. Abby's eyes didn't leave Diego's as they sucked the salt off each other's wrists.

A second's pause. The alcohol hit Abby immediately, striking her in the knees.

"Say no," Diego warned. "It's okay if you say no."

She didn't want to. All she had was yes, a great swarm of yeses buzzing under her skin. She had no voice left, but she didn't need it—her body was such a huge yes yes *yes*.

She didn't find her voice until much later, when she was roaring through her third orgasm, his mouth at her core, her fingers clutching the sheets she'd bought with Scott in mind, her brightly colored widow's duvet pushed to the floor. Her voice came back, and she screamed so loudly she felt him jerk below her, but his tongue never stopped, never paused what he was doing so well.

Then she locked her fingers into his shoulder blades and dragged him up her body. She slid herself down, bucking her hips to take him inside her again. When she started crying, though, when she started sobbing, he stopped. He stilled completely inside her. And even though he was hot and hard, and even though she was slick, and even though she was still bucking frantically underneath him, he moved his hand to her wet cheek.

"I'll stop," he said.

"Never," she said, and she meant it. She had nothing to do but this, nothing to do but fuck this man—this stranger who was somehow related to her—from now until they died of exhaustion, of dehydration, of starvation.

"But . . ."

She hit at the tears on her cheeks with one hand and gripped his side with her other. She tilted her hips so that he was inside her deeper again. "I'll stop crying. I promise. I'm fine. *Fuck* me."

"Hey." His mouth caught hers again, for the thousandth—the millionth, the first—time. Against her lips, he said, "You can cry. Don't stop for me. I just need to know you're okay."

So she tipped her hips again and ground against him. She cried harder, so hard it felt like she was raining. High black clouds parted in her chest, rumbles of thunder roared through her head. The sobs made the next time she came even bigger, and as she clenched around his cock, he yelled something in Spanish that she didn't understand and then before he stopped moving, he kissed every inch of her face, her neck, her breasts. When he reached her belly button and the soft part of her stomach, she stopped sobbing and started giggling, and by the time he'd dropped kisses down her inner thighs, to her knees, to the bottoms of her ticklish feet, she was laughing so hard she got a cramp in her side.

Still giggling, Abby said, "This doesn't have to mean anything, you know."

He laughed, too. His dark eyes were clear. "I know. But *fuck*, you feel amazing."

It was the perfect answer. Abby felt something in her chest

break, like the glass in the sink, and then she felt the shards cut her inside, so sweetly. The pain was flawless.

She rolled under Diego, wrapping his arms around her shoulders, pushing her nose into the still-sweaty spot between his ear and neck. She didn't get that old feeling she used to get after sex with Scott, that feeling of being safe, that nothing could ever hurt them.

Nothing was safe.

Trust, the thing she used to think she needed for good sex, wasn't in the room anymore. Sex was just sex. And she was still alive.

Diego said, "Shit. Matty's backpack." He kissed her forehead. "Go."

On the floor next to the bed, Tulip groaned and flopped over. In bed, Abby did the same.

Diego pulled on his jeans.

He let himself out.

Abby rolled again. And then, alone, she slept.

chapter *thirty~seven*

S ex was just sex.

And Fern needed it. She didn't have a motherfucking job until all this was fixed *(if it could be fixed—god, it had to be fixed)*, so she didn't need to wait till midweek to get some.

She'd been in the hospital—spitting with fury—until six p.m. the night before. She had sent Diego over to get Matty's backpack at seven. He'd come back with it at eleven, not meeting her eye. If he'd had sex with her . . .

Abby couldn't have her family. Not after she'd been the reason Fern had lost everything. First the child support (okay, maybe that wasn't exactly Abby's fault, except that Scott had left, and then he'd married her) and then Fern's job. The two things she'd blithely thought would always be there until Matty was eighteen.

Fern had been so naive. So intentionally cheerful, sure that if she believed hard enough, everything would always work out.

So she didn't ask Diego what he'd been doing for those four hours. She just took the backpack and texted Gregory. *Tomorrow. Any time you want. I've got the whole day free.*

Gregory was out of his class at noon. They met at his place at twelve fifteen. They barely made it to the bed. Fern dropped her jeans, shirt, and underwear in the kitchen, and if Gregory hadn't had a belt malfunction, they would have had sex on the floor next to the stove.

Afterward, he rolled over onto his back. With satisfaction, Fern watched the sweat slip along his hairline. She'd done that. She was the reason his eyes were glazed. *She* was why his lower lip was swollen. Was it possible to have this? To actually keep it? This gorgeous (almost) string-free sex with someone she really liked?

"I needed that." *Here's your one chance, Fancy,* sang Reba McEntire.

"Me, too," he said.

He had no idea. She had *really* needed it, had needed to know that her body still worked. There was nothing wrong with her libido, with the way she got wet, with the way she made Gregory lose his shit. So she'd had a seizure. It was her body's way of overreacting, that was all. Reacting to Abby. To her being in their lives.

"So," he said.

"Yeah?" She moved her head up his arm so that her temple rested against the muscle of his shoulder. He smelled like sweat, and she liked it. "Talk to me."

"You—" He broke off.

Uh-oh. Fern felt a cool draft on her stomach and wished suddenly that they hadn't pushed the bedcovers to the floor in their eagerness. She couldn't handle it if he went back to the whole love conversation. She just needed this—exactly what they had now—to keep going. A little longer. She could break up with him in a month or two. Maybe three. Three more months of Wednesday afternoons with this man, of sex like that, such perfect fucking sex it was ridiculous . . . "Yeah?"

"Is it real?"

Her stomach slid into her kneecaps. "Gregory . . . I can't—"

He tightened his arm around her and kept his gaze upward. "No, I want to know. Are you really coming when you make those sounds?"

"What?"

"You can tell me."

"Gregory—"

"No, really. Linda was the one who broke it to me." He gave a short laugh, but there was no humor in it. "On our seventh anniversary. She told me that all women fake it. I mean, I knew some of that. I knew women could do that. I just never understood why anyone would want to. You know? And since then, I've asked a few women." The tops of his cheekbones colored. "They've all admitted it. That they've done it. And it's fine. If you do. I just . . . I don't know. I just want to know."

"Gregory, I came so hard I don't think I'll be able to walk. Maybe ever again."

"You don't have to make me feel—I know that most women don't orgasm from vaginal intercourse alone."

"Whoa. Sexy talker." She rubbed her eyes. "I come that way." She wished she could leave it there. And she knew she wouldn't be able to. So there she was. Taking care of him. Of course.

"You really do?" His voice was brighter. Hopeful.

It made her want to jab her finger into his side, giving him a mostly innocuous but still unpleasant surprise. And she knew she was a shit for feeling that way. Gregory needed reassurance. He was asking for it, which was a damn sight more than most men could do. "I don't come *just* because your penis is inside my vagina." They were such ugly words for such amazing body parts. "There's sensitive tissue called the cavernosum near my vagina that is connected to my clitoris. When you're on top and I push upward against you, I'm rubbing my clit against your pubic bone." She pitched her voice so she sounded like a sex-education high school teacher. "My vagina also clenches, which is pleasurable. When suitably and persistently aroused in a regular pattern with either a male penis or an expensive but realistically shaped dildo, I can achieve a satisfactory and highly enjoyable orgasm."

"Fern. God."

"What the hell?" Fern pushed herself backward, moving his arm so that it was between them. "I just told you how I come in the most precise terms available. I thought you'd be happy."

"What's your problem?"

I'm on medical probation. I'm not going to be able to make the house payment. My son isn't going to pass science because his project tutor probably fucked his uncle.

"My problem? *Que madres.*"

Gregory sat up and scooted to the headboard, reaching for a clove. "I'm glad you come that way, don't get me wrong." He flicked the lighter, and with his first exhalation, the room smelled like church again. "But after, you push me away so fast, every single time. . . . I'm just not sure I can keep up."

"What is that? A threat?"

Instead of answering, he sighed and drew deeply on the clove. It made a crackling noise.

"God, I knew this would happen." She should pull a pillow over her body—she should hide her breasts, the vee at her legs. But no, wait a minute. She was fine like this. With all of her solidity on display. She sat up and faced him, crossing her legs, feeling the coolness where she was still wet. "I knew it." She would have to break it off with him. The thought—just the thought of it—made her gut feel empty. Then she'd have no job, no money, and no Gregory.

She laughed. Then, in a move that surprised her to her core, she said, "I'm out of work. That's why I can be here on a Monday."

"What?"

"Seizure."

"Shit, are you—"

Fern pushed back his hand. "In public. Abby called 911. Because of her, I'm out for three months at least, on probation for six. If I get my job back at all." Sandy Taylor hadn't gotten hers back. Not after her seizure in Safeway. She never got behind the wheel again.

"What are you going to do?"

The laugh wanted to turn into a sob, but she choked it into submission. "Sell my blood? Do they still do that? Maybe I could take up tarot card reading. How hard can it be to tell a fortune?" It was easy enough to see into her future, anyway.

"Start your business."

"Pffft."

"I mean it."

"I have nothing to offer."

"You have time. Talent. You look at numbers and see

patterns. This is why you've been taking classes. This is what you've been *waiting* for. I know you can do this." His smile was brighter than the afternoon slant of light coming through the blinds behind him. "I'll make some calls. I know a guy who's starting a wine distribution group. He'll need a bookkeeper. And a sales team."

"No."

"Let me."

"Don't you get it?" Her words were a metal file's rasp. "I want to accept your help. But if I do, that would mean I need it, and that terrifies me." Just the admission of it struck such deep fear into her she thought she might burst into tears or something equally embarrassing.

His hands stilled. "Just *accept*."

"Fine." It wasn't fine. But she could try. Couldn't she? "Give me his phone number. Maybe I'll call him." She honestly thought it was enough. That she was trying.

"For god's sake, Fern." There was real anger in Gregory's voice—alive and hot—and it shocked her more than if he'd reached out and slapped her across the face. "Why do you make everything so hard?"

She felt her mouth twist, and even though she hated herself for saying it, even though the words felt dirty in a bad, soap-scummed way, she said them anyway. "Baby, I know what I could make hard again."

He stood. The slam of the bathroom door was her answer.

chapter *thirty-eight*

Abby went to the video game store, and it felt more like arriving in Las Vegas than it did visiting a shopping mall.

There were lights everywhere, flashing and strobing in neon. Abby didn't understand a single thing. Used-car sales words such as *pre-owned* and *trade-ins* jumped out at her, reaching to grab her legs from the stacked boxes. The store wasn't large, probably less than two hundred square feet, but it seemed like a million miles to the back wall of Hot Releases.

Research. Abby's body ached to turn around and run. Just a few doors down was a national chain that sold cakes of soap and bars of bubble bath. Once she'd gone in with Brook, and Abby had felt viscerally confused, as if every scent were a sound that she had to untangle and trace to its beginning. She'd left with a headache that Brook had put down to the smells that weren't natural, like their own soaps and oils, but

Abby had known it wasn't that. It was the *volume* of the store. The sights, colors, sounds, and smells had added up to a cacophony of confusion.

She felt the same way in the games store.

But this was research, the kind that might help. Maybe. Someday. In the space of five weeks, Abby had gone from being a wife to a widow, from having no family to having . . .

Well. She still had no family.

What Abby had was a house. She had a garden. She had a tall, thin Great Dane who was probably at that moment chewing down a retaining wall, a dog she had thanks to Matty.

Matty wasn't returning her texts.

Neither was Fern, except for the one that read, *Don't need your help with Matty anymore since I'm off my bus. Thanks.*

Those six simple letters—each one an insecticide-soaked spike: *Thanks.*

Abby had fucked everything up. Unintentionally. But she had. And then she'd literally fucked Diego, a fuckup to end all fuckups. Guilt twisted a dirty rag in her chest.

Abby took another three steps into the noise of the store. It sounded like a war zone—blurts and beeps and whines of sirens—enhanced by two boys bellowing war cries at a console to the right. The store smelled of ink, a bright chemical smell that couldn't be good for anyone.

This was wrong. She'd have to do her research another way. She turned to leave.

"The worst, right?" said a woman standing next to a spinning rack of what looked like electronic Ping-Pong paddles but probably weren't. She was short and round and blond, wearing a black skirt that was rumpled in the back and a red sweatshirt that was snug at her waist. "Those are mine over there. Where are yours?" She peered over Abby's shoulder as if she were hiding a kid or two behind her purse.

"I don't . . . I have *no* idea what I'm doing here."

The woman sighed. "You're spending too much money on something that's only going to rot their brains and probably ruin their lives in the long run."

"Ah." Abby nodded and tried to sound as if she agreed.

"So. The new COD?"

All Abby could think of was cash-on-delivery, something they'd stopped doing by the time she was old enough to have cash for any kind of delivery. "Sorry. What?"

The woman's red sunglasses wobbled on the top of her head. She pushed them more firmly into her hair. "You *are* new to this, aren't you? Call of Duty. The new Xbox version just came out."

"Is that . . ." There'd been a *New Yorker* article on it. "Isn't that a violent one?"

The woman gave a descriptive shrug. "Eh. They say twelve, but you know. How old is the kid?"

This, at least, Abby knew the answer to. She was grateful for its nonambiguity. "Eleven."

"Mature?"

"Yes! I mean, I think he is. I don't know him that well."

"Oh." The woman looked Abby up and down once, quickly, as if she were judging Abby's birthing hips. "Yeah, so that's my eleven-year-old over there." She pointed at the two boys now hooting at something on a screen. "With his thirteen-year-old brother. And I've got an eighteen-year-old working at the barbecue place in the food court." The woman smiled as she pointed out the games store door down the bright sidewalk.

She was objectively cute. In a bar, she'd get drinks bought for her. "You can't be old enough," said Abby.

The woman brightened. "Aren't you sweet? I was a child bride. And a child divorcée, obviously, or their father would be doing this errand, not me." Her green bag buzzed violently. She pulled out her cell and glanced at the face of it before dropping it back in with a grimace. "You want game advice?"

Hell, yes. She wanted everything advice.

"Are the games for keeping at your house or for your boyfriend's house?"

"Oh. No. Not a boyfriend. Matty's a . . . a friend's kid. So for my house. For when he comes over." If he ever came back.

"Get an Xbox. Other people will say PS4, and that's fine if your kid's into single-player games. They're cheaper, too, and so are the games. But I gotta tell you, the kids still want the Xbox. Better for playing with friends, too."

"Xbox. Check."

"They're not cheap. But in terms of keeping 'em busy, there's nothing else like it. If I let them, my boys would sit in front of it all day in nothing but their underpants. Add some Cheetos and you're going to be the best babysitter in the whole world."

"Underpants," Abby echoed. "Cheetos."

The woman walked briskly to a shelf, motioning Abby to follow her. The dark-haired clerk, who couldn't have been more than nineteen, watched them without saying anything.

"So, here you go. Games. Start with these. Call of Duty—we talked about that. Halo, here. Not too violent. Kids today are tough. Don't worry about that. And WWE."

Abby stared at the cover of the heavily muscled man wearing a Speedo. "Really?"

"Oh, yeah. They eat that shit up. That's Drake's favorite." She pointed at the shorter boy. "Oh, here. Final Fantasy.

That's still big. And Minecraft. Does he have that one? They all have that one."

Abby vaguely remembered Fern telling Matty to go play it in his room. "I think so? But should I have it, too? What *is* it?"

"It's like solving puzzles. I even like it. And it doesn't make me motion sick like the others do. My kids keep talking VR to me, but I'd hurl for sure."

Abby held the stack carefully, as carefully as if Matty had picked them out himself. "Hey," she said. "I have a question for you."

"Shoot."

Abby arranged the words in her head before she said them. "What can I do that will make him happy?" *Besides getting a dog. Besides buying all the video games. Besides all the hope in the world.*

The woman's phone buzzed again. "Damn it. I'm so sorry. Boys! Now!" Without saying anything else, the woman waggled her fingers and left the store, her cell at her ear, the boys trailing slowly and listlessly behind her, short sailboats with no wind.

The young store clerk swiped Abby's card for an exorbitant amount. He placed her purchases in an enormous shopping-cart–sized bag.

"Thank you," Abby said automatically, taking the receipt.

"Listen."

Startled, Abby stopped moving. She faced the young man. "Yes?"

"Not to me. To him."

"Sorry?"

"The kid you're babysitting. Just listen. Don't push. Everyone pushes boys to talk, and he won't want to." The clerk touched the top of the counter lightly with his fingertips, tapping lightly. "Just listen to him talk about the game. It won't seem to matter. But it will."

"Thank you." Abby meant it. This man had been a boy, what? Five minutes ago? "What about mothers?"

"Huh?"

"How old is your mom?"

He blinked and a game's siren howled behind him. "I think she's forty-two. Maybe?"

"What does she want the most?"

His answer was too fast to be anything but true. "A raise."

"What does she do?"

The young man scratched his eyebrow and glanced over his shoulder. "This is, uh, weird."

Abby slid a twenty across the counter, feeling brilliant and idiotic at the same time. "I can't tell you how much I appreciate your help. What's your name?"

"Robby."

"I can't wait to Yelp how incredibly helpful you've been, Robby. So. What does your mom do?"

The twenty disappeared. "Answers the phone at a glass company."

"So she wants a raise. What else does she want?"

"A nap. She's tired, like, all the time. She has something . . . chronic fatigue? She takes pills, but they don't help, and the good pills aren't covered by her insurance, so she just sleeps on BART on the way home. Once she went all the way to Fremont, and our stop is Bay Fair."

A keen sense of disappointment sliced just above Abby's eyes. "Ah. A raise and a nap." There had to be more. She already knew that Fern could use both of those things. *And a job. To replace the one Abby had lost for her.* "Anything else?" Please, let the boy know the magic answer.

He shook his head. "She says she needs a *new* job, but there's nothing out there, and she says she needs more sleep but can't get it because my sister is only six and she's a little monster, I shit you not. Like, literally a monster. I was living with my girlfriend, but we got kicked out of the apartment, so now I'm back with my mom, but I can't even be in the same room with my little sister, no joke. She bit me the other day for no good reason." He poked at his arm as if testing it for soreness.

There's nothing out there. Fern might lose her job for good. She'd have no money. And she wouldn't *take* the money Abby wanted to give her. She wished she could slide it across a counter to Fern like the twenty that now rested, warm and folded, in the young man's pocket.

"What about school? Can she go back to school somehow? Change her job?" She knew as she said it she shouldn't have. People couldn't just take time off their paid work to learn a new trade, unpaid.

Robby stared, and then yanked the receipt from the machine. Her twenty was obviously spent. "Dunno. Anyway. Here's a survey. If you call this number and answer seven questions, you can get ten percent off your next purchase of fifty dollars or more." He gave her a slip of paper. "And here's your bag. Thanks for your business and, um . . . ." He trailed off, his eyes focusing above her shoulder as if he'd remembered something important.

Hope battered the top of her lungs. "Yes?"

"Um. Have a nice day."

chapter *thirty~nine*

Dinner was a planned attack. Fern was staging it, special chicken mole and all. Their mother's sole successful recipe, it was Diego's favorite. Matty loved it, too, especially when she served it with corn tortillas fresh enough from Mi Pueblo to be steaming inside the plastic bag when she tossed them on the counter.

Nervous, Fern tied her apron tighter, made sure Captain America's shield was front and center. Matty had gotten it for her the previous Christmas. It was too big, obviously made for a dad, but that was okay. She liked the way the ties were long enough to double around her waist and tie in the front. And she'd always liked being the man of the house.

Until recently.

In the living room, she heard Matty yelp and then give a howl.

Thumping footsteps were followed by Matty barreling into the kitchen. "He said I suck at Minecraft Parkour."

"*Do* you suck at it?" Fern said, stirring the sauce. It was perfect, thick and red–brown like dark clay.

"No!"

"Then why do you care what he says?"

"God. You don't *get* it. And it smells terrible in here."

"What? You love my mole." Even though it was her mother's, they'd never called it *Abuela*'s mole. The cirrhosis had killed Fern's mother long before Matty had ever come on the scene. He'd never had an *abuelita* of his own. One of many things he'd never have.

"I hate it."

"You do not!"

"You don't ever *listen* to me when I talk!" Matty's voice had hit its seriously upset range. "You say you hear me, but you don't remember *anything*." His face was bright red, and he looked like he was about to cry.

"Dude." He was actually upset. What was this? "Is this about the game?"

"No!"

Diego entered the kitchen, looking guilty. Great.

"Honey, your uncle didn't mean to upset you. I bet he wants to apologize."

Diego nodded. "I sure do. I'm sorry you suck so much at launching off walls."

Matty went redder and his fists balled at his sides.

"Diego!" Fern wanted to throw a tortilla at him, the hotter the better. "Can you apologize to him, please?"

But Matty didn't wait for any apology from his uncle. "I'm

not mad about the *game*. I'm not mad at Uncle Diego. It's *you* I'm mad at!"

Fern didn't point out that she wasn't the reason he'd run into the kitchen at high speed. "Okay." She softened her voice and made sure she turned her body to face him. She hoped that maybe her head on top of Captain America's shield and bemuscled body would soften Matty's emotions. "Tell me how I can help."

Matty made a noise of pure frustration, a guttural growl that a grizzly bear would have been proud of. "Chicken."

"What about it?" Matty loved chicken. He loved wings and drumsticks and chicken tacos.

"You buy factory chicken. They cut off their beaks." Each word was spit in her direction.

"Oh, honey. No."

"They do. If one gets sick, the others *eat* them. And they're as smart as dogs, did you even *know* that?"

Fern doubted this. "I think you've been reading too much on the Internet. This is the same chicken you grew up on. The same we grew up on."

Diego, no help at all, flexed. "And look at me now!"

Matty ignored him, keeping his rage focused on Fern. "They can't even move in their cages. They're stuck in there. They hate it."

"Who told you this?" Who should Fern thank for this fight? Yeah, she would have bought the college-educated free-range organic chicken if she could have. But even if she could have afforded it, her supermarket didn't even carry the fancy kind. They carried cheap and cheaper.

"Abby told me."

Fantastic. "I thought you were mad at her."

"She didn't mean to do anything bad. She said she feels *terrible* about calling 911."

Fern's skin prickled. "Did you see her? When did you see her?"

"I didn't." He crossed his arms stubbornly. "But I want to."

"Then how do you know how she feels?"

Matty folded his lips.

"Matias." Captain America's chest broadened. "Tell me."

"Text. Whatever."

Fern blew out a quick breath, a barely concealed curse. "How does that even come *up* in a text?"

"She said she was thinking about getting some." Matty looked up at the ceiling as if he were getting his words from there. "Some chickens. For the yard."

"With that dog of hers? *Fffft.* The chicken is fine. It's just a freaking chicken. Right, Diego?"

Diego, no help at all, just shrugged guiltily and tucked a chip into the beans and crunched it over the stove. He *had* slept with Abby. Fern would lay money on it. Goddamn him. She couldn't even handle that. Couldn't think about it.

Matty was who mattered right now. "They're happy. They even say it on the package now." She remembered noticing that. "Happy chickens."

"Show me."

Fern took a deep breath. "Okay." Please, for the love of god, let her have gotten the right kind of fucking chicken. Whatever had been on sale, that had been the right kind.

But luckily, there it was. "See? It says they're happy. Right there. That chicken is fully smiling."

Diego chimed in, "They can't print it if it ain't true."

"Humph," said Matty.

But the fight was over, as suddenly as it had begun. Matty set the table without protesting. He woke his grandfather in the living room, and he knocked on Elva's door, inviting her politely to the table. Fern made plates bigger than any of them would be able to eat.

She was buttering them up. Pouring on the fat and the sweet, before she hit them with the bitter.

Elva sat carefully and poked at her hair, pulled back into a dancer's bun. One errant gray lock stood straight up, waving back and forth with every move. "This looks wonderful. Can we say grace?"

Fern sighed. "Okay."

Grandpa Wyatt said, "I got a grace to say."

"Please," said Fern. They just needed to eat. She needed to get this over with.

"Here you go. Dear Lord, please fix my broken molar and make this food mushy enough for me to eat." Grandpa Wyatt slapped the tabletop. "Amen!"

Fern was speechless.

Diego laughed, the traitor.

And Matty just grinned and started building a mole taco with a tortilla.

"Are you serious, Wyatt?"

Wyatt stuck out his neck like the chicken they were eating. "Broke plumb clean in half."

Matty said, "Doesn't it *hurt*? Show me!"

Mouthful of beans and all, Wyatt dropped his jaw. The broken dark space on the right looked awful.

"Oh, god."

Diego said, "Appetizing!"

"Wyatt. You have to get that fixed."

Grandpa Wyatt shrugged. "I checked and it ain't covered on the insurance. I'll just eat on the other side."

Carefully, Fern made the perfect forkful: heavy, mole-soaked chicken, dipped into the rice and beans. If she was cautious enough, if she stayed still, maybe everything would go back to the way it was two months ago. Before everything broke.

"Eight hundred dollars!" Wyatt held his butter knife into the air. "I could do a lot of things with that kind of cash and fixing my teeth isn't one of 'em. Me and Elva, we'd go gamble on the ponies, right, Elv? If I had it, that is."

Elva shook her head and rolled half a tortilla into something that looked exactly like the blunts the guys on the bus rolled. "I'd make you fix your teeth, crazy old man."

"Once, at the tow yard, I used epoxy and wood glue to make a mouth guard for a fighter who drove for us. It worked good, and in his first fight, he only lost a couple of teeth. Wonder if I could craft my own tooth? You think Krazy Glue works in wet places?"

Fern needed to find the money to fix Wyatt's tooth. She wondered for the hundredth—the millionth—time how much money her mother's collection of Mexican coins was worth. It wasn't like they were in mint condition or anything. Every coin had been handled. Loved. But still, it had to be a lot of money. Thousands, probably. Enough for the tooth and to cover the next month's mortgage . . . If she could only bring herself to take them to a coin shop. There was one in Alameda—she'd gone as far as to look it up. She could just go get them appraised, right? They did that? The very thought made her soul ache. But if they didn't fix Wyatt's tooth, all the rest would fall out and then he'd probably get something terminal, too, for good measure.

Jesus. If she lost her job permanently, she and Matty wouldn't even have *health* insurance.

Diego caught Fern's eye. No. She wouldn't accept his help. If he wanted to put Wyatt's tooth on his credit card, that was his business, but she wouldn't take the money.

But he only said, "This is good."

"Good." Fern straightened, wishing she hadn't taken off the apron before sitting down. Captain America was pretty good armor. "Hey. Guess what? I've been offered a part-time job at Ensenada Taqueria. Tamales for everyone!"

chapter *forty*

"Huh? Ensenada like the restaurant?" Matty gave that sideways head tilt that always tugged at Fern's heart. "Why?"

"Just till I get back on the bus."

"The place you used to work at? By the BART station?"

"You remember me telling you that?" She'd worked at Ensenada as a waitress when she was in high school. A million years ago.

"You tell me that, like, every single time we go past it."

She probably did. "Yeah, that place."

DMV would get the report of her lapse of consciousness soon enough, and as soon as she got the notice in the mail, she wouldn't be able to drive even her own car, let alone the bus. The restaurant was close enough to walk to in less than thirty minutes. She'd just have to hope to get off shift early enough so she didn't have to walk the sketchy part of Bancroft after dark. She wouldn't be able to risk driving—she'd researched it online, and the punishment for driving with a suspended license in California was a mandatory thirty-day impound on the car driven. Grandpa Wyatt had confirmed this was true, and had pointed out that with tow-yard storage at more than a hundred dollars a day, she'd never be able to pay to get her car back at the end of the month. *That's how my boss got all the cars he sold at auction. Rich motherfucker. No one could afford to pick up their wheels after a whole thirty days.*

Fern continued. "Just think about it, all the bean dip we want, right?"

Diego nodded. "Sweet. Like, doing their books?"

The heat that hit her cheeks was painful. "Kind of."

Diego's eyes narrowed. "Kind of?"

"I'll be handling money." It was true, after all.

"You're gonna *waitress*?"

Fern looked at his plate, then at Matty's. Their plates were still full. "Water? Anyone want some ice water?"

"Oh, good," Diego said. "Getting some practice in?"

"Don't be mean."

Matty just looked confused. "What's wrong with wait-ressing?"

Diego banged his fork against the tabletop. "She's better than that, that's what wrong. And she knows it."

"That's not true." Ciela, who'd inherited Ensenada from her uncle the year before, had spent twenty years waitressing before taking over as manager, and she was as smart as anyone who'd gotten any kind of degree. They'd started together there when they were both sixteen. They'd bonded over how they could make change in their heads, and laughed at the girls who had to use the sticky calculator next to the water station.

Elva said, "I was a cocktail waitress in the seventies. I could go home with five hundred dollars in ones. That was when I wore the heels. But boy, my dogs barked."

"Dogs?" Now Matty just looked confused.

"She means her feet hurt," said Fern. "Honey, waitressing is a good job. Your uncle is prejudiced for some reason, even though his last girlfriend was a barista at the airport, isn't that right?"

Diego ignored the dig. "It's a step down. You *know* that. You shouldn't have to do that."

The frustration on her brother's face was the hardest part to take. *"I'm a bus driver."*

"Yeah, well, you're unionized."

"Yeah. So are janitors. Makes you think, huh?"

"Why the hell have you been doing night school? What's the goddamned point? You're never going to use your book-keeping skills? Not good enough? You remember when Mom got that waitressing gig at the diner by the jail?"

That wasn't fair. That diner had a full bar and a line of guys planted on their barstools who were always more than happy to buy the little Mexican waitress a shot of tequila when she got off shift (or earlier). Their mother had had a disease. Fuck Diego, and fuck his morals. "It's temporary."

"That's what she said, too."

"This is *exactly* why I worried about telling you."

"Because you know I think you're better than that."

Grandpa Wyatt and Elva had apparently tuned them out, and were shoveling mole-soaked chicken in their mouths while talking about a reality television show that either was or wasn't airing that night.

Matty was still listening to them, though.

"I can't *wait* to get back to it. I was a kick-ass waitress back in the day. I love making people happy." She grinned at Matty, hoping he bought it. "I love surprising them with ice cream when it's their birthday."

He blinked. "But if they told you it was their birthday, then it's not a surprise."

"Hey." Time for a counterattack. "What did Mrs. Hutch say about a new science project?"

"Huh?"

Did he always have to say that? With his mouth open like that? "Your *science* project, genius?" She regretted the last word as soon as it slipped from her mouth. Mrs. Hutch had told Matty once that not all kids got to be geniuses and that he shouldn't worry about it. Somehow the teacher had thought that was supposed to make him feel better, and had been aggrieved when Fern called her on it. She was as terrible a teacher as Fern was a mother. Awesome.

Matty blinked again, that hurt-owl look of his. "I don't have a new project. Just the old one. She told me it was too ambitious. And that I was too stubborn. I hate her. I really, really do."

If Matty was stubborn, he got it from her. Pride curled through Fern. "There's no such thing as too stubborn. But what old project? You're not still doing the onion knitting thing." With Abby. He wasn't doing that anymore.

"Yeah."

"Yeah, what?" Fern's bite was cold and she let the chicken fall off her fork in a glop. "You *are* still going to do it with her?"

He stuffed a bite of the mini-burrito he'd made into his mouth and said, "Yeah."

"Matty."

"I *told* you. She knows she got it wrong. She feels bad."

Fern's eyes stung, as if the cayenne she'd sprinkled so carefully over the mole had suddenly gone airborne. Had Matty forgiven Abby? So easily? He'd been so furious, and even though she knew it wasn't the right way to feel, it had felt *good* to have her little Captain America so righteously angry at Abby. "Have you . . . started already?"

He stared into his burrito as if the answer were tucked somewhere inside it. "We've just been texting. But I want her to help me. I want to knit and stuff. And then dye it. I *want* to. I'm supposed to ask you if I can go to her house tomorrow after school."

"Oh, yeah? So when were you planning on asking?"

"I'm doing that now." He jabbed his fork into another tortilla. "So can I?"

"Matty." Disappointment laced through her veins, a slow poison.

Diego leaned in. "She's kind of a witch, y'know." He waved his beer bottle in a circle. He caught Fern's eye and corrected himself quickly. "Abby! Not you."

Matty's eyes widened. *"Huh?"*

"Una bruja. A good one, I mean. Like the stuff she does with the plants. Kind of magic."

Fern said, "I think that's still illegal without a card issued from your doctor."

The corner of Diego's mouth twitched. "Like basil. She said it could help you find love and guarantee fidelity."

"What's fidelity?" asked Matty.

"A convenient fiction," said Fern, hoping he'd forget to look it up online later. "When was she telling you all this, huh?"

Diego didn't answer, just took another huge bite. The way he was sitting, bent forward, shoveling food into his face, he looked like he had as a teenager—big, broad, always hungry, always wanting more.

He'd always liked the *güeras*.

"So? When? When you were over there getting Matty's backpack?"

"Yeah. Then."

"And?"

"And we went out for dinner last night."

He wouldn't.

But he did, and he had. The betrayal rose in her throat, thicker than the mole, and more slippery.

Matty said, "Camo-something."

"What?" She heard how thin her voice was.

"It's a white flower. Camo-something. Makes tea."

"Chamomile?"

"Yeah."

"Like Peter Rabbit. Remember that?" Once, when Matty was about five, he'd asked to try the tea that the mother rabbit gives to Peter and his siblings, but when she'd brought home the green box and brewed him a cup, he'd roundly rejected it, calling it grosser than cough medicine.

Matty's eyes slid to the left, as he made the connection. "Oh, *yeah*. That's it. The same thing. She gave me some dried stuff the first day we hung out, after we found Tulip. . . ." Then his face went guilty, his lower lip twisting, his gaze suddenly fixed.

"Wait. Was *that* what was under my pillow?" She'd found dried detritus, and she'd blamed Elva, who always insisted on drying the sheets on the line even though she dropped them on the ground half the time. "Why?"

"It's supposed to be good for . . ." Matty broke off. Then,

defiantly, he continued, "You're always complaining about how bad you sleep. I was trying to *help*."

"Oh, Matias. That's pretty adorable."

The word lit Matty like he was a firecracker. "It's not *adorable*. It was just *nice*. I'm just *nice*. But you don't care about me. At all."

"Matty—"

"You care about whether I'm happy about the same amount as you care about how happy a chicken is." He thunked out of the chair and thundered down the hall, slamming his door before she could say a word. Elva and Grandpa Wyatt barely glanced up, still arguing in soft voices about the television show, something about a naked person living in the woods.

The bass in Matty's room thumped with the sound of a video game, all guns blasting. Zero to a hundred in two seconds, and Fern couldn't do a thing. She couldn't chase him and drag him back like she had when he was six. She couldn't hold his shoulders in place anymore. She couldn't face him and demand he finish his dinner, or listen, or follow her instructions. She couldn't demand he love her. She couldn't tell him to never see Abby again. If she did, he'd disobey. She would have if she'd been him.

Fern would have to call Abby. Tomorrow. She couldn't do it tonight. "Seriously?"

Diego dragged a last tortilla through the red sauce on his plate and said, "Well, yeah. The chamomile thing is pretty fucking adorable. I wouldn't have told him, though."

"You know what's not adorable?"

"Mmm?"

"One guess, smart-ass."

"Me being friends with Abby?"

"*Friends?* That's what you're calling it?"

"Know what? I'm not going to waste time justifying it to you because, with respect, it's actually none of your god-damned business," he said.

He was right.

And it made her want to run away from home, even though she sure wouldn't get that far on foot. So instead, Fern cleared the table as Diego argued with Grandpa Wyatt in the living room over which direction to face the old TV. When the dishes were dried and put away, she scrabbled through the big, low drawer next to the sink until she found that old green box of chamomile tea. Six years old. She should have gotten rid of it ages ago.

Standing in the backyard, she ripped open each dry paper packet, letting the tea fly into the wind, over the fence, and into the neighbor's perfect, perfect garden. The lopsided moon hung almost close enough to touch, and she said the only incantation she knew: *Estamos completos. Siempre vamos a estar completa. Siempre.*

But when there were no more tea bags to open, no more chamomile to scatter, she wondered if she was just plain wrong. Maybe they weren't complete.

She'd been wrong about so many things.

Maybe Abby was someone who was *supposed* to come into their lives. Maybe Scott, against all odds, had been the mechanism for that.

A younger Fern would have believed that easily. The old cheerful, open-armed, wide-eyed Fern would have embraced Abby faster, harder. When had she gotten so tired that she didn't trust a person who just seemed to want to know her sweet boy?

Fern raised her chin. She looked the yellow moon dead in the eye. "I'm listening." She waited a beat, the low roar of the city filling her body, weighting her so that she didn't float away. "I'm trying."

It was *so* close to true.

chapter *forty~one*

"Can you park a few doors down?" Matty was poking and prodding at his backpack as if he was looking for something important.

Abby didn't want to ask, but she couldn't help it. "Okay. Why?"

"I can't find my key."

Tulip leaned forward from the backseat—an easy thing for him to do—nudging Abby wetly in the neck. "Ew. Stop. Attack that guy, not me," she said, pointing at Matty. As if the dog understood, he nosed Matty, ruffling the back of his hair with his sticky breath.

Matty giggled. God, Abby loved the sound of it. He'd giggled earlier when he kept dropping the second needle every time he reached the end of a knitted row. The wooden click of the needle hitting the floor made him laugh. That was a good thing, she told him. Most new knitters got frustrated and wanted to hurl their knitting against the opposite wall. *Nah,* he'd said. *I'm good with my hands. Mostly.*

Abby had slipped up then, saying he'd come by it naturally.

Really? His voice had been so eager. *My mom is a total klutz, except when she drives the bus.* He'd paused. *So, my dad . . . ?*

His father had been good at everything, she'd told him, and it was true. From mowing lawns like it was a sacred vocation, to the way he'd touched her in the middle of the night (she didn't say *that,* obviously). Scott had been good at things like car repair and hanging Christmas lights, all the typical manly things he was supposed to do, but he was good at unexpected things, too: bookbinding (they'd taken a class) and fixing her broken jewelry and dancing. He'd been such a good dancer. Abby's jaw ached with missing him, the pain surprising. She'd known she would keep grieving Scott, even though she'd been leaving him. That was natural, of course. But she hadn't expected the piercing shaft of old, leftover longing. She hadn't seen the sadness coming—the knowledge that they would never, ever fix themselves. Abby had thought she'd given up hope for them, but apparently, a pocket of it still lingered, deep in her lungs.

Now she turned off her car and focused on Matty, the boy next to her. The boy who remained. "Why am I parking down the street? You said your mom was okay with you hanging out with me."

Matty dodged the question and held up a key on a blue lanyard. "Found it! Hey, did my dad ever try knitting?"

Abby's heart dropped, landing in a cool puddle of regret. "He did." She should have thought of that earlier. Maybe she'd been blocking it out.

"What did he make?"

Scott had lied. He'd lied so beautifully, and for such a good reason. One afternoon near Halloween, he'd asked her to teach him what she was doing with her sticks and string. His usually nimble fingers struggled at first with the basics, the wrap of knit, the backward loop of purl. When it seemed like he was getting it, a few hours later, he took his increasingly even stitches off the needle, pulling the yarn, balling it back up. *Yeah. That's not for me. I was just wondering.*

But he was so good at it, she'd told him. He should keep going.

Nah. She'd never seen him touch the needles again.

Then, that Christmas, he'd given her a red scarf. It was almost perfect, with only one dropped stitch near the edge. He'd worked on it in secret, stealing time in parking lots when he was between clients, knitting in his office, ignoring the mocking of Charmaine, of the guys he employed. It had been her favorite piece of clothing for years, until she'd been visiting a friend in New York and left it behind in a cab.

"He made me a gorgeous scarf. I lost it, and I'm still mad at myself for that. I'd love to be able to show it to you."

Matty's eyes were so disappointed by this that Abby almost wished she hadn't told him. But then he recovered. "You think that's why I'm such a natural at it?"

Abby laughed. "Probably. Yes."

"Next week we'll dye it?"

"Maybe. Sometimes your first attempt isn't the one you want to save. The science fair isn't for another two months. You have time. Lots of little attempts add up." She cleared her throat and wiggled the key in the ignition. "Speaking of attempts, I'm going to give it one more try and ask you why we're parked here. I texted your mom. It's not like this is a secret." Brief texts that said almost nothing. Such an awkward, unwieldy conversation. She'd wanted to apologize for calling 911. But she couldn't—she would do it again if she were in the same situation. What if something worse had happened? What if Fern hadn't started breathing again on her own? Abby wanted to apologize for everything, but hadn't known where to start, using texts as a medium, and then Fern had texted Matty would be at Abby's house at three thirty, that he'd take the bus. *Take the bus.* The one Fern wasn't driving.

"Yeah." Matty yanked the backpack zipper closed and ripped it open again. "I know."

"What's up, then? I do *not* want to piss her off any more than I have."

"She told me to take the bus home. She, like, made me promise."

"But I . . . Why didn't she just come get you, if she didn't want me driving you?"

Matty looked at her like she was stupid, and perhaps she was. "She can't drive."

"I thought that was just the bus."

"At all. For three months, and that's just to start. It's like the law. They suspended her license."

"Holy crap. *Shit.*" She glanced at him. "Sorry. But damn. So, I bet she actually wants to kill me. Like, for real. With a pitchfork or something, huh?"

Matty appeared to think about the question, as if weighing methods Fern could rid the earth of Abby—guns versus knives, fire versus plague. "Yeah. I think so. But you know what? I think she understands why you did what you did. Like I do. But deep down, maybe—maybe she has to blame someone, you know?"

Abby's arms felt as heavy as garden pavers, her fists lumps in her lap. "That's pretty smart."

Matty sighed. "It's so boring when adults are always *surprised* by a kid actually being smart. Like we're either about to rob someone or we're smart like the Wise Men or something. We're just *kids*."

"That's a genius thing to say." She waited a beat. "Kidding."

Matty laughed. "Get it? Ha."

She laughed again. "*Kid*ding!"

"Heh. That's just dumb." But he kept laughing.

"I know." It felt good, to sit with him in the dark, giggling. She didn't want to ruin the slim, sweet moment. But she had to know, so when his laughter died down, she asked, "What is she going to do now? Like, while she waits to get her license back."

Matty shrugged as if he was irritated. "Waitress. I guess."

The shock was a cold thud. "Where?"

"This Mexican place she worked when she was in high school."

"Is that . . . a good thing?"

"They have the best tamales in town. That's what she always says."

"Well," she said weakly, "in Oakland, that's saying something."

"I don't know. My uncle is mad about it."

She'd seen Diego for the second time on Saturday night. He hadn't said a word to her about his sister. Then again, they hadn't said much of anything, had they? There had been words, many of them. But none of them had really mattered. He'd asked if she wanted to go out to eat, but it had seemed prescribed, a question he had to ask. Cutting to the chase, she'd used TaskRabbit to deliver a pizza and a six-pack. They'd eaten on the patio and after the sun went down, she'd taken him to her bed. She'd loved the way he felt, but more than that, she adored the way his voice sounded in her ear. It didn't matter what he said and it didn't matter what language he said it in. She just wanted his voice to keep talking, to keep making sound, and he'd complied with her desire until she'd fallen asleep, lulled by the dark, comforting timbre of his words.

When she'd woken in the morning, he was gone. The pizza box was in the trash, the napkins in the washer, the beer bottles in the recycling outside. "Waitressing."

"I guess."

"Dang it. I have to walk you in, dude."

Matty jumped. "I'm *pretty* sure you don't want to do that."

Apprehension was a dull buzz behind her eyes. "Oh, you are so right about that."

Fern had a level of control over her face that Abby admired. Her expression appeared open. Neutral. Her lips were curved in a small (very small) smile, and her forehead stayed smooth. Even her hair seemed tamer than normal, as if she'd just run a brush over it.

Only in her eyes did her anger show. The normal brown of her irises was almost black, and heat snapped in their darkness. She sent Matty to his room with a flick of her wrist, and without a word of protest, he went. Abby planted her feet in the low pile of the threadbare carpet. "Don't be mad at him."

"I told him to ride the bus home." Fern's voice was as neutral as her body language—open hands, her hips squared to Abby's. "I'm not sure why he wouldn't tell you that."

"He told me." Abby didn't mention he hadn't told her until they'd pulled up outside.

Matty's grandfather Wyatt, sitting on the couch, didn't even try to hide his fascination, setting his pad of paper and pencil on the table next to him. He rubbed his whiskers eagerly. From the kitchen, Abby could see Elva peering out.

"I didn't say it on the phone last night—I didn't know about your driver's license then." Abby shoved her hands into her jeans pockets as if she had something to hold that would steady her. "But I'm sorry."

"For what? Calling 911?"

She couldn't—wouldn't—lie to Fern. That wouldn't be fair. "No. I'd do that again in a heartbeat. I thought you were going to die."

"But Matty—"

"Matty's a *child*. You were writhing on the floor. I was the only conscious adult there."

Fern's mouth snapped shut. She blinked.

Abby wouldn't lie, but she could tell the truth, stripped down to its basics. "I *am* sorry my actions have had such a major repercussion in your life."

To Abby's surprise, Fern laughed. "Fancy words for the shit I'm going through."

"I know."

Fern blew out a breath and pushed a frizzy curl off her forehead. "I appreciate you helping Matty with his project." The words sounded heavy and expensive, as if she could barely afford to part with them.

"You're welcome. He's welcome."

"Okay, then."

Abby realized Fern was nervous. It helped her move forward with her crazy idea, knowing that.

"Hey, I need help."

"Sorry?"

"I mean, I would love your help. To sell my stuff, the stuff I make. Like you said I should."

"God, Abby. I can't keep up with you."

"I know it sounds crazy, but I'd pay you."

Fern looked over her shoulder at Wyatt. "Are you hearing this?"

Wyatt nodded. "Seems she wants to make you her employee."

"No—" The last time she'd half-assedly mentioned she could use Fern's help, Fern had gone into seizure. What the hell was she thinking?

Fern's face was storm-dark. "Come on, Abby. Can't you use oDesk or something for that? What did Diego say you called to bring you beer? TaskBunny or something?"

He'd told her? About that second night?

But that wasn't important. Abby scrabbled in her mind for the right words—any words—that wouldn't keep igniting Fern's anger, that wouldn't accelerate her overreaction any further. "First of all, calm down. Getting mad at me can't be good for you."

Fern's eyes widened. "You tell *me* to calm down? Let me tell you something, *mami*, the other day? That was not *you* that made me have a seizure. I need you to know—"

"*¡Cállate la boca!*" It was about fifty percent of what Abby remembered from high school Spanish, but it worked. Fern's mouth snapped shut, and Abby went on. "*Not* an employee. The opposite. My partner."

chapter *forty~two*

*P*artner. The word knocked the wind out of Fern, like a big fist sailing into her gut. It had happened twice on the job over the years, the punch she didn't see coming, the one that left her gasping in shock.

The secondary feeling was the same—not pleasant.

"Did you hear me?" Abby's face was red.

"Yes." Had this woman actually told her to shut her mouth in Spanish? Where had that come from? "I heard you."

"And?"

"And give me a minute." She needed to breathe. "Jeez."

"Fine." Abby crossed her arms and scowled. Elva had scuttled in from the hall and Grandpa Wyatt was openly staring.

"Outside. Backyard, okay?" Fern gestured into the kitchen, through to the door. All the way out—she didn't want this conversation to happen in the kitchen any more than she did the living room. The kitchen was her safe zone, and this didn't feel safe. "Keep going. Out."

Abby looked over her shoulder. "Are you going to lock the door on me as soon as I'm out there?"

Fern made a *humph* in the back of her throat and said, "You want a beer?"

"Really?"

"Give me a second."

At the sink, Fern leaned on the cracked porcelain and took a breath. Then another one. She searched inside herself for what feeling she should carry outside with the beer bottles—fear? resistance? caution?—and came up empty.

So she popped the caps and carried them out. She held one out and said, "Interview."

"For you or for me?"

"Both."

"Yes," said Abby, and if she was surprised, it didn't show. "Go."

Fern took a long sip of the beer and looked up at the box elder's limbs stretching overhead. The setting sun streaked the one lone swatch of fog pink, and two planes lumbered across the sky so slowly it seemed they must fall, that the crash was imminent.

"What do you want me to do?" The words came out wrong, implying that Fern would just *do* whatever it was Abby wanted. And that was so wrong. "I mean, what do you—what are you talking about?"

"I don't know."

"Awesome."

"The idea just came to me in the car."

"Spontaneous charity? Even better. Did Matty tell you I was going to wait tables at the taqueria?"

"Could you just *not* be a bitch? Huh?"

Abby's voice was sharper than Fern would have imagined it could be, and she felt the scowl rip across her face like a strike of lightning. She couldn't have stopped it if she wanted to (which she didn't). The problem was that the urge to laugh followed straight after. Even she could see that Abby was trying. God knew *what* she was trying to do, but it was something. "Well, now. That's not very charming of you. Isn't that your thing? Charm?"

Abby looked chagrined, her knuckles whitening on the Corona. "Just listen to me, okay? Maybe it's a fucking terrible idea, but I could use the help."

"What kind of help?"

"You were right. I could sell a lot more of my product if I actually put more into it. More time, more investment. I have orders I haven't been able to process, and I got a request from a lifestyle magazine for an interview, but I need a proper Web site first."

"Why, though? You don't need the money." Better to be blunt.

"Because my pau d'arco liniment helped my friend sleep when her rheumatism wouldn't let her. Because the sage and burdock tonic helped another friend deal with chemo side effects. Because this one shop in Cambria sells my dandelion-burdock tea in bulk to a man who's dying of liver cancer and says it helps a little. Because what I make *helps* people, simple as that. And because you were right."

It would have been so easy to mock Abby then. To take her words and squash them, the way older kids did on the bus to the younger ones, socking her verbally until she cried uncle.

But Fern didn't want to. She didn't want to be that person. "Go on."

"I'm not trying to be trendy. I'm not trying to be all

Pinterest about it—I don't make it because it's pretty or hip or because I'm trying to impress anyone. I make my stuff because I love learning what herbal remedies worked in the past, and I like trying out the old recipes with the things I grow myself."

Fern sighed. "You know we'll have issues with promises?"

"I don't need you to promise me a damn—"

"Not me. In terms of packaging and liability, I mean."

Abby blinked.

"Have you even thought of that?"

"No."

Of course she hadn't. "What you promise your users matters. If you say it will ease certain aches or pains, and it doesn't, then you're in trouble."

"Of course."

"Wait, now that I think about it, you might be in trouble even if it does get the job done. I'm assuming you don't want to go the whole FDA route."

"Sorry?"

"No promises of health, then. Just the suggestion that such and such herb has been known to help shit."

"Um . . ."

"And if they turn out to be deathly allergic to the kind of ionized water you put in there, the liability lands on you, you know that, right?"

"I knew that."

"What have you done about it?"

Abby tilted her head. "I hoped really hard it wouldn't happen. And so far, that's worked."

"Just a matter of time. That's okay—we can get insurance for that. Easier if we incorporate—have you done that?"

"Are you kidding me?"

"LLC?"

"What?"

"Do you even have a brand name?"

"I've been calling it Abby's Alimentary."

"I have no idea what that even means."

Abby nodded. "I hear that a lot."

"If you can't spell it or remember it, you can't Google it. First rule of business. Be discoverable." Over the fence, Fern heard Maria Silva's hose snap and spit as it was turned on. The sound was as familiar to her as Grandpa Wyatt's snoring, as Elva's humming over a pot of something unidentifiable. "Okay, then. If we did this, what do you envision my role being?" That sounded good. It struck the right tone.

Abby set her beer bottle on the cold rim of the fire pit and pressed her palms together, as if she were going to snap a *namaste* at Fern or something. Her face was eager, her eyes bright. "Selling."

"Marketing," Fern corrected.

"See? That. I make, and you sell."

"And my cut is?" If she'd learned anything in her night classes, it was that you asked about compensation up front, that it was all written down in black and white, so all parties were safe.

"I thought—fifty dollars?"

Fern frowned. "For what?"

"An hour?"

"An *hour*?"

"You're thinking more?"

Fifty dollars an hour for labeling bottles? For putting them online? Abby lived in a whole different world. Or this really was her fancy way of doling out charity, and Fern wasn't sure which concept was worse. "Holy shitballs. No."

"What's reasonable, then?"

"You don't have any idea how the real world works, do you? How much was Scott billing when he died?"

Abby picked her beer back up and took a sip. She was stalling, Fern could tell. "I think it was double that. Ish."

Fern whistled. "Wow." She breathed carefully through her mouth, hoping her hands weren't shaking. "I make twenty-seven an hour." And she had thought that was a lot of money. It never went as far as it should—taking care of three other people would do that to you—but she'd always been proud when she thought of her wage, the hourly rate that rested in her hands, which didn't sit on the backbone of a college degree or anything else just handed to her. She earned her money. At Ensenada, she'd be lucky to take home thirteen bucks an hour, even with tips. It had been hard enough when she was a cute nineteen-year-old with sky-high tits and hopes to match, slinging four-dollar plates of rice and beans. Tacos were still a buck fifty each, but she was almost twenty years older. Grandpa Wyatt needed a new tooth. The hole in Matty's backpack was patched with duct tape.

Fern ached to just say, *I'll take the life insurance money.* It would make everything so easy. She could actually rest a little. Not waitress. She'd managed to take Scott's money, after all. But that was different. He'd owed his son that much. The life insurance was different. It was his wife's money. Abby owed them nothing.

But if she worked for—with—Abby, she'd be an equal. Accepting money for real, honest work, work she would be good at. *Running a business.* That was the goal, the reason she went to night school in the first place.

"Business partners. Not friends."

Abby pulled up her chin. "Why not both?"

Fern let out the breath she'd been holding. "Girl, I need money way more than I need friends."

"I'm going to hope for both." Abby tilted a crooked smile at her.

"Let's start with business partners, huh?" Fern was proud that her voice was as strong as she wanted it to sound. "And my brother is off-limits."

Abby tucked her lips in, briefly. Then she said, "I'm sorry about that. I really am. It just happened."

"Twice?"

She colored, but she nodded. "Yeah. It just happened twice."

"Well, he would have to be out of the picture." That had to be part of the deal. No negotiation.

Abby paused.

Fern counted one breath. Then two.

Then Abby nodded. "Okay."

"That was fast." In a twist of emotion she didn't see coming, Fern wanted to know why Abby could just give up Diego like that, that quickly. He wasn't good enough?

"It's not a problem." The look on Abby's face was unreadable.

"Huh. 'Cause he said he saw you Saturday night."

"We'll make that the last time."

"And I get twenty-five dollars an hour."

Abby blinked twice. "Are you seriously negotiating me down?"

"I can't believe you're insulting me by offering me more than I'm worth."

Abby nodded. "Fine. Accepted. Plus twenty-five percent of the profits."

"Now you've just lost your goddamned mind." Fern's arms ached with the weight of all of it. She wanted to ask why Abby would choose them, would choose Fern and Matty over a few more rolls in the hay with her brother. She wanted to know why they were so important to her. It couldn't just be about Scott, not anymore. But she had a feeling the answer might bring her too low to the ground, and she was scraping the earth with her bare knuckles as it was.

"I told you, partners. I meant it. I get twenty-five percent, too. The rest, after expenses, goes back into the business. Marketing, like you said."

"Why me?"

Abby looked at her like she was an idiot. "Because you're Fern. And your son is Matty."

"*Ay, madre.* You have to understand that there's a limit to generosity."

"Why?"

"Are you serious?"

Abby set the bottle down on the edge of the fire pit with so much force that Fern was surprised it didn't break. "People think there has to be a limit. Why is that true? Why can't we just give as much as we can give right up to the point we can't give anymore?"

Fern didn't have to think before she spoke. "Because your house would fill up with homeless addicts. Because some people are made to give and some are made to take, and those roles don't change. If you give too much, you'll end up with nothing." Ask her how she knew. Fern would fight to the tooth for her house, for what it represented in terms of protecting the ones she loved. She cared for the people who got on her bus, the ones she was paid to protect during her shift, but the ones

THE ONES WHO MATTER MOST

who lived in her home? Her family? She'd do whatever it took to keep them safe from everything—from burglars and fire and crazies and zealots and earthquakes and from the very hand of God if it came to that. God was big. But her love was bigger. She would die for the ones under her roof. That was how you knew you were alive. "Because you're living in the wrong kind of world otherwise. It's not fair to those who can't pay it back." Did she really have to explain this to an adult? "You have to live in the world that's in front of you, don't you get that? Not the one that you make, not the world that you think is better than it actually is."

"What if other people are just seeing it wrong? What if I'm the one who's right?"

For calling Fern an idiot, it wasn't a bad way to do it. "Abby's Aliment-a-whatsit isn't going to work. Have you thought of any other names?"

"I did think of something. Maybe." Abby kicked at the base of the fire pit. It left a black mark on the white toe of her sneaker. "Taking Care."

Fern saw Scott's scrawled handwriting in her mind, that addendum to every check she'd ever cashed. *Take care.* Did Abby mean it as a fuck-you to Scott? She searched Abby's face. Her gaze was clear. Open. But there was possibly the *slightest* hint of mischief behind her dark, curled lashes. It was, Fern knew, nothing Abby would admit. She might not even know it.

But it was kind of awesome.

"Okay, then," said Fern. "I guess I'm in."

Abby held up her bottle. "To Taking Care," she said.

Fern clinked her bottle with the neck of hers. "Fuck, yeah."

chapter *forty~three*

Two weeks later, Abby leaned backward and groaned. "I could not possibly care less about a Twitter account." The chaise in her office was dark red and heavily pillowed, and each pillow conformed exactly to the shape it was needed for—under a knee or behind a head. It looked decadent and a bit slovenly, the velvet's pile ancient, and Abby loved it. "You make all this crap look easy."

"It is easy."

"Humph."

"It's just time-consuming." Fern pulled her curls back with a red rubber band. Two or three spirals sprang wildly to the side. Her nose was shiny. She was pretty. Abby wondered how much prettier she'd been in person when she was younger. Fern seemed to be one of those people who was probably growing into her looks. If Scott had stuck around, he would have known that. Fern continued, "That's the only reason you never got around to it before."

"You're giving me too much credit."

Fern bent forward, staring at the Photoshop window. They'd done a photo shoot earlier in the morning, when the light was bright and clear: the blue and green bottles gleaming on a wooden bench they'd propped over a stand of newly sprung forget-me-nots. The calligraphed tags (in blue ink, Abby's hand) fluttered in the wind. Now Fern was cropping and putting filters on the photos, and they looked more professional than Abby could ever have imagined. Fern frowned and swore, making a white box jump forward and then minimizing it again. "It . . . Oh, never mind."

"What?"

"Nothing."

"No, tell me. Do you not like it? I can tell by your face. Do we have to reshoot?" Of course they would—it had been too easy. "Should I go set it up? Move the bench to the irises, maybe? Tulip has probably chewed on the bench a little more by now, made it look even more authentically aged." Abby peered out the window, and sure enough, Tulip was happily gnawing on the leg of the picnic bench.

"It's not that. I just . . ." Fern turned in her chair to face Abby. "I wish you wouldn't say you can't do simple things. Matty says that when he's feeling lazy."

Abby pulled her legs up, the old velvet prickling the bottoms of her feet. "Oh."

"I don't mean it like that. You're not lazy."

Heat started at Abby's hairline. "I'm not an imbecile, you know."

"I know you're not."

"It's just I didn't know where to start. Or, when I'd started, where to go next. Instagram, Pinterest, Twitter, Facebook—you know you've set all those up within a week? That's just when you've been here. I know you've been working on it at home, too." Fern was keeping an Excel spreadsheet of her hours.

"I could have done it faster if Gmail hadn't been acting so stupid about confusing your computer with the new address. That took, like, half a day."

"It would have taken me a whole day just to figure out Instagram."

Fern rubbed her eyes. "That's not true."

It was an exaggeration. Wasn't that obvious? "I know it's not *true*. I know how to make up a password and open an account. It's just that when I'd set it up, I wouldn't know what to do with it. I don't understand hashtags, why you'd even need them in the first place." Fern had started posting almost immediately, adding *#TakingCare* to every picture, to every tweet. "Who are you talking to right now, anyway? Who's going to read these things?"

"No one."

"Awesome."

"But they will. One person will find the Etsy shop—then they'll search for your Web site."

"Which I don't have!"

"But which you will have in about an hour. Then they'll see your Twitter account, and click over there to see if you're active."

"Like yeast." Abby pictured the Web site growing in a bowl, bubbling under a tea towel. They would set it in a warm place and in the morning, they'd have to punch it down so it could grow some more.

"Like professional. Then they'll buy something, and when they get it at their house, they'll hopefully post something with our hashtag, and other people will click on that, and see our pretty things. Get it?"

"I *get* it. I understand the concept. I just don't think any-one will actually do it."

"Oh, they will."

"Your lips to God's ears."

"I hate that phrase," said Fern absently. Abby watched as she changed a blue bottle to faintly iridescent green and back again.

"Do you ever like anything? Right off the bat?"

Fern finally turned to look at her. Abby tightened her arms around her knees but stayed still.

"Yes."

"That surprises me," said Abby.

"I'm kind of known for liking things," said Fern. "That's who people think I am at work. Or who I was at work, any-way. I like my riders. I like my coworkers. I like driving in the rain, and I like driving in the sun. I'm the cheerful one. The funny one. I never take life too seriously."

"What happened?"

Fern looked back at the screen. "Do you prefer this photo? Or this one, with more of the yellow base?"

"You won't answer the question?"

Fern sighed. "Life happened. And I hate that I'm the kind of person who's letting that get her down. That's never been me before." A short pause. "You blew up my life. Twice."

"Yeah. I'm kind of actively trying to not do that right now."

"Did you and Scott ever want kids?"

The abrupt change in topic felt like a change in elevation. Abby could almost hear her ears pop. "Yeah. We tried."

"Tried?"

"They didn't stick."

"Oh." Fern's cursor stopped moving on the screen. "I'm sorry."

"Some women are made to pop 'em out. I'm not, I guess. I was getting okay with adopting, but he said no."

"That sucks."

"Then I was going to trick him. To try again for a baby, once more. But he got a vasectomy." The bitter laugh was more of a choked-off breath. "A secret vasectomy. That's why I was leaving him. I was furious. I guess I still am. But I think I was just as bad as he was. We were both trying to trick each other about the most important thing of all."

Fern spun in the office chair to face Abby fully, her palms flat on her thighs. "I don't—I don't even know—"

"It's fine," said Abby. "You don't have to say anything. Really. And I'm sorry I blew up your life, by the way. Twice. Both times unintentional, you know."

"Sure. Damn, girl." But Fern's voice was light. Something had shifted in the room, as if a cloud had scudded away from in front of the sun. "Eh, I've forgiven you."

Abby's blood warmed. "Really?"

"Mostly."

"And now you . . ." *Kind of like me. Don't hate me. Could see being friends with me someday.*

"No way. Don't make me say it."

Abby thought she could see something behind Fern's eyes, something she wanted to tease out, to put in a warm place next to her bubbling business bowl. "*Come* on."

"You're fine."

Abby cupped a hand behind her ear. "I'm what?"

"You're all right, I guess." The corner of Fern's mouth twitched.

"You don't hate me."

"At this very moment?"

"At this very moment. And don't forget I was about to go make you another cup of coffee."

"A cup of coffee with cream, you mean?"

Abby nodded, her heart unfolding. "With cream, of course." What she meant was *Everything, anything.* She would make her a loaf of bread, a bubble bath, an oil painting—anything she could figure out how to make, she would do it for her. "A cup of coffee with cream for my friend."

Fern laughed lightly, the sound warm and round. "Don't push it"—a comma's breath—"friend."

chapter *forty-four*

The bus was so full that Fern had to stand up for the first twenty minutes, something she hadn't done on a coach in too many years to count. She laughed and ignored Gilmore when he told her just to get on, dumping her money in the fare box just like anyone else. "What, my money ain't good enough for you?"

"Why you gotta do that, lady?" Gilmore had put on a few pounds since she'd seen him last, and his hips spread over the edge of the wide seat. They'd started together, in the same training group. He ate two egg-salad sandwiches for lunch every day, without exception. Once his wife had sent him to work with peanut butter and jelly because the store had been out of eggs and he'd been so mad he spent the next three nights at their coworker Rizelli's house, going home only when Rizelli's wife threatened to make Gilmore start cleaning the bathrooms for his room and board.

"Yeah, yeah." She could almost afford the $2.10. Kind of.

"Hey, how long you off work?"

"Another nine weeks or so." It made it sound as if she was coming back, as if they'd let her, when she cleared medical probation. Fern grabbed the pole behind Gilmore's head, ignoring the flash of envy that raced through her at the way his fingers fit around the wheel. She missed the sound, the smell, of the bus—the mixture of rubber and gasoline and weed and body lotion and lunch meat. It smelled like perfume to her. She wished she could ask Abby to bottle the smell somehow, but she'd be the only customer for it.

"So you hit that cush disability gig, huh?"

She smiled. "That what you heard?"

He winked over his shoulder. "Yep. I heard you pulled a fast one."

"That I did, my friend. I can highly recommend it. Good stuff."

A lie. She'd filed immediately with human resources, but they said the state could take up to six weeks to even *start* paying her out, and no one seemed sure about retro pay. Linda had an e-mail in to Ivy, who had called the state twice already, but every question Fern asked raised two more. The transit district lost people to disability all the time, she *knew* they did. How was it that they didn't know their asses from a timetable? Fern didn't have six weeks. What she had was a father-in-law with a tooth that needed work, and a mortgage that was still late, still gathering charges and writhing like a dragon.

The check Abby had just given her burned in her back pocket.

Fern had been in love with a boy in high school—Romano. He lit his smokes with a Zippo, the only kid who hadn't used a cheap plastic lighter. After he'd kissed her for the first time, he'd let her take the Zippo home with her. "For tonight. Think of me. Then bring it back tomorrow." It had seemed like a declaration of love, that overnight loan. She'd slipped it into the back pocket of her jeans, and it sat there, a small hard lump. By early evening, her right butt cheek burned. She thought that was love, too, but then it started to itch *and* burn. It had leaked, and the lighter fluid caused her skin to rise in teeny-tiny bumps. Romano had taken his lighter back without comment, and she'd wondered how many other asses he'd burned with it.

The check felt the same way.

She hadn't had the guts to look at it yet. She needed a few more minutes. A few more turns on the bus, a few swings around a couple of tight corners. That would make the feeling in her body settle, would bring her back into herself so she could decide what to do next. (She already knew what she had to do—it was why she was on this bus going this way instead of the shorter way home on the 53.)

"How do I pull that off, you think?" Gilmore smiled at an old woman who took off a yellowed glove to extract the exact change out of a tiny pink pocketbook.

"I'll tell you how," said Fern. "Just fall over in the middle of something, the more public the better. If you can pretend that you're foaming at the mouth—that's good. If you bite your tongue, it's even more effective. Blood and foam is damn impressive. You know what I mean?" She knew he did. Because passengers were so often among the ranks of people whose medical ailments were untreated, seizures weren't uncommon on the coach. She had to get radio to call 911 for an ambulance at least once a month, from as minor as a trip on the last step to the old guy on the 61 last year who had stopped breathing in the back row and never started again.

"You know I do. No fallin' out, you hear me? I ain't in the mood."

"I hear you, friend."

A long, slow nod. "Good." He eased the coach into traffic like it was the tongue of a zipper. Gilmore'd always been good.

A woman wearing a black cutoff sweatshirt that slid off her shoulder *Flashdance*-style spit angrily into her phone. "This bus is *supposed* to be the fast one. Seventy-two R—that's why it's *R*."

Fern caught Gilmore's eye in the bigger mirror and they shared a tiny smile. Restricted buses were technically supposed to be faster, with fewer stops, but in rush-hour traffic, nothing was sure. The normal 72 sailed past them on the left.

"They *came* at the same time. That's why I chose this one!" The woman was yelling into her phone now. "I could've been ahead of this bus, but this driver is so fucking stupid, he don't even know what he's supposed to be doing. Can he hear me? Yeah, he can fucking *hear* me. He's right in front of me. I'm sitting right up front. He can fucking hear me."

Fern would lay equal odds the woman wasn't even talking to anyone on the other end of the phone. She was probably just trying to make her point. There was something almost soothing about hearing the abuse. It was a language she spoke, something that cheered her up in the way it never changed. She could tell by the jaunty way Gilmore saluted at a kid getting off that he was amused, too.

At the next stop, the woman swung angrily off the bus. Gilmore gave her a cheery, "Have a great day!"

"Fuck off! Do your job!"

The woman ran to catch the 72 that was stopped half a block up. Then, with a jolly honk, Gilmore passed it. Fern could feel the satisfaction in her very fingers, the way it felt when the universe was in order. Like that.

She needed her bus. Oh, god. What if she never got it back?

At the next stop, Fern was pushed farther into the bus by a large crowd of schoolkids headed toward the Coliseum. When two kids finally pulled their tongues out of each other's mouths and noticed their stop, hurtling out of the bus like they were horny crickets, she scored a seat.

Finally, thirty long minutes after Abby had pressed the check into her palm, Fern worked up the courage to pull it out of her pocket. When she'd accepted it, she'd only been able to nod and say, "Yep." She'd folded it in half and then in half again, casually, sticking it into her back pocket as if it were a receipt from the drugstore, the kind that was a million miles long, printed with coupons that never came in handy. It was working—the whole helping Abby out. It had only been a couple of weeks, but it was really working. Fern could even admit it was sometimes fun. At least once or twice a week, Matty rode the bus over after school and worked on his knitted hat in front of the TV downstairs. Then Fern rode home with him. He leaned on her if it was crowded. She loved that.

She unfolded the check. It was light blue with darker blue stripes at the bottom. Heavy paper. She could picture Abby writing it out, could imagine that it came from a leather full-sized folio kept in a walnut secretary, so different from the vinyl-covered checkbook Fern threw in the kitchen drawer next to the scissors.

Fern's full name was written out in Abby's pretty, careful

handwriting. Six hundred twenty-five dollars. Twenty-five hours last week, at twenty-five dollars an hour.

In the memo line, it read, *Taking Care*, followed by a smiley face.

For a moment, Fern tried to imagine what she would have done if Scott had ever included an emoticon on his check. She probably would have ripped it into tiny pieces and then immediately regretted it.

Out the window, the neon lights of the Chinese gambling place on Broadway caught her eye. This was where she needed to get off.

"Excuse me. Coming through." No one in the pack of kids moved, and for a second, she imagined what it would be like to be older, feeble. Invisible. She tried again in a louder voice. "My stop, let me out." The kids seemed to huddle tighter, the passage impenetrable unless she crawled up and over them like Diego climbed trees. Gilmore heard her—she knew by the way he was holding the bus steady, doors staying resolutely open even though no one was getting on. "Hey, you little shits, *move*."

A small gust of appreciative laughter breezed through the teens, and they split, letting her pass. She waved at Gilmore up front and stepped down onto the sidewalk.

Taking a huge breath in and holding it, she turned to face the bank's double doors.

She went inside.

She filled out the slip.

She deposited the check. It was money from Abby, but it was money she'd *earned*, doing the thing that she'd wanted to for a long time, using her business brain. It wasn't half as hard as she'd thought it would be. Actually, it felt damn fine, putting that money into the stripped-bare account. Simple, really.

She caught another bus home (a new driver she'd never seen before, a young guy who barely met her eyes) and was home an hour later, the door closed and locked behind her. She sat alone on the broken sofa. Her perfect, sagging, ripped-to-shreds sofa.

Taking care.

It was simple if you could breathe, and Fern could. It was still her air, the air that smelled like home, like dust and Matty's shoes and cumin and oregano and old wood.

She could breathe.

chapter *forty~five*

Abby sat in the waiting room of the emergency vet and tried to fight the urge to throw up.

Tulip was going to die.

The strong, young Great Dane whose muscles flexed like an Olympian's, who had seemed completely invincible as he thumped through Abby's empty house, thundering up and down the stairs with man-heavy footsteps—he was going to die and it was all Abby's fault.

He'd eaten all the onions. All of them. For days, he'd been snacking on them, and she hadn't noticed. He'd pried off the lid on the box behind the shed, where she didn't go unless she actually needed some of the stored bulbs. Pounds and pounds of them. It was all her fault.

All because she thought he was safe outside. He chewed furniture, yes, but that didn't seem hazardous. She'd been writing new labels with a fountain pen, watching the rain (unexpected and welcome) fall outside. She'd been trying to impress Fern with fresh-ground cinnamon in her coffee. She hadn't been trying to impress Fern with her extended knowledge about historically accurate dye recipes from the nineteenth century, or even with something like the ability to navigate her new Pinterest page. No, just a cinnamon-dusted *coffee*. Tulip's huge feet were muddy after he'd gone out to pee, and she hadn't felt like having to mop, so she'd left the dog out there under the magnolia tree. He didn't mind. He wouldn't get into trouble.

An hour after Fern left at six, she'd called him. He came, but he was slow to do it. He peed on a solar garden light, and his urine was dark red. Then he'd fallen sideways, heavily. He'd just panted after that. She'd loaded him into the car immediately, almost dropping him as she tried to lift his heavy back half—but by the time they got to the emergency vet clinic, he was barely moving. It had taken two interns to help her carry him in.

The waiting room of the clinic was cold and sterile, separated into two parts. One enormous yellow sign shouted CATS over a left-pointing arrow. Abby sat under the blue DOGS sign on the molded plastic seat that clearly had never been meant for a real person to sit in—it was square, the back at a right angle to the seat. (Maybe it was supposed to feel that way, hard and cold and terrifying and guilt inducing.) The walls were white, their starkness alleviated only by a cat calendar—on the dog wall—which featured a cranky-looking Siamese caught in a wide-mouthed yawn.

The receptionist, somewhere in her forties with bright red glasses, had been professional enough, but her smile hadn't reached her eyes, and when she wasn't typing on the desk computer, she was whacking the touch screen of her phone. After each flurry of smacks, another ding sounded. Any minute she was going to hurl the phone through the small plate glass window that faced dark and rainy University Avenue.

Tulip was probably going to die. Abby's stomach roiled, and she measured the distance to the bathroom again, for the tenth time. She would make it if she had to. Just in case, she noted the placement of the trash can. Then she made the mistake of imagining what might be *in* a trash can at an emergency vet's office, and felt even worse, like the ground was heaving below her.

A phone's low buzz. A few murmured words. Then a few more anger-slapped texts, a couple of corresponding dings, and the receptionist looked up. "You can go in."

Was Tulip dead? Was that what they would tell her? Abby tasted acid at the back of her mouth. No, no, no. She hadn't planned on falling in love with the damned dog. She'd only taken him home to please Matty. To tempt him. Tulip had started out as a bribe, and she'd known it. But that first night, he'd let himself out of his crappily made though shockingly expensive crate. Abby had heard him breathing heavily at the foot of the bed. She'd lain still in the hopes that he'd just curl up on the floor. That would be okay. But then she'd felt the bottom of the bed dip. Curious and vaguely amused, Abby had kept herself motionless.

Tulip had dragged himself up on the bed, one paw creeping up after the next one. He'd pressed his long body flat at the bottom of the bed, curving himself so that he wasn't lying on her feet.

The fact that he'd sneaked his way on (and knew it) had struck her as sweeter than honey. She'd let him stay, resolving the next night she'd figure out a way to close the crate more thoroughly. Maybe a twist tie. Or a padlock.

But when she'd woken the next morning, Tulip had moved. He was lying next to her, right where Scott had slept. His big square head rested on the pillow like a person's. His back was to her, and she'd had her arm slung around him.

She had spooned the damn thing.

He was hers then.

"Is he dead?" Would the receptionist tell her if he was?

The interior door buzzed. "Push," said the woman. "Room three."

The little patient room was even worse than the lobby. The seat was metal, like at a bus stop. The sink looked scrubbed clean, but it was rusted at the corners. It smelled of bleach, and Abby couldn't help thinking about what they might use the bleach for. "Mint," she whispered to herself. "Ginger. Blessed thistle." Maybe just whispering the anti-nausea herbs to herself would help.

She checked her phone. Seven thirty-two p.m. She'd been waiting in the room for ten minutes now. She'd give it two more, and then she'd bust out and go looking for Tulip's body. They couldn't keep her from knowing the truth. Not one second more. What would they *do* with him? Cremation? Was there a red button somewhere for the bereaved? What about that huge head of his? That nose that wouldn't jam itself impolitely and hysterically into her crotch every time she walked in the front door? No, she wanted to bury him. There should be a place where you could dig the earth yourself and put your pet in the ground. A pet cemetery. Then in her mind, she saw the cover of *Pet Sematary* by Stephen King, and that, in turn, made her feel like she was going to throw up again.

The doctor entered, gray-haired and slump-shouldered. The white coat over pink kitten scrubs seemed too young for her.

"Tulip's going to be fine."

Abby's mind went blank. How could an almost-dead dog become fine? "Sorry?"

The vet rubbed her temples as if she had a headache. "Just fine. We induced vomiting for the toxicosis, and you're right, that was a lot of onions. He also needed a blood transfusion. He's resting now. We've got him on IV fluid for a little longer—it'll help him feel better later, since we just assaulted his system pretty rudely."

"Yeah." Relief flooded into her system like she was the one hooked up to an IV—it was cold and delicious, and the nausea abated immediately.

"You okay? It can be pretty scary, I know."

"I can take him home?"

"Yep. Probably be about ten or fifteen more minutes, then a tech will bring him to you. Sorry it took me so long to get out here to talk to you. Busy night. Hey. Are you really okay?"

"Yeah," said Abby. Then bile rose and she clapped a hand over her mouth. She raced to the bathroom and only just made it.

Half an hour later, she gave the receptionist the equivalent of a double car payment. Tulip sat on her foot and made no sign of wanting to leave. He panted happily and drooled on her leg.

"You both look a lot better now," said the receptionist, whose phone was nowhere in sight. Abby wondered if it was outside in the rain.

"Yeah. Well."

"Pregnant?"

Abby tilted her head, as if she could reframe the word, make it mean something else, like plant or puppy or present. "No. Tulip's actually a boy dog. I know the name is confusing."

"Sorry. I meant . . ."

"Me?"

"So sorry. You had a look. I apologize. You came in looking like I did with my first two."

"What?" she said again stupidly. Something shot down into her knees, a metallic adrenaline rush.

"Kind of green. But not like with flu."

"I'm not pregnant."

"Of course." The receptionist didn't look convinced as she pushed the receipt and the credit card across the counter. "Just one signature here, and then I'll get you a complete printed record to give to your regular vet."

"You thought I was *pregnant*?"

The woman blinked. "So sorry."

Abby loaded Tulip into the back of her car and hoped he'd stay there for once. It was hard to see around him when he sat on the passenger seat. "I'm not pregnant," she told him. He just panted, his breath antiseptic-smelling with an oniony afterburn.

"I can't be pregnant." She settled into the driver's seat and tried not to pant the same way. She pulled up the calendar on her phone.

She counted.

Then she counted again.

And once more, because counting was hard when you suddenly didn't have a single brain cell that seemed to be willing to be devoted to the task.

She was late. Two weeks, almost three. It had been only a month since she'd had sex with Diego the second and last time. Was that even possible? She would have been ovulating . . . yep. That was about right. Shit.

She had used condoms with Diego. She wasn't a fucking moron.

Abby wasn't pregnant.

It was what she said to herself all the way to the store. She said it to the cashier, because the more she said it, the better chance she had of forcing it to be true. "I'm not pregnant."

The sloe-eyed cashier just rang up her box, obviously knowing better than to comment.

Abby drove home, Tulip slobbering in her ear. The dog was alive. She had managed to keep the dog alive. That was something, wasn't it? Something important?

Abby wasn't frightened.

What she felt in her body, what pressed at her lungs and pulled at her gut, was so much bigger than fear. She was shaking with so much *hope* that it was rattling out of her body. She had to kick her way through it to the car, she had to shovel it off the sidewalk in front of the house, and when she sat on the toilet and peed on the stick and then stood to wait, trembling, the hope threatened to bury her alive and she knew she would willingly die underneath it, her mouth open to breathe more of it in, more hope, more hope, always more, even when it made no sense at all.

chapter *forty~six*

Fern's cell phone rang twice. The first time, she checked that she didn't know the number and sent it to voice mail. The second time, she and Gregory were both recovering, sweat drying, hearts slowing. "Just making sure Matty doesn't need something."

It was Mrs. Hutch, Matty's science teacher.

Fern mouthed the word *Shit* to Gregory and rolled to a sitting position.

"I need to talk to you briefly about Matty's ambition."

Well, that was something, at least. Mrs. Hutch had never started out that way before. Maybe there was hope. "Okay."

Fern started to stand so she could move to another room, to do this by herself, but Gregory cupped her free elbow and made her feel caught in a good way, caught as if she'd been falling and hadn't known it until her downward trajectory had been halted.

"Well, you know. We've talked about this before. Not all children can be at the top of the class, and sometimes we have to help them help themselves."

Is he on welfare or something? "Okay . . ."

Gregory lit a clove cigarette, and before he could even inhale, Fern took it from him. It crackled, and the smoke felt thick in her mouth. Protective.

"It's the science project. I feel . . . he's taken on a bit too much."

Fern's brain felt light, a feather in her head. "He said you approved it."

"I did. I didn't quite grasp, at that point, how much he was trying to do."

"It's not that much."

"Mrs. Reyes." She pronounced it Ray-jus. A *güera* trying to affect an appropriate Spanish pronunciation. "Matty's trying to learn a new motor skill while proving a theory about chemical composition and transformation within a classroom setting he already finds extremely challenging."

Motor skills. Like her kid had trouble walking or something. "Matty's a smart boy."

Silence met her words, and Fern's blood pressure shot up to the top of her head. What was the damn teacher's first name again? "Jane. Can I call you Jane?"

Another pause. "Actually, I prefer Mrs. Hutch. It keeps it simpler in regards to the parent–teacher relationship. I'm sure you understand."

"Of course." Fern literally saw the color red against her eyelids, but she managed to keep her voice even. "My son is more than intelligent enough to successfully complete the assignment. I'm fully confident of that."

"I wonder, Mrs. Ray-jus, do you remember our pencil conversation?"

Of course she did. Mrs. Hutch had asked her to keep Matty supplied with a full box of sharpened pencils because his need for a newly sharpened one during the middle of class was distracting to the other students. "He has pencils every day. I've been making sure of that."

"Well, be that as it may, he's still getting up in the middle of class to use the sharpener."

"It's hard for him to sit still." *When he's in a place he hates to be, that is.* Of course Matty got restless. He was a kid and he knew his teacher didn't like him. What kind of motivation was that for him to sit quietly in one spot?

"Mrs. Ray-jus, I'm thinking we should get him tested."

"For what, fleas?"

Another silence was her punishment.

"I'm sorry. Go on."

"I'm concerned he might have ADHD." Was Fern imagining it, or was Mrs. Hutch enjoying this? The carefully dropped voice, the acronym almost whispered as if it were a dirty secret.

"He doesn't."

"Yes, I find that's normally the response parents have at first."

Something about the woman's voice made Fern want to hurt her, to resort to actual physical violence. A quick pinch to the upper arm, a knee to the crotch. Poor Matty, having to put up with her for five hours a week. This woman brought out the worst in Fern and she had adult levels of impulse control. "Well, I'd have no problem if he did have ADHD, but he doesn't. In fourth grade, his teacher actually thought he might have it, too. So we tested him. He doesn't have it."

"Oh."

Yeah, *oh*. Bitch.

"Well, I'm relieved to hear that. I didn't see that in his file."

Fern waited for the apology, but it didn't come.

"So I'd like to talk to you about assigning him an easier project."

She leaned into Gregory's thumb. He rubbed a spot on her shoulder she hadn't even known was tight. "Like what?"

"Germination. I think he'd enjoy that."

"Germination?"

"Putting seeds into dirt, watering them, measuring the results."

"I *know* what germination is." Sweet baby *Cristo*. "He loved that project when he was six. It was very exciting back then. We got radishes." They'd had radishes for months. Those damn things were the only thing her backyard had ever really liked growing besides those weird black-and-white tulips the dog was named after. Nobody in the house would even *eat* the radishes. "I think you're underestimating my boy. You're aware his father died recently?" There. She'd done it. She'd played the dead-dad card, and she hadn't even seen it coming—it was so inappropriate she hadn't ever bothered wasting time worrying she might do it.

"Yes. I'm sorry for your loss." Mrs. Hutch's voice was flat. "I'm also aware they were estranged."

Fury leaped through Fern's body—an electrical storm of anger, perforating her skin and bone. But there was no good answer. It was true. Matty was mourning a shadow. She took a shaky breath. "What you're obviously *not* aware of is who he's working with on the project. His stepmother is a renowned botanist. Great woman. I mean, Scott obviously had good taste." Gregory snorted next to her and grinned. "She's also grieving, of course, I'm sure you can understand. I think it's been doing them good to work on this together, even though it's hard for Matty to get to North Berkeley to work with her every day as he has been. But my kid's dedicated." *Gets that from me.*

"Ah. North Berkeley?"

It was sick, terrible, that she knew what to say, and how to play it. "Up by Solano, you know the area? *Huge* house, enormous garden, which has been a boon to the project. Would it help if she came in to talk to you? If we came in together?"

"Well. I didn't know he had an actual botanist in the family."

Of course you didn't. "I'm sure she wouldn't mind." And Abby probably wouldn't. She'd jump at the chance.

And then, in Fern's chest, something released. It relaxed the same way the knot in her neck was loosening under Gregory's hands. Abby would help.

More than that, bigger than that—Fern would let her.

The knowledge felt like being on Gregory's bed. It was one of those memory-foam mattresses, and when she'd first lain on it—okay, she hadn't noticed a damn thing the first time she'd put her back on it, because she'd been fucking Gregory. But the second time, she'd thought it was wonderful, the way it held her up, the way her body sank down only an inch at most. The firmness felt like strength, something she didn't have at home when she lay on her old, sagging mattress with the springs that squeaked no matter how quietly she tried to get up in the morning.

Fern hung up the phone, shoving it away from her. Curling into a tight ball, she turned so that her forearms were against Gregory's chest, her legs tangled with his. His breath warmed her forehead. "Bitch," she said.

"Sounds like it. What are you going to do about it?"

"Play the game." Fern shut her eyes. The darkness felt warm, there in the circle of his arms. *I want a comfortable bed that won't hurt my back.* Lucinda Williams wasn't wrong about that.

"Games are okay sometimes. They get the job done."

She imagined Matty, the way his face looked when he was playing Minecraft. His jaw went slack, as did his shoulders, but his eyes stayed focused, his alertness high. He held both in his body—keen attention and total relaxation—at the same time. "I can't stand it that she makes these judgments and doesn't play fair. How the hell am I supposed to motivate him to keep fighting her? To keep winning?"

Gregory's lips touched her hairline. "You can tell a lot about a person by what he does when he loses. What does Matty do?"

The time he couldn't figure out how to make the tetherball work. Long division. That city-building board game that his friend James had loved but made him feel all thumbs. It had been impossible to motivate him to keep going, to keep trying at any of them. "He stops playing. It's not fun for him anymore, so he just stops, no hard feelings."

"So if he's playing a rigged system, he'd stop playing, right?"

"You think that's what's happening in her class?"

"Sounds like he can't do right by the teacher. Why would he keep trying?"

Because that's what you do. Even when you can't win, you keep driving the fucking bus as long as they'll let you, as long as your body doesn't let you down. You hold it all together.

Gregory was right. Matty was smart enough to know that the system was rigged. And he wasn't motivated to win the way some people were, like Fern was. Matty just wanted to have a good time. That was his motivation. There was a clean, sweet relief in the realization, along with the frustration that went along with it. "So, what, he just gives up as he goes along? Where does that leave you, if you don't play the game the right way?"

Gregory pushed the edge of the pillow farther under his cheek. "Well, if you get a master's in economics and don't want to go into the family business because your old man's a jerk and instead decide to move to the Bay Area, where you can rent a one-bedroom for an amount that would keep a thousand families alive in the Sudan, and then decide to become an adjunct professor at three different adult schools, guaranteeing you'll never make enough to pay off your student loans, well, then . . . You end up in bed with a pretty woman, sweet enough to make you fall in love with her and stubborn enough to try to stop you—well, I'm just saying. He could end up worse off."

Fern touched Gregory's face, traced the line at his nose that ran into a dimple farther south, an inch above his jaw. "I'm not sure what part of what you just said is the nicest."

"Sometimes the ones you can't motivate turn out just fine."

"Says the guy who's in debt, in a rental, and in a couple of jobs he doesn't like."

"And in your arms." He grinned.

It was possibly the cheesiest line Fern had ever heard. And she loved it. "Technically, I'm in yours."

"Even better." He kissed her eyebrow again. "Let him be who he's going to be."

"What if that's a burned-out skater living in a squat?"

"He's a great kid. He'll be fine. The squat will be better for him being there."

"You don't even know him."

"So introduce me."

chapter *forty-seven*

Abby hid. Rather, she dropped. Off the radar, out of sight—she was a chunk of concrete dropped off the Bay Bridge pedestrian walkway, invisible six inches from the rail, completely nonexistent by the time it hit water.

She wouldn't be able to hold this baby inside her body (who was she kidding, even trying to?), but she also wouldn't be able to keep it a secret from them, from Fern and Matty, the ones who mattered the most now. She couldn't keep that kind of secret. She just couldn't. They might hate her—they might think this had been her plan (it hadn't—god, who made a plan like that?). Abby felt in her bones that the knowledge of this baby might destroy every chance she had with them.

She had no idea what to do. All she knew was she had to figure it out—she had to find the time to determine exactly how she could hurt the fewest people, for the shortest duration.

She needed time to think.

She sent an e-mail to Fern: *Great news! I got a fellowship at a botany retreat. The bad news is I'll be gone for three weeks. If you could just keep track of the hours you work, I'll settle up as soon as I get home. Tell Matty to keep knitting. And to get some onion skins. He should be able to get some from any produce market, just by asking to clean out the bin. We'll do the dyeing when I get back.*

She hit send, even though she had no idea how she'd be able to stand being near Matty, knowing she was carrying his cousin, knowing she would lose it (kill it—her body *killed* babies) like she always, always did.

She e-mailed Kathryn: *Last-minute chance to get out of town. Will call you when I'm back in three weeks.* Kathryn would know a fellowship at a botany retreat was bullshit. The less lying, the better.

She didn't have to explain a thing to Brook. "I need to get out of town for a while. Can you take me to the airport? And can you watch Tulip for me while I'm gone?"

Brook only said, "Pack me in your suitcase? Please?"

The next morning, Brook drove Abby to SFO. Tulip panted in the car's backseat, no worse for the onion wear. "Sorry it's so early," Abby said. "I appreciate the ride."

Brook looked pleased to have been picked. She parked in the white zone and touched Abby's hand. "I'm just stoked you're doing something to make yourself happy. Are you sure you don't want to tell me where you're going?"

"I told you, I don't know. I'm being totally honest. I want you to get a surprise postcard from me."

"Bora-Bora?"

"Maybe."

"Edinburgh? Reykjavík?"

"Wait for the postcard." Abby kissed Brook's cheek. "Thank you for taking care of Tulip while I'm gone."

She waved the car out of sight, and then she entered the international terminal. Inside, the ceilings soared over her, and the clamor of passengers made her hands shake. She held her suitcase handle more tightly. She'd packed for contingencies. She'd put four books on her Kindle, all travel memoirs (China, Italy, Antarctica, and Russia). She'd packed a bathing suit and a heavy sweater. Heels and hiking boots. She would just walk the terminal until she saw a sign that pointed somewhere she felt like going.

But what if a flight was enough to do it? To shake the fetus loose? Abby cupped her hands at her low belly, a move that she'd done so many times in the past it felt natural. And useless.

Abby turned and headed for ground transportation. She bought a BART ticket to North Berkeley. On the train, she closed her eyes and pretended to be one of those commuters who were so tired they fell asleep on their way home. She couldn't tell if anyone was looking at her, but with her eyes shut, she felt invisible.

She walked home from the station.

Then Abby dead-bolted the door and then drew the chain, something she almost never did. The house felt emptier than it ever had, even emptier than it had right after Scott died. She'd gotten used to Tulip's thumps and snorts, the way his nails sounded on the hardwood, the sound of his jaws chewing something inappropriate, the edge of a door or the top of a table.

She took off her clothes and got in bed, folding her hands again over her belly. It wasn't even noon. She had three weeks of aloneness. Maybe she could send a fake postcard or three and push it to a month. Working on this, the only important project in the world.

She'd have to tell Diego eventually. Abby knew that—she

just didn't know how to *do* it. If she were a different person, she'd never tell him at all. If she could, she'd stay here alone, all biological needs paused except the need to grow this child.

Wishes.

Later today Abby would have to get up and drink water—the filtered water from the Brita. She'd have to eat—she would order organic fruit and meat from Andronico's and have it delivered.

She had no intention of hurting herself, which, she realized, was the way it might look to the outside world.

It was the opposite, in fact.

She wanted to take care of herself. She'd done it wrong the first three times. Maybe this time, if she stayed still and quiet and alone, maybe if she kept her feet up, maybe if she ate right and drank right and slept right and hoped right—maybe if she hoped so hard that the wish became a bright color, a sweet scent—maybe this would stick. Grief filled her limbs, old blue-green algae that threatened to swamp her body when she rolled from one side to the other. Had this been what her mother had felt after losing Meg, when she was carrying Abby? The surety she wasn't enough to make a viable baby? (But, Abby! So viable! Still viable, even after three miscarriages. Still breathing. Hoping.)

Maybe this time Abby would be enough for a baby. Or (just maybe) the baby would make her enough. Redemption. Poor thing, to have to hold such an enormous, inappropriate word in hands that were probably still webbed, a clump of cells that couldn't survive outside her body.

But maybe. Abby clutched the word in her hands, storing it at night under her pillow next to the sachet she'd filled with lemon balm and nettle leaf and hope.

chapter *forty-eight*

The trip to the farmers' market had been Gregory's idea.
"Almost every stall has bins of onions. We'll ask for
them. It's not like anyone else uses them, right?"

Fern had Googled onion skins—turned out they weren't
just something you could go out and buy. "That's a good idea."

"And, hey. I could meet Matty then." Gregory said it so
simply that it actually sounded that way. Uncomplicated.
Sure, why not? Matty was old enough. He understood that
she dated. He'd never expressed interest in meeting anyone
before, but that was probably due to the fact that she'd never
been serious about anyone before.

Not that she was really serious about Gregory. Fern might
be clearer in her head about him if she didn't have Abby so
heavy on her mind.

Damn Abby and her skipping out, just like that. Who
promised to help a kid with a science project and then took

off? Fern had been fine for the last three weeks—she had plenty of Taking Care work that she could do from home. But Matty looked worried when he held out his almost-completed hat (*Is this part supposed to look like this? Did I do this right?*), and Fern had no idea what to tell him. Abby had been supposed to be home three days ago, but she hadn't returned any of Fern's e-mails yet.

Disappointment split the lanes of worry in her mind like a motorcycle threading traffic. What if Fern had just been plain wrong to go into business with Abby? The worry was electric, reminding her of the way she felt before a seizure— a mental wind that kicked up tiny but devastating dust storms. After the first two weeks of Abby's being gone without a single text or e-mail returned, Fern had stopped putting Ciela off. She'd worked three shifts at Ensenada so far. Abby wasn't coming back, if in fact she'd ever even left. Botany fellowship. Fern had a built-in bullshit detector, and that sounded like nothing more than total crap.

The money was good enough at the restaurant, the change and dollar bills heavy in her pocket as she left, making up for the physical stress of the job.

She'd had a seizure after her first shift. She'd been at home, blessedly alone. She'd come to alone, and she'd cleaned up the blood from her mouth alone. Diego had brought Matty home soon afterward, and even though he *thought* she'd had a seizure, he couldn't prove it. What could she do? They needed the money.

The worst part was that Fern knew she'd never drive her bus again—one seizure from stress was one thing, but two? She wasn't safe, not anymore. She couldn't take the job even if they offered it back to her. Fern could see this truth in the corner of her eye—she could *feel* it—but she tried not to look at it. It was too hard, too painful. Like staring into the sun.

"Fern?" Gregory was still there, still looking at her.

Then, because Gregory's eyes were soft, because he was there, because he seemed to really *want* to be there, to be wherever she was, and because all of those added up to something happy and warm in her chest, Fern said, "Yes. You can meet Matty."

On Saturday, the farmers' market at Jack London was in full swing. The first truly warm day of spring, there was an excitement in the air that had nothing to do with baby broccoli or the shilling of lemon-verbena handmade soaps. Leaves were full on the sycamores. Tulips, planted by the city, bloomed happily in the huge ceramic urns. (*Don't think of the dog,* willed Fern, watching Matty's face. *Don't think of that damn Tulip.*) The estuary sparkled, boats bobbing past Alameda on their way to the bay. The air smelled of diesel and salt and heated caramel from the kettle corn sold from every other booth.

At the dock, Matty hung over the railing and watched the kayakers paddle past. "Can I do that someday?"

He could do anything he wanted. Fern would give him everything she could. "Okay."

"This summer?"

"Maybe. If we can get the money together for it."

"Sweet. I can get a job."

"You don't need to do that, *mijo.*"

"Under the table, I mean. Sergio's brother is thirteen, and he's making like fifty bucks a night busing tables at his dad's restaurant."

"I think that's illegal. Watch your elbow." Something

white and soft was smeared on the railing, a gift from a passing seabird.

"Ew! Bird caca! I almost touched that! No, he's just helping. His dad calls it his allowance."

Numbers spun sweetly in Fern's mind, a well-oiled wheel. "How many nights a week?"

"Is this a trick? Are you going to get him in trouble?"

"Do I look like a narc to you?"

Matty giggled, and a child wobbling past on shaky toddler legs laughed as if in agreement. "I think they let him work every night he wants to. Which is like every night, because he's saving up for a Mustang, one of those old ones, when he's sixteen. He's all responsible and stuff, I guess. I just want the new WWE. And to kayak. That's all."

Fern ignored Matty's puppy eyes. There would be no new video game, and if he thought about it, he would already know that. "So you're saying he gets an 'allowance' of three hundred fifty dollars a week? That sounds more like a paycheck to me. Which is, like I said, illegal."

"Whatever it is, it's good. He buys a Frappuccino every day before he comes to school and those are like five dollars or something."

The wind ruffled Matty's short hair and Fern stuck her hands in her jeans pockets so she wouldn't do the same. "You don't even like coffee."

"That's not even coffee, Mom. It's like a milk shake."

Mom. It used to be *Mamá.* Before that, it was *Mami.* Did they send out little-boy memos? When would he get the one that said he had to turn sullen? When would he get the one that said he could no longer hang out with her on the water in bright spring sunshine, watching the ducks bob and dive in the oil-sheened water?

"Where's your boyfriend, anyway?" Matty looked at his phone. "He's late."

"By like one minute. And there he is." *He's not my boyfriend.* She should have corrected him.

But damn. In that second, as she saw Gregory grin. Oh, god. He *was* her boyfriend. As usual, she was practically the last to know.

"Hi," he said to her. He looked off-balance, moving as if to kiss her, and then stopping himself. Awkwardly, he held up his palm, and just as awkwardly, Fern high-fived him.

"So. This is Matty."

"Matty. Hiya." Gregory was nervous, she realized. "It's good to meet you, man."

Man.

Matty gave a tight, polite smile. "Hello."

"So." Gregory rocked back on his heels, but the concrete step he stood on wobbled, and he pitched backward. "Shit." He righted himself before he fell. "Shit, shit. I mean, sorry for swearing. Fuck."

It couldn't have been planned, but it worked. Matty snorted. "Smooth. We have a swear jar, you know."

"How much?"

Matty cocked his head. "Five bucks."

Gregory got out his wallet.

"Matty! We don't have a— Where did you even *get* that idea from?"

"Mrs. Simms has one on her desk in math." Matty grinned. "Just kidding. I wanted to see if he would believe me."

"Of course he would. He already knows you don't lie."

"Yeah, I *never* lie." Matty rolled his eyes. "Ever."

Gregory laughed.

It was funny. There Fern was, having a funny moment with her son and her boyfriend. A fishing boat blasted its horn as it made its way around a small sailboat awkwardly tacking toward the cranes. A seagull complained cheerfully overhead. She wrapped her arms around herself and hugged because her arms needed to hug someone, and neither of the guys looked like he would appreciate her doing it to him. Not right now. Later, she'd hug both of them so hard they wouldn't know what hit them. Fern, the bus of love.

"Speaking of lying," said Gregory, "this was kind of just a ruse to get you both down here. I know a better place to get onion skins than begging all these vendors, one by one."

"You do?"

"You willing to take a chance?"

Matty lifted one shoulder and let it drop, but his face was bright, probably brighter than he knew. "I guess."

"Fern?"

"Okay?" *Don't hurt my boy.*

He held up three slips of paper. "When was the last time you took the ferry to the city?"

Dios. Matty had always wanted to ride the ferry, but on her days off she never had time to waste an hour going to the city and an hour back just to be on a boat. He'd been supposed to go to Alcatraz on a school field trip when he was eight, but he'd had strep throat that week. She'd never gotten around to making it up to him.

"Seriously? Mom?" Matty's eyes looked desperate, as if he thought she might say no.

"Are you kidding me? I can't fucking wait." It was a

deliberate curse, one she could just afford. She dug the five-dollar bill out of her purse and handed it to him. "Here, take this for the boat instead of ye olde nonexistent swear jar. I think they have hot chocolate on board."

"Oh, *yeah*," said Matty, and started off toward the ferry waiting area at a pace faster than a jog, slower than a run. His knees were stiff, locked as if he were a robot, which at that moment in his mind, he probably was. Matty was still young enough to pretend, and old enough to know he shouldn't tell anyone that's what he was doing.

Gregory took her hand. "What a nice kid." He pulled away, and her fingers felt cold immediately. "Crap. Is this okay?"

Fern glanced ahead—Matty was out of sight, on the other side of an orchid vendor. She turned to face him. She went up on tiptoes and kissed him. "Yes."

Gregory looked up at the blue sky overhead. "There's no fog."

"For once."

"We've never kissed outside before."

"I bet you're right."

"I'm not saying I have to kiss you all the way to San Francisco."

"Good."

He grinned, and Fern's stomach tightened. "But I'll want to. Just so you know."

"Good," she said again.

chapter *forty~nine*

Three weeks and three days after she'd left on her nontrip, on a sunny Saturday afternoon Abby finally managed to get out of bed and actually go outside. Her drip irrigation had kept the vegetables alive—the kale was still coming in even though it was warming up, and the parsley was growing as if its goal was to take over the yard. But something was eating the onions, and her hellebores had withered, as if they missed her daily pep talk. Her coreopsis was failing to thrive.

She knew the feeling.

There was a hole in the ground just to the south of the shed. It was a good, sunny spot. She'd been going to put in a pomegranate tree, planning to keep it small and espaliered. She'd bought a bare root one and left it in its burlap bag. Now it was dead, a dry stick with no promise left.

The hole was still there, though.

Abby stood on the edge of it, her bare toes dipping down. Loose dirt tumbled in. The hole wasn't bigger than a foot across. It wasn't good for anything but planting a tree in.

Or a phone.

Diego had texted her twice while she'd been "gone," sweet notes. Apparently his sister hadn't told him that she was off-limits, and Abby hadn't had a chance to. *Would love to see you again. I know that's crazy. But crazy can be good sometimes. . . .*

Kathryn had texted, too: *I thought you'd be back by now. Call me when you're home, I'll bring over some homemade granola, the crunchy kind you like.*

Abby held her iPhone above the hole. She could just drop it. That's all it would take. She could bury it, kicking dirt over it, scrabbling earth into the hole with her bare hands. In a year, a message tree would grow. It would look like one of those fake trees, the ones they put on hillsides, the ones that were actually cell phone towers made to look like trees (Abby always spotted them, the desperate evenness of their branches, the way no tree in the world would be so symmetrical). From its branches would flow voice mails of guilt, text messages of disappointment, e-mails of blame.

Abby sat, heavily, her feet shoved into the hole. Maybe if she waited long enough, someone would cover her feet with the extra dirt. They would fertilize her (no, wait, she was already fertilized). She would grow into something that looked more natural than a cell phone tree, but produced the same amount of dismay and disruption.

Her phone buzzed—she'd managed to silence it, but she hadn't figured out how to turn off its vibration. It was angry, a cursing wasp.

It was a photo text from Matty. His hat. It was still the

light silver of the wool she'd given him, still undyed. And it was perfect. She could see, even at the small resolution, how well he was making his stitches now. His decreases were even and perfectly placed.

Her heart gave a thump that threatened to kill her right there, her feet still in the hole. He must have learned how to decrease like that from someone else. Or he could have learned from YouTube. She didn't know which would be worse. It was followed by another text that read, *I'm getting onion skins right now. I'm on the ferry!*

While she was looking at the phone's face, it rang.

Diego.

She hit ignore on the phone.

A minute later, she had a voice mail. *Voice* mail. It struck her as archaic—the voice, used as a communication device. Most people either e-mailed or texted when they needed something, but Diego had admitted to her that he wasn't good at spelling and that he'd always been self-conscious about it. On one of their two nights together, he'd held his hands up toward the ceiling and moved his fingers. "Good for nothing but gripping trees."

Abby had been able to think of a couple other things he'd already shown her his hands were pretty good at. "Don't you use gloves?" she'd asked.

"Supposed to."

"But you don't?"

"Sometimes you just need to feel the bark. These big old things can't type on a tiny cell phone. If I have something to say to you"—he'd turned to her with a grin—"I'll say it with my mouth. The mouth is the best thing for communicating there is." Then he'd moved down her body and proved it.

Now, her feet still in the hole, she listened to his voice. "I'm up a tree right now, pretty near your house, over by the new Catholic church they're building. They need a sick poplar taken out. I just thought . . ." He cleared his throat. "I just thought if you were back in town, and if you got this, you could call me back. Or come see me. Maybe you can convince me you haven't changed your mind about being Fern and Matty's friend. 'Cause I think they might think that. And that—I gotta tell you, Abby—that would piss me off. I'm fine. You don't have to see me again if you don't want to. But them—anyway." The message clicked and went dead.

Abby's car coughed when she started it. She hadn't driven it in weeks. It felt funny to be behind the wheel. The seat belt was shorter now.

Diego's truck was in the dirt parking lot near the new church. She scanned the trees for the diseased poplar he'd mentioned, and she found his orange vest high up in a wildly overgrown tree, at least a hundred feet up.

It was probably for the best that Diego didn't text much. *I'm pregnant.* Her text—invisible and dangerous—flew with a swoop out of her phone, across the dirt lot, over the construction, and up the tree.

She watched him. He was too far away for her to make out his features. She couldn't see his expression. But she could see his limbs—she watched him swing sideways, reach an arm out to steady himself. He would be looking at his phone—he'd told her he kept it tethered to his body with a small bungee so that if he had to glance at it, he couldn't drop it and kill someone standing below.

His body stiffened.

The fuck.

She tapped a message back. *I don't want anything from you.*

The tiny orange figure swung wildly, legs kicking.

Is that u? In the parking lot?

What had she been thinking? What if he shimmied down—no, she could still hit the engine, peel out, beat him to her house, shoot the dead bolt, hide under her covers. *No.* A stupid, necessary lie. *I'm only telling you because it's the right thing to do. It won't stick.*

Her phone buzzed furiously in her hand. Of course he would call her. She was a fool for not thinking he might.

Abby hit the answer button. "It never sticks. This will be the fourth child I've lost."

"You know you could have *killed* me?" One orange arm was raised, as if he was shaking his fist at her.

"I'm sorry." She should have thought. Why had it seemed like a good idea? She'd just wanted to watch him find out. . . . She hadn't thought further than that.

"We used condoms."

"Well, yeah. One must have failed."

"Failed? Shit. Are you sure it's mine?"

It felt as if his tree had fallen directly on top of her. She was smashed, flat, almost dead. But she supposed it was a fair question. Her husband had only been dead three and a half months. "Yes."

"You're sure. Because I've never knocked anyone up. I thought I couldn't do it."

"You can."

"Well."

It didn't sound like a question, but she answered it anyway.

"That's why I took myself out of the equation. I'm just kind of . . . waiting. Just till it passes." *Maybe it wouldn't pass. Please let it not pass.*

"Abby." The orange figure swung back and forth slowly, a tiny plastic-looking pendulum. He'd taken his feet and hands off the tree and was hanging by his harness. "How can I help? Tell me what to do."

She was the same, dangling in midair. "Don't worry about it. Like I said, I lose babies. Give me another couple of weeks and I won't be pregnant anymore."

"So you don't want to be pregnant."

"I *do*." Should she even admit that to him? How was that fair?

"What does the doctor say?"

"That I'm having a baby." The doctor was the only other one who knew. She hadn't even told Brook yet. She'd taken Tulip back and closed the door, refusing to say where she'd been. She didn't know what to say . . . not yet.

"Jesus Christ. When?"

"In December." It was a stark and impossible eternity of good luck away. "But it won't stick."

"That's what you keep saying. What do you want me to do?"

"Nothing. I don't want anything from you. You don't have to be involved at all."

"Then why the *fuck* are you telling me?"

Why was she? She touched the steering wheel lightly with her left hand. "Because."

"Great answer. How far along are you, anyway? Eight, nine weeks? That's how long it's been since you called me, by the way. And telling me now that the baby I might have fathered is about to die inside you, no matter what, am I getting that right?"

He was getting it right. Abby was the one who'd gotten it so very, very wrong.

His words were low and urgent. "The right thing to do would have been not to run away. The right thing would have been to let me help. A *baby*." Something on the line crackled, either his voice or a branch. "What do you want me to do here, Abby?"

"Nothing. I'm sorry. I thought I had to tell you. . . ."

A heavy sigh. "Of course you had to tell me. But this was the wrong way."

He didn't say good-bye. The only thing she heard was a click and then silence. The distant orange man reattached his limbs to the tree, and started climbing upward, his tiny movements measured. Sensible.

And Abby, still sitting in her car, dropped through the air. Miles and miles of coldness opened beneath her and she had no harness.

There was nothing to catch her, nothing at all.

chapter *fifty*

Matty talked about the ferry ride all the way home. "And then we saw the dolphin!"

"We weren't sure it was a dolphin, you know that, right? Take this corner slow, okay?"

Gregory nodded. John Prine's "Angel from Montgomery" crooned low from his stereo. *Just give me one thing that I can hold on to.*

"Because the Ybarra kids always play kickball on the sidewalk, and every once in a while, they pop out into the street like a Ping-Pong ball."

From the backseat, Matty laughed as if the words had been dirty somehow. "Ping-ping singsong," he said and laughed again. "Ping-poingy-poing."

Gregory grinned.

"I'm serious. Two of the kids have been tapped by cars already. Not hurt, *gracias a Dios*, because there's no other reason for it. Their idiot parents don't tell them to stay out of the road. What if the bus ran here? Instead of a block away."

"Then they'd probably keep their kids out of the street," Gregory said lightly.

"Maybe."

"I'm being careful, Fern."

"I know." He was. He was a gorgeous driver. He would be good behind the wheel of a bus.

"Ping-Pong! Dolphin! The captain said it could have *totally* been a dolphin."

The man Matty had spoken to hadn't been a captain—he'd been the bartender, serving mochas and vodka tonics. But he'd worn a captain's hat, and had let Matty wear it for a minute, too. Matty was convinced he'd seen a dolphin leap near a leg of the new Bay Bridge, and Gregory, bless him, was backing him up now. "Coulda been. Looked like it."

Gregory had been good with Matty. Not in a creepy way, not in a dad way. Just in a guy way. Agreeing with him on the dolphin. Disagreeing with him on *Mad Max*. Talking to him like he was a person, not just some kid.

"And the wind! It blew that tourist's hat right off his head into the water. That was *hilarious*."

Gregory pulled up in front of the house. She swore the front gate was even more crooked than it had been when they left— was it possible that gravity had a greater pull in this corner of Oakland? It would explain why nothing stayed standing in this neighborhood the way it did elsewhere. In Montclair and Piedmont and Rockridge, old houses just got old. They didn't slope and slant until they tipped right over. They held up. Here, it was like the earth quaked more. Harder.

"The wind didn't take *your* hat, though," she said.

Matty tugged it lower on his forehead. "That's because it's made good."

"That's probably it. And maybe because you never took your hand off it once." He hadn't—while they'd been up on the top deck, watching the city get bigger as if it were magically growing—he'd kept one hand on his head the whole time. Just in case.

"It would have stayed on, though. Even if I hadn't."

"I know." Stupid hat. What if her suspicion was right? What if Abby really never came back?

Matty *needed* her to come back. Why couldn't he just get hurt by an eleven-year-old girl at school? A simple Valentine's Day failure, a playground misunderstanding. He'd been hurt by his father for so long—it was beyond unfair that his first heartbreak by a woman might be by his father's wife.

But Abby would come back. She would.

Fern hated that she couldn't tell whom she was hoping it was true more for: Matty or herself.

"Look! Maybe he brought pizza!" Matty was out of the car and running up the walkway toward Diego before Gregory could finish putting the car in park. "*¡Tío, Tío!* Did you bring pizza?"

Diego nodded, and Fern's heart lifted. Pizza. Her brother. Beers on the front porch. Or in the kitchen, or in the backyard—it didn't matter where they hung out. She needed—wanted—to be with her brother tonight.

"Heartstopper from the Lanesplitter," he said.

"*Yes,*" yelled Matty. "That's my favorite kind!"

"You sure this is still okay?" Gregory's voice was quiet next to her. "You don't have to introduce me to everyone in your life all in one day."

"I'm sure." For once, something was easy.

Gregory followed her up the walkway. "Diego, this is Gregory. Gregory, my brother." She felt heat rush to the base of her skull. "Matty, go get some paper plates."

Matty boggled. "Really?"

She'd bought them for his ninth birthday party. The hundred-pack had been on sale at the SavMart. Fern hoarded them. Doing dishes was cheaper. But what else did she have them for?

"Go on." She looked at Diego. "Are Grandpa Wyatt and Elva here?"

"They are. But they went into Wyatt's room." Diego waited until Matty had run inside and then he switched to a stage whisper. "I heard a couple of things I wish I hadn't heard. I brought enough pizza for them, too, but I think we should wait a while. If you know what I mean."

"No, no, no. Stop talking. We'll stay out here. I hope Matty is quick."

Gregory sat on the top step. Fern sat on the swing next to her brother. Night was falling like purple velvet, a promise of the summer to come. Two of the Ybarra kids raced past the house, laughing, followed by two new white puppies. None of them spoke for a moment. It could have been an awkward silence, but it wasn't. She leaned companionably on Diego's arm, and Gregory looked upward at the rosy clouds. In another town, this would be the time for the fireflies to come out and dance. Here, they had mosquitoes and motorcycle exhaust, but those were just as welcome to Fern. This was *her* over-grown yard, *her* purple-and-red-streaked sky, *her* boys bump-ing around her, knocking into her knees, holding up her heart.

Matty ate pizza with his mouth open and told Diego about the dolphins and the captain and the fact that he had two entire grocery bags full of red onion skins from the vendor guy Gregory knew at the San Francisco Ferry Building.

"You're gonna dye that hat, huh? For your project?"

"Yeah!" Matty tugged it lower on his head.

"When's the science fair?"

"Three weeks."

Fern could almost *see* her brother thinking about Abby. She tapped Matty's woolen head. "We make a good team, this kid and me. He's been doing the knitting on his own with some help from YouTube, but I found the Web site on natural dyeing. We're good to go. I mean, just in case Abby doesn't get home from her trip in time."

"But she will," said Matty.

"Yep." Fern was the one helping Matty now. She'd even picked up a pair of needles, too, something she hadn't done since she was a kid. YouTube had reminded her that she still knew how to knit, and she was still pretty bad at it. Suddenly, her shoulders ached, as if she'd been carrying Matty's backpack all day instead of just the last few hours of their trip.

Diego grinned at Matty. "You're gonna show that old bitch of a teacher, huh?"

"Diego!"

"Come on. We all hate Mrs. Hutch."

Matty laughed. "Yeah, Mom. We all hate her."

"We're not supposed to admit that, though."

Gregory wiped his mouth with a paper napkin. "Even I hate her, Fern."

"Good man." Diego pointed a finger gun at Gregory and shot. Then he turned back to Matty. "But you only have the one hat? How are you going to set it up, like, so that she sees the original color, and then sees you dyed it red with the onions?"

"Technically"—Matty pronounced it carefully in four syllables—"it's going to come out closer to brown or orange, not red, like you'd think. It's chemistry. We tried it on a little bit of white yarn the other night. And I'm just going to make another hat. Maybe two more. To show."

"Just like that."

"Yeah, well, now I'm faster." The Ybarra kids and dogs ran past going the other way. Matty threw down his paper plate. "I wanna go see those puppies."

Fern sat up straighter. "Be careful. Don't run into the road."

"Not a moron, Mom." He clattered out the gate and chased after the pack.

He wasn't a moron. He was smart enough to get by. Like her. Like her brother. Fern bumped Diego's shoulder. "What did we do to deserve pizza, huh?"

She expected him to say something disparaging. Something funny to make Gregory laugh. Instead, he said, "Ah. You know."

"What happened?"

"Why do you think something happened?"

Her spider-senses went on alert. Something to do with Abby. It had to be. "Think? I know."

"Nah."

Gregory glanced at her. "You want me to take off?"

"Yes," said Fern, the word automatic. Worry juddered in her chest, and she didn't care that she sounded rude.

"You're cool, man." But Diego's legs jiggled and he thrummed his fingertips against the arm of the old porch swing.

"Yeah, well, I have a million midterms to grade and even though I've been damn good at keeping them out of my mind all day, I can't put them off much longer." He rubbed his hands on his thighs and stood. "Diego, man." They shook hands. "Good to meet you."

"I'm sorry—" Fern didn't waste time trying to make her words convincing. Something was wrong with Diego and she was irritated with herself that she hadn't noticed right off the bat. "Okay. I'll walk you out?"

At the car, she kissed Gregory hard, because she meant it, because she meant a lot of things she didn't feel like saying.

But he pulled back. "Who takes care of you?"

"What? Diego does." She tried to laugh it off. "He brought pizza. That's not bad, right?"

"I'm not going to wait forever."

It wasn't like she didn't know what he was talking about. "I know."

"I want to be with you. That means something to me. I fit into little pockets of your life, but I know I don't fit in here, with your family. That's been fine up till now. But someday it won't be fine."

Fern looked at the ground. "I'm sorry."

"I just need you to know. I'm pretty patient. But I'm not a saint. Someday I'll want more." Gregory's eyes were impossibly, heartbreakingly kind. "Or I'll want less."

"I know." Her voice was almost a whisper. It was all the breath she could grab.

He said, "What about you, Fern? When do you get your turn?"

She would have said, *I'm good,* but she couldn't—she wasn't—so she tugged the strings of his A's hoodie and kissed him one more time, hoping he'd feel what she meant, what she couldn't say.

chapter *fifty~one*

When she was back on the porch, Diego said, "I'm glad you didn't make me witness that good-bye." He smiled vaguely. "Kissing stuff. Super annoying."

Fern shook her head to clear it. She would have to worry about Gregory later. "What happened?"

"Eh."

"What did she do?" It was Abby. It *had* to be Abby.

"It's what we did." He blinked, and for a sudden terrifying moment, Fern thought her brother was about to cry. But then, the next second, there was nothing on his face but anger, so stark and white it scared her. "She's pregnant."

"The *fuck*."

He slumped. "Exactly what I said."

Fern hit him on the shoulder. She wanted to do it with her car. With her bus. "*¿Tu eres un idiota?* Seriously?"

"We used condoms."

"Then she can't be. She's lying." Oh, god. Abby had *tricked* her brother, like she'd been planning on tricking Scott. "Were they *her* condoms?"

"Does that matter?" Diego scrubbed at his face. "She said it won't last."

"What the fuck does that mean?" But Fern knew. *They didn't stick.*

"She said she'll have a miscarriage." For the first time, Diego met her eyes, and at that moment, Fern would have happily killed Abby for putting that kind of agony into his gaze. All her brother had wanted from his wife was a kid. Just one. "She sounded sad."

"Sounded? You didn't see her?"

"She texted me while I was up a tree. I called her back and she finally answered. She was in the parking lot across from the church construction. Said she wasn't, but I know it was her car."

The swing was moving too fast—Diego's nervous legs pumping it back and forth. Fern slid off and down to the top step Gregory had vacated.

A child.

A child she'd lose.

Oh, god, what if Abby didn't miscarry?

Math—it was math in her head, only this time the numbers mattered more than they ever had before. A child. It would be Diego's son or daughter.

It would be Matty's cousin.

Forever. There was no getting around blood. It was okay that Abby had left them (no, it wasn't, it was *not* okay, but it was what it was) because she wasn't blood. Fern should never have let down her guard in the first place. She'd let the wrong person in, and then they'd been hurt, and that was the way life went.

But a baby would be forever.

Abby would get the family she'd been looking for. All built-in, tied up in a cute little package. Just like she'd wanted.

The problem was, that family was *Fern's*. If she could have dropped some kind of dome around the house, some kind of invisible shield, one straight out of one of Matty's comic books, she would have. No one in, no one out. She would give everything she had left (the box of coins, her less-than-five-year-old water heater, her health) to pay for it. If they starved to death together inside, they'd at least be together at the end.

"Where's Matty?" She needed him here, next to her on the porch, inside her imaginary shield. "Matty?" Her voice was too loud, too shrill.

"He's fine. He's playing." Diego's pupils were large in the darkening night. He'd had that look long ago, the first night their mother didn't come home at all. He'd had it again when his wife had left him.

"Matty!"

"I'm here!" The gate bounced open, and one of the Ybarra boys laughed. "What?"

"Nothing."

Matty gave her a suspicious look but then seemed to shrug it off. "Here, I got your mail." He dumped a pile of bills—always bills—into her lap. "I'm gonna go play WWE. *Tío*, you coming?"

"Yeah. Just a minute."

The door slammed shut behind him.

Fern didn't have the right words. She had no words at all. "Diego . . ."

"I don't know what to do."

His voice cracked, and Fern felt something in her chest

crack along with it. "Do what you would do if she wasn't Abby."

"Like . . ."

"Like if she was just some girl you met at a bar. What would you do?"

"Offer to help."

"Did you do that?"

He glared at her. "Of course I did."

"I know you did. What else would you do?"

"Try not to fall in love with her."

Fern's heart ached. "Would that be hard?"

"I don't know. Depends on how much she ends up hurting you. Matty. Us. If she does, fuck her. But, Fernandita— I want the baby. I want the baby so bad I can't stand to think of it not working. Not *sticking.*"

It took all her courage to say the words: "Tell her, then." *If he did, if the baby stuck, if Diego chose her . . .* Fear was a solid wall hit at sixty miles an hour.

"What?"

Desperate to put something—anything—in order, she flipped through the mail, her fingers thick and clumsy. All bills, two advertisement flyers, one slim envelope addressed to her. She arranged them by size. "Tell her you want the baby."

"I can do that? I mean, I know I *can*, but that's . . . that would be okay?"

"Only if you mean it." She slit the smallest envelope with her first finger, ripping it.

"I mean it. I would fucking mean it."

Fern looked at the slim piece of paper in her hand. *"Que cabrón."*

"What?"

The silent explosion inside her head made her rock backward in pain. "It's a check."

A check, made out in Abby's clear hand. Five hundred and twenty one thousand dollars, fifty-two cents. It was drawn on a personal bank account. Not a money order, nor a cashier's check—nothing as secure as that. A fucking personal account.

The memo line didn't read *Take care* like Scott's checks had. And it didn't read *Taking Care* like Abby had written cheekily on the one work-related check Fern had received.

In tiny, cramped handwriting that barely fit in the small space, it read, *I'm sorry I hurt you. I won't do it anymore. You're off the hook.*

"She just fired me."

The worst part was the knowledge of how much it was going to hurt later, like getting a burn that blistered from accidentally touching a hot stove. It stung badly at first, yes, but the fear—the knowledge—that it would get worse before it got better was the terrifying part.

Fern would deposit the money, because she would have to.

And if the baby was born full-term, she would have to see Abby sometimes. So she would have to be cordial.

To someone she'd thought was becoming a friend. A real friend.

This was why—Fern knew—*this* was why you kept the door closed. You had to keep it shut against the danger, against the potential damage. If you didn't, everything rushed in like a flood, stripping away everything you loved.

chapter *fifty~two*

The pain came the next Wednesday morning. Abby felt it in her sleep, a low twinge that would soon translate to cramps and then to real pain. She didn't have to wonder what was going on—she knew.

What she wasn't prepared for was the weight of the sadness that parked itself on her chest, pinning her in place. The fear was bigger than Tulip and had the weight of a black hole. She'd thought she'd felt all of it in the past. No matter what happened, she'd thought, if this pregnancy turned into a loss, it couldn't be—it would never be—as painful as the first three she'd lost.

But she'd been wrong. This one cut deeper. Even though she'd tried not to let herself hope, she had. In deep and secret moments, just before she fell off the ledge into sleep, she'd thought about the heft of a baby. Nothing more concrete than that. Just how a baby would feel in her arms, a fat, happy baby that had spent a full forty weeks inside her body, a baby that was outside her body but in her arms, breathing air but drinking her.

She rolled sideways in bed, moving slowly to the edge. The pain was sharper. It would get worse, soon. In the bathroom, she wiped the first blood away.

She could have called Diego, if she'd handled it differently. But she hadn't. She didn't deserve his sympathy (or, worse, his possible relief).

Kathryn answered quickly, her voice hoarse with sleep. "Are you okay?"

"No." It was a sob, a scream, a wail, even though the word itself was almost inaudible.

"Oh, my girlie."

"Can you take me to the hospital?"

A pause. "What's wrong? Are you going to finally tell me? Are you sick?" Panic rattled at the edges of Kathryn's voice.

"I was pregnant. I'm quickly becoming unpregnant. Again." Abby wondered if Kathryn remembered the garden conversation they'd had, when Kathryn had told Abby to sleep with someone. Anyone. She had. And this was her punishment.

Another long pause. "Do you think you need an ambulance?"

She needed a lot of things. She needed a god to pray to. She needed more time with the creature inside her, the tiny sea monkey she couldn't will to be any bigger. She needed her mother. (Fourteen years now she'd been gone—such a long time. Abby wasn't even sure what her mother would have said to her. She'd lost the sound of her voice years before.) But she didn't need an ambulance. "No, that's okay. There's no real hurry."

"You're bleeding?"

"It's not bad yet. Take your time. Get your coffee."

Kathryn lived fifteen minutes across Berkeley, near the tunnel. Abby knew she'd be pulling up in ten.

Abby dressed. She got her wallet, her medical ID, and the book she was reading. Raspberry leaves, in a small ziplock, for a successful pregnancy. It was already too late, but why not? She pulled out the bag with her knitting in it—if Kathryn insisted on staying (and she would), Abby would need something in her hands that she could fiddle with while Kathryn chatted with her. Darling Kathryn. She'd say light things, loving soft things. It would be unbearable, but the thing that was breaking in her body was worse.

In the car, though, Kathryn didn't say the soft things Abby thought she would. "What the hell were you thinking?"

"What do you mean?"

"Not telling me?"

"I didn't tell anyone." It wasn't a good excuse, but it was all she had. "Except the father, but I told him not to count on anything, so he won't be disappointed."

"How long were you planning on keeping that up? Not telling anyone?"

"Until this morning came. Whenever that was."

"What are you talking about?"

"You know I don't keep babies. I'm not . . ."

"Not what?" Kathryn's voice was short.

"I'm no good at it." *Not enough.*

"Bullshit."

Abby shook her head and looked out the window, gripping the seat belt as she tried to decide if another cramp was coming.

Kathryn stomped on the brake harder than she needed to.

"Not that you're not good at some things. That's for damn sure. You *suck* at some things."

Abby just stared at the red light, willing it to go green.

"Do you know how I felt this last month?"

"I'm sorry."

"No, you're not."

Annoyance brushed against Abby's skin. "I said I was. I meant it."

"I know you better than anyone else, you know that? I've known you since the day you first drew breath. I was the third person to hold you, and let me tell you this." Kathryn slammed the stick into first and lurched through the light. "You're better at hiding from yourself than anyone I've ever known."

"I don't know what you're talking about." Abby suddenly felt sixteen, caught sneaking out of the house to meet Robby Wilkens.

"Oh, honey." Kathryn took a deep breath, her voice suddenly softer. "Ever since your parents died, you've felt like you needed to make a family, instead of seeing that you have one already. Me. Rebecca. Brook. Your friends. I thought Fern and Matty might enter that category sometime, too."

Something cracked inside Abby's chest, higher than the cramping. "Kathryn—"

"But then you push everyone away when what you need is to trust them. To trust us. Who's the father?"

Abby took a breath and released it shakily. "Fern's brother, Diego."

"Jesus, Abby. Seriously?"

"No, it's okay. It's fine, really. I don't *need* him." All she needed was this to work, this tiny flutter of life to stay with her. "I swear."

Kathryn sucked in a quick breath and then rolled down her window. She turned left and pulled into the ER parking lot. "For the love of god, dear heart. That's what I'm trying to say. We all need people."

Abby hobbled the few feet into the doors of the hospital. Then came more pain, dull and throbbing, and then came the rote formality she'd been through before—signing the paperwork, sitting in the waiting room with her hands at her low belly. A man bellowed his way in, his fist wrapped in bandages, the blood dripping through and down his shirt-front. Some kind of machine accident. He was admitted quickly. Then a kid having an allergic reaction to milk—they pushed him right in, too. Everyone was having a higher-priority medical emergency than she was. That was okay. She wouldn't die from this. Not physically.

She sat in the hard plastic chair, her fingers knotted together at her waist. She should get out her knitting, or her book, some-thing, anything, to take her mind off what Kathryn had said.

What if she already had enough?

It was a traitorous thought.

But yet.

A yellow heat flooded into her, moving from the top of her head, all the way through her body, right down to her toes.

What would the knowledge that she was already enough feel like? Would it feel like the warmth that was rushing through her? Would it taste like relief?

A woman entered the waiting room. She was wearing a red head wrap and carrying a small child on her hip. Her head was high, but she was crying silently, tears dripping from her chin to her chest. Behind her, a man followed. At the desk, she whispered something to the triage nurse, who nodded and pointed to the entrance door, the one Abby still hadn't been cleared to go through. The woman turned and quietly transferred the child to the man, who spoke softly into the boy's hair, words Abby couldn't understand. Then the woman walked through the door into the next room. Her shoulders were straight, her neck long, her body tall.

She was alone.

Abby's own tears started. She watched the man put the child on a plastic chair and give him his phone to play with. The man swiped his hand over his stubbled mouth, then stared straight ahead, obviously lost somewhere else in thought. Maybe in his thoughts, he was in the next room with his wife, who was sick. Possibly very sick. Maybe he was in his home country, resting on a bed more comfortable than he ever slept in here.

Abby, though. She was right there, in the same exact room with him, but they were both completely alone. The baby inside her wouldn't live to be that child's age. Abby would leave the hospital walking next to Kathryn, but they would both be alone as they passed under the EXIT sign.

The woman in the head wrap had gone in, alone, without her family.

And maybe that was okay.

Maybe it was enough, just being near one another. Maybe . . . that was the whole point. They were all enough by themselves, and a bit more, together.

The thought was big enough to make the ground shake, to make the building slide sideways, to make the sky crumble. Those things *should* have happened, but they didn't, and for a moment she was surprised, as she looked around, to see nothing had moved.

So Abby let it all go. It was an experiment, really. To see if she could. That's all it was.

She let go of her expectation. She let go of her hope, and her excitement, and her sorrow. She let go of the image she had of herself as someone strong enough to get by until she turned into the person she was meant to be. She let go of her need to be a mother. To have a child cling to her, to have a child to cling to. She set all of it down on the floor in front of her—invisible, vast, everything she'd ever thought she needed.

There was nothing to hold, nothing but emptiness. So she let it all go, and she was left with open space.

She was left with just openness, terrifying and brilliant and ungraspable. The experiment (because that's all it was supposed to have been) turned real.

When Kathryn finally came into the waiting room a few empty and equally glorious minutes later, Abby's tears had turned to incredulous wonder.

"Are you okay? Why are you still out here? They should get you in. I'll go talk to someone, all right?"

"I'm okay," Abby said in surprise. "I think I might be okay right here. As long as you're here with me. I'll be okay."

chapter *fifty~three*

"No, Mom, you're doing it wrong." Matty leaned forward, pausing *Poltergeist*. They were working their way through the tamer horror movies because Matty said he wanted to be inoculated to, as he called it, the "hard-core stuff." Pointing out to him that he wasn't eligible to watch the rated-R stuff until he was eighteen had only earned her a beatific smile. "Unless a grown-up is with me. A supercool grown-up. Luckily, I know one of those." She knew he didn't mean her, and had answered that Diego wasn't actually *that* cool.

"Look," he said, pointing to the knitting in her hands. "That's totally wrong."

"What do you mean? Looks right to me."

"You're doing your stitches, like—" Matty grabbed at her knitting and peered at her stitches. "Dude, you're doing them backward."

Fern held it out and looked carefully at her ribbing. "Dude. No, I'm not." She'd known how to knit, a million years ago, and it had felt like it was coming back to her. She'd learned at a friend's house when she couldn't have been more than ten. Her friend's aunt Rita, that's who had taught her. She remembered the feeling of the movement of the needles.

"Look at the leg of the stitch you're going into. That's wrong."

"But the finished stitch looks exactly like yours."

"It's still not the right way to do it."

From the kitchen, she heard Elva giggle. Grandpa Wyatt said something that sounded inappropriate, even though she couldn't quite make out the words. Then she heard, "Hey! My tooth! Not *that* hard! You sexy beast!"

Elva tittered happily. Matty snorted.

She hadn't told Grandpa Wyatt yet that his tooth would be paid for as soon as she put the check in the bank. He was phobic about the dentist (thus the break), but she'd made an appointment for him for the next Monday. She'd tell him that morning, right before she loaded him, yelling and protesting, into the cab that would be suddenly available in the tooth budget, too.

The box of old Mexican coins had been her last hope. It shouldn't have been such a surprise, but it had still felt like a sick thud: they hadn't been worth thousands. The coin dealer had been nicer than he needed to be, surprisingly gentle. He'd probably seen her type before. Maybe he saw her type every day. "Look, these silver fifty-peso pieces?"

"Yeah?" Silver was silver, right? Always worth something.

"Silver plate. People always make that mistake." The guy had a waxed mustache, had probably had it decades before it was hip. He looked sad for her. "All ten of them are worth about twenty bucks."

Fern had dropped into the cracked leather chair on the other side of his desk. "Oh."

"But this," he hastened to add, "this one! The five-centavo? This is worth real money here. I'll check the rates, but I'm thinking at least two fifty." He clarified quickly, "Two *hundred* fifty." He turned his computer screen and showed her the resale sites. He seemed hurt by not being able to give her more.

All told, the box went for $472. Not even enough for the tooth. Fern kept her favorite coin, the silver 1945 fifty-centavo piece, even after she'd learned it was actual silver. She would need something to tuck in her palm to sleep with, once the rest of her treasure was gone, once she'd cashed the enormous check that would make them rich. The check that would hollow her out, leaving nothing but a husk of a woman behind.

Fern turned back to Matty, reaching for her half-knitted hat. "Explain to me how it is that if I'm getting the exact same result, you're still saying it's wrong?"

Matty tossed the hat back to her. "So . . . it's like when I get As on the math test but I don't do my homework? If I get the same results, it doesn't matter how I get there, right?"

"Smart-ass."

"You get what I'm saying, though."

He had a very good point. It was one she wouldn't admit, either. She'd try to do it his way, that was all. "Hey."

"Hey what?" Matty peered down at his own knitting.

"You never said what you thought of Gregory."

Matty set the remote on his thigh and jiggled it, obviously impatient to get back to the movie. "Yeah."

"Yeah?"

RACHAEL HERRON

"He was fine, I guess."

"Can you be a little more neutral, maybe? I thought you'd liked that whole dolphin thing. And the fact that he got us all the onion skins we'll ever need for all our yarn-dyeing needs forever."

Matty shrugged. "Yeah, he was cool. I just figured he wouldn't come back, so I didn't bother spending any time on him in my brain." He tapped his forehead. "Very smart up here, you know. Lots to do." He switched to a robot voice. "PRI-OR-I-TI-ZING."

"Why did you think *that*?"

He raised his shoulders again and let them drop. "Because you don't let anyone in."

Her throat was tight, like she'd tried to swallow a dry dollar bill. "What?"

"You want me to hit play?"

"What do you mean?"

"HIT. PLAY," said the robot.

"I don't let anyone in? I let way too many people in." That was where she'd gone wrong with Abby, after all.

"Whatever. I just don't think he'll stick around."

Stick. "I invited him to spend time with you and me that day. That's no small thing, bucko." Matty didn't have to know what a big deal that was. She shouldn't have even brought it up. Her throat was tighter now.

Matty just rolled his eyes.

"What?"

He looked at her. "Come on. You let him sit on the porch for like five minutes before you and *Tío* kicked him out, right?"

"Not fair." He was exactly right, and that was the worst part. Fern had already let Gregory too far into her circle. That

~ 376 ~

was why she hadn't told him about the baby Abby was carrying. Gregory knew something was going on, but when she'd seen him on Monday, he hadn't even asked. They'd just had sex, and then he'd smoked his clove. They'd listened to Lyle Lovett and talked lightly about the singer's hair. Then he'd said he had more grading to do.

Fern yanked at her next stitch, making it too tight. She'd regret it on the next row. "Know what? It's time for bed."

"Hey!"

"It's almost ten. You're supposed to be in bed by nine."

"I have a *bedtime*?"

He was only partially kidding. They'd always laughed about the fact that she'd never enforced a bedtime with him, trusting him to sleep when he was tired. It had been a joke, except that she didn't think it was funny anymore. Yeah, he had a bedtime, yet another ill-chosen, arbitrary rule that Fern had made up in her head and then hadn't bothered to ever back up.

"This weekend we can work on trying to dye the first hat, right?" He'd made two, one for contrast. He'd sped through the second like his fingers had been on fire.

"Sure. Hey, Matty?"

"Yeah."

"It's in three weeks."

"That's plenty of time."

"Abby might not come back . . . before then."

"It's okay. I bet she does come back in time. But even if she doesn't, I want to do it by myself. I've been Googling the onion dye baths and stuff. I can do it."

"We have no idea what we're doing. Maybe you can just turn in the hat. We'll make up some crap about something. Tying knots to change string into fabric."

"No. I'm going to do it *by myself.*"

"What about Mrs. Hutch? Is she still after you?"

"Mrs. Hutch already thinks I'm going to fail. It doesn't matter what I do or don't do. At least this way I'll be doing what I want to do."

"But shouldn't you aim for a good grade? If you can?"

Matty's body went seizure-rigid and he slid off the couch to the floor. *"Mom."*

Fern was tired. God, she was tired. And she had to work a split shift tomorrow. "We'll finish the movie another night."

"Whatever," said Matty. "Not like I haven't already seen it at Jorge's."

Ow. "You have?"

"Twice."

His door slammed.

Shit. She'd managed to blow that, hadn't she? Again.

In her pocket, her phone vibrated.

I think she lost it.

For a second, Fern thought Diego meant Abby was losing her mind, and then she realized that the actual meaning of the words was even worse. Her fingers hovered over the tiny virtual keyboard. What should she say? What *could* she say?

She wouldn't wish that loss on anyone.

Shit. Are you with her?

It happened this morning, She sent me a text on her way to the hospital and now she's not answering me.

Oh, god. Keep me posted.

Fern's gut was even tighter than her throat now. She would *not* cry. Why on earth was she tasting salt water at the back of her throat? There was no reason for that. It was just a miscarriage. Without stopping to wonder why she was doing it, she pulled the circular needles from her stitches. Then she yanked on her working yarn, hard. She kept pulling. In three minutes, she'd destroyed the hat she'd been making. It was red, a bright, fire-engine red, and she had loved what she'd done so far.

In minutes, all that work was gone, a pile of crimped, forlorn yarn in her lap.

Fern tugged a few inches of it between her fingers. It was strong stuff, and even stronger when it was doubled. She had an urge to take the ball of it outside. She sat silently, her eyes closed, doing the math, estimating the length of the house, adding the width, doubling it, adding a bit for the laundry room extension. Judging by the yardage on the ball band (223 yards), she could wrap it around the house four times. Plus a little bit. Four-ply around the house? It would be pretty strong. It would be hard to open any of the doors if she did it right.

But it wasn't strong enough.

Oh, god. Poor Abby.

Poor Diego.

For one bone-achingly cold moment, she imagined that happening to her. Not getting pregnant with Matty would have meant no marriage, no house, no house payments. No tripping over Grandpa Wyatt's slippers. She wouldn't know that Elva cried every Memorial Day for her father. Fern would live somewhere else, maybe even in a different city. She might have ended up married to someone else, with different children.

The thought was so unbearable it made her chest hurt.

Matty was in bed, playing with his phone. He looked up, his eyes narrowed. "I'm *going* to sleep."

"With your phone in your hand?" It was an automatic argument, and she didn't mean to say it. "I'm sorry. I'm . . ."

Matty waited.

Fern perched on the end of his bed. "I'm sorry, *mijo*. You're right. I guess I do."

"Do what?" Still suspicious. Of course he was.

"Keep people out."

His face—his darling face, the one she loved more than any other face in the whole world—softened. "It's okay. It's just who you are."

"I guess. But I can try harder." She imagined Gregory at her kitchen table, listening to Grandpa Wyatt talk about the different towing capabilities of full-sized trucks. She knew he'd really listen, and that he'd want to. "I used to be less serious, you know. I was a grasshopper."

"Huh?"

"You know that story about the grasshopper and the ant?"

Matty rolled his eyes. "Yeah. You're totally an ant."

"No way. I've always lived in hope." Now she didn't have to. She could deposit the check, and hope would be a moat filled with dollar bills, keeping Matty safe. "Totally carefree."

Matty raised an eyebrow. Fern hadn't even known he could do that. Was that new? "Yeah. That's you all right. *Estamos completos*."

Her throat ached. "What do you mean?"

"I just think if you were a grasshopper, you wouldn't mind so much when things change."

"I don't mind when stuff changes!" It was such a lie that she almost laughed. When *had* she gotten so serious? Was it when she met Abby?

No. If she looked at it truthfully, it had been when Scott had left. Maybe even before that. The moment she'd learned she was pregnant with Matty, maybe. That was when she'd become a worker ant.

And she hadn't even noticed.

"It's fine, Mom. We're good this way. We *are* complete."

"Mijito." If he was trying to make her feel better, it wasn't working.

"I thought Abby was getting in with us for a minute, but then when she stopped answering her phone and stuff, I figured maybe it's for the best. Like with Dad, you know?"

"Dad?" Fern's fingertips went cold.

"I know he left because of whatever—like—I know you said it wasn't me and all, but I know you kept him out to keep us safe. To keep us complete, just like we were."

"Matty—" It was so terrible. And so true.

He plugged his phone in and set it on his bedside table. Then he tucked his hand in hers in exactly the same way he used to when he was little. "We're good, Ma. I like us, too."

Her voice was so thin she didn't recognize it as her own. *"Estamos completos."* Maybe if she kept saying it, it would be true.

He smiled and closed his eyes.

Fern stayed with him until his breathing slowed, trying not to listen to the ragged edge of her own.

When she went back into the living room, she moved to the front door. She turned the dead bolt, feeling it slide into place in her heart, knowing the metal might kill her and that if it didn't, the words surely would, but she whispered them to herself anyway. *"No somos suficientes."*

Then Fern sat on the couch and while she stared at the frozen image of a woman screaming on the screen, she rewound the yarn into a ball.

Abby would be so sad.

Fern cast on again. One more time.

They were *not* enough, not the way they were. Not yet.

chapter *fifty~four*

For a guy who didn't like to text much, Diego was getting good at it. Abby's phone pinged every hour or so.

What about now?

Still pregnant.

An hour later: *Now?*

Still pregnant.

Every time she texted the words, her heart felt like it would pound right out of her chest in sheer happiness that could still break, but not yet—right now it was real.

She was still pregnant.

The ER doctor (fresh on his shift and as chipper as if he'd just slept for three days straight) said, "Well, this kind of thing is normal."

"I know."

"So go home. No special instructions for you."

She blinked in surprise. "No D and C this time?"

"No!" He'd grinned. "Sorry! Thought the nurse told you! Nothing abnormal in your ultrasound. Just a little spotting. Happens sometimes." He flipped a page or two. "Yep, you have some history. Looks like your OB is already watching you carefully. You can expect a call from her by the end of the day. But it looks like everything's good."

"The pain?"

He shrugged. "You're still feeling cramping?"

"No." She hadn't since she got out of the car.

"Happens."

"I'm still pregnant." Abby had looked toward Kathryn desperately.

Kathryn gave a bark of laughter and gripped both of her hands. "This one, girlie. *This* will be the one."

Kathryn took her home. Abby slept the afternoon away, then the early evening. She woke up and cooked a sweet potato from the garden. She ate the whole thing, along with four pieces of jack cheese and two apples. Then she went back to bed and slept until morning.

The next morning, her cell phone was full of texts, running over with them. Diego had gotten her text message late, and he was obviously panicked. Apparently he'd come by last night, but she hadn't heard him knocking.

I'm still pregnant, she texted. The phone made the sweetest sound as the words flew outward.

He was at her house within twenty minutes.

They talked. They'd talked and argued and he was right, and then she was right, and then both were furious and both of them were wrong.

Then they'd agreed.

They would do their best.

In the backyard, the morning sun was thin and clear. They kept their eyes fixed on the eucalyptus overhead.

Abby said, "It still might not work out."

"I know."

"There's no way to protect myself from that, though."

"Nope."

"You knew that already."

"Yep," he said. "Worrying about something doesn't make it happen. It doesn't make it not happen. And it sure as hell doesn't get you ready for it if it does. It just feels shitty."

Simple words. Abby smiled. "Yeah."

Diego took her hand. She let her fingers lace with his. His knuckles were thicker than Scott's had been. They watched Tulip ravage a marrow bone. It was so big it had barely fit in the freezer, but in Tulip's wide maw, the bone looked almost dainty.

"What are we doing?"

Abby knew what he meant but asked anyway. "You mean us?"

"Yeah."

"I have no idea. What do you want to do?"

"I want to have a baby with you."

"But what if this—" She touched each of their interlaced fingertips with the pointer finger of her free hand. "*us*—doesn't work?" How could she possibly know what she'd feel in the coming months? She was still in shock over Scott. Diego felt amazing. But would that last?

He leaned his shoulder against hers, just enough weight. "What if we don't name it?"

She knew he wasn't talking about the baby. "Don't we have to?"

"I don't think we do."

"Then what do we do?"

"Whatever we want to. Maybe we date. I'd love that. I'll take you to your doctor's appointments and we'll go to matinees afterward. I'll buy you whatever you're craving to eat. Maybe we fall in love. Or maybe we just stay in like, and get ready to make a family together. A lot can happen in the next seven months."

A long time and she'd never keep this baby that long—

"Don't," he said. "Don't get that look. If we lose the baby, then we're both exactly in the same place we are now, right?"

He was right. "I'm scared."

"I'm fucking terrified," he said. "Tell me again what the doctor said."

Abby was happy to repeat the words. "That no one can know why I miscarried before, but that it might have been about the combination of me and Scott. Maybe this combination is a better one. There's no physical reason to think it won't work this time."

Diego's face was bright, and his shoulder was warm against Abby's, and something like peace rested just above her heart. "Ah," he said. "So good."

"Did you tell your sister?"

"All she knows is that last night you were at the hospital."

"So she doesn't know." That there was still a chance of a baby, a real child.

Diego shook his head. "I haven't talked to her yet."

"Let me tell her? Unless you mind?"

He took his eyes off the sway of the branches overhead. "Why?"

"Because I owe her."

chapter *fifty~five*

Fern could have sworn she saw her brother's truck pulling away from the curb at Abby's house, but by the time her Uber got to the driveway, the truck had sped away.

She stood next to the mailbox and dialed Diego's phone. She got his voice mail.

That was fine. She didn't want to talk this over with him, anyway. Not before she talked to Abby.

For a long moment, she stood in place, looking up at the house. An amazing-looking place, really. It *looked* like money, with its window that shone high and clean, its paint unchipped and not peeling. This part of Berkeley smelled like money, too, of fresh air and of someone else pushing the lawn mower.

But for the first time, Fern realized she didn't *want* anything better than the house she had. So her home wasn't in the best neighborhood. So it was kind of falling down. So it was small and sometimes smelled like curry, other times like rice and beans or sweat socks or burned toast.

It was hers, and it was filled with the people she loved.

This big house just had Abby.

Fern knocked.

Nothing sounded inside, not even Tulip's bark. Abby's car was in the driveway, though, so she was probably somewhere close by. She could call but didn't want the possibility of Abby hitting the ignore button.

Fern knocked again, then tried the door handle. Locked. Damn it. The gate was too high on the side of the house for her to climb. She looked up—there were open windows on the second floor, but with her luck, she'd fall on the brick-work below. On a hunch, she pulled back the doormat. Sure enough, a silver key gleamed underneath.

Of course Abby was lax about security. People who had a lot worried about everything less than those who didn't.

Fern unlocked the door and poked in her head. "Hello?"

Nothing.

She went through the foyer (perfectly tidy, fresh iris blooms in a crystal vase) and into the kitchen. "Abby? It's Fern."

The countertops were clear, the appliances wiped shiny and clean. The only thing on the long dining room table was a slim paperback.

Baby Names and What They Mean.

"Oh." Pain socked her, a thump to the chest. Before she'd gone to the hospital, she'd gotten out this book? Judging by the dog-ears and the creased cover, it wasn't new. Fern flipped the pages. There were red stars next to "Sally" and "Greta." "Dagmar" and "Rodney" were fervently crossed out. *"Dios."*

She put the book back exactly as it had been, open and facedown on the first page of G names.

She called up the stairs, "Abby?" Still there was no answer. And no Tulip.

Outside, then.

"Abby?"

There was a low, hoarse bark, and Tulip ran at her. He pushed his nose into her crotch ecstatically. "Hey, boy," she said. "Down. Quit it. Nothing to see here. Where's Abby? Hey, Abby?"

The door to the potting shed was ajar. Fern crossed the lawn.

At first she thought the space was empty, but as her eyes adjusted, she could see into the corner, just past the second long table.

Abby was down, lying on her back in a pool of red.

Red, red—god, blood? Adrenaline spiked through Fern and she reached for her cell phone as she plunged forward. "Abby! Jesus!"

But the red was a heavy blanket. And Abby, her eyes now open, looked perfectly surprised, round mouth, wide eyes. "Fern! What are you—?"

"You scared me. Are you okay?"

"I got tired. I decided to lie down. I had just closed my eyes."

"Out here? You have a whole *house*."

"But this is my favorite place." Abby sat up. "Your brother just left."

"Are you sure you're okay?"

Abby's radiant smile was as unexpected as an earthquake. "I'm wonderful."

"Sorry?"

"I'm still pregnant."

"Holy shit. But I thought—"

Abby patted her belly. "Yeah, we all thought. False alarm. I'm healthy. We're healthy."

Equal parts fear and joy flashed through Fern's limbs. She felt queasy. "Wow."

"Exactly."

Then Fern was being embraced by Abby in a hug so tight it felt like she couldn't breathe, but that was okay, because she didn't *need* to breathe. Not this exact moment. For a few seconds, she could hold her breath and hope as hard as she could.

"I'm so glad you came," said Abby in her ear. "I wanted to tell you myself. I'm so glad."

Fern pulled back, feeling awkward, her movements jerky. This gardening shed was, after all, the place she'd had her first seizure in years. Even though it smelled heavenly, of dirt and lavender and sunshine, she wanted out. "Can we sit outside?"

"Of course, of course. I was going to call you as soon as I took a nap. I'm so tired," said Abby. "And it's wonderful to feel this exhausted for a reason."

They sat in the Adirondack chairs that faced the garden. There were two long rows of something green growing, something with clear plastic that flapped.

"What's that?" Fern didn't actually care. She just didn't know what to say next.

"I'm experimenting with germinating early hyssop outside."

Silence dropped hard between them. Fear reared up again inside Fern and she wasn't sure if she'd be able to stay seated. "I'm really mad at you."

"I know," said Abby. "I would be, too."

"You sent that check."

"Is that why you're here? I won't let you give it back to me." Abby turned in her seat, pulling up her legs. Soon, Fern thought, she wouldn't be able to do that. Her belly would preclude that kind of graceful move.

"That's not why. You *fired* me."

Abby looked at her knees. "I was scared. It wasn't about you."

"It wasn't about us when Scott left, either."

"Sorry?"

"I know that now. It wasn't about us. It was just him. It was just Scott being Scott. The problem with him leaving was that I tried to fix things for Matty. That's all I did, for years. I tried to make things right, to make up for Scott being nowhere in the picture. It was exhausting, and in a perfect world, I wouldn't have had to do it."

Abby kept her lips closed. She nodded.

Fern felt her upper chest tighten. "You hurt my family. You left Matty wondering what he'd done wrong. You left him to finish the project alone. Who does that to an eleven-year-old?"

"Me," said Abby. "Apparently I do."

"You left *me* wondering what I'd done wrong, too. You know who else did this to us?"

"Scott."

"Yep."

Abby tilted her face to the sun briefly. Then she said, "I'm sorry. Those words don't sound like much, I know that. But I do mean them. I'm *so* sorry I hurt you."

"Yeah, well." Fern felt a tremor in her fingertips, but it wasn't an impending seizure. It was just fear, plain and simple. Big words—she had the *biggest* words to say to Abby, and what if she got them wrong? "Family does that to each other."

Abby's knees jumped, but her face stayed still, as if she were frozen. "Pardon?"

"I made you something last night." Fern dug in her purse. She gripped the red hat firmly but gently, like it was a kitten trying to escape a box. "Here." She felt stupid handing it over. She'd made a hat, using Matty's pattern, and she was giving it to a real knitter. What was she thinking?

"You made me a hat?" Abby's voice was thin as a penny pressed in a souvenir machine.

"It took forever. Like, almost all night. I couldn't sleep anyway. I thought it would go way faster than it did." Fern flexed her wrists and shook them out. "It has a couple holes that I couldn't figure out. And my hands hurt."

"I can't believe you . . . Why? Why did you do this?" Abby pulled it on. It made her look like an adorable elf.

"Matty told me. About the red scarf Scott had knitted."

"The one I lost."

"I thought maybe that meant you liked red."

"I do." A shine rose in Abby's eyes.

"Don't you dare cry."

"Wouldn't," said Abby. "No way."

Fern felt the feeling again, the one she'd felt last night, when she'd thought Abby was miscarrying. *Protective.* "You want my family."

"No, that's not—" Abby blinked. "Fuck it. Truth? I did. I do. I *do* want your family. I want Grandpa Wyatt to tell me tow truck stories. Matty says he has a million of them, all of them only half true. I want to eat Elva's cooking, no matter what it is. I want to be the cool aunt—or whatever I could pretend to be—when Matty needs to run away from your house when he's a teenager."

"Diego?" Fern prompted.

"I want him, too. I don't know how he'll fit. Neither of us do, but we're going to wait and see. And I want this baby." Abby's voice was as fierce. Ragged at the edges, just like any mother's voice. "Yeah, you're right. I wanted your family. I do want it. But I know I blew it."

Fern could barely speak around the lump in her throat. "You can have it."

"Pardon?" said Abby again.

"*No chingues*, you're so fucking *polite*. Who says *pardon*? You heard me. You can have my family. But look. You have to *be* there. You have to *stay*."

"Fern." It was a gasp. "I'll stay. I swear I'll stay. Is this about the science project?"

"Fuck the project. He's gone stubborn and wants to do it all himself."

"Is it about the job?"

"Honey, I'm going to deposit that big-ass check. I've gotten okay with it. It's the right thing to do, I guess. So I don't need the job. But I'll help you. If you want me to."

"I do. I do."

"I think I'm going to be one of those online business assistants. Gregory showed me a site where you can set your own price. I'll be good at it."

"No more driving?"

Fern shook her head. Her lungs felt tight. "Nope."

"I'm so sorry."

"It's not your fault." It would have been so much easier if it actually had been. But it wasn't.

"Fern—" Abby leaned forward, but Fern interrupted her.

"You have to know this: I am never going to lie for you like I did for Scott. I tried like hell to make him sound like a stand-up, decent man whenever Matty asked about him, even while I knew he was a piece of shit for leaving his son behind. You, I won't lie for. You leave us, you hurt Matty one more time, I'll tell him exactly what I think."

"I won't."

"Won't what?" Fern needed to hear the words.

Abby was crying freely now, tears streaming down her cheeks, but she was smiling. "I won't disappear again. I won't hurt him." She rubbed at an eye and tugged the hat straighter. "I realized something in the hospital."

"What's that?" Fern tucked her hands between her knees, trying to still their trembling.

"I'm . . . okay. This way. Not a mother. I want to be one, but if I don't get my wish, it's okay, because it has to be. That's life. So I guess I'm saying that I understand. If you change your mind."

Fern shrugged, as if it were unimportant (it wasn't—it was so important that she ached). "Why would I do that?"

"If I lose the baby. Family might be . . . family is maybe a bigger concept than I'd thought it was. And I understand I'll be . . . that you'll let me be part of your family—if it sticks."

Family as a bigger concept. Maybe that was true for Fern, too. She took a deep breath and then jumped. "Yeah, well. I figure you're ours even if it doesn't."

Abby stared.

"Scott had good taste. And don't say *pardon* again," Fern warned. She wouldn't cry. She would *not* cry. It ached so much, opening like this. Her chest creaked with it, and it was hard to remember the combination to open the locks she'd put around her heart. Which reminded her. "I can't believe you leave your key under the doormat."

"Oh, my god, you totally broke in."

"Is it breaking in if I have a key?"

Abby didn't say anything. She stretched out her legs to the grass and leaned back, then reached to take Fern's hand.

It felt weird. Fern was used to holding Gregory's bigger hand. Matty's small one. She held the hands of old women getting on and off the bus, their skin thin and brittle. Abby's hand was warm and dry, the same size as her own. Her fingers felt strong.

They both looked up into the sky. Clear, blue, and so bright. It might get too warm to sit here later.

But for now, they sat together in the sunlight.

chapter *fifty-six*

Abby curled her fingernails into her palms and kept moving forward, her heart hammering so loudly the kernel growing inside her was probably dreaming of monsters. She'd known that the science fair was a big deal, but she'd had no idea how *very* big a deal it was.

The entire auditorium was full of *things*. Rows and rows of tables, each one holding something that squawked or moved or rolled or grew. Parents yelled as kids raced from row to row. Two young teachers with whistles around their necks looked almost ready to cry. Three people bumped into Abby within seven steps of the front door.

"Holy crap," she whispered to herself. Three grades of kids, the entire middle school, each kid with a project. And each of them with a family coming to view the work. How the hell was she supposed to find Matty?

And then, like she'd wished them into existence, Fern

barreled through the main door with Grandpa Wyatt on one side, Elva on the other. Wyatt held a cane, and Elva's red dress was hitched up into her stocking.

Abby rocked on her heels, feeling more off-balance than she'd ever felt before. This was it. The test. The first time she'd seen Matty in long, long weeks. It was official. Abby had *never* been this particular kind of scared, not when she'd had her miscarriages, not even when she'd been on the floor with Scott, doing CPR, waiting for the medics. Those times she'd been scared of losing something—someone.

This new kind of fear was unfamiliar. She'd *already* lost these people. She'd pushed them away, and run from them when they tried to help her. They were allowing her in, and oh, god, she wanted to stay.

But no matter what, she would be all right.

It was her mantra now. *It will be okay.* The words helped her to breathe. For the last few weeks, the words had put her to sleep, and they were the first things she thought in the morning.

It would be okay.

If she really did lose the baby.

If she never got to look at Matty's dancing eyes again.

If she never got to hear Fern's laugh.

If Diego never sat next to her on the porch, if he never kissed her again.

She'd be okay.

But sweet baby *Cristo*, as Fern would have said, it was all right to *want* this.

"Hi," she said.

Fern smiled. That was all.

And it was all she needed.

"How many kids does this school *have*?" Grandpa Wyatt

lifted his cane as if he wanted to joust with one of the students running past.

"All of them, I think." Elva had worn black kitten heels and was teetering slightly.

"Holy shitballs," said Fern. "How are we supposed to find him? He didn't tell us."

They moved forward together, one of a number of small clusters of people. Those clusters, Abby saw, were families, all clinging together. Like them. Happiness filled her like helium. If she spoke, she might sound like one of the Chipmunks.

"Here." Her voice didn't squeak. She pointed at a laminated poster at the end of the first row. "A map."

"Great," said Fern. "His class is row eight. Now we just have to get there. How are we supposed to get through this mess?"

A small robotic cupcake ran across the aisle in front of them, followed by a huge cupcake on wheels, driven by a kid wearing a frosting hat. Somewhere a rooster crowed. There was livestock in here? Maybe they should be thankful Matty had been only knitting and dyeing things for the last two months.

"Wait!" Grandpa Wyatt raised his cane and almost hit a woman in a green sweater in the eye. "I got an idea! Go with me on this. Give me your sunglasses."

"Oh, no." But Fern took them off the top of her head and handed them over.

They were too wide for Wyatt's narrow face. He swept the cane back and forth in wide arcs as he moved forward.

Without missing a beat, Elva yelled, "Blind man coming through! Step aside. Hello? Yes, you, please give way."

Fern looked horrified but followed in their remarkably wide wake. "Come on, Abby. Sorry, ma'am. Oh, *dios.* Sorry, sir," she said.

"Oh my god, he's amazing," said Abby.

"How are you?" Fern didn't look at her, just kept moving forward, her hands out as if Grandpa Wyatt might topple backward any second.

Abby swallowed hard. "Just entered week thirteen."

"Oh, damn." Fern grinned at her. "That's amazing."

"I know." Joy felt like the parade she was in right now, the wobbly line of people she cared about, cutting through the jostling of the crowd.

At row eight, Grandpa Wyatt made a sharp right turn. "Here we go," he said.

"He's healed!" said Elva.

"I'm assuming you've pulled this routine before?" said Fern.

"How do you think we get the best samples at Costco? There he is! My grandson! The scientist!"

Matty stood behind his table, next to four full-color signs. The first sign was hand-drawn knitting moves, cartoonlike and arrestingly clear. They showed the slipknot, then the first row of upturned loops, the way a knit stitch pulled out of its turn before tucking back in, the way a purl caught itself.

The next sign depicted an onion's growing season. Abby's heart tripped faster. Her favorite plant, drawn by Matty.

The third sign was a chemical description of what happened in a dye pot, and the fourth had three hats he'd knitted pinned to it: the first, undyed and simple. The second, dark tan, almost brown. The third was lighter, and a bit splotchy.

Three! He'd knitted three hats! And dyed them! He'd done all this himself! If Abby felt proud, how must Fern be feeling? But before she could turn to look at Fern, Matty leaped around the table like he was a baby goat. "Abby! You're here! You're here!" Then he looked behind her. "Did you bring Tulip?"

"Not this time," she said.

"That's okay." He flung his arms around her. "I knew you'd come. I told everyone you would."

Abby caught the sob where it started, at the back of her throat. "I missed you," she said. "I'm sorry I didn't help you more."

"It's okay. I wanted to see if I could do it myself. And I did. You can help me with the next one."

Abby felt baptized, newly born and perfect.

Matty hugged Fern and Elva and his grandfather. Then he quickly moved back into place, guarding a pot of steaming water propped over a can of Sterno. "Mom." His voice was suddenly desperate. "She won't let the water boil."

Matty looked like he'd gone right to panic as soon as he'd looked into the pot. "She said I have to blow out the flame when it starts to bubble." He flailed the way he had when he was small and frustrated. *"Safety."*

Fern looked around. "There's like a thousand people in here."

"What?"

She raised her voice so she could be heard over the clamor. "And there are little kids running around. She just doesn't want someone to get burned."

"You're on *her* side?" Matty was incredulous. "I'm going to fail. I fail everything with her. She hates me and I hate her, and . . ."

"Hello, Matias." Mrs. Hutch was dressed up in a blue dress

exactly the color of the auditorium's walls, exactly the right color for creeping up on students.

"Hi." Bright pink lit Matty's tan cheeks. Watching, Fern felt the same heat light her own face. Her kid. This was *her* kid. She was so goddamn proud, and if Mrs. Hutch pulled a single thing, if she said one word against him or his work, so help her god . . .

Her arms crossed, Mrs. Hutch leaned forward to check the flame on the Sterno. "Not boiling, right?"

Matty poked miserably at the lukewarm onion skins. "No." Fern felt his misery creep into her own skin. Poor kiddo.

"Mrs. Ray-jus?"

Fern took an indulgent second to memorize the tightness of the teacher's voice so she could imitate it to make Gregory laugh later. He was taking all of them out to dinner. Somewhere nice, he said. He wanted to help Matty celebrate his project. And more than that, Fern was going to let him. "Yes?"

"Your son did a great job on this project. You should be very proud of him." Mrs. Hutch stalked away to terrorize the next table.

"Holy shit," said Matty.

"Hey! Language," said Fern. "But holy *shit*."

"Dude!"

"Good job!" Grandpa Wyatt gave Matty a high five, but Matty's missed, as his gaze whipped to the right, toward Abby again. His eyes lit up in that way that sometimes made Fern feel like she could fly.

"Did you hear that, Abby? Are you going to stick around?" Matty asked. "Do you want to go to dinner with us later?"

Abby looked at Fern.

Fern nodded. It was okay. It was better than okay.

"I'd love to," said Abby. "Diego mentioned it to me, but I didn't want to accept without your approval. It's your day. He's right behind us, by the way. He had to drop off a chain saw at a job, but he said he'd be here soon."

Fern wondered what Matty thought about Diego and Abby, if he had any thoughts at all. Maybe over dinner, if it felt right, they could tell him about the baby. It was Abby's call, of course. She was the one most scared, most cautious, about sharing the news.

But Fern was scared, too. Terrified. There was *so much* coming up. Her family was bigger now, and it would probably keep getting bigger as the years went on. By choice. Abby had made the first move. She'd chosen them.

Then they had chosen Abby back.

Diego and Abby might not stay together. The baby might not live. Gregory might decide Fern wasn't worth the effort. Grandpa Wyatt's bad teeth might give way to heart problems. Elva might keel over in the kitchen and drown in her own soup. There was no safety, no guarantees, in any of it. Life came with no money-back guarantee.

But maybe it was like being on the bus. The passengers (like Fern, because that's what she was now, just a passenger peering out the side windows) didn't get seat belts, because statistically, they were safe enough without them. They dropped their thin coins in the fare box, then rode, hopeful.

Safe enough.

Safe enough, when it was combined with family, might be all anyone needed in the end.

Fern marched around the table and kissed Matty on the top of his head. He squawked like a chicken but didn't look displeased. Then she went around again, kissing Elva on her right cheek and Wyatt on his left. His stubble scratched and Elva's face lotion left her lips smelling like violet.

Then Fern wrapped her arms around Abby and gave her a hug, the kind Fern used to give all the time, the kind she wasn't going to forget how to give. A full-body hug, boobs to bellies to thighs. She planted a smacking kiss on Abby's cheek and then stepped back, folding her arms.

"Where's that Mrs. Hutch? I think I'm going to kiss her, too."

epilogue

LIFE SCIENCE PROJECT
by Matias Reyes for Mrs. Hutch

In our class this year, we talked about changing states of matter. Everything can change from one state to another (liquid to gas, gas to solid), even though it might take a whole lot of pressure or energy or extreme temperature to do it. In this experiment I'm not going to change a solid to a liquid or anything, I'm just taking one solid in one form, applying outside energy and heat and chemicals to construct a solid in another form.

Sounds fancy, right? *STICK AROUND BECAUSE IT JUST GETS BETTER.*

First, you need a ball of yarn. White is best, although my father's wife (not my mother), Abby, explained that it isn't really white, it's off-white, because that's the way it came off the sheep. In this case, it came off a Blue-faced Leicester, which is a kind of sheep, and it doesn't have a blue face (disappointing!), but the blue veins can be seen through its white hair on its nose, which is why it's called that.

Then get two circular knitting needles, size US 8. You can use YouTube to understand these directions because I'm supposed to keep it to three pages and I can't teach you to knit in that time.

Cast on 88 stitches and join them in a circle. Knit 2, purl 2, all the way around until you have a tube that's nine inches long. (This will take longer than you think, trust me on this one.)

Then the recipe (it's not called that, it's called a pattern, but it's basically a recipe for actions) goes like this:

Round 1: Knit 2, purl 2 together, repeat that all the way around.

Round 2: Knit 2, purl 1, repeat that all the way around.

Round 3: Knit 2 together, purl 1, repeat that all the way around.

Round 4: Knit 1, purl 1, repeat that all the way around.

Round 5: Knit 2 together all the way around.

Round 6: Knit all the stitches.

Round 7: Knit 2 together all the way around.

Round 8: Knit all the stitches (you only have 12 left or you messed something up, but if it looks like a hat, don't worry that much about it).

Round 9: Knit 2 together all the way around.

Then cut your yarn, leaving a long tail, thread it through a big tapestry needle (or you can make one out of a paper clip if you're that kind of creative person like I am), and pull it through all the stitches. Sew up the ends and hide them the best you can. It's not that hard.

GUESS WHAT? You used the *kinetic energy* of your hands (converted from the food and water you put into your body) to make something that didn't exist before. A hat!

Brag to your friends! But it's white (off-white) and that's no good for when you crash while you're skateboarding or when your friend is eating spaghetti too close to your head, so now is the time to use naturally occurring chemicals and heat to change the color, like magic, except it's *science*!

Go to the grocery store and get one of those plastic bags near the apples. Take all the red papery onion skin in the bottom of the red onion bin. If they ask you what you're doing, make your eyes really big and say it's for a science project. They won't charge you, because you're a kid and adults like kids who do science projects. The more you get, the better. I got mine from a cool dude my mom's boyfriend, Gregory, knows, but I bet you could get a lot just by going back a few times to the same store.

Put them in a pot (check with someone first, I used Elva's favorite pot and I got in trouble even though it was just *onions*). Boil, and simmer (that means little bubbles) for an hour. Take out the onion skins with a fork. Get the hat wet under the faucet (so it's not shocked by the water in the pot) and then, while it's still dripping, put it in the pot of water. Keep it simmering for about an hour, stirring and poking to make sure the dye gets all over all the strands. Whatever you do, don't forget you're doing this. You should stay in the kitchen and do your homework or watch TV or something. Abby told me once she forgot a dye pot and came back and her knitting was on fire. Turn off the heat. Let the hat cool in the pot along with the water. Overnight is best. And then let it dry! In the sink is best, since if it drips on the floor of your bedroom, your mom will be irritated with you. Ask me how I know.

Your hat will be an awesome brownish orange color, and NO ONE ELSE will have one just like it. And it's all natural, all organic, from a sheep and some onions and some water and the kinetic energy you put into it. And when you get an A on the project (HINT, HINT, MRS. HUTCH), you will smile and feel happy every time you wear the hat that reminds you of your family and how sometimes it's fun to learn.

(But don't quote me on that.)

acknowledgments

To my ever-excellent editor, Danielle Perez, thanks for always managing to see what I *mean* to do and helping me get there. To Susanna Einstein, love and thanks. You're the best agent in the whole wide world (with the cutest kids), and I'm glad we're on this wild publishing ride together. To AC Transit and the bus drivers who are superhuman in their kindness and dedication, thank you for letting me imagine what it would be like to be a part of your ranks. Any mistakes are mine, as are any liberties I took with the funeral industry and the valuable information I got from Oakland's Chapel of the Chimes. Thanks to my sister Christy Herron and my friend Rachel Harvey for sending me wonderfully detailed reference e-mails about what eleven-year-old boys are really like. Cheetos and underpants, check. Your boys' quirks and sweet-nesses helped make Matty real. Thanks to my sister Bethany for being the best partner in playing hooky. As always, thanks to the friends I can't and won't do without. When I need to bury a body, Cari Luna will provide the dark, lyrically dense soundtrack, Sophie Littlefield will pour the Islay Scotch while using her iPhone as a torch, and Juliet Blackwell will wear something sexy and say something wise and comforting while we all take turns wielding the shovel. And always, to Lala Hulse, all my love. If we end up with a Great Dane, it will be only partially your fault now.

the ones who
matter most

RACHAEL HERRON

This Conversation Guide is intended to enrich the
individual reading experience, as well as encourage us
to explore these topics together—because books,
and life, are meant for sharing.

a conversation with
rachael herron

Q. How did you get the idea for this book?

A. The original idea for any of my novels usually gets buried so deep that by the time I've finished writing, I can barely remember what the first idea was. This book, though, was different. The first scene *was* my original idea. A woman makes the agonizing decision to leave her husband, tells him, and then he drops dead.

Questions, naturally, follow that first idea. My first big question was, *How do you mourn a person you were abandoning?* My second question, the question that became the impetus for the rest of the novel, was, *What secret might you find in a desk drawer?*

Q. Do you always know the endings of your novels when you start them?

A. I wish! I know writers who know their endings and aim for them like marksmen. Rather than apples to be hit with arrows, though, my endings are always asymptotes. I write toward them forever, getting closer and closer but never *quite* getting there. Usually I have to revise the whole book (minus the ending) a few times until I figure out what should really happen.

In an early version of this book, Scott was a philanderer. He was a hackneyed cliché, and he bored me to death. Abby's discovery of his affairs was certainly a good reason for her to leave him, but it was hard to understand why a smart, kind woman would choose a jerk like him in the first place.

When I realized that Abby's main focus was *family*, I nixed his cheating ways. Scott became who he was meant to be, a well-intentioned man who'd never quite pulled it together, the guy who'd never quite grown up. A secret vasectomy would, for Abby, be the ultimate betrayal, not an affair. Figuring that out made lots of other things drop into place. When those magical things shift around in a manuscript, writing becomes a purely joyful act.

Q. *What might surprise a reader of* The Ones Who Matter Most?

A. Writing the scene in which Abby is scrabbling through the rolltop desk's drawers was a special treat. Writers are incorrigible thieves, stealing bits and pieces of their lives to provide sparkle and heft. We can't help populating our books with parts of ourselves. I share Abby's optimistic naïveté as much as I do Fern's ruthless practicality.

But beyond the stolen personality pieces, we steal actual objects. In my first novel, I borrowed a Canadian friend's cat, Duncan. I lifted him, huge and orange, out of my mind's eye and plopped him into the book (and, at one memorable point, into a bathtub). I absolutely forgot that's what I'd done until the book was published, eighteen months later. I got a congratulatory e-mail from my friend, who said, "Good book. But is that my *cat*?" In another book, I put my incurably horrible (and dearly beloved) cat Digit on a boat, because I'd always thought he'd like life at sea. He was a tuna guy.

For the book you're holding, I stole even more from myself (always a little safer than stealing from other people). That's my desk in Scott's office. As Abby explores the many small drawers, Abby wonders why they aren't being made *useful*. They could hold hair bands and gum and those wonderful yellow Paper Mate pencils. In my office, those drawers *do* hold those things. Found in an antiques store in a defunct chocolate factory in Oakland, my desk waited for me to stumble over it. As my eye fell on it, a solo spotlight hit its polished oak highlights and a heavenly choir sang one high, perfect note. I hadn't been looking for a rolltop desk, especially not one as unwieldy as a drunk cow. It was in my office the next day.

I have a wee drawer just for shawl pins. I have one for stamps. There's one for Sharpies, and one for Post-its (that's my favorite drawer). One of the side drawers has a *fake back*. I could totally hide something behind it! Well, now I can't, since I've told everyone about it right here. But the fact remains that I could. It made me happy to plop that desk, candy drawer and all, into Abby's house.

Another stolen shiny object is the café Abby and Fern meet in. I've written parts of each of my books at that exact café in San Leandro. I adore the kids who run it (as soon as you hit forty, you can call the twenty-somethings kids, right?). It closed for a while, and the whole community was bereft because we treated it like our living room (we put our feet up, Skyped with family, sang Christmas carols by the tree). Then Sarah bought it and reopened it, leaving it exactly the same (only better! Beer and wine now on the menu!) and it's our place again. It's a family there, and I'm so proud to be a part of that community that it's a joy to bring it into this book.

Dropping pieces of nonfiction into fiction creates a small, tangible connection: real life intersecting with the imaginary. Characters meeting "characters." The whole book, of course, is mine. It came out of my head, so it belongs to me (and really, I belong to it). But those tiny real-life cameos can help bring books to life.

Q. If you based a couple of past cats on real cats, is Tulip the Great Dane based on a real dog?

A. No. No, no, no, no. Nope!

Of course, my wife *just* e-mailed me a picture of a partially blind four-year-old black-and-white Great Dane who needs a forever home.

THIS MEANS NOTHING. (Although I can't get over the image I have of a Great Dane carrying our elderly five-pound Chihuahua in a wee backpack . . .)

No. No, no, no.

Hmmm.

questions for discussion

1. What role does Kathryn play in Abby's life? How has she helped shape Abby's life trajectory?

2. Do you think Abby will be able to carry this pregnancy to full term? What echoes do her past miscarriages present in her current life?

3. "Chosen family" is a theme of *The Ones Who Matter Most*. What other themes do you see in this novel?

4. How has Abby changed by the end of the novel? Is it for the better? How do her decisions as the book progresses affect this change?

5. Same question for Fern: How has she changed? Is it for the better? Is life pushing her? Is she pushing life back?

6. Fern thinks of herself as stubbornly independent and actively wants Scott to stay out of her and Matty's life, yet she's been taking checks from him since he left. Is this a contradiction? Why or why not?

7. Matty learns several skills through the course of his science project. What's the most important thing he learns? What will serve him the best as he grows up?

8. What do you think Matty will be like at sixteen? At twenty-five? At forty?

9. When Scott left Fern and Matty, his father, Wyatt, chose the ones left behind. Do you think he made the right decision? Why?

10. *Estamos completos*: "We are complete." Is there a complete family by the close of this novel? Is this something a family can truly attain, or is it a dream on Fern's part?

11. Is most of your family related to you by blood or by choice? Of course you wish for health and happiness for your family, but what else do you wish for the ones who matter most to you?

Courtesy of Bethany Herron, 2014

Rachael Herron received her MFA in English and creative writing from Mills College and when she's not busy writing, she's a 911 medical/fire dispatcher for a Bay Area fire department. She is the author of *Pack Up the Moon* and *Splinters of Light* as well as the Cypress Hollow romance series and the memoir *A Life in Stitches*. She is an accomplished knitter and lives in Oakland with her wife, Lala, and their menagerie of cats and dogs.

CONNECT ONLINE

RachaelHerron.com
twitter.com/RachaelHerron
facebook.com/Rachael.Herron.Author

CONNECT VIA MAIL

Rachael loves snail mail. Feel free to write to her:
3542 Fruitvale Ave. #135,
Oakland, CA 94605